Praise for the First E

"Essential reading for anyone involved in Women's Studies."
—*Library Journal*

"This unsparing account of the troubles that beset Women's Studies programs should incite vigorous debate." —*Publishers Weekly*

"Feminists should read this book seriously and debate it vigorously."
—Joan Mandle, former director of the Women's Studies program, Colgate University, and author of *Can We Wear Our Pearls and Still Be Feminists? Memoirs of a Campus Struggle*

"This book seeks not to kill Women's Studies, but to save it. Feminists should listen closely." —*National Review*

"This book is certain to start a firestorm within the North American academic feminist movement." —*Asahi Evening News* (Tokyo)

"The answer that emerges from *Professing Feminism* is clear: Whatever Women's Studies in its present form may be, a scholarly or intellectual enterprise it is not. . . . This witty and informative book also is an excellent read." —*Washington Times*

"It is impossible not to admire the courage and integrity that inform *Professing Feminism*, although, as the authors know full well, it will provoke many feminists to condemn them as traitors and deny their claim to write as feminists at all."
—Elizabeth Fox-Genovese, author of *Feminism Is Not the Story of My Life*

"In this illuminating book, Patai and Koertge show that . . . in many universities Women's Studies programs have been transformed into political pressure groups or religious cults. The authors' analysis of the situation, based on expert examination of eyewitnesses, leads to the inevitable conclusion that Women's Studies, as presently professed, represents a giant step backward into educational fundamentalism."
—Mary Lefkowitz, Wellesley College

PROFESSING FEMINISM

Education and Indoctrination
in Women's Studies

New and Expanded Edition

DAPHNE PATAI

AND

NORETTA KOERTGE

LEXINGTON BOOKS

A division of
ROWMAN & LITTLEFIELD PUBLISHERS, INC.
Lanham • Boulder • New York • Toronto • Plymouth, UK

LEXINGTON BOOKS

A division of Rowman & Littlefield Publishers, Inc.
A wholly owned subsidiary of The Rowman & Littlefield Publishing Group, Inc.
4501 Forbes Boulevard, Suite 200
Lanham, MD 20706

Estover Road
Plymouth PL6 7PY
United Kingdom

British Library Cataloguing in Publication Information Available

Library of Congress Cataloging-in-Publication Data

Patai, Daphne, 1943-
    Professing feminism : education and indoctrination in women's studies
/ Daphne Patai and Noretta Koertge. — New and expanded ed.
        p. cm.
Includes bibliographical references and index.
    ISBN 0-7391-0454-3 (hardcover : alk. paper) — ISBN 0-7391-0455-1
(pbk. ; alk. paper)
    1. Women's studies—United States. 2. Feminism and education—United
States. I. Koertge, Noretta. II. Title.
    HQ1181.U5 P37 2002
    305.4'07—dc21

                                                                2002011041

Printed in the United States of America

♾ ᵀᴹ The paper used in this publication meets the minimum requirements of
American National Standard for Information Sciences—Permanence of Paper for
Printed Library Materials, ANSI/NISO Z39.48–1992.

For Gerald
—D. P.

For Deborah, Matthew, and Emma
—N. K.

Lying is done with words, and also with silence.
—ADRIENNE RICH

Every revolutionary ends by becoming either
an oppressor or a heretic.
—ALBERT CAMUS

CONTENTS

ACKNOWLEDGMENTS

IN WRITING THIS BOOK, we have been aided by the contributions of a great many people. First, we wish to thank the dozens of feminists—mostly women, but a few men as well—who shared their experiences of Women's Studies with us, either in tape-recorded interviews or by letter and E-mail. It is customary to mention that some of the folks whose help one is acknowledging may not agree with parts of the book. In our case, given the critical message of this work, there are undoubtedly people to whom we are indebted who will disagree with practically everything we have written. So be it; still, we thank all of our fellow feminists, even those who think we are wrong-headed, for demonstrating what should be abundantly clear to all, that women can be just as brave and cowardly, generous and selfish, thoughtful and obtuse, insightful and insensitive as the other half of the human race. The failures of feminism are no different from the failures of all grand schemes that have set out to improve human society in one fell swoop, and they remind us of how important it is to have enlightened institutions and traditions that foster open discussion and critical debate.

We also wish to thank Peter Edidin, formerly of New Republic Books, who first encouraged us to write this book and then provided editorial advice. Special thanks go to Angela Ingram and

Edward Grant for their useful and detailed comments on the manuscript. We are grateful, as well, to Claudia Van der Heuvel for expert transcribing and research assistance and to Teresa Anderson for turning barely legible scribbles into word-processed prose.

Daphne Patai   *Noretta Koertge*
Amherst, Massachusetts   *Bloomington, Indiana*
1994

I n preparing the revised edition of this book, we were aided by the research of David Shumaker. Different versions of some of the material in our new chapters first appeared in the following: Koertge: *A House Built on Sand: Exposing Postmodernist Myths About Science,* ed. Noretta Koertge (Oxford: Oxford University Press, 1998), and in the journals *Philosophy of Science* and *British Journal for the Philosophy of Science.* Patai: *Academe, Academic Questions, Chronicle of Higher Education, Gender Issues, Partisan Review,* and *Sexuality & Culture.*

DP and NK, 2002

INTRODUCTION TO THE NEW
AND EXPANDED EDITION

EIGHT YEARS AGO, in the first edition of *Professing Feminism*, we voiced our concerns about Women's Studies. Our mood was one of sadness and disappointment. How did it happen, we wondered, that an academic enterprise to which so many talented women had devoted so much of their energy had turned out to be so problematic in so many respects—and what could be done about it? We reported on the experiences of women who had become disillusioned with institutionalized Women's Studies and we drew attention to recurrent mistakes and self-defeating stratagems on the part of Women's Studies programs.

Although they boasted about the revolutionary contributions they were making to scholarship, feminist academics too often were letting their ideological commitments serve not just as a motivating and heuristic force but also as a filter that removed recalcitrant evidence from the final product and predetermined the conclusions of their research. In a healthy academic environment disciplines can survive the incursions of a lot of dubious scholarship, especially when it is as clearly labeled as were feminist tracts. But we worried about the students in Women's Studies classes. Women's Studies claimed to be empowering these (mostly) young women by preparing them for life in a patriarchal world. Yet the very skills and attitudes that make a liberal arts education so worthwhile were systematically disparaged.

Logic, the analysis of arguments, quantitative reasoning, objective evaluation of evidence, fair-minded consideration of opposing views—modes of thinking central to intellectual life—were dismissed as masculinist contrivances that served only to demean and oppress women. And the great classical and civilizing works that anchor studies in the humanities were mocked as either irrelevant or dangerous productions of Dead White Males. A whole generation of idealistic young women were not only being cut off from a liberal education but actually inoculated against it.

No doubt there were students who gained confidence and a sense of belonging from the sharing, caring, and calls to empowerment that pervaded feminist pedagogy. But we found that others felt excluded by the strict enforcement of whatever the prevailing feminist norms happened to be. And those who did fit in were taking on a worldview that militated against anything but a life as a feminist activist—and this by design. It is right for women to be alerted to the possibility of rape and violent assault and apprised of methods of prevention and legal recourse. But if such topics are to be discussed in a classroom setting, they must be dealt with carefully and analyzed as a complex social issue using the tools of social science. All too often the definitions and doctrines espoused within Women's Studies seemed calculated merely to make women feel besieged. Their sensitivities were being sharpened to such an edge that some were turned into relentless grievance collectors or rendered too suspicious to function in the workaday world outside of Women's Studies and were left with few possible roles in life beyond that of angry feminists.

Our tales from the strange world of Women's Studies were indeed cautionary, as the original subtitle declared, but the book ended with a call to turn from dogma to dialogue and to reinstate the liberal values that once undergirded feminism. We were apprehensive for the future but not quite ready to give up. There is always a place in the academy for applied programs designed to relieve drudgery, suffering, and oppression and improve the social weal—one thinks not only of the medical sciences but also of gerontology, ecology, social work, criminology, sex research, and clinical psychology. And there is always excitement over a new (but, one hopes, not uncritical) approach to understanding the human condition, be it that of Freud, Marx, Arendt, or de Beauvoir. But practical disciplines must be, well, practical. Their proposed remedies have to work, and that entails a willingness to submit them to empirical test. Interpretative disciplines also must be prepared to accept criticisms of their limitations and false directions, as well as be scrupulous about not overstating their case. We were concerned that although feminists prided themselves on debating their subtle theoretical differences, they were oblivious to the tenuousness of the fundamental doctrines that were so widely shared.

Eight years ago we felt that the future trajectory of Women's Studies was still an open question. Were the problems that we had documented ones that would be ameliorated as the field matured? Revisiting academic feminism in this new and expanded edition, we ask: What has happened in the intervening years? What sort of programs are scholars moving into? Some Women's Studies units have changed their name to Gender Studies. Many of the original founders are now retired or close to retirement age, and the new appointees are typically women whose graduate training has been mainly in Women's Studies, a field in which growing numbers of doctorates are now completed each year (the vast majority with subspecializations in literature and history). Women's Studies programs are also much less marginalized now in the university than they were twenty or even ten years ago; there is a significant number of name chairs and degree programs in Women's Studies, and their courses fulfill general education requirements. In view of all these developments, one can now put the question: Has Women's Studies mellowed with age? Or have the old habits become even more entrenched and intractable?

In the three new chapters that constitute Part Two, we take seriously the critiques made of our first edition for including narratives by unnamed women. While noting the irony of such a stricture coming from feminists, who have made much of hearing women's "voices"—in whatever form they reach us—and of the concept of "the authority of experience," we have responded to this criticism by concentrating our appraisal of the current situation of Women's Studies on recent feminist writing. In addition, we again use many documents issuing from Women's Studies programs or departments to convey how the field defines itself and what it takes to be the components of a Women's Studies education. We also have the writings of other feminist critics to draw on, memoirs by "founding mothers," and scholarly books that make large claims for the validity and sweep of a feminist perspective. And, finally, we have letters and comments by named (and, yes, a few unnamed) women dedicated to Women's Studies who have found their confidence in it eroded by the practices they observed and encountered in their own Women's Studies programs.

In our new Part Two, we have adopted a division of labor that corresponds to our activities over the past eight years. Daphne—though she no longer teaches in a Women's Studies program—has continued to follow these programs and their writings and has remained active on the Women's Studies E-Mail List, which now has approximately 4,500 subscribers and is a crucial source of information on the concerns, problems, and attitudes prevalent among feminist academics. She reports on her research in chapters 10 and 11. Noretta has continued to work on feminist (and other) critiques of and attacks on science and provides an analysis of several key works in this field in chapter 12. We have reviewed, commented on, and edited one another's work and jointly assume responsibility for all the chapters that follow.

Amherst, Massachusetts, and Bloomington, Indiana
January 2002

I

CAUTIONARY TALES FROM THE STRANGE WORLD OF WOMEN'S STUDIES

PROLOGUE
On Airing Dirty Linen

THIS BOOK began eight years ago, with a number of long conversations under the honey locust trees in the courtyard of The Runcible Spoon coffee shop in Bloomington, Indiana. Daphne, on leave from the University of Massachusetts at Amherst, was spending the year as a fellow at Indiana University's Institute for Advanced Study and offered to be a visiting speaker for Women's Studies classes. Noretta was teaching a seminar on Concepts of Gender and Sexuality at the time and invited Daphne to lecture about her research on sex role reversals in utopian fiction. As we became friends, our conversations meandered from the political commitments of novelists to the social responsibility of scientists, from complaints about lazy students to cynical remarks about university administrators—the standard chitchat of academics, except for the fact that almost everything we talked about was informed by, or at least flavored with, ideas and analyses that had developed within contemporary feminism.

But there was another thread that ran through those early conversations. As we got to know each other better and spoke more frankly, we began to discuss our concerns about the direction in which Women's Studies programs and feminism in general appeared to be heading. At first, we tended to view the unpleasant little anecdotes we reported to each other—irregularities in the way programs conducted their affairs or odd methodological turns in feminist research—as isolated excesses or local anomalies.

As the years passed and our conversations continued, usually long distance, first by post and then by electronic mail, it became increasingly clear to us that what we were really saying, if only we had the courage to admit it, was that many of the central tenets and favored practices of feminism within today's academy are seriously flawed. But it is one thing to convince yourself that the Empress has threadbare clothes and quite another to shout it in the streets, as the difficulties we experienced while we worked on this book demonstrated to us.

In many ways, ours was an unlikely collaboration. We were born on opposite sides of the globe; we have different computer preferences, sexual preferences, politico-economic philosophies, and disciplinary backgrounds, and, as we quickly discovered, quite different writing styles. But each of us in her own way has invested a great deal of intellectual and emotional energy in feminism and Women's Studies. We each identify strongly with the feminist movement. In criticizing certain aspects of feminism, we are therefore not only repudiating some of our own previous beliefs and practices but also jeopardizing friendships with many colleagues and allies. Even the people who basically agree with us often remarked during interviews how important it is not to criticize feminism in a way that would give legitimacy to the political and religious right. The old saying about not airing dirty linen in public kept popping up.

Nevertheless, in the end, we decided we should speak out about the troubling aspects of Women's Studies as we see them. Perhaps it was in part our feminist training that spurred us on. After all, does feminism itself not counsel women to refuse to be silenced by coercive ideological systems? Does feminism not tell us to criticize and dismantle traditions and institutions that harm women by impeding their development in all spheres, including—we would say, especially—the intellectual and moral? Does it not warn us about the costs of political expediency, and has it not encouraged women not to shy away from espousing positions that may be unpopular or misunderstood? And is it not feminism itself that teaches us how difficult and also dangerous it is to try to keep dirty linen within the household precisely because the boundary between private and public is so porous?

We believe that it is feminists, not their opponents, who must speak out about contemporary feminism's tendency to turn into a parody of itself. Where did things go wrong? And why? Answering these questions is hard enough; it is even more difficult to suggest solutions. But just as naming and examining the problem was an important accomplishment of the women's movement in its early days, so, we are confident, it matters today that attention be paid to the harm done to contemporary feminism by the ideological policing and intolerance going on in its own ranks.

From our personal experience we knew that some programs, in their fervor to use the academy as a staging ground for the liberation of women, were not doing a good job of educating them. But what we did not know was how widespread and deeply rooted these failures were, nor how serious their adverse effects. To find out, we began our research in typical feminist fashion—by asking a variety of women to talk about their own experience in Women's Studies.

When we told colleagues in Women's Studies that we were doing research about problems within contemporary feminism, some assumed we were referring to "the backlash"—a pejorative that is today slapped onto any and every criticism of feminism and whose main function seems to be to shut down discussion. Others thought we would write about lack of administrative support for Women's Studies. When we said, no, we were dealing with internal difficulties, our colleagues' conjectures turned either to racism and other diversity issues or to doctrinal conflicts over pornography, postmodernism, psychoanalysis, and the like. But as we began to speak of "ideological policing," "intolerance," "dogmatism," we evoked a different kind of response—knowing looks and sighs, a host of nonverbal admissions that things were not quite right after all. These gestures, however, were routinely and rapidly followed by expressions of concern about "horizontal hostility" (women criticizing other women), or about the possible appropriation by political enemies of any open critique of feminism.

It was only when we talked to some "exiles" from Women's Studies—colleagues who still considered themselves to be feminists and whose work and lives have been deeply marked by feminism, but who for one reason or another had withdrawn to other departments, or were contemplating such a move—that we found women who were prepared to admit the seriousness of the issues we were raising. Each of these women who has walked away, taken what we call "inner flight," or in other respects has become alienated from the enterprise of Women's Studies contributed a portion of the analysis we present here. Some complained to us of improper academic procedures or the tyranny of "consensus" in decision making; others were put off by personalistic and haphazard academic proceedings; still others resented the bullying tactics of militant students. Some felt that the pedagogy in many Women's Studies courses was thinly disguised indoctrination; others feared that the emphasis on "support" and "finding one's voice" threatened to turn Women's Studies classes into twelve-step programs or group therapy sessions. All expressed concern, disappointment, and unhappiness.

Academics are notorious complainers, and in every department and discipline one is apt to find faculty grousing about falling scholarly standards, undeserving colleagues, and students who are either too docile or too aggressive. But the tales we collected from women who had lost some or all of their confidence in Women's Studies stood out both qualitatively and quantitatively from the general background of academic grumbling. Furthermore, there was a pattern to the complaints that transcended local peculiarities and personality conflicts.

Again and again, women told us that they had long wanted to discuss their concerns but had felt isolated and hesitant to express opinions they knew could be dismissed as the experience of one disgruntled woman unable to thrive under the new feminist regime. Many of the women who were willing to talk with us were pained or distressed. No enemies of feminism lurked among them. Instead, we found sincere and thoughtful individuals, providing accounts of troubling experiences and disappointed hopes.

Our inquiry is concentrated on feminism as it is practiced in Women's Studies at colleges and universities. The reasons for this focus are self-evident to us. First of all, the academy is the scene we know best and care most about. More important, we recognize it as the setting that has provided a fascinating and—we think—revealing testing ground for feminist principles and claims.

Women's Studies programs have enjoyed the substantive protections afforded by the principle, and indeed the reality, of academic freedom. It is, in our view, the existence of the essentially liberal value of academic freedom that has allowed Women's Studies programs to develop in the diverse ways in which we observe them today. But our own experiences and those of many colleagues with whom we spoke have led us to conclude that some programs now deny the very values that allowed them to come into being. If Women's Studies does not promote, indeed does not stand for, open inquiry, critical exploration of multiple perspectives (even threatening ones), and scholarship not tethered to the political passions of the moment, what is there to be said for its presence in the academy?

Academe is in many respects a sheltered arena in which ideas and persuasions can be developed and thrashed out largely unconstrained by the world outside. But feminist academic behavior is not "academic." Feminism in the lecture hall, seminar, or committee room provides us with a virtual laboratory in which to study in microcosm the likely effects of social changes, were they to be set loose in the larger society. If even in the relatively protected world of the academy feminist endeavors, controlled by feminists themselves, too often run aground, should we expect them to do any better in the world at large?

The academy is also, as it turns out, a highly visible stage, upon which feminism's excesses have been plain to see for some time now. We are not claiming that every single Women's Studies program throughout the country displays the problems described in this book. But far too many do so for these matters to be buried or left unaired any longer. And this simple fact should be of major concern to feminists, wherever they are located. Important allies have already been lost. Too many among the first generation of feminists in the university, those who organized and fought for Women's Studies programs, are now profoundly alienated from these very programs and endeavors. More are on the verge of becoming disenchanted. Feminism cannot afford such a brain drain. Among women students—the next generation—"feminist" has already become a label many prefer to avoid. It is naive to imagine (or pretend) that this is all due to media malice and misrepresentation. Clearly, academic feminism must begin to acknowledge and address its considerable problems, or else shrink into an introverted and marginal sect.

A NOTE ON METHOD

Thirty women from around the country contributed their experiences and reflections to this work, in the form of lengthy and detailed taped interviews. Most of these women are or have been faculty members; some are or were students and staff members in Women's Studies programs. We have also utilized material offered to us from correspondence, memos, and journal entries, as well as communications from the International Electronic Forum for Women's Studies (WMST-List, run by Joan Korenman, the director of Women's Studies at the University of Maryland, Baltimore County), a rich source of information. While we have not conducted an exhaustive inventory of Women's Studies programs, everything we have learned convinces us that the voices heard in this book, and the problems discussed, are characteristic. Such a view is confirmed by the fact that many other women spoke to us of friends and acquaintances who had encountered similar situations, explaining why these individuals were not likely to be willing to talk to us.

In open-ended interviews (conducted between January and July,

1993) that lasted, on the average, three hours, we attempted to allow people to speak of their own experiences, their own hopes and expectations of feminism and Women's Studies programs, their own appraisals of the proper relation between educational and political commitments, their own pleasures and pains in the classroom and in their universities. Nearly every woman who figures in this book requested that her name, affiliation, and other identifying features be disguised. However alienated and disappointed these women (and we ourselves) felt, the desire not to embarrass colleagues and institutions continues to be strong, as is the reluctance to publicly acknowledge the failures of feminism in the academy.

We also note, with regret, that the desire for anonymity reflects some of the very problems this book aims to analyze: the tendency of feminism to stifle open debate and create an atmosphere in which disagreement is viewed as betrayal. We have honored all these requests and, for uniformity's sake, have incorporated many of our own accounts into the book in the same way.

1

Introduction to the World of Women's Studies

CHANGES IN THE STATUS OF WOMEN are undoubtedly among the most important social developments of the twentieth century. Each demand for equality has been contested; each step has made a vivid impression on the women who lived through it; each advance has become part of the birthright of the next generation. Despite the apparent lull in—and to some extent, even reversal of—women's gains during the 1950s, the contemporary feminist movement in the United States, now in its fourth decade, has carried the redefinition of women and their roles steadily forward.

In important ways, both intellectual and practical, this movement's agenda was shaped by the work of feminist scholars in the academy. The result of their efforts has been an enormous flowering of Women's Studies programs, feminist scholarship, and women's culture, as well as an increasing public awareness of job discrimination, domestic abuse, sexual assaults, and other impediments placed on women in the public and private spheres. Complementing all this attention, albeit on a more modest scale, have been political and economic gains for at least some women.

Women's Studies, which began in the late 1960s as individual courses typically offered through humanities departments, proliferated throughout the United States during the 1970s and 1980s. Now, after two and a half decades, there are more than six hundred undergraduate and several dozen graduate programs at colleges and universities. This success drove, and in turn was driven by, a spate of scholarly publications in various fields. During this time, too, the use of gender as a powerful conceptual tool and a key category of analysis in the humanities and social sciences transformed entire fields, of which feminist literary criticism was the first to attain national prominence and respectability.

Why, after these successes, have Women's Studies programs turned into such a combat zone? Some reasons are fairly ordinary. One is their anomalous position, which made them simultaneously contest and exploit established institutional structures. Another is frustration not only over the difficulty of getting more faculty positions but also over the slow pace of material change generally. Paradoxically, discontent and infighting also reflect the great achievement of Women's Studies. The study of gender is no longer news, and thus Women's Studies may seem to have lost some of its revolutionary appeal. Incoming students are no longer astonished to find Women's Studies programs in place; they take such programs for granted and are either attracted or hostile to them in advance.

Then, too, given the current economic and political climate, there is less optimism that the academic study of women and gender is itself an effective agent of change. Women's Studies programs also continue to experience conflicts over their acceptance in academe, and it is hard, over the long run, to sustain feminism's moral presuppositions and activist style unless new issues can be found around which to crusade.

But the deeper and far more disturbing reasons for the problems currently visible are, we believe, to be sought elsewhere: they are the direct result of self-destructive habits and assumptions that have grown up within Women's Studies itself. Long before the term "political correctness" gained currency in its present conservative/ ironic sense, ideological policing was a common feature of Women's Studies programs. Women appraised one another; and, too frequently, found reason to judge others deficient, undeserving of the accolade "feminist."

Whereas feminists originally argued for a loosening of gender roles, now there is great pressure from within for conformity. Feminists used to urge women to explore their own sexuality freely, but now there is a figurative policing of the bedroom. At an early stage of second-wave feminism, consciousness-raising groups helped women work toward self-actualization and develop a nonstigmatized identity, but now women are pressured to conform to the microstereotypes of identity politics. In feminist pedagogy, the new valorization of women's modes of communication and interaction has led to the use of sentiment as a tool of coercion. Many feminist classrooms cultivate an insistence on "feeling," which, on examination, turns out to be the traditional split between intellect and emotion recycled, with the former still assigned to men and the latter to women. The characterizations of male and female have not changed; instead, the plus and minus signs associated with each gender have been reversed.

In yet another significant area of feminist endeavor, the early assumptions about women's "commonality" gave way to crucial realizations that not only gender but a variety of other important factors such as race, ethnicity, and sexual identity shape women's private and public selves and their life opportunities. In particular, "minority" women have increasingly entered feminist debates, which had too often neglected the problems these women face. But this valuable corrective now threatens to degenerate into a host of particularisms that could turn feminism into little more than a gathering of competing narrow "identities," each hotly promoted. Such wars have already been fought over sexual orientation, and we know how destructive they can be.

In each of these instances—as in many other aspects of contemporary feminism that we will explore in this book—we are witnessing the progressive deterioration of a vital movement. This has now reached the point that, today, distinctions between style and substance are blurred, escalation of rhetoric replaces real gains, and ostentatious posturing is taken for achievement. In the process, many women have come to feel marginalized by the coercive treatment received at the hands of some feminists and, as a result, are increasingly alienated from—and puzzled by—a movement they once embraced.

What troubled us most was that many of the aspects of Women's Studies that distanced, and in some cases drove away, women were the very features in which advocates took particular pride. The still-hopeful supporters of Women's Studies with whom we spoke often revealed, through their own accounts, the same landscape as that portrayed by the disillusioned. Where critics objected to emotional coercion in the classroom, advocates talked about the importance of transforming students' consciousness. Where dissenters saw feminist ideology distorting scholarship, advocates praised the virtues of research guided by political commitments. Where exiles complained about an atmosphere rife with hypocritical avoidance and shunning, advocates claimed to have found a sanctuary from patriarchal strife in groups based on the cultivation of women's "difference."

From the outset, Women's Studies occupied an unusual position in academe. It was not just multidisciplinary but had a dual agenda: educational (the study first of women and then of gender) and political (the correction of social injustice). As stated in the constitution of the National Women's Studies Association (NWSA):

> Women's Studies is the educational strategy of a breakthrough in consciousness and knowledge. The uniqueness of Women's Studies has been and remains its refusal to accept sterile divisions between the academy and community . . . between the individual and society. Women's Studies, then, is equipping women to transform the world to one that will be free of all oppression . . . [and is] a force which furthers the realization of feminist aims.[1]

Inevitable tensions have resulted from this grand, not to say grandiose, vision. As a brave new field that sprang up from grass-roots efforts—first motivated by the student movement of the 1960s, and later spurred by the example of Black Studies programs—Women's Studies faced many obstacles within the university. The legitimation of any new academic field is a long process, but feminists believed that the challenges they faced were invariably manifestations of sexism. This sense of vulnerability contributed to the development of a siege mentality.

At the same time, Women's Studies was always allied with university reform: affirmative action, offices of women's affairs, and so on. Commitment to good causes meant that Women's Studies, in order to be effective, could not withdraw but had to play academic politics. This entailed a constant negotiation between feminist ideals (even assuming all feminist faculty agreed about what these were—which was hardly the case) and the pragmatics required to build a program in an academic setting. In the post-1960s atmosphere where in-your-face political activism was valorized above all else, feminist academics were often accused of being ivory-towered recluses, far removed from the barricades, and many academics accepted this characterization and felt guilty. Today, women "in the movement" are still leveling such charges against feminists in academe.

Confronting competing demands and pressures, Women's Studies adopted two self-defeating practices: academic separatism and a deference to political activism. These two strategies, as we shall see, are closely connected and reinforce each other.

Separatism has been a dominant theme since the inception of Women's Studies. The biblical injunction to "set yourself apart and be a separate people" describes a time-honored method for building group solidarity and is undoubtedly an effective way for a minority community to resist assimilation. But it cannot be a good long-term strategy for changing the ambient culture, and it is certainly incompatible with creative intellectual inquiry.

Today, separatism in Women's Studies is readily and graphically illustrated by the widespread exclusion of male authors from course syllabi, assigned reading lists, and citations in scholarly papers. In particular cases, there can, of course, be practical reasons for mentioning only female sources, and probably scholars in every field tend to overcite close colleagues and allies. But a systematic refusal to read or respond to male authors harms feminist scholarship in many ways. In addition, the separatist agenda has caused many Women's Studies programs not to seek collaboration with and support from male colleagues, as if mere association with men would contaminate feminist purity. Such moves are debilitating to the cause of feminism, and they may lure female students into the—obviously false—belief that all intellectual work produced by males is irrelevant to, or in conflict with, feminist projects.

Some feminists would argue that they were forced to set up their own programs, found their own journals, and form their own intellectual networks because the academic mainstream (or "malestream") would have nothing to do with them. This may well be so. But even if academic separatism was necessary in the past, it seems clearly counterproductive today, for gender analyses and the study of women have succeeded in making widely acknowledged contributions to the humanities and, increasingly, to the social sciences as well. In the hard sciences, feminist scholarship has been less influential, but the best way of gaining recognition there is by engaging in open dialogue with both male and nonfeminist female scholars. Separatism unavoidably discourages such dialogue. Instead, it favors dogmatic assertion, a standard tactic of ideologically inflamed movements, whether religious or political.

While academic feminism has tried to keep the rest of the university at bay, it has energetically fostered an intimate relationship with feminist political initiatives, both inside and outside the academy. Arguably, some forms of participation in these initiatives have been appropriate. For example, a professor might give her textbook order to the local feminist bookstore, thus offering financial support to a woman-owned business while also ensuring that her students are exposed to the novels, T-shirts, records, buttons, and periodicals of feminist popular culture.

But at other times academic feminism has made itself subservient to activist agendas. Consequently, in many programs, the appointment of faculty has hinged on the candidates' commitment to community organizing or other forms of feminist activism, rather than on the strength of their academic credentials. Some programs have adopted course and instructor evaluation forms that encourage students to judge the quality of their education in terms of its direct relevance to a rather narrowly defined and constantly shifting political agenda. It is not uncommon for students to be urged to engage in nonscholarly internships and practicums, for which they are able to earn academic credit. The degree of supervision of these internships, like the extent to which they include academic components (such as writing a final paper), varies enormously from program to program.

The American university accommodates many academic units that, like professional schools, provide intellectual service to various constituencies in the "real world." But these units typically maintain a certain critical distance from their practical objectives. Schools of education, for example, train teachers, but they also theorize about pedagogy and school policies. Forensic science departments offer courses of use to police officers and probation counselors, but they also scrutinize the operations of the criminal justice system. The ivory-tower model of inquiry has always been recognized as freeing the scholar from the need to demonstrate practical relevance, and the whole point of academic freedom and tenure is to protect the scholar from political pressure.

An unfortunate reversal of these tenets occurs when a program sees itself as a site of correct political action and therefore promotes not independent inquiry but adherence to a particular line of analysis and to the activities that follow from it. In such cases—as we find in some Women's Studies programs that attempt to minimize the difference between themselves and groups engaged in feminist activism outside the university—educational aims are made entirely subordinate to political goals.

Academic units that manage to balance these internal and external values do so by maintaining high intellectual standards while also using as texts some material selected for its political utility. Thus, a sociology department, for example, may have a Marxist orientation while insisting on excellent scholarship and publication records from its faculty and all-around competence in sociology from its majors and graduate students. Such a department sees its mission as providing a solid education shaped, but not outweighed, by a political commitment that many (but rarely all) faculty in the department share. But Women's Studies has never even acknowledged that achieving such a healthy balance is a worthwhile goal as well as an inherently difficult feat. Instead, both academics and activists have tended to repudiate the very desirability of such a balance and have agreed that "Women's Studies is the theory and activism the practice"—as if the relationship between the two were both comfortable and obvious. And because "activism" has had the brighter luster in feminist rhetoric, many Women's Studies programs have felt compelled to embrace and promote an activist stance.

The yearly NWSA conferences have always dramatically exhibited the uneasy mingling of academic and nonacademic concerns within Women's Studies—and this quite apart from the charges of racism that nearly destroyed the organization at its 1990 meeting in Akron, Ohio. Thus, the typical NWSA program includes not only symposia on Emily Dickinson or on the depiction of women in Hindu temple art, but also panels on how feminist organizations can get tax-exempt status or on how lesbian couples can practice do-it-yourself artificial insemination. Publishers' displays of academic books stand side by side with booths featuring crystals, drums, massage oils, and the other paraphernalia of "women's culture." Over time, the nonacademic components of the annual meetings have come to predominate, perhaps because activists outside the academy provide an important portion of the market for books in Women's Studies. Not surprisingly, many serious scholars stopped attending the annual NWSA meeting because (so they told us) they felt it was no longer a worthwhile professional endeavor. Here, too, people could, after all, vote with their feet—the "exit option," as some political scientists call it.

Activism as a legitimate goal of Women's Studies has certainly been communicated to students. When we put the question "What do you think Women's Studies is all about?" to approximately 150 undergraduates in Women's Studies courses at two contrasting institutions—one a large research university in the Northeast with a twenty-year-old, highly political program, the other a former teacher's college, now a university, in the Southwest, whose Women's Studies program is less than ten years old and quite unpoliticized—most answers touched only the practical side. Students wrote: To "raise women's self-esteem," "create a less patriarchal society," "break down sexism," "empower women," "lessen discrimination against women," "help women find a career centering on improving women's lives," and so on. When we asked "What do you think *other* students at your school think Women's Studies is all about?" the vast majority of the respondents answered with some form of the notion of "male bashing"; and a few added "a touchy-feely class," "militant," and "raging militant feminists." This negative image, too, should be of concern to those responsible for Women's Studies.

The twin tendencies toward academic separatism and deference to activism have developed in concert. Academic feminists who either felt rebuffed by the established disciplines or wanted to develop a radically different approach often turned to the welcoming audience of cultural feminists and activists. As they elaborated their writings in response to the concerns of this largely nonacademic audience (an important market even for university press books), much of their research tended to become both less accessible and less acceptable to colleagues in the mainstream disciplines. Traditional academics, moreover, could readily be denounced for their "elitism" and narrowly academic concerns. As a result, those Women's Studies faculty whose own research remained connected to the conventional disciplines have come under increasing pressure from activist students to base their courses on more radical or less scholarly texts.

In such an atmosphere, scholarship itself becomes suspect as faculty members feel constant pressure not to betray the cause. One result is the rhetorical assertion that scholarship *is* politics, an insistence that only signals the devaluation that scholarship has already undergone. A feminist professor who says, "My scholarly work is my form of activism," or even, "Teaching is my form of activism," is thus inevitably affirming that "activism" is indeed the correct measure of all aspects of Women's Studies.

Women's Studies, in its early phases, had a choice. Its justified critique of much traditional knowledge as biased and limited (if not overtly misogynist), and therefore ultimately erroneous, could have led it to claim the high ground by insisting on broader, more balanced, less biased curricula and research. But this is not the choice many programs and Women's Studies faculty made. Instead, at every juncture at which feminist bias emerged, it was justified by reference to the prior bias of men—as if emulation of the thing being rejected had, unconsciously, become the feminist agenda. Such inconsistencies are unworthy of a feminism that hopes to have a future. By capitulating to them, Women's Studies has become the defender of the faith within the academy's walls. In the chapters that follow, we explore the ideology constituting that faith and see why it has become impossible for some feminists to adhere to it.

2

Cautionary Tales from Women Who Walked Away

WHEN WE BEGAN conducting our interviews for this book, we expected to elicit strong opinions from our subjects, for Women's Studies is not a field that attracts the dispassionate or the impassive. We were not disappointed. The stories we collected from faculty, students, and staff members in Women's Studies programs are vigorous, concrete, and often eloquent. The experiences recounted in them—many happy, many painful—were vividly recollected and proved highly informative. Most of all, we were struck by the sharply contrasting judgments we heard. Some students had "found their voice" and gained self-confidence from feminist classes; others felt they had been "silenced" and ostracized. We heard from professional and clerical staff with intense personal commitments and loyalty to the programs they worked in, and from others who found their allegiance sapped by selfish or hypocritical faculty and students.

But it was the interviews with faculty members that proved most revealing—and most disturbing. Even the most enthusiastic among these women acknowledged serious tensions. We encountered tenured members of Women's Studies programs so dissatisfied that they had quietly withdrawn or taken inner flight: they continued to teach their courses, though estranged from the whole Women's Studies enterprise. Others had taken the next step and actually resigned from their programs, choosing to work, instead, in more traditional departments. Not surprisingly, it was those who had initially given their best to Women's Studies and had then become disillusioned who offered the keenest insights into the problems we were trying to analyze.

Among our informants, three women told stories that seemed to us emblematic of the dissatisfactions now besetting Women's Studies. All three define themselves as feminists and are still engaged in research that is informed by feminist perspectives. All were enthusiastic participants in and supporters of Women's Studies programs earlier in their careers. All of them have now given up their official involvement in Women's Studies and have returned to their respective discipline-based departments.

Jeanne, as we will call her, is a well-known and widely respected historian in her early forties. She began her present position, at a large state university, with a joint appointment in Women's Studies and history, which provided her with a perspective from which to evaluate the operations of two very different programs. She considers leaving Women's Studies the "most difficult thing" she has done in her professional life of nearly fifteen years.

Anna, a prolific and highly visible scholar in one of the social sciences, has been involved with feminism throughout her professional life of more than twenty years. She first joined a Women's Studies program in the fall of 1973, "full of excitement." But after consistently unpleasant experiences in feminist programs on a number of campuses, she is thoroughly fed up. "Sooner or later people are going to have to face up to this crap," she says.

Margaret, now a professor in a humanities department, directed a Women's Studies program for over a decade and was also very active in the National Women's Studies Association. She describes the rupture with her former associates this way: "I experienced it as a divorce; that was my metaphor for it. And, obviously, if you get divorced, the marriage wasn't happy. It was a very isolating experience. I was such a true believer, and I worked so hard for so many years."

There are important and interesting differences among the stories these three women have to tell and in their present attitudes toward Women's Studies programs. But what they told us is marked by so many points of agreement that we have not found it difficult to assemble, from their narratives, a coherent picture of the unhealthy conditions and self-destructive tendencies that appear to be intrinsic to many Women's Studies programs.

STUDENTS WHO STOMP IN SEMINARS

When asked about the circumstances that led them eventually to abandon Women's Studies programs, all three women said they had found it increasingly difficult to do intellectual work in a hostile and intolerant environment. Each of them attributed a large share of the blame for creating an inhospitable atmosphere to militant feminist students, and each described how such students tried in various ways to impede open class discussion of ideas that did not conform to these students' politics.

In Anna's case, such students seem early on to have decided that she was not "the right kind of feminist":

> I began to get some bad vibes, as we used to say in those days, when I started teaching a feminist theory class which became a standard offering for the Women's Studies curriculum. And what I did there was to rehearse the different feminist positions: radical feminist, liberal, Marxist. The psychoanalytic feminists were just beginning to make an impact. And, of course, I would come into class and offer what I thought were balanced views of these different texts. Some of my comments were very critical, because I thought the texts were philosophically incoherent and politically disastrous—not to put too fine a point on it. I mean, they weren't scholarly texts—books like Shulamith Firestone's *The Dialectic of Sex*—they were really polemics. But that was the feminist literature of the time, it had that character, and I thought it was important for students to

work through them and to hone their critical skills on them, to
be able to separate some of the texts from one another and to
be able to ask themselves, "Now, what kind of world would we
live in if this person got her way? Is it a world that would be
more just, more equitable, or is it a world in which you'd sort
of change one class of oppressors for another?"

And that started to get me into trouble. Some students were
tremendously irate, and would run and tell tales out of class.
You weren't supposed to criticize the feminist text. One of
them said to me that she was shocked and horrified, and it was
very upsetting to her that I was criticizing the historical accuracy, for example, of parts of Firestone's account, where I said,
"The scholarly literature does not support these claims." So
there were students who were being perturbed by this, and I
thought: Well, that's okay; they need to learn how to deal with
this.

Then, at the request of the Women's Studies people, I
signed on to do a senior seminar. As it turned out, this was a
ghastly experience, one of the worst I've ever had in my life. I
was doing a topic on mothers and daughters, which is probably like a red flag to a bull in a bullring. And there was a group
of really tough students—they called themselves "dykes," actually—who, in the first class meeting, just launched an all-out
assault on me for having men on my reading list.

They came prepared with all this animus. One group sat in
the back and actually stomped their feet and kind of hooted
sometimes when they heard things they didn't like. And, by the
way, this particular group, at the end of the semester when I
was passing out teaching evaluations—you just pass out a stack
and they grab one—they all took two apiece, and they were
marking the lowest category for everything. They were sort of
trying to stuff the ballot box with bad teacher evaluations. I
caught them at it.

I was told later, by a graduate student who felt guilty about
the whole thing, that she in fact had sat in on a strategy session

where specific plans were made—and she swore to this—to disrupt my classes and those of another professor, because we were not doing the right thing. And this was confirmed later, that this meeting had in fact taken place. Now, whether there were faculty instigating any of this, I don't know. But it happened. Needless to say, experiences like this start to sour you.

It is worth pointing out that Anna can hardly be considered an ineffective teacher. She is, in fact, the recipient of a distinguished teaching award for her work in her social science department.

Margaret recalled similar difficulties in the early days of Women's Studies, caused, in her case, by students who identified themselves as "radical lesbian separatists":

I remember the atmosphere then. I remember feeling afraid in the classroom. One time when I was teaching an advanced seminar, the class was totally polarized, literally. The lesbians sat on one side, the straights on the other, and I was constantly terrified that they would attack each other physically, hate each other, hate me, that the class would completely break down. In this particular class the heterosexual women were intimidated. And this was often the case. They would feel intimidated, silenced, and later they would come and cry and tell me that they just couldn't go on this way. Yes, I'm sure they assumed I was heterosexual myself. I don't think I declared myself. I remember really not liking to feel that I had to do that, and resisting that.

This particular course was on literature and gender representation. It was really about women's writing, and, like everything else, the locus of debate, or the terms of debate, came to be whether or not the books were offering positive images of women—that was part of the theoretical discourse of the time. And the activist issue was right there. The lesbian students wanted to look only at works that were in some way able to help women. That was their idea of what women's writing

should be. They had no interest in any aesthetic questions, in
any structural questions. They were not even interested in
reading against the grain, let's say, or reading works that one
could see were, in spite of themselves, "subverting the patriarchal discourse."

Jeanne, too, expressed much dissatisfaction with the behavior of
Women's Studies students, and she wonders what they were taught
in their other Women's Studies courses to produce the attitudes they
brought to her classes:

> You have to know something in order to think critically. Now,
> if your project is to deconstruct, you have to know what it is
> that was constructed to begin with. For example, I teach
> Freud, and I understand the feminist critique of Freud, but
> he's not someone you can just dismiss out of hand. And I
> remember starting out one of my classes, the one where we
> were going to be taking up Freud, and I asked students to
> write on a piece of paper: "Free associate. When I say the
> word *Freud*, what do you think?" And these students would
> come up with statements such as: "He's like Hitler" and "He's
> the most damaging person to women in modern history."
> These were the undergraduate Women's Studies students.
> Now among the other students [those not in Women's Stud-
> ies], some just had very simplistic notions, and others said,
> "Well, I really don't know very much about him and I'd like to
> know something"—you know, they had an openness.
>   You need to read Freud, you need to read Marx, you need
> to read Adam Smith. I mean, you need to read all of these fig-
> ures if you are going to develop a feminist critique. And where
> do they ever read them? What I hear from the Women's Stud-
> ies students is a kind of automatic rejection of people who
> have made enormously important theoretical contributions
> because they are "patriarchal," or, even worse, simply because

they are "male." It's just an utterly knee-jerk, "dead-white-male" kind of thing.

My teaching evaluations are hilarious. I always know which are from the Women's Studies majors because they'll also write comments like, "This was not really a Women's Studies course," "There's not enough radical feminism in this course." That's what I'll hear. They want a course that is more explicitly political. I think what I do *is* political. But what they're looking for is something more programmatic, that results in an agenda.

You know, the argument for complexity is a very hard case to make to people who are eighteen, nineteen, twenty years old, especially students here who, I think, are uncomfortable with intellectual work. They don't come out of an environment in which they're comfortable arguing about ideas. So it's difficult, because there's a certain kind of true-believer desire among many Women's Studies students, and that's not what I can give them.

POLITICAL PURITY AND HOSTILE COLLEAGUES

Even more disturbing to these professors than the troublemakers in their classrooms was the realization that they could not discuss their concerns about this belligerent anti-intellectualism with other faculty members in Women's Studies. In part, this was because they suspected that some of these colleagues were, by their teaching, reinforcing the students' tendency toward disruptive behavior. Anna reports hearing strange stories about one of her colleagues:

She started to do some really bizarre things in her courses. For instance, she put reserved reading in brown paper bags in the reserve room, and instructed the students in that class to not even permit a man to peek at it. Seriously, I have this on good authority. Students in her classes were to keep the material in these bags, and they weren't to let a man look at it, because some of it was really hot stuff, like information about women's bodies that the male medical establishment had tried to keep hidden.

I also, by the way, had two students, who were taking a class, who came to me complaining that they were being treated unfairly because they were heterosexual women. They and the other heterosexuals had been asked to identify themselves at the beginning, with the suggestion that by the end of the term, if the course were successful, there would be no heterosexuals left. One of them had been asked to do extra papers. I actually went to the ombudsman about this, because a married woman with kids was being asked to do extra work as a kind of punishment, because she'd been stubborn about her sexual orientation.

Jeanne recalls that the constant emphasis on political purity, coming, as it did, from both students and professors, early on created an atmosphere in which it was impossible to have an open discussion aimed at the resolution of conflicts:

Before there was a name for it, I certainly experienced what we now call political correctness in Women's Studies, in the sense of not being able to speak freely. I think there's a lot of fear about being publicly denounced. There's so little margin for error, for saying anything that's even experimental. People are so ready to pounce.

And that came from all kinds of different people. It wasn't one single political line. So I think it was happening very early in Women's Studies, but there was no language for naming it, and then, of course, the right picked up this terminology and painted all of us with that brush.

Part of the problem is the lack of—for want of a better

term—professionalism. Professionalism is seen as something bad. It's seen as something masculine or patriarchal. But to me that is the way you function in an institution. It allows you to have a disagreement and yet be able to work with one another. And what seems to have happened in this program is that everything is deeply personalized, and people hold these grudges for decades. It's really interesting to me to hear how people are always referring to history, the historical precedent, and frequently these precedents are figments of somebody's imagination, or very partial recollections of what actually happened. But it speaks to a way in which there's all this personal conflict exerting a hold over the program.

In my other department, we'll have a conflict, we'll vote on it, people will say, "Okay, I lost," and then we move on. I think the problems in Women's Studies have to do with the specific temperaments of this group of people, which is, I think, an unusual cast of characters, and the kind of political purity that many people are committed to. I have studied left-wing politics, and this kind of factionalizing and purity and rigidity is very much present in leftist movements.

Margaret, too, commented on the inability of Women's Studies faculty to resolve differences amicably. As director of the program in her university, she was especially aware of the tendency of members of her program always to assume the worst about one another:

At one point my colleagues decided they wanted to hire [a well-known African-American woman], and I was supposed to do something to make this happen. But I had to wait for the Afro-Am department to write me a memo about it. They never got me the memo, and I was blamed for this not working out. I was in effect accused of being a racist. . . .

There was a lot of appearance of solidarity, but not a lot of exploration of difference. There was certainly awareness of difference, and the disciplines were dividing lines, as well. I think people really did have a hard time dealing with conflict. And a lot of conflict was suppressed. But sweeping problems under the rug was part of the rhetoric of the women's movement, which was "sisterhood," and that meant no conflict, which was ridiculous—anybody who has a sister laughs when you say that.

Increasingly, Margaret found herself dreading going to her office:

I felt lonely. I would walk into the office, and I could feel real antagonism from the staff and not very much connection to the other faculty. I felt I was lacking real colleagues, and I very much needed and wanted to have them, in order to develop in my own work and just to be able to have some fun. The program was getting bogged down with the race issue and the sexual preference issue—there was just so much argument and so much antagonism and self-interrogation and daily confrontation.

It wasn't clear to me what was feminist about any of this. I came to feel that it was just pathology, that it was just individual and group pathology. I thought that too much behavior, bad behavior, was somehow rationalized in terms of feminism and that there had to be other categories for me, or I just couldn't go on.

One of the things that became boring to me was this inward-looking mentality—people so convinced of their superiority and acting like a club. I never liked the clubby atmosphere. To me, it just didn't belong in a university.

As time went on, Margaret began to "think longingly of traditional academic departments as a haven and a refuge." The irony of this nostalgia was not lost on her:

This program, this very entity that we had created supposedly because we were all being oppressed in our so-called traditional departments, seemed even worse than most departments, and people started talking about that privately. The more I got out of the program, the more I presented papers, the more I was in the world, at conferences that were not Women's Studies conferences primarily, the more I thought: This is really nuts! Because the people I was with outside of Women's Studies were interested in what I had to say and what other people had to say. There is a genuine discourse of feminism which can critique the disciplines and is not done in a hostile way, where you're not made to feel like shit.

"WOMEN'S STUDIES CAN BE HARMFUL"

The excesses of Women's Studies affected not just faculty, but, even more so, students. And the deepest outrage of our three informants was directed at the miseducation suffered by the students they had left behind.

Anna, the social scientist, says flatly, "Students are being cheated":

> Over the long run, the students are the ones who suffer, and that's the sad part to me. I mean, what kind of mentoring is it, for God's sake, where a whole range of issues is just not to be discussed? And if they are discussed, it's only to denounce those who raise certain questions. This really does not serve students well. Once they leave the university, the world is an ambiguous place, it's filled with ambiguity, it's filled with irony, and not to be able to handle that does not serve them very well. The world is filled with disagreement among people who are people of goodwill. The students, poor things—I feel really bad for them, because they're not being given an education. And, you know, once they're in Women's Studies, it's like the

Stepford Wives! Women's Studies turns them into ideologically inflamed Stepford Wives!

I was always able to recognize them, these kids who come in, kind of zombified, who start uttering stock phrases. And you say, "Well, so-and-so certainly put her bootprint on these kids." Because it's obvious they're terrified of a thought, because if they ever had a serious thought, they might start reflecting on this stuff they're taught to repeat. I don't want to make it that clear-cut, but the ones who identified themselves as Women's Studies students were the worst. It was just a relentless dogmatism: "We will not talk about this!" Any criticism is because you're homophobic, or you're a patriarchalist in disguise, or you're this or you're that!—whether the criticism came from me or from other students. Politics is driving out their ability to think!

You see, what "feminist process" in the classroom winds up being is a push toward conformism and toward silencing dissent. It's all done under the rubric of being nice and open, and not being an authoritarian, old-fashioned type of teacher. But this winds up being tremendously more coercive. Because with authoritarian teachers you *know* they're being authoritarian, and you can resist. You know who's doing what to you. But this other way is manipulation, which is far worse than straight coercion, because students are being led someplace without any clarity as to who's accountable for what and who's leading them there. And since it's all supposed to be for *your own good*, you see, there's this terrible paternalism, or should we call it maternalism? "It's all for your own good." And I think that's *far* more dangerous than a more old-fashioned, straightforward authoritarianism, because it's harder to resist that kind of maternalism than it is the other, and to be clear about what's going on.

Jeanne had similar criticisms. She told a story of a very bright student who was "jerked around intellectually" by her Women's Studies professors, and she commented on the emotional stress to which all students in such classes are subjected:

> I can't speak in terms of numbers, but what I can say is that I've had some really fantastic students who I think have been ruined by this program, intellectually and, in some ways, emotionally. There's one in particular who studied with me when she was a sophomore, really smart, really creative, very committed to both intellectual work and political action. She took a course with one of my colleagues and sort of went off the deep end into a kind of radical feminist mode for a while, then came back to take another course with me, and we had a lot of conflict. I felt that her reading of the pornography debate was completely wrongheaded. She was unable to listen to any contrary evidence. I thought, Well, maybe she'll grow out of this. And she was very much involved in the campus women's center, where they have this violence-against-women training—it doesn't problematize the relationship between pornography and violence against women; it just says they're essentially identical. And she was very much involved in this.
>
> And then I went on leave, and I saw her when I came back, at graduation. I asked how she was doing, what she was doing. And she said, "Well, I'm really glad to be out of this program. I'm going to work for a little while. Maybe I'll go to graduate school, but I will *never* do anything in Women's Studies."
>
> She had taken a course with a black colleague, in womanist theory—yes, this student was white, and Jewish—and she told me about this experience, in that course. She had raised certain questions about anti-Semitism, and had been viciously attacked for her views by students in the class, with the support of the professor.
>
> She said to me, "You know, they didn't have to agree with me, but no one would even listen." She was shouted down. She was doing a presentation and she was shouted down. It's unconscionable. She was really shattered by this experience.

And she was one of the smartest students I ever had. I think
she was jerked around intellectually. That's my reading of it.
You know, she goes into one course and becomes a true
believer in the radical feminist position. Then she goes into
another course and it's something else.

That was the worst case, partly because the student had
so much promise. But I've had other good students as well
who just couldn't figure out what was going on. They're in
this classroom in which things are exploding, in which they
are made to feel guilty because they're white or because
they're heterosexual or whatever, and they just don't know
how to even begin to think about it. If a student feels that
there's no space for her in a classroom to make a response
unless it is the response expected of her, I don't think it's
very healthy.

These are young people who are not only trying to figure
out what they believe intellectually, but are also emotionally
fragile. It's a period, you know, of youth typically questioning
their own identity, sexual issues, all of it. And it's dangerous.
Women's Studies can be harmful.

Margaret, as a longtime program director and a founder of the
NWSA, speaks of having grown "embarrassed to be representing"
the later developments within Women's Studies:

By the time the eighties came around, it just didn't seem that
there was much new being developed within the program, and
some of the really exciting developments, in the country and in
the world, weren't finding their way into the program. And
there evolved a kind of language, which was almost like a
"committeespeak," of how each course was described, and
they all started to sound the same: "issues to be addressed will
include:" and then the list—pornography, rape, abortion,
those things. I think there's a leveling there, for want of a better term, that I found boring. It was not challenging.

She believes the insularity of Women's Studies was in large part responsible for the paucity of students entering the program:

> I think lots of young people were afraid, felt intimidated, felt unwanted. I had lots of students who told me so—because I taught big courses—who felt that they themselves were not radical enough, or that they would be rejected because they were with men. Men felt that they would be rejected because they weren't women. We have all heard stories about that. The insistence on "women" as opposed to "gender" had something to do with it, though gender came to be used more frequently over time. But in my particular program there was a solid commitment to being on the side of women's issues, and not so much the study of gender, which would have to include men, male experience and male sexuality.

In speaking of the general intimidating atmosphere within Women's Studies, Margaret concludes:

> I'm really opposed to it, totally opposed. How can that be an education, a liberal education? No, I don't think it's retrograde to believe in a liberal education. I think we have real struggles now to make sure that things don't go completely over into thought police. I see it in other areas of the university, too, but nothing like in Women's Studies.

"THE CHICKENS COME HOME TO ROOST"

The women who withdrew from organized Women's Studies programs have spent much energy trying to gain some understanding of what went wrong. All agreed that Women's Studies programs had from the very beginning been impaired by deep internal flaws, and that the programs they knew best could not pretend to be academically respectable.

But our narrators expressed very divergent views when asked to explain just what they thought had gone wrong. Their diagnoses range from psychoanalytic conjectures to suspicions of personal nest feathering.

Anna notes a line of continuity between the political ethos of Women's Studies and the protest movements of the sixties:

> Some of the people who have written about this, Roger Kimball and others, their books are certainly very exaggerated. But they are on to something, which is that the academy has become a sort of redoubt for 1960s radical politics. When you're not getting very far with the working class, the academy becomes an outlet for all your energy. As it turns out, the academy is a rather fragile place, and more easily manipulatable as well, and a lot of people went into it for this reason.
>
> I think a lot of it has to do with having as much power as you can get in a particular local situation, and the last thing you want is a debate. The politics of the 1960s was not very generous in its approach to disagreement, and I think that the kind of moralistic fervor—where you're absolutely convinced of the rightness of your own position—carried over, and the idea that people could actually disagree was simply not considered appropriate. Plus, of course, you could also draw on a theoretical position, or a quasi- or pseudo-intellectual position, which says that, basically, there's no truth anyway, and everything is just a matter of someone arbitrarily imposing something on somebody else. So it's our turn to impose now, and you can't come in and make an argument based upon truth or historical accuracy or any of those old-fashioned values, because we know that all of those things are just constructions and have no absolute validity in any case.
>
> It took me about a year to realize that a lot of what was

going on had to do not with intellectual issues at all, but with a political strategy. The question really concerned the big philosophic difference over: Is Women's Studies primarily about scholarship? Is it an intellectual enterprise? Or is it primarily about pushing an agenda, turning gender into one of those major categories, like race, where special interests are involved and special needs have to be met, and you have a very close tie to the campus women's center?

The intellectual orientation women brought to their programs also affected their ability to handle conflict. Anna continues:

You know, having thought about this for a while, I decided that one of the problems from the very beginning was that the Women's Studies faculty was overloaded with people from literature, people who didn't have any training in the social sciences. And so, because we were raising certain kinds of questions that were foreign to them, they just decided our way of approaching problems was somehow masculine. For us, gender couldn't be the all-determinative category, because we knew that there were other issues that divide people.

Where there are separate Women's Studies programs, there has been a tremendous animus against the social sciences. Philosophy can be more loosey-goosey too, like literature, but in the social sciences, every now and then you really do have to deal with the *facts*. There *are* facts in the world; there are phenomena; there's real evidence out there that's intractable; there's real *data* about what people are thinking about a certain thing, or how they voted, or what's happening with education and income levels. You can't just wish all that away, and I think this determination to, sort of, wish away the real world is easier to accomplish if you're not compelled to deal with it as part of your professional work.

A friend of mine in economics was describing to me some

things that were going on in a faculty seminar set up by Women's Studies people. One time, she was tremendously upset because she had been accused by one of the Women's Studies people of exhibiting "masculinist categories of thought," simply because she was an economist. I said, "Quit going. Don't put yourself through this crap. It's just not worth it." But she hung in there for a while.

Anna suspects that if Women's Studies faculty were all housed in regular departments, some of the problems of factionalism and policing would decrease. Such a change might also lessen the hostility stemming from professional jealousy, which she and other feminist scholars have encountered. There were always those in Women's Studies, she says,

> who did have both scholarly and political passions, who really were determined to do good work and be good historians, good sociologists, good whatever, and to do this under the rubric of Women's Studies. But there were also others who, it seems very clear to me, were very weak in a scholarly sense, whose work was almost entirely a form of special pleading or polemic, and the only way they were going to make it in the academy was by validating this as a legitimate academic activity.
>
> I think that, with something like six hundred Women's Studies programs throughout the country, we now have a situation in which there is a lot of animus against women who do well in scholarship and are succeeding in it. And this comes from people who could not pass rigorous muster in a department of history, for example, and who are holed up in Women's Studies and carp from the sidelines at the women who are doing good work, by charging that somehow they've sold out or they're male-identified or they're all the other labels. We can all point to really terrific scholars in the field of Women's Studies, so you know I'm not making a blanket indictment, but there's absolutely no doubt in my mind that that carping was part of it.

Anna believes that a major problem with Women's Studies programs that continues to this day is what she calls a "rush to a kind of groupthink" and an unwillingness of many participants to engage in, or even to allow, self-critical inquiry into the aims and practices of their procedures:

> Absolutely nothing! There was no such inquiry. And just to let you know how hard it is for people to even think about that: I did a presentation at a conference at another university, at which I talked about feminist studies and feminist rhetoric. I talked about the strategy of women as the universal victim, and how this approach did not exactly yield the best scholarship in the world. And even at that late date—and this was probably toward the mid-eighties—there were women jumping up and having fits. And the irony for me was that I had gone over these different strategies and resoundingly endorsed one that I thought yielded a tremendous amount of important and interesting scholarship. And I talked about that scholarship, and talked about the fact that there *is* bound to be a relationship between feminism as a political enterprise and Women's Studies, but that you *can't* collapse the two, because then everything Women's Studies people do is judged by some political result, and then it's not scholarship anymore, it's something else. And it was just amazing, the ire of the people in the audience, the women jumping up, and one of them was so angry her voice was quivering. There was to be no criticism! Just no criticism!

Anna comments on the current allegations that Women's Studies programs are dominated by the agenda of white bourgeois women:

> It just reminds me of all those strands of Marxist revisionism and deviation—where a position that lasted for twenty years then gets accused of hopeless deviationism and it's all trash and you move on. I mean, it's the same kind of sectarian battle,

you know. The idea that the program [at this university] was
somehow racist seems to me ridiculous. For example, if one
teaches Western political thought, the fact that the great masters of the canon, to anyone's knowledge, were not black,
should not surprise anyone, for heaven's sake. There you're
dealing with historical issues where you can't invent people
who didn't exist. That's just not taking account of the very his-
toric contingencies that they say determine everything.

To make those charges is part of the ongoing need, I think,
to set up a Manichaean universe, where you've got these horrible people who used to do horrible things, and now it's going
to be wonderful and pure and virtuous. But, trust me, ten years
from now the people doing all of this denouncing will themselves be denounced for some crime or other. They're going to
be denounced, because this *is* like Communist politics.

Jeanne, who is the youngest of these three women and whose
experience with Women's Studies dates back only fifteen years, gives
the least pessimistic analysis of the causes of the malaise in the particular program that she left:

I assume it all has something to do with the origins of Wom-
en's Studies in a specific political movement. Clearly, Women's
Studies needed that political movement to even develop, but
at this point in time, when it's institutionally entrenched—I
mean, this program is not going to disappear unless we cause it
to, unless we destroy it—the conflict between being in an academic program and part of a political movement helps to generate what happens in the classroom.

But she also offers a different kind of explanation:

I hate to reduce things to the psychological dimension zone.
It's not my usual mode of interpretation, but in this case I
think there just are some temperaments that are really trou-

bled. I think we act like a dysfunctional family. The Women's Studies faculty is locked in a set of dynamics that it cannot escape from. And I think that to have a program that would bring in all, or as many as possible, of the faculty at the university who are working in feminist scholarship in some way—and there are *huge* numbers whom we never see, who never cross the threshold of our program—that would diffuse the conflicts that we have as this small group. It's not that they would disappear, but they would be diffused by just the sheer numbers. So if there's a way to solve the problems of Women's Studies, I think it is to change the structure to a true program, with people housed in regular departments, and not have faculty lines in Women's Studies.

Jeanne comments on what she calls the current "challenges of women of color," and she describes the effects on Women's Studies programs:

I feel compelled by the challenge of women of color, whoever they are, however you want to define that—African-American women, Hispanic women, Asian women, et cetera—to change my courses. I mean, race has always been central in my courses, but it was always a biracial analysis—black women and white women. And now I'm feeling much more compelled to try to think about ways to really talk about the diversity in American women in a way that's not just a salad bowl—"we'll spend this day on Asian women"; that's totally unsatisfying to me. So finding some analytic tools for an historian to convey what this might mean historically, how these dynamics played out in significant ways historically—I am compelled to do that.

But I also think there's a gigantic amount of static around these legitimate issues that has to do with local politics, individual self-aggrandizement, motives that are not highly intellectual. It's hard to separate out these moves. But trying to position yourself so that you are really engaged in what needs to be addressed and what needs to be changed and at the same time saying there's a lot of bullshit going on here—that is the difficult thing to do. Right now there's a privileging of racial categories. This is not legitimate, and it ought to be resisted. And how to be as a white person is also a very difficult question, now, because when you know that what you say is going to be discredited, well then, do you say it anyway? It's not made easy for you in a situation in which deviation gets labeled racism, you know, because it's so hard to take that label, to be called a racist.

I think it would help the program if it acted as though it were an academic program, rather than one in which political purity was a requirement. I think it would help all of us. But the program hasn't changed; it was always political. I mean, ways of behaving that were there from the day I set foot in the program have continued, and they've just reached the breaking point. And a lot of this does have to do with racial politics, which were not as palpable in the mid-eighties, although there were racial politics going on. I think it's all just reached the point of explosion over the last year or so. But this was already there; the seeds of this were already in the program when I came. I think the chickens have finally come home to roost.

"WHO OWNS WOMEN'S STUDIES?"

Given her extensive administrative experience, Margaret not surprisingly offers a diagnosis that centers on institutional aspects of Women's Studies. She speaks in particular of the nonacademic goals that many programs adopt, their reliance on professional staff who lack academic credentials, and feminist antipathy for traditional governance procedures:

I think that the program was always confused about its identity and its purpose institutionally. And having started as a kind of adjunct to the campus women's center was a really strong part of that. For a long time our office was adjoining the women's center, and there was an absolute confusion of who did what. I remember even resentment on the part of some of the staff of the women's center that we were getting a little too academic. You know: "Isn't Women's Studies really The Women's Movement?" Well, no, not exactly. And that was in the origins of the program—this confusion between academic and activist goals.

We were supposed to be the public institution where we could be down and dirty, so to speak, and real politicos, real hard-line politicos and not afraid of struggle and storming barricades and demonstrations.

As director, I felt a very strong sense of mission—that it was *my job* to help all women on campus who wanted and needed support. This was the rhetoric of the program. But I always felt that you can't do everything and do it with a high quality.

I thought I was being hired to be an academic. But I saw, of course, that it was a very complicated organization. There were seats on the program's executive board for staff, for the women's center, for the community, for this, for that. And during the first years of the program not too many people were involved who were really academics. That's where, I think, some of the conflict arose about who were "the faculty," who was "the program." The faculty, who had appointments in other departments, had tremendous power, because they *were* faculty; and almost everyone else was not faculty, including me, because I hadn't yet completed my Ph.D.

There was always a kind of two-tiered system. There was "the faculty"; and "we" all know that they're prima donnas, and we have to do all the dirty work, while they just do what they want to do. And then there's "us," the staff, and we're the *real core* of the program. It was a matter of loyalty, as that was

enacted at the time. And there was also the question of owner-
ship—who owns Women's Studies? These were the old arguments, but I think they originated way back there.

Because staff people participated in the program's governance—
in accordance with the feminist principle of operating as a collec-
tivity, regardless of rank or position—they were able to impose
their views:

> The way this program started, the whole business of having
> professional staff as opposed to faculty—I still insist that this is
> at the core of the whole conflict. I was very slow and stupid. I
> didn't understand *for years*, because I *was* a true believer—and
> I'm not saying that there was nothing good in there, because
> obviously there was—but I did not understand how much self-
> promotion was involved, how strategies and courses and struc-
> tures and ideas were being rationalized to serve a particular
> agenda that was at once personal aggrandizement or security,
> job security, as well as a particular ideological agenda.
>
> Some of the staff didn't think that Women's Studies ought
> to be academic at all, because they either couldn't make it
> themselves in a regular academic context, or they so despised it
> and were envious of it at the same time, while wanting all the
> perks. They really wanted to have it both ways. I think they
> wanted it to be pretty much what it ended up being—a pro-
> gram that had people working for it who were legitimate
> enough in the eyes of the rest of the university to get the
> resources and the institutionalization that it needed, and then a
> privileged existence in a separate realm that was unassailable,
> so that they would have the same status as Afro-Am, where
> people would say, "You can't touch them."
>
> People were threatened by the accomplished women on the
> faculty, those who had achieved what seemed unattainable to
> others. Probably the unconscious fear was that if we were to
> hand the program over to them, then people like "us"—the

ones who started the program—wouldn't be acceptable. I think any woman who was really accomplished in a scholarly way was suspect to some. Such women were criticized for a number of things, but people saw that we were going to need to be able to demonstrate scholarly qualifications if they were going to get tenure; and if they didn't get tenure, there wasn't going to be much in the way of clout for the program. But I don't think there was genuine respect for scholarship. I never felt there was much interest in people's scholarship. There wasn't at that time an environment that could promote it.

I think what was so distressing was that everything seemed to become exacerbated. It's hard to know whether that was a function of working so closely with people who were, in some sense, not my peers—the staff. Much of my time was spent in doing what I thought was pacification. I had to hide my own ideas and abilities to some extent, because of this notion of "leveling"—that we are all the same.

This effort at "leveling," also noted by other Women's Studies faculty, has led some to observe, ironically, that the feminist notion of "empowerment" seems to result above all in the equal disempowerment of each by all. Margaret remembers having to fight for control of the budget. Some of her colleagues in Women's Studies wanted every single budgetary decision to be submitted to the plenary group, which met once a month. The idea was dropped only after Margaret's unrelenting insistence that such a restriction would make it impossible for the program to function at all, since she had to make decisions about money on an almost daily basis. Nor was this Margaret's only experience of staff members' resistance to allowing distinctions among program participants:

I remember there was a big hassle about whether I should even have a vote on anything. There was a huge fight about even using the word *director*. For many, many years I was called "coordinator," and people on the staff certainly did not want that to change, because they thought that the name *director* carried too much power. They didn't want anyone to have any power in that position; they didn't want "stars."

It was all about having to know your place! And this was the rhetoric from the very beginning. It seemed to me that there was a strong desire to have staff people who would "do the work," as they called it, and not necessarily new faculty. There was always some resistance to getting new faculty in the program, because that threatened the position of the professional staff.

The things that I heard, the kind of bad-mouthing of faculty on the basis of their so-called politics or their personality or their research or hearsay about their teaching—this was done in an absolutely unchecked way for the whole time I was there! And the power of the staff to determine how faculty were seen by students, and also their egging on of the students—that was the locus of what I'd call politics at the time. The students were being encouraged to rise up, to find the program wanting, to attack us. The staff was doing this, in their clubby atmosphere. I overheard many things that were deeply shocking to me.

Like Jeanne, Margaret is in some measure attracted to psychological explanations for the problems in Women's Studies:

I think you have to ask what kind of personalities and temperaments and psyches are attracted to Women's Studies, as opposed to those who aren't. I mean, is there a psychological profile that can be discerned? The tendency—which I've always thought of as, in psychoanalytic terms, a borderline personality disorder—to always take an either/or, an us/them, an all-good/all-bad approach, this tendency very much characterized Women's Studies. And I always wondered about that. Is there something about those of us—including me, of course— who were attracted to this? I'm not sure.

But certainly there seemed to be, as time went on, an increasingly almost violent acting out against one another. There was a certain process of Othering, which is not too different from what you see in the rise of nationalism. It's almost like the Balkans. I found this also among some of the European feminists, not just the Americans. I remember European conferences where there was screaming and yelling and accusations directed at other women. But I also remember Monique Wittig, whom I very much admire, telling everybody, "C'est un scandale!" that women are acting this way toward each other.

For all the anger that was acted out, there was, it seems to me, a deep fear of confrontation. This was couched in terms not unlike what is done in the black community where you're not supposed to accuse in public or in front of the Other. But even privately there was no openness. I mean, our retreats didn't really get at what was going on. People spoke in politicized terms, arguing over how we define ourselves as a program. But I found myself increasingly coming to think in almost pathological terms about our problems, because it was a pathological situation in Women's Studies.

Does she attribute this deplorable environment to a lack of respect that women display toward one another?

I wouldn't want to generalize from that experience, to assume that women generally don't respect each other—I'm not sure that's true. But there was certainly envy that was not dealt with; there was competitiveness; there was anger—I mean, the whole range of traits that academics have in common, or the problems they share, which have to do with a general feeling of being undervalued or insufficiently appreciated or not rewarded tangibly.

I also think there are just tremendous feelings of inadequacy and insecurity in Women's Studies, vis-à-vis other disciplines. It's the flip side of "We are better, more important, more radi-

cal." The other side of that is: "Are we as good?" It's what I
would call "splitting," in that it makes for a very uneasy sense
of self, individually and collectively. It isn't just taken for
granted and then you go on. It's always reproblematized,
somehow, every day. Every day the territory has to be con-
quered again, somehow. I really hate some of the thought-
police stuff that's going on now in universities, and it was going
on earlier in Women's Studies than elsewhere. Absolutely, I
think it was. I think there was silencing of people, there was
exclusion, and certainly there was shunning.

SCHOLARSHIP IN A
SEA OF PROPAGANDA

Despite their negative conclusions and outlook, our narrators are
convinced that much research inspired by feminist commitments has
been eminently worthwhile. They expressed serious misgivings,
however, about whether Women's Studies programs, in light of their
history, could reliably serve as sites for such research.

Jeanne, the historian, speaks enthusiastically about the many contributions feminist scholarship has made to her field:

For one thing, just on a very fundamental level, a compensatory level, we now have all this history of women's activities—whether they be public contributions or household labor,
mothering, and so on—which was completely ignored in past
historical scholarship. Increasingly, there is now a turn to analyzing gender as it affects power relationships that may not
have anything to do specifically with the relations between
men and women—for example, the gendering of the welfare
state. And all of these ideas about how social life, institutions,
ideologies are structured in certain ways by gender—that gives
us a wholly new way of looking at history. So the questions that

historians ask have changed. What historians used to see as significant in history has been contested by feminist scholars, and pretty effectively.

She also welcomes research that is inspired by feminist politics, as long as the work conforms to disciplinary standards:

> You know, there are historians who work "on women" who are clearly not feminist. I think there is a distinction, and I would say the work I do is "feminist," even when I'm disagreeing with a lot of feminist scholarship. I place myself within a feminist discourse, definitely.
>
> If it is to be feminist research, there has to be, at some basic, common-denominator level, a belief that women have, in the past, been oppressed or repressed, and that we are looking for ways to emancipate women, to give them greater freedom and justice. And I think that you bring that perspective to your work.
>
> In its fine points and its details, this can mean many different things. But it's more than simply working on the subject of "women." I have no problem with work coming out of a political impulse. But when this impulse takes over the work, then I think it becomes a problem. You know, what I tell my graduate students is that the questions they ask *can* be informed by their politics—and inevitably will be—and the more conscious they are of that, the better. But when they're devising ways to find answers, they have to adhere to the methods of our discipline, because it *checks* them against their assumptions and their biases, and in some ways their politics.
>
> There are historians who err by putting ideological considerations before scholarly ones. But history is a field in which you don't see that happening very often, because of the way the discipline works, because of the empirical standards to which we subscribe. The advantage that history has—and, again, it depends on the individual historian—is that there are definite standards for what constitutes a good historical study.

And it's not just that there is evidence, for example, but that you actively seek out evidence that, if it existed, would contravene your assumptions. There is an understanding of what the proper relationship should be between evidence and claims. These methods help to mitigate some of the political thrust you bring to your work. Because we hold to these standards, we are more likely to acknowledge the truth claims of other people if they can back them up, if they can substantiate them.

Anna, too, readily recognizes the important contributions made by feminist scholarship:

I could point quite happily to all sorts of important work that's come out, that's made a big contribution to knowledge. The most important ones to me are actually not from my own field; they're from history. The new social history has been looking at the whole issue of women's work historically, at women and the family, at relationships between women and how these relationships had political and social implications that have not previously been examined, at women's labor unions, at women as political actors, at women as resistance fighters. I think the scholarship in social history has been tremendously important.

Also the anthropological work that has specifically looked, or looked again, at some societies and asked: Were some things missed about the power and authority that women in fact have? Maybe they weren't the powerful ones juridically, but they do have evident power—let's examine it. I think that's a tremendous contribution. Some of the new work which gives a more complex account of the history of Western political thought also is a contribution. And economics—well, isn't the household a part of economics? So I think there's been a lot of interesting work. And in literature, too, though I must say I'm tired of the trendy lit-crit stuff. I think the women and moral reasoning issues raised by Carol Gilligan and others, those are interesting and important debates and contributions. So all of that has been valuable.

Then there are the feminist commentaries on the fieldwork of people like Jane Goodall, her work with the chimpanzees, and Dian Fossey's work with the mountain gorillas, and Cynthia Moss's work with elephants. It's interesting that a lot of this pioneering work in watching animals in the field has come from women. It's not explicitly a critique of science, but it stands as a critique of the laboratory versions of trying to figure out what these creatures are about. So all of it I find very interesting.

One question I have, and I don't know how to answer it, is: Would all this have happened without Women's Studies? But this might be the entry point for a more basic question, which is: Has Women's Studies served a purpose? To the extent that it has supported and sustained these scholarly efforts, and given people an academic place, a toehold, so to speak, and helped to legitimize these scholarly efforts, of course it's been worthwhile. But to the extent that Women's Studies has become a refuge for a kind of overpoliticization that pushes certain dogmas, it's done a real disservice. So I would say my report on it is mixed, and I would say, also, that my evaluation of it would in itself be a historically contingent one, which is: Did Women's Studies serve an important function at one point that it no longer serves?

But, of course, as soon as you say that, people are going to ring your home and do voodoo chants, because that's where their jobs are, that's where they've got a vested interest.

As to the future of Women's Studies as an academic enterprise, Anna is very blunt:

Sooner or later people are going to have to face up to this crap. There are too many nasty things going on out there.

I think the change will come from generations of young scholars, black and Hispanic and women and so on, who really want to go out into the world and be the best historians they can be, and the best economists they can be, and who may in fact come to see being defined exclusively by programs like Women's Studies and Afro-Am as itself a marginalizing thing. I don't know how soon this is going to happen, but that is one possibility.

Another sign of hope is that a lot of parents are getting fed up with paying for education that doesn't seem very much like education, and I think there's a little bit of reaction setting in. Sometimes this can take forms that are not particularly attractive—that kind of parental ire. But I think some people feel that their kids are getting a little bit cheated on the intellectual content of the education they're receiving, and that's coming to the attention of college administrators.

And after all, money does talk. It may even talk louder. And if they say, "Well, gosh, what are the stories I've been hearing about this place? Is my kid going to get caught up in all this?"—that might lead people to think twice about some of the virulence and aggressivity they are displaying, and about the tremendously bad impact and chilling effect, as they used to say in the old days, it's having on free speech.

Let's face it, however, a lot of the people we've been talking about are tenured, and they're going to be around forever, and they can't *do* anything else. I mean, it's not as if they could be integrated into other departments. They don't have the qualifications in many cases to say, "Well, I've had it with this program; I'm going to go have the sociology department take me in." That's kind of a built-in problem.

Margaret, who feels that Women's Studies has never developed a clear view of itself as an academic discipline, concludes:

I personally am not interested now in being active in Women's Studies on an institutional basis. I'm entirely involved with what I'm doing in my own department. But within my work there, there *is* women's studies. I encourage that in every way I can, with individual students, with my own courses, with my research. I was a feminist before I came to Women's Studies, and I still consider myself to be one.

3

Ideology and Identity:

Playing the Oppression Sweepstakes

THE STORIES in the preceding chapter stand on their own as poignant recitals of great expectations reduced to bitter disappointments. But they also touch on all of the issues that any critical discussion of feminism in the academy must engage. This is why we have singled them out. From these stories, and from others that appear in later chapters, emerges a portrait of the problems besetting Women's Studies today: saddening accounts of shunning, personal betrayal, and unkind practices—all perpetrated amidst avowals of sisterhood; but even more evident are the shocking instances of unprofessional behavior and subversion of normal academic standards and procedures—all carried on in the name of feminism.

Perhaps most disturbing were the tales of feminist pedagogy that too often looked like indoctrination and harassment in the classroom. As we listened and read, we slowly began to realize that some of the things we heard about not only were affecting the lives of Women's Studies faculty (a relatively small group) and their students (a much larger group), but also were having significant repercussions outside the narrow circle of Women's Studies. Ideas central to Women's Studies were being taken up by secondary and even elementary school educators and policy makers. If, as we suspected, these ideas were not, in fact, working well within Women's Studies but no one was saying so, did feminists not have an obligation to address these problems frankly before the rot spread any further? But to do so, we had to go beyond "speaking bitterness" and attempt to understand the underlying issues.

UNRAVELING THE WEB OF FEMINIST DISCONTENTS

Reviewing the trajectory that goes from hope to despair is a melancholy business. Like all those we interviewed, we had started out excited and energized by Women's Studies and its challenges. What had soured the stew? An assortment of superficial and partial rationalizations were offered to us by women we interviewed. Just as feminist discontents are part of the folklore of feminism, so there are many folkloric explanations of why feminists have trouble organizing themselves and getting along with one another. As with the attempts to understand a suicide, probably there is a little truth in each explanation; at one time or another we entertained all of them ourselves. But we now think they fail to go to the heart of the matter. In brief, our narrators offered the following analyses and rationalizations, which we used as a springboard in formulating our own hypotheses.

A few of our informants felt that the problems in Women's Studies are only growing pains and will disappear as the field gains definition and acceptance. A greater number tended to blame patriarchy for all these problems and held that men and male institutions gain by keeping Women's Studies weak, isolated, and marginalized. Small wonder, then, that the bonds of sisterhood get strained and people lash out at one another in frustration over their inability to make headway against the system.

In a more ambitious try at explanation, some of the people we spoke to pointed out that because of previous oppression, both faculty and students bring a lifetime of experience in dysfunctional nuclear families to Women's Studies programs. All academic departments have internal problems, but women's oppression in patriarchal society makes Women's Studies faculty and students play out their tensions in particular ways. Too much is expected from women; thus, blame is cast more fiercely and hurt is more deeply felt when things do not go well. We have not recovered from our resentment against our mothers. We cannot accept Women's Studies as a "good enough mother" (to use the famous phrase of the British psychoanalyst D. W. Winnicott).

Moreover, according to this attempt at analysis, we have internalized some of the gynephobic elements of the patriarchy, and we harbor a lot of "horizontal hostility" because patriarchy has taught women to distrust each other and look only to men for leadership. As Adrienne Rich writes in "Women and Honor: Some Notes on Lying," under patriarchy women can only survive by lies and manipulation; we then carry these weapons into relationships even with those who do not have power over us—other women.[1] Rich exhorts us to learn to deal openly and honestly with each other.

From well before adolescence, this line of argument continues, we have been socialized to form cliques, to be gatekeepers, and to engage in what might well be called "social sorting." We protect our own status and limited possibilities by discrediting other women, just as proper Victorian wives would open their homes to a male adulterer in their social circle, but not to his mistress. Not surprisingly, then, what we see in Women's Studies is an intellectual and personal preoccupation with the tasks once assigned to Victorian women: to keep the language pure, to act as guardians of morality (feminist morality, now), and to spread tales about those who do not measure up to the prevailing norms (whether it be questions of etiquette or political correctness). From this point of view, Women's Studies as theory reflects the traditional location of women in domestic arrangements, while Women's Studies as practice derives from the sort of tribal/consensus/shaming strategies that work best in family-sized groups.

Still others blamed the media representations of feminism: Because feminist gender analyses have been so distorted by enemies of feminism, many people are resistant to the new perspectives that Women's Studies offers. Other feminist scholars, however, suggested that the very success of feminism may also be responsible for students' alienation (a point alluded to in chapter 1). Though social problems and inequality persist, they said, gender is no longer news. Incoming students no longer find the feminist analyses presented in Women's Studies programs novel and original. Women's Studies, unless it can continually find new issues around which to crusade, may seem to have lost some of its raison d'être.

Moreover, some of our narrators noted that, in the current economic and political climate, the academic study of women (and gender) seems less promising as an effective agent of change than it had once appeared to be. Social transformation turns out to be a long and arduous process. Nevertheless, some activists criticize and even disdain Women's Studies as "merely" academic. Whether voiced or not, such a perspective hangs like a menacing cloud over many Women's Studies programs today. In fact, the more established and successful such programs become, the more vulnerable they are to this sort of accusation. In other words, Women's Studies programs cannot fail to be subjected to a kind of undermining from within. Most other academic programs are immune to this sort of attack: Their self-definition as "academic and educational" does not invite such assaults from within or without, and neither "backlash" nor complacency haunts them.

Other women we interviewed offered more particularistic explanations. Some activists felt that Women's Studies has become too immersed in arcane theory; others blamed "white privilege." And one feminist, now a dean, insisted that Women's Studies had no greater internal difficulties and bad vibes than other academic departments. Women, she said, get "demonized" when they behave the way men do.

Even those feminists deeply distressed by the internal problems faced by Women's Studies tended to blame them on outside forces and suggested that they would wither away "after the revolution." Sadly, we cannot agree.

Although we see some truth in most of the preceding arguments, we find that, upon reflection, all are insufficient to a greater or lesser extent. And so we opt for a different approach, one that looks more closely at Women's Studies programs as an outgrowth and embodiment of a specifically feminist ideology. It is not the personal or institutional relations, in other words, that deserve scrutiny, but rather the explicit premises and practices on which Women's Studies was built. Such a perspective gives quite a different meaning to the oft-cited definition of Women's Studies as "the academic arm of feminism." Responsibility for the difficulties faced by Women's Studies lies, in our view, not primarily with malevolent patriarchy and its effects but with the ideological variant of feminism that has been embraced by and incorporated into the academy.

We are aware of an immediate skeptical response that may be raised against our endeavor to understand Women's Studies as an expression of feminist ideology. Does it make sense to talk about a "feminist ideology" when every student in a feminist theory class has learned to differentiate and contrast the various "feminisms"? There are socialist feminism and Marxist feminism, psychoanalytic feminism and postmodernist feminism. There are radical lesbian and womanist approaches, and others as well.

We acknowledge the existence of this proliferation of feminist positions, and we know that this very pluralism of views makes for interesting debate. But we also hold that the feminist academic community embraces a particular cluster of elemental precepts and patterns of response to social and educational issues, and that it is these basic precepts and patterns that are responsible for the sorry situation in Women's Studies. We use the word *ideology* in the common sense of a set of general ideas people have about the world (more specifically, about human society), which influence what they believe, what they find important and valuable, and how they think people ought to act. For our purposes, we prefer this term to *worldview* or *philosophy of life*, because *ideology* connotes that some of the ideas people hold are unarticulated and unacknowledged. Furthermore, in certain of its usages, *ideology* conveys the suspicion that the basic beliefs in question may be distorted and self-serving. Thus, one speaks of "analyzing" a philosophy of life but of "disclosing" or "unmasking" an ideology—the implication being that the person who subscribes to an ideology will be either reluctant to own up to it or unable to examine it critically.

The identification of someone's allegiance to an ideology normally rests on indirect or circumstantial evidence. One looks for recurring patterns of behavior and characteristic locutions as well as explicit formulations. What the investigator in effect says is: "You are comporting yourself as if you were acting on the ideology I have attributed to you." The investigator cannot prove that her interpretation is accurate. She can only show that, if correct, it will explain behavior that would otherwise appear strange, or even bizarre.

People usually adopt ideological stances unknowingly and rarely subject them to systematic scrutiny. Their beliefs tend, therefore, to be not only vague and incomplete but also often inconsistent. Since this is certainly true of feminist ideology, we do not attempt to offer a set of propositions with the pretense that these define the feminist ideological canon. Instead, in the next few chapters, we describe and analyze a series of maneuvers that we have found popular in contemporary academic feminism. We call these maneuvers "games," partly in an allusion to the concepts of "language games" and "forms of life," as developed by Ludwig Wittgenstein. But primarily we wish to emphasize the fact that these patterns of behavior incorporate conventional rules that the participants could, if they wished, agree to change. We definitely do not mean to suggest that these games are frivolous or recreational. Those involved in them take them very seriously, and—as we show later—the games have consequences for real people in real life. In the long run, the players can only come out as losers.

Despite the underlying seriousness of these games, we have not attempted to suppress the satirical tone that has often crept into our descriptions of the games feminists play. Once these ideology-based maneuvers are exposed, it is difficult not to treat them in a deprecating manner. We hope that other feminists, too, will see the absurdity of these games and acknowledge their self-defeating nature. That is surely the first step toward a turn to good sense and professionalism.

IDPOL: IDENTITY POLITICS AND
IDEOLOGICAL POLICING

We begin with the most popular game of all: identity politics, or what we call IDPOL. (We note with satisfaction that it could also stand for ideological policing, an enduring feature of feminist politics.) The central mission of feminist activism is to put the needs of women first. Its single criterion for appraising a political initiative is: Will it help women? Such a focus may be entirely appropriate for rallying support around particular issues. But we need to examine the consequences of allowing such a mission to be embraced by an academic program. What happens when the activist notion of basing politics on identity is allowed to shape the ethos of Women's Studies?

Social scientists use the term *identity politics* in a neutral way to describe the various methods that social movements employ to "alter the self-conceptions and societal conceptions of their participants."[2] But in recent years, identity politics has come to mean something quite different. IDPOL now stands for the attempt by a particular group to gain a political advantage from whatever makes it identifiable *as* a group. Its practitioners wield IDPOL as an instrument for disadvantaged or oppressed groups to seize their rightful share of power in the world.

Seeking favors for one's own group is as old a practice as politics itself. But while lobbyists for special interests rarely own up to their quest for disproportionate benefits, feminist players of IDPOL proudly demand preferential treatment, claiming that their history of oppression entitles women to special consideration. Much can be said for what Aristotle calls "rectificatory justice," but it immediately raises two very complicated questions: Who should decide what is just compensation for past inequities, and who should pay the retribution?

By and large, feminists offer a simple answer to these questions: Oppressed people are uniquely situated to say what they should get, and the oppressors are morally obligated to acknowledge their claims.

According to feminist epistemology, the knowledge produced by those in power (typically, white European males) inevitably reflects their partisan interests and is prejudicial to all those not in power. The knowledge needed for liberation must, therefore, be generated by the oppressed themselves. In addition, feminists often claim that the morality and value systems of oppressed groups are inherently superior to those of the oppressors, whose long history of exploitative behavior has demonstrated their moral bankruptcy. Last but not least, it is assumed that the only way for an oppressed group to remedy its unsatisfactory situation is by single-mindedly pursuing the needs of its own members.

As long as gender was the key variable in defining identity, it was men and a few "male-identified" women who were seen as oppressors, while most women occupied the status of victims. In time, however, other stigmatized identities emerged, and soon nearly everyone could lay claim to some need for special treatment. The result has been a degrading struggle among members of identity groups for the recognition of each group's oppression, generating an atmosphere of condemnation directed at anyone who could be labeled a member of a more privileged group. Comparing types and degrees of oppression is a tough business, and, not surprisingly, it has led to much hostility as one group elbows another for pride of place in the contest for "most oppressed" status. Rather than contributing to an atmosphere of collegiality, self-pity and allegations of guilt lead to suspicion and mutual recriminations. As played today, IDPOL is more than the ugly spawn of old-fashioned special-interest jockeying and ethnic politics. In recent times, this offspring has been further crossed with oppression analyses coming out of the left to create a virulently personalized form of IDPOL that is perhaps the single most destructive aspect of Women's Studies programs today.

Certainly, feminists neither invented IDPOL nor monopolize its use today. But many feminists have found it a thoroughly congenial tool. In turn, they have often seen it aimed at themselves. After all, no one has an unassailable identity. To recognize this simple fact is the beginning of humane fellow feeling. If seriously played, the game of IDPOL would leave only corpses on the field. It divides allies from one another as it feeds its appetite for ever-new targets to attack. Formerly devalued, now highly prized; formerly on top, now at bottom; the cast of characters changes, but in the game of IDPOL the clock never runs down.

The Amazon Laughed: "Tell Your Brothers"

When we talked to people about difficulties in Women's Studies, a recurring theme was the "problematic" presence of men in Women's Studies classes. Some said male students interrupt women, talk too much, question the authority of the female professor, are defensive when the topics of rape or wife battering come up, and in general "just don't get it." Others, however, were appalled at how rudely the more radical women students treated any males who strayed into "their" classes. And although some feminists have said that male undergraduates should be forced to take at least one Women's Studies class in order to confront their own sexism (and, indeed, some colleges now have compulsory sensitivity training sessions or require all students to take a course on gender and diversity issues), there was wide agreement that Women's Studies classes go more smoothly when men are not around.

Men who have strong sympathies with feminism are frequently surprised and hurt when they find they are not welcome in feminist circles. In an unpublished novel called "The Amazon's Brother: Testimony of a Committed Coed Feminist," Allan Hunter, then an undergraduate, wrote allegorically of his disappointment:

> He was sternly informed that [joining his sister to live with the Amazons] was out of the question, and was told of all the terrible man-crimes and man-ways that made male presence in their land intolerable. Said he, "I am not like that; try me for any such crimes, and if your court finds me innocent of [them], allow me to pass."

The Amazon sentinel laughed and told him that they had far more important things to do than evaluate each individual man who claimed to be different from the rest, saying, "I have yet to meet a man who did not think himself to be the single exception."

The young man protested. "I agree with your way of thinking about many things, and I want to share your lifestyle as an equal, for you are like unto neither the women nor the men in the maleworld, as you call it, and life there is intolerable."

Again the sentinel laughed and said, "Tell your brothers."[3]

Writing ten years later of his experience in a feminist theory class, Hunter, now a graduate student in sociology and Women's Studies at the State University of New York at Stony Brook, says that his attempts to debate theoretical issues in this class invariably led to "the constant question of 'Who asked you? Why should any of us give a damn if YOU don't like the direction that feminist theory is taking? It's our stuff, not your stuff.'" He finally concluded that it is conceptually problematic for any male to be a full-scale committed participant in the political effort to transform patriarchy.[4]

Nor is Hunter alone in having reached this conclusion. One consequence of a strict interpretation of gender IDPOL is that only women can be fully engaged in women's liberation. If Women's Studies is conceived of as an academy for training young feminists, it makes no sense to devote energy to male students, and males will not be welcome in Women's Studies classrooms. But this attitude cannot coexist with the broader feminist goal of educating everyone about gender issues. From the beginning, therefore, IDPOL was destructive to feminism's long-term aims.

Some feminist faculty recall their own discomfort with the way in which gender IDPOL was being played out in their programs. Linda, a white woman in her fifties, is a historian at a large research university. She has been involved with her school's Women's Studies program from its inception, more than two decades ago. Deeply committed to the ideal of community, she has reflected extensively on the causes of the lack of civility and the absence of tolerance among feminists:

> I have felt this all along, since the early seventies. This is nothing new. Lack of tolerance for high levels of diversity has been endemic to the program from the beginning. I would trace it to the inability to deal with a fundamental difference—and that is men. Once you've defined the world as a world of women, and you have decided that men cannot be assimilated into the way in which you develop your theory and methodology, and the way you interact socially, then you've already placed yourself in a curious contradiction to the whole concept of diversity. This feeling I've had has, I think, affected my social relationships with members of Women's Studies.
>
> I don't really want to sound as conservative as I'm going to sound right now. Let me just lay out this position for a second and then take it back, or qualify it. I do believe in divorce, but I think the ease with which people's intimate relationships are dissolved—whether they're married or nonmarried—because they can't get on with one another, because they are incompatible in some fundamental way, and the degree to which our culture has fostered the notion of not struggling together to work on differences and accept conflict, is also a reflection of what I call the separatist tradition of American society.
>
> That goes back to the Puritans separating from the Church of England in order to set up their ideal City on the Hill. We have had a profoundly separatist mentality in which denominations separate from one another, political groups separate from one another, rather than struggle together to work on their differences, to find modes of accommodation and pluralistic solutions. That separatist mentality was there in a very powerful way by the sixties in marital relationships and ultimately in women *needing* to separate from men. . . .
>
> There's no question in my mind that women *had* to separate

from men, that most of those partnerships were probably hopeless. But that became a way of not facing that there might be lots of situations where that was not the best solution, where working with men and learning how to deal with profound differences might have been a better way of handling things.

Because Linda believes that the organization of Women's Studies as a separate department generally exacerbates intolerance and the playing of IDPOL, she does not favor such a structure:

I think one reason for the difficulties at my university is that Women's Studies has to make political appointments. We have to hire people *in* Women's Studies. My theory is that we were *much* better off before we were a department. When you do those things—hires, fires, reappointments, tenure, all this personnel decision making—power enters. Not only does power enter, but also the question of, Who do you want to work closely with? Do you want a clone? Or do you want someone very different from yourself? And on the whole, I think that women—and it may well be because they've had enormous difficulty dealing with the otherness of men—want clones. Maybe they wouldn't say they want clones exactly, but they want people with whom they would feel a high level of rapport ideologically and personally.

There is an alternative to polarization and separatism, one that Linda much prefers, but she did not see this alternative model developing within Women's Studies:

It would have been an inclusive model. Before you get to the point of adding issues of race and ethnicity and religion and sexual preference and the disabled and all these other categories of difference, there has to be a respect for other people's decisions to live certain kinds of lives, whether it's to have children or not to have children, to be married to men or not to be married to men. These choices can't be seen as excluding someone from being a thoroughgoing feminist in theory or in practice. And I think there was this problem of exclusion from the beginning.

Having embraced exclusiveness and hostility toward those identified as outsiders, women, perhaps inevitably, soon turned on one another once the category "women" began to fragment along identity lines.

Sleeping with the Enemy

If, at first, women in the feminist movement considered gender the source of their primary identity, it quickly became apparent that this classification was no guarantee of internal unity. Many activists also identified themselves as lesbian. But since, according to the logic of IDPOL, one can only trust the perceptions and values of people who share one's identity, it is not surprising that conflicts arose, especially as the process of "coming out" and positively affirming a gay identity had been such a significant feature of lesbian existence.

The idea that the definition of one's identity incorporates political commitments is a central tenet of gay liberation analysis. As long as being homosexual was defined by traditional religion or by psychoanalysis, it was very difficult for gay people to view themselves as anything other than sinful, sick, or freaks of nature. By redefining themselves instead as gay (in both senses of the word), people of a same-sex orientation could begin to shed their stigmatized identities, to use the phrasing of Erving Goffman.[5]

But lesbian feminists then proposed a different and more radical definitional shift, one that led to political realignments. Feeling that it made better political sense to separate lesbians from the gay male liberation movement and wanting to form stronger alliances with nonlesbian feminists, they suggested that *lesbian* be redefined as "woman-identified woman." This change, they said, would remove sexual preference as the defining criterion of lesbian identity, and thereby would create potential common ground among lesbian feminists and other women interested in liberating women from male domination.

There were lesbian and heterosexual activists who argued that they should be able to work together, since both lesbian identity and feminist identity hinged on commitment to women. The liberation of women envisioned by feminists would automatically liberate lesbians, so the argument went. Instead of talking simply about patriarchy, these groups spoke of "heteropatriarchy," and in a famous often-anthologized essay called "Compulsory Heterosexuality and Lesbian Existence," Adrienne Rich contended that any woman who questioned male privilege and put emotional energy into women was part of the "lesbian continuum" of women-identified women.[6] Sexual preference was only one aspect of the feminist project of concentrating on women's needs and potentialities.

However, these attempts by theoreticians to build bridges between heterosexual and lesbian feminists were not very successful. Lesbians never forgot that Betty Friedan and other founders of NOW had called them the "lavender menace,"[7] while heterosexual women resented being told that they were "sleeping with the enemy." Furthermore, lesbians often felt that they were putting more than their fair share of energy into the new feminist institutions, such as battered women's shelters and Women's Studies programs, and that straight women did not appreciate their contributions. As one woman, Silvia, told us bitterly: "We worked our asses off, but we were told to be invisible because it would be bad for the big picture if the movement was cast as a bunch of radical dykes. The idea was to work for the rights of all women with the belief that the gains would trickle down to us. It simply never happened." Nonlesbians, on the other hand, noted that lesbians now seemed to be trying to turn *feminist* into a codeword for *lesbian* and were thereby using feminist organizations as a kind of cover to deflect stigma.

The logic of sexual identity politics also played itself out in the classroom. Just as radical feminists had argued that works by men had no place in the syllabus, radical lesbian feminists now demanded that the syllabus include *their* people. And Rich's concept of the lesbian continuum, which some had hoped would forge bonds between feminists of different persuasions, was used instead as a yardstick to determine the depth of one's commitment to feminism. Not surprisingly, Women's Studies students who talked about boyfriends or whose dress seemed intended to attract male attention did not measure up very well on the lesbian continuum.

Quite different tensions developed when feminists who had previously identified themselves as heterosexual decided that it would be politically preferable to sleep with women. These so-called political lesbians, unaccustomed to the courtship patterns in the lesbian subculture, were often accused by "born lesbians" of exploiting the latter's erotic energy. And although many political lesbians aggressively displayed their newfound sexual preference publicly as a badge of their feminist commitment, when springtime came they frequently found themselves falling in love with men again. When the failure of the feminist attempt to redefine sexuality in terms of polymorphous sensual sisterhood became apparent, lesbians then felt that it was they who had been tricked into sleeping with the enemy. Resentment of bisexual women increased dramatically as the AIDS epidemic worsened.

Silvia, the lesbian cited earlier, reserved her deepest criticism for the doctrinaire attitudes that developed within feminism itself as these conflicts were played out:

> I do what I interpret is precisely the main feminist message: to be independent, to think for myself, to question assumptions and stereotypes, and to claim an empowered life outside the realm of tradition in which a woman had to be "completed" by a man. When I heard those messages, I was excited, overwhelmed with enthusiasm, and thus naively believed what was

said. I set out to be independent, to think for myself, to question things, et cetera. However, when I entered into the realm of the "movement," I found that this wasn't what feminism was "about" at all. My experience has been that feminism has been just as conformist and stifling of creative thought as the most right-wing religious groups.

It seems that many in the feminist and lesbian subcultures require that you meet all of their criteria and address their agendas before they are willing to listen to what you have to say. We—women, feminists, lesbians, whatever—so often make statements or wear buttons proclaiming "Question Authority" or "Question Everything." However, we rarely, if ever, question feminism. Is it justifiable for women to trash or embarrass a male in a Women's Studies class on the grounds that men have done the same to women for ages? Questioning the authority of feminism or the heavyweights within the movement is akin to heresy, and is basically treated as such.

I have watched with great interest (and sometimes sadness) as the feminist and lesbian subcultures evolve. My latest barrage of criticism came when I made the statement that we lesbians have treated our bisexual sisters much the same as heterosexual society has treated us, and that we should be ashamed of ourselves because we should know better.

As we have seen, feminists had argued that women must isolate themselves from men. By the same logic, faults quickly appeared within feminism along lines of sexual preference. Many other fissures were to open in a chain reaction that, eventually, would threaten to leave feminism splintered.

Dismantling White Women's Studies

In 1977 a group called the Combahee River Collective issued a "Black Feminist Statement":

We believe that the most profound and potentially the most radical politics come directly out of our own identity, as opposed to working to end somebody else's oppression. . . . We realize that the only people who care enough about us to work consistently for our liberation is us. Our politics evolve from a healthy love for ourselves, our sisters, and our community which allows us to continue our struggle and work.[8]

This manifesto became an important statement of the growing belief among African-American women that "white feminism" was in many respects ill-suited to their political needs. One vivid example arose in connection with the feminist stance on rape. Whereas the official feminist analysis held that there is a very strong presumption that any female who alleges rape is telling the truth, black women remembered too many cases in which black men had been lynched as rapists simply on the say-so of a white woman. In their version of identity-based epistemology, then, race was sometimes a better guide than gender. And there were many other grounds on which they felt uncomfortable with the feminist agenda. Abortion on demand, for example, was not a good issue around which to organize grassroots support in the black community. And all the energy that early white middle-class feminists had devoted to liberating themselves from the "feminine mystique" seemed pretty silly to black women who had grown up with hardworking mothers who were outspoken and strong-willed.

Black women activists were faced with a confusing array of identity niches. Some joined African-American studies programs, but others found those arenas too male-dominated and turned to Women's Studies. Black lesbians had even more decisions to make. For example, when they attended a NWSA meeting, should they work through the black caucus or the lesbian caucus? Or should they form a black lesbian caucus?

Similar decisions faced the well-meaning feminist instructor who wished to design a syllabus that reflected all the major identity groups. If she devoted only one assignment to the concerns of, say, black lesbians, she was likely to be accused of "tokenism." Some students even went so far as to argue that a course should not be offered until the requisite number of works by authors of "proper identities" were available. As one professor reported: "That is exactly what a white Women's Studies student last fall commented on my course, in a tone of high censoriousness. She wrote that if I didn't know of more than one work by a black writer that fit into my rather specialized course, I damn well shouldn't be offering the course until I'd researched the subject thoroughly."

Such dilemmas arose in connection with scholarly publishing, too. Black feminists complained that they were invisible or, at the very least, underrepresented in feminist journals and anthologies. White feminists countered that for a variety of reasons, some of them demographic and others having to do with the history of racism, there was a dearth of material written by black women. But the perspectives of black women were taken to heart, and it quickly became a standard trope of feminist criticism to claim that any work of feminist scholarship that does not explicitly focus on race is seriously defective. A white woman professor told us that when a book she had edited got blasted in a feminist journal for not containing a sufficient number of articles by and about women of color, a concerned friend informed her that she was "dead" as a scholar because of the imputation of racism.

On the other hand, it is usually considered inappropriate for white women to do too much research on minority women. After all, how can they pretend to have genuine insight into another identity? Are they not simply usurping the voices of women of color—engaging in ventriloquism? And it has also become very difficult for white women to reflect critically on anything written by a woman of color. A white professor reports:

In one of my classes a student made a criticism of a metaphor utilized in a novel by a black writer. One of the Women's Studies majors sniffily observed that it was not up to us, as white women, to criticize a black writer's metaphors. A rather shy student in the same class, who was also a Women's Studies major, confessed in paper after paper her guilt over her "white-skin privilege" and her status as "oppressor." And why not? I have repeatedly heard a black colleague of mine declare: "There are two kinds of people in the world: oppressors and oppressed—and these correspond to white and nonwhite."

IDPOL can also readily lead to disputes about grades when teachers and students belong to different identity groups. Another Women's Studies professor wrote to us:

> There is a professor of history here who teaches the course Women in History (a core component of the program), who is being raked over the coals for not including [in her syllabus] all women of all countries. . . . At the last meeting at which this problem was discussed, a student who is a woman of color said that she got a 78 percent on her paper—which she considered to be a poor mark—because the faculty member involved, not being black, did not understand her. The whole issue has become very scary to me, and the instances of people either losing their jobs or leaving voluntarily are increasing.
>
> What most bothers me personally is the way people measure their words in order not to offend. Let's face it: people can be offended over virtually anything, and if we spend our lives worrying about it, we really will not have too much to say. As Susan Sontag says, we must be against censorship and self-censorship and for the right to offend. It is frustrating to me to be told that I cannot respond or speak a certain way because I am of a certain skin color. I thought we were supposed to have gone beyond all that. There are racists and there are sexists. I am not one of them, and I do not like being accused of being one simply by virtue of my appearance.

Silvia, the lesbian critic of feminist orthodoxies whom we quoted earlier, also protested against what she called "this double standard stuff":

What could possibly be more racist and/or condescending than to expect less of an individual, to allow an individual to present positions (and even praise them) that are riddled with inconsistencies, or to hold another individual to higher standards of rigor, based upon their ethnicity or race? Sometimes I am ashamed to call myself a feminist, and I often feel that I have to add so many qualifiers that it is hardly worth it.

IDPOL has also frequently led to charges of racism concerning administrative decisions. This was the experience of one of the authors of this book when she served briefly as program director. A particularly nasty blow-up occurred when new funds could not be located for an elective course proposed by two minority graduate students, who were to be the instructors. At about the same time, the director had used the last of the existing budget to hire the most experienced graduate student (who was white) to teach a required course for which no faculty member was available. The minority students protested and accused the director of being racist:

At a large meeting of our governing board, I attempted to explain how the two, quite unrelated, decisions regarding courses and teaching assistants had been made. A young black colleague said (as I had heard her say on other occasions) that when a woman of color states that she has been the victim of racism, *she* is the authority on that experience and cannot be challenged. I replied that this assertion made examining any problem impossible. That comment only made things worse. No one supported me in trying to move our discussion to a different ground. More accusations followed: I was said to be guilty of racism personally, while the program was tagged as pervaded by "structural racism." The white graduate student announced that she could not, in good conscience, teach the course for which she had been hired.

By now I have learned that the only acceptable response in feminist circles when accusations of racism surface is, "Mea culpa." It was also clear, even to me after a while, that a power play was going on. Accusations of racism gained for the accuser points of some sort. Keeping others on the defensive seemed to have become a strategy no one was willing to challenge.

But I believed that the issue of the truth or falsity of particular accusations needed to be addressed. Knowing the "identity" of accuser and accused simply was not enough to resolve a grievance. I denied the charges—which only brought a storm upon my head. The result was that I found myself increasingly isolated as memos flew about, accusing me of one thing and another, while my "friends"—senior, tenured faculty in Women's Studies, who were in perfectly secure positions—tried feebly to support me behind the scenes but were unwilling to say anything in public.

Evidence of my "racism" was produced, such as a memo I had written to a Women's Studies committee urging us to attempt to work together without casting blame or attaching labels to one another. My suggestion that it did not help matters to bandy about terms such as "Eurocentric" and "racist"— which by then had become virtual synonyms and were repeated by our students—was itself cited as a further mark of my "racism." Long afterwards—small comfort—one of my former friends, who had remained publicly silent throughout this depleting episode, said to me: "You did nothing wrong, and race had nothing to do with it." That was one of the few times reference was ever made to what had happened. None of the principal belligerents said a word to me later about their accusations.

In such a climate, professional decorum, concepts of collegiality, and proper academic procedures are quick to fall:

A colleague of mine, I later found out, allowed two of her students that semester to do an "analysis" of racism in the program which highlighted that same memo of mine—a confidential memo addressed to a Women's Studies committee.

Toward the end of that semester, a group of graduate students proposed that, during the following term, they team-teach a course on indigenous women. My colleagues accepted the sketchy proposal without asking any questions about it, over my protests that we needed time to consider the proposal calmly. One voiced the predominant view: "We can't afford to turn it down"—this, despite the fact that there was no detailed course proposal on the table before us, merely a couple of lines followed by a listing of half a dozen North and South American "identities," which would presumably serve as the subjects of the course.

These episodes cost me any lingering faith I had in our program as a place where serious academic work—not to mention normal collegial relations—could exist.

Denunciations of homophobia and racism can, of course, just as easily be made by heterosexuals or whites as by actual members of oppressed groups, and some of the most bizarre situations arise when it is white women who are accusing one another of racism in situations where no women of color are directly involved. Often the allegations seem to be serving primarily as ammunition in personal struggles for power.

What is the atmosphere like in a program that has gone through such battles? One professor wrote as follows:

I have no doubt that in our Women's Studies program, each of us felt that we were working in an extremely hostile environment, surrounded by women who for the most part had no respect or liking for one another. One day, after a particularly tense meeting, I imagined how the scene might look to a being from another planet. Such a creature's account might go like this:

"I descended to earth one afternoon and found myself in a room filled with beings colorfully dressed. From their discussion I understood these were, or were acting on behalf of, a group called 'women'—a category apparently suffering some sort of disadvantage in relation to another category named 'men' who did not seem to be present. These women, if such they were, were of a variety of colors—some pale ivory, some dark brown, some beige, some pinkish. Though to my senses they looked very much alike—all had two eyes, a protrusion centrally placed on the face and serving I know not what purpose, a pink-colored opening from which sound emerged, and shell-shaped appendages on either side of the face from which pieces of stone and glittery metal sometimes dangled—it was clear that they saw themselves as very different from one another, and made much of these differences. Foremost among the distinctions was the hue of the skin—all used the phrase 'women of color' repeatedly—and I sensed that some of the darker-complexioned among them harbored a particular grievance against the others that was often on the verge of exploding but equally often expressed in innuendo and gesture. The lighter-skinned, by contrast, were nervous, poised as if prepared to receive a blow and, judging by their expressions, awash in feelings of conflict and guilt ill concealed by their apparent acceptance of angry words from the others. Fear was evident in all these beings, mingled with hostility and resentment, over I knew not what."

IDPOL based on race can, of course, also lead to animosities among women of color. A black Latina woman speaking at a conference session that one of us attended told of participating in the first Latin American meeting of women who identified themselves as black (many Latin American women do not, either because they have no African ancestry or because they downplay it). The speaker reported that the organizers had decided not to admit lighter-skinned women of African descent to the meeting. She personally had seen a light-skinned, straight-haired woman challenged at the conference door with, "What are you doing here?" In recounting the episode, the speaker seemed to applaud this procedure. She reported that when she conducted interviews, she made it a point to challenge light-skinned women who spoke to her about their "black grandmother." While many in the audience squirmed uncomfortably, noting that the speaker herself had far lighter skin than many blacks, she declared in tones of moral righteousness that she would not let such interviewees "get away with denying their light-skin privilege."

Many of the white Women's Studies professors we interviewed seemed genuinely puzzled over what could be done about the allegations of racism they had encountered, and the ritualistic denunciations and confessions of "white-skin privilege." These accusations seemed especially troublesome to them in light of the frequent and rather desperate searches for "affirmative action" candidates to fill "special opportunities" positions within their departments. Moreover, many white women teaching in Women's Studies programs had never been guilty of "ignoring" women of color in their courses, a common charge. Linda, the history professor cited earlier in this chapter, who has been very active in her university's Women's Studies program for the past twenty years, analyzed the situation this way:

> There is a tendency to mythologize the seventies as being unaware of the issues of race and ethnicity. Quite honestly, I was then teaching my women's history course very little differently, in terms of its race component, than I do now. That is, I always taught a lot about women under slavery, I taught a lot about ethnic and immigrant cultures. I think the major change is that I deal much more now with indigenous American women, Native American women. But my course was always pluralistic. So it's not like this became a sudden new agenda in the late eighties. It was there all along, it just took on a much greater urgency and intensity in the mid-eighties.

The most common response to the angry allegations of racism has been to elevate this issue to the theoretical level, where calls for an "integrated analysis" of race, gender, class, sexuality, ethnicity, and so on, are recited "like a mantra" (as several of the professors we interviewed put it). In practice, this means that, whether discussing a novel or a social problem, one must always focus on race, gender, class, sexuality, and so on, and demonstrate how these factors interact. Proponents of "integrated analysis" always claim that the forces that create oppression (and the privilege that is its counterpart) are systemically related and that unless all are removed, no real or lasting progress will have been made. Mysteriously, the central force or forces that this integrated analysis purports to expose are never specified, beyond rounding up the usual suspects: hierarchy, heteropatriarchy, contempt for the Other, phallocentrism, multinational capitalism, imperialism, hegemonic nationalism, worship of "power over" instead of empowerment, and on and on.

Black women, on the other hand, have grown increasingly angry at what they view as the refusal of white feminists to admit their own racism. They favor the term *structural racism* to refer to institutional arrangements dependent on both the heritage of racism generally and the subtle complicity they allege exists between white women's self-definition and the white American male's assumption of an identity constructed on the oppression of African Americans.

This sweeping charge was spelled out in detail for us by Marilyn, a black professor in a social science department who is also active in her university's Women's Studies program. She identifies herself as a "womanist," using a term popularized by the writer Alice Walker to refer to nonseparatist black women who see their struggle as one on behalf of black women *and* men.[9] "*Feminist*," Marilyn says, "for me, is too narrowly associated with white women. And most women of color who have issues and are active around them are not feminist, do not define themselves as feminist." Women's Studies, in Marilyn's view, is *white* Women's Studies:

I would like to be able to see students of color who are attending predominantly white institutions be able to study themselves in relationship to whites and other women of color, and to get their degree doing it. Right now, in order to get their degree, they still have to predominantly study whites, and I think that's inappropriate. But that's the only Women's Studies there is. We don't have a nonwhite Women's Studies; we have white Women's Studies. Everybody else kind of plugs into it.

I happen to be at this school, but there are plenty of schools where there's *no* people like me. So, therefore, I'm saying that the mass of the curriculum that's available for anybody who's doing Women's Studies is a white curriculum. When I teach a course, I'm plugging my little bitty course into this big white curriculum. It's a fly in a glass of milk. So I don't see that as change.

What would it take for real change to occur? Marilyn outlines her vision:

I think it's going to take white women dealing with their complicity with white men, and I don't think they will do that. I don't think that they want to look at that. You know, white women, on the one hand, are willing to acknowledge the way the whole women's movement itself really caught fire on the coattails of the black movement. People will give lip service to that in an intellectual form. People don't want to think about the pragmatic, practical implications of that, in terms of what this program should be looking like. If the black movement gave birth to the women's movement, why aren't black people central in the women's movement? Racism, that's why.

What I'm saying is that if it's ever going to change, that change has to be an internal one, in those women who currently hold power in Women's Studies. What needs to happen is for those women to be able to *acknowledge* the way in which their efforts to include themselves in a particular group of power has exclusionary tendencies. Even when people of color are invited by them, there are ways in which people of color who have been invited in are constrained in their opportunities to articulate *their* vision of what the program ought to look like. That constraint is specifically designed to make the people who are the *core* of the program—i.e., the white women— feel safe. And so, until white women who are the core of these programs are willing to look at that, and to give up some sense of that safety, and to take more risk, I don't think we're going to see a change, no matter how many creative courses people of color create.

Marilyn explains what she means by the "power" that white women exercise in Women's Studies:

These women have white privilege—that's their power. I'm not saying that they run the university. I'm not saying that they have the power to make their Women's Studies program or department whatever they wanted it to be. But I am saying that they collude with the university in the maintenance of white power—white privilege. And even their subordination is part of their collusion—in the same way that the subordination of white women to white men made white male supremacy possible. That's exactly what I'm saying.

I'm saying that white women as a class of people had to allow themselves to be subordinated by white males in order to reify this notion of white supremacy. So white supremacy in a general sense applies to all white people, but in a very specific, analytical sense it mainly refers to white male supremacy. And white women have always known this. They have generally raised their sons to be white male supremacists. I think that the interest of a woman in doing that is that she will have a dominant white male son who is able to gain greater access to the available resources than most other people on earth.

To a question about whether some of Women's Studies difficulties might be due to lack of respect or civility among colleagues without this having anything to do with race, Marilyn responded emphatically:

Well, this is one of the places where you and I probably differ, and I know this is very much because I was born in a black body and you weren't. But in my opinion, it's completely ludicrous for me to hear you say that those particular kinds of problems that you just described don't have anything to do with race. White women don't know who they themselves are in isolation from women of color, and white women don't know who they themselves are independently of the construction of male power. So it makes sense to me, since vertical oppression—that is, oppression by males against white women—always produces horizontal oppression—that is, people fighting among themselves. So I see that as a racial phenomenon. It doesn't bother me that you don't, but I think that until you *can*, we won't ever solve the problem. I don't know why you're not willing. I suspect it's fear, fear of what could happen with the relinquishment of authority.

"Definitely one of the disappointments of my adult life," says Marilyn, "[is] that I fail to see more emphasis on people of color in most Women's Studies programs." Although their complaints differed widely, everyone we talked to was disappointed at the way Women's Studies programs had negotiated issues of race. Whatever their take on the nature of racism and what should be done about it, our narrators had all expected Women's Studies to be a strategic site for making some progress on these problems.

We submit, however, that IDPOL, which has been the main strategy for addressing the problem of race (as well as gender), does more harm than good to this cause. According to the logic of IDPOL, one must always act in one's own group's interest as long as that group is oppressed. Oppressors are assumed to be doing the same for their side, but they should be castigated for doing so. Thus, a man who does not support a feminist cause is automatically a sexist; a white person who disagrees with a black person's position is a racist. The reverse, however, is not the case. Consequently, those defined as oppressed place a high premium on keeping that identity.

Patriarchy and Pigs at the Trough

The logical result of extreme identity-based politics is tribalism or balkanization, the partitioning of a complex system into small ethnically and culturally distinct units of homogeneous identities, none of which seeks coalitions with any other unit (not unlike the situation that has been occurring in the former Yugoslavia).

The expanding intricacies of IDPOL have led to the creation of entirely new categories of oppression. At many feminist public events there are now special scent-free seating areas for the "environmentally disadvantaged" who cannot tolerate the smell of deodorants or hairspray. Feminist institutions, not surprisingly, have become notorious for their factionalism. The large annual Michigan Women's Music Festival has even introduced segregated seating, drawn on identity lines, for its concerts and camping grounds. Feminists are proud of their abilities to accommodate the needs of diverse women, but they also joke uneasily about this multiplication of "identities" and realize that it is apt to lead to a splintering and trivializing of the feminist movement, so that it loses its potential for genuine political action.

A recent college graduate reported to us on how the focus of concern in the "Take Back the Night" marches in which she participates gradually changed from dealing with college jocks who harassed the marchers from the sidewalks to trying to maintain harmony among different groups of feminists:

> Being on Internet gave me an opportunity to meet people and receive information—like a twelve-page list of activities, meet-

ings, conferences, and receptions to be held prior to the march [sponsored by] Catholics, Jewish women, lesbians, bisexuals, polysexuals, African-American women, women of Spanish descent, Greek women-loving women, reformed Catholic lesbian women loving Greek women with tattoos. The list just went on and on. There seemed to be a little subgroup for every single person who categorized herself as "oppressed"—or maybe just a special interest.

Yes, I fit into more than one of the above categories, and I understand the ideas behind separatism. But what do we have now? We have a women's movement made up of all these little tiny groups, because each one wants special attention. There's no solidarity, because we're all so interested in making sure the world knows that people are diverse. We don't come together often enough anymore. It's becoming too segregated. And there's no utopia for people who want different things, unless those different things balance each other out. But they can't balance, because one thing they want is the same: recognition and respect. If ALL the groups have that, no group is "special" anymore.

Contrast this with the hopes of the early days of Women's Studies. A historian who, in the late 1960s, taught one of the first women's history courses left this field because of her unpleasant experiences at the hands of other feminists. She expresses the sense of loss that, years later, still overtakes her as she recalls her original expectations:

I'll tell you the kinds of ideas I used to spout, back in 1969 and '70 and '71. I would say things like, "We're all women—what does it matter that this one is a lesbian and I happen to be married and this one has chosen to do this or that? Isn't the umbrella big enough to shelter all of us?" I really did believe once upon a time that all women could be sisters.

I think that's where the rage in me comes from: that there

are so many powerful things that should be binding us, that we should be able to acknowledge, to create a forum where we really could share these things and talk about our pain and help heal one another and really be together, and, if we wanted to change the world and make it more in our image, to truly stand shoulder to shoulder to do that.

It makes me feel terrible to have lost that part of what I believed could be so. . . . [sobbing] Part of me wanted to believe that could be possible for us. And to see us more divided and less able to deal with the things that are really important, and less able to give young women like my daughter the tools that she needs to go out and lead her life. . . . —it not only feels sad to me, but it feels like such a missed historical opportunity.

I don't blame us; I don't think it was our fault. It feels sad for me to definitely let go of that part of my life and to recognize that I have done so.

Another pernicious aspect of IDPOL is the now-popular practice of stating one's identity (in terms of the key bases of race, ethnicity, sexual orientation, and class, at the very least) whenever one speaks or writes.[10] For more than a decade it has been customary—sometimes even obligatory—for feminist authors to publicly "situate" themselves in their books and papers, especially if their identities are multifaceted. Thus, a volume of feminist essays on mothering carries a blurb on contributors that begins: "I am a lesbian socialist-feminist mother of a twelve-year-old interracial daughter. . . . "[11] However, the author of this blurb, who is white, played IDPOL imperfectly, since she apparently took for granted, and therefore did not specify, her race. (One may wonder whether, had she not been white, this woman would so readily have announced her daughter's interracial heritage.) And as we have noted, it is customary for feminist reviewers to comment (generally unfavorably) on the identity distribution of the subjects and authors of articles that appear in journals and collections of essays.

Furthermore, group identity is assumed to determine all arguments a person makes or any actions she takes. When practical questions arise, however, identity politics is apt to break down. Which kind of faculty member is most needed as a role model for students: a Native American, a woman with disabilities, a lesbian, or someone from the "Third World"? Who has a better claim on scholarship funds: older returning students with children or young Chicanas for whom English is a second language?

Feminists regularly get themselves tied in knots dealing with such questions. In order to resolve them, it seems that one should have a clear hierarchy of oppressions so that the most oppressed always gets the nod. But no one can agree on how to rank competing oppressions. Black women are widely viewed as the most oppressed, but Hispanics and Native Americans are now putting forward their claims. People are starting to ask: "Is it really true these days that black women professors have a harder time than whites getting tenure, and that they draw lower salaries?"

Meanwhile, some white women with limited financial resources are getting tired of being portrayed as paragons of privilege. A white woman who has worked for years as an activist and lobbyist for Indian causes in South Dakota told us of how "a craze for labels" had disrupted collective efforts. The Native American women in her group began to refer to the white women members as "women of privilege." "For God's sake," the activist exclaimed, in recounting this development to us, "I've been a welfare mother most of my life!" She was also dismayed when a Native American employee of the organization began to reply to every criticism of her work with a shrug and, "You just don't understand how we Indians do things."

Despite their awareness of these difficulties, the primary response of feminists to this—as to any other problem—is to blame patriarchy. As one woman said, referring to the need of different programs at many universities to compete aggressively for special faculty lines for "minority" members: "If there were no patriarchy, there would be no oppression. If there were no oppression, there would be no need for affirmative action. If there were no affirmative action, we wouldn't be here acting like pigs trying to shoulder each other away from the trough!"

Opponents of feminism will indeed be happy to watch the various factions exhaust each other in the fight for scraps. But friends of feminism must begin to ask whether this kind of self-defeating behavior cannot be brought to an end.

THE PRICE OF OPPRESSIVE PRIVILEGE

As we have seen, the strategy of IDPOL is to demand that special consideration be given to the interests and opinions of members of an oppressed group. In addition, such people must be presumed to be especially knowing and virtuous, at least with respect to situations related to their oppressed condition. This strategy of demanding special privileges inevitably leads to hostilities among oppressed groups and to lessened sympathy among those identified as being outside these groups. But IDPOL is destructive in more ways than these. It does harm to the very individuals who identify as members of victimized groups. The price of playing identity politics is the cognitive and moral debilitation of the oppressed.

Why does such harm occur? First, the characteristics forming the basis of membership in oppressed identity groups are, by and large, immutable. One might seek transsexual surgery, dye or straighten one's hair, or lose one's accent and assimilate; but, as a rule, one cannot change membership in the groups under discussion. Class, by contrast—especially in America, where one's social position depends more on income and education than on birth and cultural heritage—is much more labile.

On the other hand, individuals do have a choice in the extent to which they actively identify with the group to which society assigns them. Thus, Gore Vidal, to take an example, has always refused to identify himself as a homosexual. The IDPOL strategy, however, requires that group affiliation become a salient part of an individual's personal identity. We are reminded here of the opening rituals of

Alcoholics Anonymous, where participants introduce themselves as alcoholics; in this context, being an alcoholic is clearly the most important aspect of the person and is the basis for the bonding that such rituals encourage.

IDPOL, moreover, demands that one actively identify with the worst damage that has been inflicted on one's group. As a woman, therefore, I must feel solidarity with females in other cultures—as when the feminist philosopher Mary Daly routinely proclaims in her public appearances that she feels the pain of her African sisters who are undergoing clitoridectomies.[12] But, not surprisingly, Daly's expressions of solidarity sound hollow to many people, and they are particularly objectionable to black women, who see her as "appropriating" oppression that "belongs" to them.

Within Women's Studies, women are pressured not to say things like, "I know many women are discouraged from going on to graduate school, but I always got a lot of encouragement from my male professors." As a result, women learn either to deny, or to feel guilty about, experiences that do not conform to the approved model of oppression. It is assumed that an inability to testify to personal experiences of gender oppression casts doubt on the authenticity of one's commitment to feminism.

Individuals must not only identify with a particular oppressed group but also, as far as possible, existentially participate in the sufferings and injustices of that group. The result of this pressure is that group members are constantly exposed to vivid accounts of incidents of extreme sexism. Women who have been brutalized undoubtedly find it gratifying to learn that others, too, have suffered—this is the consolation of the postsurgical ward. But women who do not feel crippled by sexism must "learn" that in fact they were—and are—victims of this cultural offense. Those whose experiences have been less negative are expected to search their memories for suppressed traumas. If they cannot locate these, they should, at the very least, maintain a sympathetic silence. And until they can come up with the requisite sufferings, they had better mute their claim to status in the identity group.

One effect of these practices is to stretch the meaning of words such as *harassment* and *racism*, so that everyone in the group is able to qualify as a victim. Another is that it hypersensitizes all those who identify with the oppressed group. IDPOL team players learn to be on the lookout for instances of injustice—especially those directed at them personally—so they will have a show-and-tell for the next sharing session.

Any undertaking involving the wholesale substitution of group norms for individual experiences, feelings, and ideas ought to be suspect. But doctrinaire feminism is particularly worrisome because it blocks the individual's ability to evaluate fairly and reasonably the causes of and remedies for her own personal unhappiness or lack of fulfillment. There are many barriers to a satisfactory life—some surmountable, others not. But the one thing all of us can aspire to is self-knowledge, along with some understanding of the constraints placed on us by our situation and of reasonable prospects for overcoming them. Feminist indoctrination inhibits women's ability to reach for this objective.

Feminism begins with the promise of liberating women from the distortions of gender under patriarchy. Unfortunately, however, contemporary feminism also fits women with blinders that keep them from seeing the varied possibilities present in their individual lives. At times this leads to paradoxical situations, as in the incantation that women are silenced and powerless, often voiced and written by highly articulate women in positions of considerable authority.

Silvia, a research biologist and lesbian activist, wrote to us:

There is no doubt in my mind that women are oppressed. However, one would think, with all of the work in Women's Studies and feminist/postmodernist theory, someone would have made the giant leap in logic that though we may not have much control or choice over the fact that we are oppressed, we do have autonomy and choice with respect to how we will respond to our oppression. *We do not have to act like oppressed people.* I learned this very important lesson from an elderly black man when I was in my early twenties. I grew up in an urban ghetto. I graduated from high school functionally illiterate. I was filled with anger and hostility, was an alcoholic, and, like most of my peers, could be constantly heard complaining about "the man." But that piece of advice from a man I held in high respect literally changed the course of my life.

When I was focused on my oppression exclusively, my creativity was stifled, I lacked vision for myself, and I lacked empathy for others. I, along with my peers, was constantly policing others for the proper attitude and behavior. Contrary to what most people on the outside believe, the ghetto isn't a place of chaos. It is a place of order. The rules and the manner in which order is maintained may be different than on the outside, but that doesn't mean that order doesn't exist. We all had a desire deep down to get out, but very few ever did, mainly because of the incessant policing of attitude and behavior. The moment that someone shows signs of making something of their life, rather than gaining the support of their peers, they are ostracized and torn down by them. It's a vicious cycle. This, in my opinion, is largely what goes on in feminist and lesbian circles as well. There is a right way to "be" and a wrong way to "be."

A rare attempt to challenge IDPOL's orthodoxy occurred on the Women's Studies E-mail list when, in 1993, the nomination of Lani Guinier as the assistant attorney general for civil rights fell through. Guinier received so much uncritical support on the list that one social scientist was moved to comment: "What troubles me is that the assumption is made by people who have *not* read [Guinier's works] that she is right and the attackers are wrong simply because she is a black woman. This is identity politics at its worst. We need to be discussing ideas, not the identity of individuals." The fact that few people in Women's Studies circles are willing even to entertain such a position, for fear of appearing "racist," merely demonstrates the hold of IDPOL on their minds.

It is indeed much simpler to flaunt an identity than to formulate a winning argument. Long before IDPOL had a name, the writer James Baldwin exposed the game when he said: "Every time I attend a conference of white writers, I have a method for finding out if my colleagues are racist. It consists of uttering stupidities and maintaining absurd theses. If they listen respectfully and, at the end, overwhelm me with applause, there isn't the slightest doubt: they are filthy racists."[13]

Given the crudeness of its categories and the problems it creates, why is IDPOL being played? The answer is that it works in the short term, at least within the progressive and sympathetic setting of the academy. Most of our colleagues—to their credit, it could be argued—*do* feel some responsibility for the past and are highly susceptible to imputations of collective guilt. But IDPOL, which is inherently unstable and promotes internal conflicts, cannot sustain a coherent political movement. Furthermore, by always giving greater weight to the testimony of members of oppressed groups, it tempts the participants to invent grievances. The greater feminism's success in raising our feelings of moral outrage at sexual harassment, date rape, or insensitive remarks in the workplace or classroom, the more likely it is that members of a protected group will find it in their interest to make a false or frivolous accusation. In a rape trial, for example, it is now ironic that, as we—properly—destigmatize the woman accuser, we simultaneously undermine the old feminist argument that the process of accusing someone of rape is so self-vilifying that no woman would ever intentionally make a false accusation.

Similar conundrums can occur with allegations of racism. In very hostile environments a victim of racism must have great courage to speak up. But in a climate in which it is assumed that every white person is a racist, it would be surprising if individuals did not sometimes allege racism when it is to their advantage to do so.

The only remedy for such abuses is to stop using identity as a passkey to all questions of truth or responsibility. Oppression will not cease because special political, epistemic, or moral privileges are awarded to the oppressed. Its elimination must be sought elsewhere.

4

Proselytizing and Policing in the Feminist Classroom

FOR MANY Women's Studies faculty, teaching is a more important, and probably more gratifying, activity than research. Indeed, feminists have been in the forefront of the current movement to give teaching and service greater recognition in the university. It seems likely, therefore, that most Women's Studies teachers start out sincerely intending to act in the best interests of their students. Given the ideology of academic feminism, however, their best instructional efforts have too often succeeded only in subverting both the values of the academy and the goal of improving women's condition.

On the one hand, Women's Studies teachers are deliberately using their classrooms as sites for the recruiting and training of students to be feminist activists. This aim tends to produce standard proselytizing tactics such as providing comfort and support for neophytes, denouncing the enemy, rejecting opinions that contradict or complicate the party line, and engaging in rituals of confession and celebration to keep the faithful pure and committed. These are all procedures that tend to constrict, rather than open, mental horizons, and straiten, rather than enlarge, argument.

On the other hand, since Women's Studies programs function as parts of colleges and universities, they are expected to offer their students at least the semblance of a liberal education; they could not otherwise justify their status within academic institutions. Despite widespread complaints about the erosion of that ideal, college students still expect the classroom to be a place for debate and the free expression and exchange of varied ideas and opinions, especially when the topics under discussion are open-ended and controversial. This opposition between politicized academic instruction and the values of liberal education explains most of the problems that erupt in Women's Studies classrooms.

Many feminists, however, resolutely refuse to face up to these difficulties. Instead, they write theoretical treatises about the virtues of feminist pedagogy and recommend that these methods be exported to the rest of the educational system. Some of the theory behind feminist pedagogy is discussed in chapter 7. What we want to explore now are the games that actually go on in Women's Studies classes, under the guise of pedagogy. Like IDPOL, what might be called FEMPED is a bewildering but destructive array of maneuvers. Who better to provide an initial description of these games than students?

SURVIVING WOMEN'S STUDIES: STUDENTS' PERSPECTIVES

The students we talked to had strong reactions—some positive, some negative—to their experiences in feminist classrooms. Caroline, a social worker in her mid-twenties, says that the one Women's Studies course she took at a private women's college was more than enough. Laura, on the other hand, who recently graduated from a state university with a minor in Women's Studies, "honestly believe[s] that everyone should be required to take a Women's Studies class." Despite this divergence of opinion, their descriptions of what went on in their respective classes are surprisingly similar. It is primarily in their evaluations of these experiences that they differ. Laura describes feminist education as "reverse indoctrination," but she thinks such training is necessary in order to counteract all that "you grow up indoctrinated with." Caroline, for her part, deplores "this ongoing knee-jerk reverse sexism which everyone tolerated and encouraged."

It did not take Caroline long to form a bad impression of Women's Studies:

The course was Introduction to Women's Studies. I was a senior, and I was, I think, pretty confident by that time, and I remember clashing with the professor very quickly. The class made me think of a skit on *Monty Python* which involves a quiz show, except the answer to every question is "pork." And whatever the quiz show host asks—for example, "What's the capital of Pennsylvania?"—the answer is "pork." In the class I took, the answer was always "men." Whatever the question was, the answer was "men." It could be, "What style of architecture is that?" And the answer is, "Men's architecture." Or, "Who contributes to all the violence in the world?" "Men." "Who's responsible for everything that we endure?" "Men" [laughing].

I was involved with a man at the time, and I thought that he didn't fit their categories of what men were like. And I also saw him as having been pressed into stereotypes of his own. When he'd been in high school, he took up computers. He'd been very nonathletic, hated team sports, wanted to read, wanted to fuss with his computers. And he was called a nerd and hassled constantly over this and abused in various ways. And I felt like I really identified with that—I hadn't been all that feminine in high school. I wore a black leather jacket, hung out with the guys, and people had made fun of me. I hadn't been desirable as a woman; he hadn't been desirable as a man. No girls wanted to date him, no guys wanted to date me. So I guess I was interested in a more global analysis, like: What is it in our society that creates some of these tensions? What is it that we're doing to ourselves here? I'm not saying I wanted the whole course to be about this, but these questions weren't acceptable at all, and I felt that the professor responded really aggressively to me.

The time that it really sort of came to a head was when we were talking about rape: "Rape—the act of violence that men do to women, that men do to women because they want to keep them down." And we got all these reasons why men rape women. And I thought, Well, there's this act of violence of men against women, and why don't we explore a little bit why people are so frustrated and so violent and so angry that they do these things? And why don't we take into consideration that men get raped too? I had a friend in high school, a man, who was raped by a bunch of other men of his age, and when I tried to enter this information, it was met with a stone wall: "Those statistics are insignificant compared with how many women are raped." And I thought, Well, how many men are reporting it? And why are you discounting what I'm trying to share here, which would be adding to the picture? And I don't remember the comment that the professor made, but it was very condescending, to the effect: "Are you saying that rapists are just poor misunderstood people who should be patted on the back and sent out?" And I'm thinking: You miserable bitch! You know, she was really like "Let me humiliate you in front of everyone," because, of course, that was not what I was saying!

I have friends who've been raped; it's not like some far-away thing to me. It's something to get really angry about and be upset about, but something to search for a better solution to than castration! But the only solution that the professor was getting at was that men are the problem and without men there'd be a solution. There was no talk of *real* solutions.

Caroline also objected to the constant representation of women as victims:

I didn't feel like a victim. I felt more responsible for the ways in which I messed up my life and the things I'd done wrong than I thought the professor was willing to allow. I find it more empowering to take responsibility for my problems and for the things I do wrong than to say that someone else has done it, because if I've done it, then I have some sort of control over my life. For example, I feel I have to take responsibility for the fact that I read *Cosmopolitan* and I look at the ads and then feel miserable. And that's got to be at least some part of me, and I can't just say, "Well, it's men." There are women in advertising, lots of women.

In her other courses at the "Seven Sisters" college she attended, Caroline had been used to studying with professors who encouraged discussions and arguments in class. But in her Women's Studies class she found a very different atmosphere:

I felt that the professor really controlled the discussion—that there were some things that she thought were appropriate to be discussed, and then there were the wrong answers and she didn't want to hear those and they couldn't be discussed. It didn't really feel like discussion. It felt like a fill-in-the-blank-type lecture, where the teacher kind of tells you what to say and you say it, and then she goes on.

I don't remember ever having the politically correct thing come up in any other class the way it did in that class. The Women's Studies class is the one which sticks out in my head—I felt really attacked as a person in a way I hadn't been in any other classes.

I just didn't feel that these Women's Studies classes had anything to offer. It seemed to me like they were stuck twenty years ago and that I could find out the information I was curious about through history classes, philosophy classes, but not through Women's Studies. There wasn't anything that a

Women's Studies class could offer me that I couldn't get somewhere else better, with less rigidity.

Laura, too, recalls such tensions in the Women's Studies courses she
attended, but she draws quite a different conclusion. She describes the
purpose of Women's Studies programs this way:

> I think that Women's Studies was created in order to
> strengthen women and to strengthen women's position in the
> world. I think it was created to—ideally?—to educate every-
> one, so that things can change, so that people will be equal.
> Practically? I think it appeals to a small base of people and that
> it is very difficult for it to educate the general population
> because the general population is not open to it. I think it
> could be better used to educate men. I mean, men ignore the
> fact that there's a Women's Studies program on this campus.
> And so women are getting all this great knowledge about
> women in the Women's Studies classes, they're learning all this
> stuff that can empower them and help them change, but it
> stays among the women.

She readily admits that men are not welcome in Women's Studies
courses and are sometimes even discouraged from enrolling:

> In the upper-level courses, if a man who's never taken a Wom-
> en's Studies course wants to get in, he has to be very strong-
> willed and has to be determined to do it, because he is going to
> run into a lot of flak—because in Women's Studies classes,
> women definitely feel like they run the show. I mean, the stu-
> dents run the show; they have a right to speak. And if a man is
> going to speak, he'd better have a *damn* good thing to say, and
> it had better be right!
>   I think it's a poor classroom atmosphere. It works for Wom-
> en's Studies only because it seems to balance out the feeling
> that everybody has from the rest of their classes. But overall, as

an education, it's horrible because people who are going to want to speak, to voice something that might differ but is just as valid, are never going to speak up. I mean, it's got to be a scary thing to sit in a room with thirty irate women.

Not that all the women in her classes formed a unified group:

The classroom gets divided. I mean, it gets divided into many small groups. There's always a small group of women who speak out. They always have something to say, they always have a comment on something, and you pretty much get the general feel of all their politics within the first week. After that, it breaks down into other small groups. There's a group that says very little. It comes down to your sexuality and your political views. It's like, it seems a lot of times if you're heterosexual, strictly heterosexual, or conservative, you don't have the right to say much in Women's Studies. You're classified with men.

Sexuality comes up all the time in Women's Studies classes. It's amazing—it just becomes an issue. People are declaring themselves, what their sexual orientation is, right away. I mean, within a week, you *know* what everybody in your class is. I don't think it should matter. And the professor's sexual orientation—that comes up as well. Why should it come up? I think it's an issue in the real world, and it should come up if people are going to be treated fairly, but in Women's Studies people get treated the reverse of what happens in the real world.

Why, then, did Laura resist the temptation to divulge that she was bisexual and thereby counteract the damaging assumptions that she was straight?

Because it seems like a cheap way to get credit. You're buying credit on sexuality. It doesn't make me a better person; it doesn't make me any different. All right, so they look at me and they go, "Ah, she's heterosexual"—great! And I go, "No, actually I'm not." I've come up three rungs on the ladder. I mean, that's reverse discrimination. Who I sleep with makes me a better person? I really believe people should keep their hands out of whatever happens in the bedroom. I think it's nobody else's business, and I'm not going to buy my credit by who I'm sleeping with.

Discussions about style and appearance were also a constant in her Women's Studies classes:

> The issue of personal hygiene and what is correct has come up in *so* many classrooms. Why should anyone care whether you shave your legs or not? I wish it were different. Women's Studies seems to get bogged down in pettiness sometimes. And that's just because it becomes repetitive—makeup, hair, appearance, what brand of tampons you use, if you use tampons, all that.

Laura's general enthusiasm for Women's Studies courses evidently did not blind her to their special problems. She had taken one course (taught by a staff member in the Women's Studies program), on women's career choices, that attracted a broader audience with less uniform viewpoints. One young woman, for example, stated that it was her aim to be married and have children. Had she made this admission in the feminist theory class, Laura says, "she might have been torn apart" by the other students, with little intervention by the professor.

> That's because [in the feminist classroom] it's mostly an open discussion. Many professors say, "This is your classroom, this is your discussion, I'm here as another participant, not as a leader," which pretty much waives the right of the professor to intervene. So it's very rare that a professor would step in to stop something like that. I mean, it winds up being this conflict between the students. I guess that's going to happen in the real

world. But I think a classroom *should* be a safe area, and I definitely feel like that girl should have been free to walk into a feminist theory class and say, "Regardless of what anybody else believes, I want to be a housewife. That would be the most rewarding life for me."

I think there should be more of that, but it's hard because you're dealing with a minority opinion, you're dealing with women who've been oppressed, and you're dealing with explosive issues to women. So any woman who is going to hold a view that might, in some minute way, support the other side, is going to be torn apart. And how do you accept her views without accepting the views and actions that have oppressed you?

All the professors would have to be made aware of this—so aware that they'd have to start really thinking about the dynamic that goes on in the classroom. I mean, obviously it's nice to have a safe haven for people, but how do you differentiate between a safe haven that ostracizes people from the program and a safe haven that also works to incorporate other people in the program?

Like Caroline, Laura objects to the simpleminded habit of blaming everything on men:

A lot of people got triggered by "men men men men men." I remember somebody just going off and saying, "Can't you blame anything else but men?" Yeah, sometimes people got furious. In one class this girl said, "All you do is blame men. I happen to like men." And she was completely at a disadvantage, because here she is sitting in full makeup, a skirt, heels, well-done hair. Guns were drawn. She was attacked. There were mainly three people who jumped in, and they just completely cut her to pieces.

You know, somebody who even looks like that and who voices this opinion is immediately going to be accused of being male-identified, which I think she was, and obviously she does not see the point in all history that men *are* to blame. I was upset by that too. I think one other person said to the class, "I think you do dwell too much on men." But by this time emotions had picked up, the snowball is barreling towards the bottom of the hill, and people aren't going to jump in the way. One guy did speak up and said, "You know, sometimes I have a really hard time sitting here because I feel like you are blaming men for all the problems in the world and here I am, a man, identifying with you, feeling the exact same way you do about feminism." And this one girl—the same girl who attacked this other girl for saying, "You always blame men"—she said to him, "You obviously have no understanding. You *are* a man. You can only try to empathize."

My brother and I are very close, and I would bring up an experience with my brother in my feminist theory class and it was like, "Ugh! You were hanging out with a man." God forbid I should bring him up! I spoke so rarely, and it was like I had to think through everything I was going to say. It came down to hostility—it was like taking a chance, a different kind of chance, in a Women's Studies class to speak out. If it becomes a personal attack and not a political attack, I think the professor should intervene, like, "You're off the subject. This is no longer political." But they very very rarely intervene.

Despite her many negative comments about the Women's Studies program in which she did her minor, Laura ends on a ringing, if somewhat chilling, endorsement:

You scratch the surface and then you go down deeper, and the more you think about it and the more you can see how it personally affects your life and your friends' lives and your mother's and sister's and everybody else's life, it's like, wow! And the whole thing starts to seem overwhelming after a while. . . . I could go into this class and learn about the persecution [of witches] in European history that I wasn't necessarily getting in my classes outside of Women's Studies, so that I know it's happening all over the place, and these aren't just isolated incidents. So, in that sense I got a firm foundation, a factual foundation, which was good.

I really honestly do believe that everyone should be required to take a Women's Studies class. In fact, I would force my friends to take a Women's Studies class if I could.

TRAINING THE CADRES

There is general agreement that students in Women's Studies classes should not merely absorb information about women's oppression and develop strategies for combating it, but should also, in the process of studying these subjects, undergo an intense feminist experience. The precepts of feminism (whatever these are said to be at a given moment) must guide pedagogical practice. As Nel Noddings puts it in *Caring*, "It is time for the voice of the mother to be heard in education."[1] Rules on exactly how political the content of the course should be, and how "maternal" the teaching, vary from program to program. Predictably, however, the ideologically sanctioned intrusion of politics on instruction is frequently disastrous.

Women's Studies professors readily admit to the political aims of the education they offer. In justification, they advance the rather tired argument that all teaching, on any subject, grinds a political axe of one sort or another. Teaching Shakespeare, unless he is read "against the grain," propounds an "elitist view" of literature and condones a hierarchical order of society. In other words, Shakespeare is unavoidably "political." Teaching chemistry without pointing to the necessity of "a science for the people" abets the "military-industrial complex." Because mathematics is supposedly a difficult hurdle for women and some minority students, it is presumed to be an inherently oppressive subject. And so on. In this essentially trivial sense, everything one talks about is political. When it comes to artic-

ulating the political ambitions of Women's Studies, however, many
feminists have something much more concrete in mind.

Typically, introductory Women's Studies courses include material
on rape, sexual harassment, battered women, child sexual abuse,
abortion, and reproductive rights, not to mention lessons on all the
current -isms such as racism, classism, ableism, and ageism. Often
the faculty members or graduate students who teach such courses
are not competent in the full range of subjects they must cover, having had little or no formal training in sociology, social psychology,
economics, medicine, or criminology. When teaching, they tend to
rely exclusively on feminist writings—particularly of the more popular and, hence, accessible sort—as their resources. As a result, students are likely to learn only what feminists say about these troubling and complex social issues. All other research is regarded as
inherently biased. Thus, not only the choice of topics, but also the
selection of study materials and the methods of instruction are dic-
tated by the objectives of feminist activists, and the range of knowledge communicated to students is tendentious, narrow, and repeti-
tive. Even committed students sometimes complain about tedious
duplication, while not realizing that this problem is rooted in Wom-
en's Studies' political agenda.

As noted in chapter 1, students in many programs can receive
academic credit for doing "internships" or performing community
service in feminist agencies, and then submitting reports on their
activities. At the university where one of us teaches, for example,
a total of fifteen credit hours out of the thirty-six required for a
Women's Studies major can be earned in this way, outside the
classroom.

Some schools require a practicum and pair their seniors with
mentors who are feminist activists in the community. The principle
that Women's Studies should train its students for political action is
at times used as a justification for appointing to the faculty women
from the feminist community who lack even minimal academic qualifications. In such instances, the political agenda leads directly to a

weakening of traditional academic requirements. One graduate student (who appreciated the mentoring practice) wrote to us about a lesbian activist brought into her program to teach a course on feminist theory: "She personally knows a lot of the theorists we read, so hearing anecdotes about them and about the movement in the 1970s added another dimension to the class. But there were drawbacks. She wasn't as comfortable facilitating a classroom as 'regular' professors are and had to get a guest lecturer in for the classes on 'postmodern feminism.'"

The importance attached to feminist credentials among both faculty and students is evident in an anxious query from the director of one Women's Studies program in which a prize was to be given to the best graduating senior. The director's problem was that the most deserving student—one who had a straight-A record, had written substantial research papers, and had contributed a great deal to class discussions—was not a feminist! The director appealed to colleagues for advice on how to handle the matter and proposed that the guidelines be tightened so that this situation would not recur.

Of course, the mere fact that Women's Studies has an explicit political aim does not by itself mean that Women's Studies education need take the form it does. As one of the women we interviewed remarked:

> Even if one were explicitly training political activists, one could do it in the traditional liberal arts mode. One would give them general historical and theoretical courses on conflict resolution, attitude change methodology, not only the tactics of Machiavelli and Mao but also those of Gandhi and Martin Luther King. One would also need general philosophical analyses of the concepts of justice, freedom, et cetera. Background in economics and history of technology would be helpful. But as you can see, this is a far cry from what Women's Studies actually is like.

Fulmination and Ferment

A major reason for the transition of Women's Studies from politically relevant instruction to politically correct indoctrination is found in the opportunities created in the Women's Studies classroom for the manipulation of students' emotions. The popular press—and particularly those elements of it that like to excoriate feminism—often portray the women engaged in feminist practice as mad (in both senses), hysterical, and certainly angry. What may be surprising to many people is that feminists of the second wave have proudly "owned" such epithets and even seem to go out of their way to cultivate anger and rage. Sometimes they make their point in jest. One popular bumpersticker, for example, reads: GOD IS COMING—AND BOY IS SHE PISSED. More generally, feminists view anger as a positive, healthy, and enabling emotion, as in the song called "Anger," by Naomi Littlebear:

> *Who says emotions are insane?*
> *Anger in a woman is the birth of freedom*
> *from the chains of your pain.*
> *Anger! Anger! Anger!*[2]

Other writers speak of nurturing their anger or practicing it like the piano. Margaret, the former program director whose story was recounted in chapter 2, commented on her slow realization that she was spending much of her time acting angry:

I was not a person who invited confrontation or felt comfortable with it. But anger was absolutely a measure of one's feminist commitment. It was taken as a sign of one's authenticity, one's radical credentials. I remember sounding angry a lot, and I remember hearing myself and thinking, This has become sort of a way that I talk. It was very strange.

Some feminist writers even speak of "tending" their anger, of periodically stoking the flames to use it as an energy source for political action.

The closest parallel in Western literature to the feminist attitude toward anger is the Greek concept of *thumos*, variously translated as Anger, Spirit, and Honor.[3] For Plato, Anger/Spirit was one of the three parts of the Soul—along with the rational and the appetitive faculties—and was a valuable source of courage and moral indignation. But when unchecked, *thumos* led to the infantile egotistical rage of Achilles (as portrayed by Homer), a man so narcissistic that he was willing to let the Greeks go to defeat in the war against Troy merely because his honor had been sullied. To warn against such excess, Aristotle called for the proper emotional balance: "The man who feels anger at the right things and against the right people, and also in the right way and at the right moment and for the right length of time is commended."[4]

If feminists could bring themselves to overlook the male referent in this passage, they might find Aristotle's message of value to them today. Women obviously are justifiably angry about many things. But to generate and cultivate anger in a classroom setting strikes us as irresponsible, especially since many of the techniques used to arouse and sustain such an emotion are manipulative, and most professors have no special ability to deal with the ensuing problems. Moreover, in the end, all such strategies are bound to prove counterproductive.

Making a fetish of anger—it might well be called ANGER-CULT—affects the Women's Studies classroom in many ways. First, doing so has a direct impact on subject matter. The topics selected for extended discussion in introductory Women's Studies courses are often lurid and charged with high emotion: rape, wife battering, incest, molestation of children, forced prostitution. One reason for choosing such topics may be practical: it is certainly easier to grip students' attention with talk of sexual slavery and clitoridectomy than with discussion of more mundane issues like the need for comparable-worth legislation or prenatal health care. In addition, feminist fac-

ulty often complain that their noninitiated students are too compla-
cent about past disadvantages and indignities, and are apt to dismiss
them as long since abolished (as many communications on the
Women's Studies E-mail list reveal). These faculty members may feel
that such students will not become activists until their sense of outrage is aroused.

Women's Studies seems to need angry students in order to "keep
the momentum going," as one feminist professor put it. Classroom
exercises can easily be designed to elicit strong emotional responses.
Another faculty member posted this on E-mail: "[After discussing
rape,] I had the women in the class do some simple self-defense rituals such as putting our arms around each other in a circle and yelling
'No!' and front snap kicking against the wall. A sociologist who
teaches at [another university] does the same thing."

The perceived need to stir up feelings of outrage among students
is also connected with the feminist sacralization of what is generally
described as a "click" experience. Participants in consciousness-
raising sessions in the late 1960s and early 1970s reported that, as
they compared notes about their experiences and began to discover
patterns in their complaints and relate them to larger political issues,
moments of epiphany would occur when everything would "click"
into place and they would immediately know that they were feminists. Like Saul after his illumination on the road to Damascus, some
feminists, such as the writers Artemis Oakgrove and Elana Dyke-
woman, even took on new names following their enlightenment.

However, while religious conversion experiences are often followed by surges of euphoria and celebration, feminist epiphanies are
more usually accompanied by strong waves of anger. It was a relief
for the early consciousness-raisers to discover that what they had
previously conceptualized as inadequacies that were either personal
or rooted in their "natures" as women were really the effects of systematic cultural and political oppression. But it was also infuriating
for them to realize that they had been dupes of patriarchy for so
long, and to find out how difficult it was to convince others, especially men, of the validity of their new feminist perspective. Hence,

irascibility and ire have come to be seen as indicators of the depth of one's feminist insight and commitment, "a sign of one's authenticity," as Margaret put it. From a feminist viewpoint, then, cultivating anger not only increases the likelihood that students will turn to activism but also serves as a precondition for equipping them with an authentic feminist conceptual framework. Those who are not full of rage "just don't get it."

Even from a feminist perspective, though, anger-based pedagogy can be a dangerous game. Free-floating anger, like lightning, seeks something to discharge itself on; thus, the oft-voiced feminist worry about "horizontal hostility" or "hazing within the community" is well justified. If, however, the anger nurtured in the program is not released, students are apt to become depressed. At the end of one recent semester, Women's Studies faculty on the Women's Studies E-mail list engaged in a long discussion of what to do about students' sagging morale. Had they overdone their emphasis on the atrocities perpetrated against women? Had students concluded that the situation was hopeless? Had they just given up? Sustaining anger, it turns out, is exhausting.

Propaganda and Resistance

The most important goal of any Women's Studies course, as is widely taken for granted, is to convert students to feminism. Feminists answer the charge that they are indoctrinating students by pointing out that all education attempts to change students; to "educate" means to "lead out" from a less into a more valued form of life. Art teachers try to expand students' aesthetic sensibilities; classics teachers try to convince students that the Great Books contain perennially valid insights. What is wrong, then, with exposing students to the sexism, racism, homophobia, and exploitation that pervade society and also affect their own lives? Why not help them change their attitudes?

Of course, feminists themselves realize that many students do not respond favorably to their pedagogy, and the phenomenon of "student resistance" is now the focus of organized discussions and scholarly papers. On the Women's Studies E-mail list an animated discussion recently took place about how to deal with female students who "just don't get it." The example that triggered the dialogue was the following:

> We were talking [in class] about how women are treated, when one student said, "I may be crazy, but I like having car doors opened for me and being put on a pedestal." Another student said, "Thank God you said that. We've [indicating the person sitting next to her] been talking about the same thing.". . . So [in this class I've] got a bunch of southern, traditional students (for the most part) who want equal rights and want to also be "ladies." [I] would like to enlighten them without alienating them.

The network generated many suggestions, ranging from a bibliographic reference to an essay on rape which argues that chivalry is a male protection racket, to a recommended exercise:

> Whenever my students raise the issue of opening doors, we eventually get to talking about holding hands. Ask your students to observe male-female couples walking hand in hand. Malls are a good place to do this. They will see that almost always the man's hand is in front. Then the students will say things like, "Well, it feels most comfortable that way!" Next ask them to observe adult-child hand holding. Again, the adult's hand is always in front. This can help them to see how this puts them in the same position as a child.

This exercise, it is worth noting, while dramatic, is not entirely honest. It is a simple anthropometric truth that when a taller person reaches down and a shorter person reaches up, the hands mesh more easily with the taller person's hand in front. Hand position may have little to do with dominance. It could be, just as the students say, more comfortable that way. Nonetheless, most of the Women's Studies people who got into the ensuing E-mail discussion felt that such a response showed student "resistance," which constituted a serious problem.

The preceding example of "resistance" is rather benign in that neither the degree of student recalcitrance nor the intensity of reaction to it by Women's Studies teachers or feminist fellow students appears to have been extreme. But at times the censoriousness of "enlightened" students toward their classmates can be much more energetic. One of the authors of this book witnessed an interesting scene that illustrates this point. It took place at a meeting at which a new antiracist curriculum was being presented to the Women's Studies students for their comments and suggestions. A white undergraduate who was very active in the program kept insisting that the Women's Studies faculty must "do something" about the many white students who sat in Women's Studies courses and studied racism but just weren't "getting it." "You can't let them get away with that," she said heatedly. "You must do something! You must do something!" Finally, in one of her better moments, a colleague muttered, sotto voce, "A firing squad, perhaps?"

When the political agenda of the Women's Studies curriculum is coupled with the favored therapeutic/confessional model of teaching, serious problems can result. Some students resent assignments they find intrusive, such as the writing of essays in which the student is expected to analyze her own racism, or the common feminist practice of requiring students to keep journals for recording personal reactions to readings. Objections to such assignments often induce attacks by outspoken feminist students, who become impatient when their peers "have trouble coming to terms with" their status as oppressors or oppressed.

One student we interviewed, who considers herself a feminist, told us of her discomfort with the dynamics she observed in some journalism courses she had taken, in which several Women's Studies students were extremely assertive: "I was surprised that they were not very tolerant—I guess that would be the word. They were very

very self-righteous, and I got the impression that they felt they were there to teach the rest of us rather than to learn what the professor had to teach us." This student is not alone in having difficulty adapting to the brave new feminist classroom in which smashing, or at least rearranging, boundaries is the norm.

Confusion and Condemnation

Although Women's Studies faculty worry about how to handle disbelieving "southern ladies," disruptive males, or unenlightened women students, they never take student resistance as a valid indication that there might indeed be something inappropriate about what they are teaching or how they are teaching it. Instead, they piously claim, as did one professor on the Women's Studies E-Mail list: "It is precisely at the point of resistance, of 'ignorance,' that there is the potential for real learning."

But what drove many of the professors and students we interviewed to despair was the "resistance" of the more-feminist-than-thou students who disrupted classes they judged to be insufficiently political. Even faculty who are still happy with Women's Studies sometimes report experiences similar to that described on the Women's Studies E-Mail list by one professor who said, "The resistance I have become most familiar with is that of female students whose expectations of 'feminist discourse' are not being met."

One reason why the views of all these "resisting" students—be they males, not-yet-feminist females, or true-believing feminists—become so visible, and hence so problematic, is the feminist encouragement of or even insistence on self-disclosure in the classroom. Feminism has borrowed pedagogical techniques from a variety of sources: Paulo Freire's practice in adult literacy classes of giving people a vocabulary to describe their oppression, the potent mixture of denunciation and exultation characteristic of revival meetings, and even the dress and demeanor codes imposed in bootcamps and finishing schools. We also find echoes in feminist classrooms of the obligatory self-incrimination demanded in China during the Cultural Revolution, and, of course, of the interventionist techniques of psychotherapy. Students are encouraged to "get in touch with their anger and pain" in discussions inside and outside the classroom, but especially in the journals they are asked to keep. They may be given assignments that require personal disclosure, such as discussing gender roles acted out within their own families, or (this, for white students) their first encounter with a person of color.

Although these techniques are in part derived from one or another of the varieties of psychotherapy, what takes place in a feminist classroom is very different from the true therapeutic encounter, in which the client can explore in a protected environment any thoughts and feelings, no matter how antisocial or bizarre. In the Women's Studies setting, by contrast, there are very definite expectations about, and limits on, the views that are deemed acceptable.

The teacher may explicitly announce, for example, that hers "is an antiracist class." Or, as indicated on the Women's Studies E-mail list, she may include in her syllabus such specific caveats as the following:

> As a white woman teaching feminist literary theory, African-American women's writing, various "minority" writings, and always affirming lesbian writing/writers, who is trying all this in a mostly white, conservative community . . . I've opened my classes and included on my course outline the following statement: "Any point of view will be welcomed in discussion except those that contend that one race, sex, or sexual orientation is superior to another." The students (particularly the young men) may not like it, but they accept it, or they leave. The ideological principle of "equality". . . works to suppress "discussion," which can be no more than a showcase for bigotry and abuse.

In other instances newly canonized views are clothed in a grudging gesture toward openness, as in the case of one Women's Studies professor who told us she said this to her students: "Personally, I can't imagine why any woman would want to have a relationship with a man, but since some do, we have to try to respect them."

As noted earlier, students are often required to submit journals giving their reactions to assigned readings. When doing so, they soon learn that only certain opinions and phrases are acceptable, as did this male undergraduate whose frank reports on his reading in a weekend "training" workshop on racism (offered for academic credit) elicited sharp replies from the two female graduate students who were teaching the course:

> STUDENT COMMENT #1 ON ASSIGNED READING: I am dominant but I am not racist. This article denies that it is possible for me to overcome the prejudice with which I was programmed. This is why the Left is failing: because it reduces all of its subjects to simpering essentialist categories and fails to acknowledge that anyone—yes, even those nasty Anglos—can rise above their cultural morass and effectively reprogram themselves. I really resented this pandering, whiny article: it's Anglo angst in rare form.
>
> FIRST INSTRUCTOR: How can you help *but* be—when you benefit and receive privileges from this racism? Your defensiveness has prevented you from understanding this article. One of the first signals to me that I have met a racist is when they insist that they are not.
>
> STUDENT COMMENT #2: In this article, Bell Hooks once again proves her worth to the Black community and to the women's community.
>
> FIRST INSTRUCTOR: Ugh! What a limitation on her contributions! Again, she is reduced to her race and gender. What a fine example of racism and sexism.
>
> STUDENT COMMENT #3: To say that all one needs is to be good intentioned is, I think, ridiculous and harmful. Everyone needs to have some sort of theoretical basis from which their action springs, not just a visceral one.
>
> FIRST INSTRUCTOR: Is this not reductionism at its finest and most limiting? Over time we have found that social change has

occurred as a result of direct action resulting from emotional strength and courage. Often the *theory* comes afterward or gets in the way.

SECOND INSTRUCTOR: "*Yes*—A very European-male opinion."

FIRST INSTRUCTOR'S GENERAL REMARKS ON THE STUDENT'S COMMENTS: Again you have effectively avoided demonstrating *any* personal awareness or at least strategies for personal action. I can acknowledge your need to make sense of such a complex "paradigm"—but I have yet to see that you actually can make sense of it at a personal level. I'm sadly disappointed by your self-protected intellectualizations. I've met far too many white men who bend over backwards to protect their own racism and white supremacy and frankly I'm utterly bored. [emphasis in original]

Students who decline to express personal views may be graded down in such courses or publicly humiliated. Those who express opinions unacceptable to feminist teachers and students are, as we have already noted, either charged with "resistance" or encouraged to drop the course. A male student, a Women's Studies major, told us that in his feminist theory class the professor did not allow discussion of divergent viewpoints and always shut him up when he made criticisms. "What about when women make the same criticisms?" we asked. "They never do," he replied. "I don't know if it's kissing ass or what, but they all seem to be in agreement with her." He was aware that he was not really welcome in the class, he said, but he had decided to stay in it nonetheless; besides, it was a requirement for all majors.

When students reveal, in class, personal traumas exemplifying the sort of damage from sexism that feminists can relate to, they may be hurt in different ways. Nonfeminist students may laugh at them or dismiss them as whiners; but ultrafeminists may also put them down if their anecdotes indicate that they are either too dependent on the opinions of men ("Sounds like you should have ditched that jerk ages ago!") or that their attitude smacks of racist, ableist, or other unacceptable sentiments ("I think we should explore the fact that you described the person stalking you as a 'big black guy'"). Even when no overt hostility or dismissive responses ensue, the student, having made her revelation, may feel vulnerable or exposed. A recent article in the *Chronicle of Higher Education* calls attention to the possible harm done to students who feel coerced to reveal painful personal material to professors, and then are embarrassed or hurt by the professor's attempts to be helpful.[5]

Equally pernicious is the opposite mode, in which it is the professor who "discloses" her personal problems to the class. Here is an example, given in a recent contribution to the Women's Studies E-mail list, by someone who teaches Women's Studies and communications:

> This semester is going wonderfully well, though mostly the reason for that . . . is related to my renewed mental and emotional health, having come to terms with what had been repressed memories of childhood sexual abuse. A good deal of what is different is that I am approaching all my classes from a position of sensuous joy and love. . . .
>
> Tuesday night I had a discussion/activity planned around dealing with a recurring question/complaint from male students (past and present): we shouldn't spend so much time looking at the terrible things men had done to women in the past but instead should focus on changing things in the present. I had the students break down into groups to discuss why it is important for us to examine our past, no matter how painful it may be, and to consider why someone might resist doing so (the "answer," of course, being that our personal identities are tied up in our conceptions of our social and cultural history, so that looking at "the terrible things men have done to women" threatens the positive identity that has been built around history as it has been taught).
>
> I also tried to get them to think about how examining a painful personal history might be helpful for them. Many stu-

dents responded in a very general way. I managed to get a few older students to give some personal examples. I ended with telling them about how I had had to come to terms with an excruciatingly painful past (explicitly identifying the problem as incest), and how until I could do that I had no future, only an endless repetition of old patterns. And now there is joy and hope and boundless energy.

This was the third class meeting (one night a week). They all sat so still, with amazement and wonder on their faces. Afterward an older student thanked me for making myself so vulnerable. I told her I didn't feel vulnerable as I spoke. I felt loved.

We merely note that, in contrast to this instructor's obviously fragile psychological condition, which she considers appropriate to "share" with her class, she holds a tough and dogmatic opinion about "the answer" to male students' legitimate questions.

Feeling Good versus Becoming Competent

Classical psychotherapy (like traditional mothering) is a very demanding endeavor. But a sort of "I'm OK—you're OK, but men are horrible" latter-day variant of it is—as we have seen—very popular in the pedagogy of Women's Studies. On this model, women "empower" themselves primarily by realizing that all their troubles result from patriarchy, and that the key to greater self-esteem is held by feminist political analysis. This can only be developed in association with other women, for many feminists—as we discuss in greater detail in later chapters—claim that traditional schooling emphasizes such "masculine" cognitive virtues as rationality and objectivity, to the detriment of women's own "feminine" cognitive faculties such as empathy and subjectivity. Students are also told that their lives provide valuable data, and they are encouraged to "own," and take responsibility for, their personal opinions.

Taken in conjunction, these propositions result in a serious curtailment of the possibilities for critical debate. The standard procedure of at least trying to separate intellectual positions and arguments from the individuals who propose them, so that the former may be examined dispassionately, is explicitly blocked. No claim is evaluated without identifying the person who originated it, and any judgments about the merits of the claim automatically reflect on the person making it. According to this way of looking at things, people and their feelings can never be divorced from their ideas. To argue otherwise is to run the risk of being dismissed as "male-identified" and, hence, subject to "compartmentalized thinking."

From a feminist pedagogical perspective, there are two ways to resolve the conflict that occurs when people make opposing claims. One can say that each person has her own perspective and all opinions are equally valid (a standard move in family therapy), or one can give preference to the opinion of the person who is most oppressed. Critical discussion becomes difficult, if not impossible, in either circumstance. When feminist classrooms manage to avoid breaking down into personal hostilities and censoriousness, they often do so only by sacrificing free and frank intellectual discussion at the altar of an appropriate feminist ambience. Even those who are generally enthusiastic about the feminist approach note the absence of critical discussion, as one student wrote to us:

> I feel Women's Studies classrooms offer a nurturing environment in which to learn. I learned a lot more in that class than I did in any undergraduate class. On the downside, sometimes people are afraid to even disagree with each other, although constructive criticism and respectful debates are very useful, I find. (Another technique we used was to always own our own opinions.) Because of this fear, the discussion sometimes lacked the intellectual rigor I craved as a grad student. People spend so much time worrying about offending others that they often don't disagree at all, and, as a result, the conversation does not move to a very deep level theoretically.

One might argue that the feminist approach, whatever its intellectual cost, is not only a more humane form of inquiry but also the one many women feel most comfortable with. For example, the authors of the much-cited book *Women's Ways of Knowing*, which we discuss more fully in chapter 7, note that, when given a choice of classroom assignments, women students rarely opt for projects involving debate. They are uncomfortable with conflict and especially dislike the idea of having to defend a position with which they personally disagree.

It is certainly true that in the domestic sphere, the milieu for which women were traditionally held to be best suited, paying attention to feelings is very important. And it may well be that many women are ill at ease with contentious modes of resolving contradictory claims. But the whole point of education is to introduce students to new ideas and methods, to expand their horizons, to move beyond what they already know and believe. Just because a student "feels uncomfortable" debating, evaluating arguments on impersonal grounds, learning statistics, or honing her skills in disputation by defending a disagreeable proposition, doesn't mean that she would not gain immensely from becoming competent in these ways of operating intellectually.

Moreover, in the name of being "supportive" to women, the therapeutic aims of feminist pedagogy too often collude in inculcating the attitude of "learned helplessness" so deplored by our earlier, tougher, feminist foremothers. Consider, for example, the following policy announced by one Women's Studies teacher, as described on the Women's Studies E-mail list:

A few years ago I started making it a requirement—a condition of my agreeing to be students' senior thesis advisor—that they had to join, form, create, find—in other words, somehow participate in, a peer support group by, for, and of others who were writing senior theses at the same time. If they ask for my advice on what to do or how they should go about it, I tell them, as a model, about a group I participated in while in graduate school. The goal of this group was to provide an intellectual community committed to doing whatever was necessary to help one another achieve the conditions necessary for work (whatever those turned out to be). . . . Among other things, one of the explicit (or implicit) goals of such a structure can be to explore feminist conceptions of colleagueship, collaboration, and cooperation in intellectual endeavors.

Is this professor merely helping her students learn how to network? Or is she telling them that it is not possible to work alone, and that one can do nothing without supportive friends? The latter claim is patently untrue (just ask Barbara McClintock!). But beyond the truth or falsehood of such advice, one should consider whether it is empowering for students to believe that they can learn and work only in a cozy Women's Studies environment. When does a support group become a crutch? When do networking and forging consensus stifle innovation and creativity? These are hard questions, but feminist pedagogues have not even asked them.

FEMINIST PEDAGOGY: A MIDTERM REPORT

The most characteristic aspect of feminist pedagogy is the value it places on getting students to "give voice" to their raw, unanalyzed feelings on any topic being discussed. But for those who believe in liberal education, the feminist mode of dealing with these personal reactions has many pitfalls. Any teacher who has ever dealt, in a classroom, with emotionally charged readings or issues knows how difficult it is to balance the students' needs to ventilate their feelings with the academic objectives of analyzing assumptions and evaluating arguments.

When, in 1969, the Ontario Institute for Studies in Education initiated a Canadian Public Issues Project, which developed curricular materials on controversial topics such as abortion, euthanasia, law enforcement methods, cultural diversity, and sex education,[6] those who designed these materials encountered a major problem in getting students to move from a mere blurting out of their subjective reactions to a reasoned analysis of the issues. Their recommendation was that teachers begin the study of each topic with one or two periods explicitly designated for "sounding off," and then—very deliberately—change the classroom atmosphere to one of a calm and careful weighing of pros and cons. The goal was to have students realize the complexity of issues and grasp the strengths and weaknesses of whatever conclusions they, individually, might draw.

Contrast this with the situation in Women's Studies. Consider, for example, a recent communication on the Women's Studies E-mail list, in which a philosophy professor described what she tells her students about the value of small-group discussions:

> I always spend time *in class* talking about the reasons why I use that classroom technique (small group discussions), and the reasons that I think it produces a superior learning experience to the one(s) that I'm electing not to use (traditional lecture, etc.). I also talk about what "counts" as "active participation"—and I make it clear that talking, per se, is *not* what is valued, but that "being engaged, both with the course materials and with the learning processes of themselves and others in the classroom" is what matters. I point out that this can include "actively listening" and "giving attentive consideration to questions produced by others" whether or not one chooses to speak up, oneself. But I also point out that this includes "bringing one's own questions, confusions, concerns and insights into the discussion" with the caveat that leaving *oneself* out is not really a way of being well engaged. [emphasis in original]

Another professor complained that feminist pedagogy's stress on personal involvement had led the students in her feminist theory class to a different kind of resistance—namely, an unwillingness to undertake serious intellectual work:

> My Women's Studies students are generally far more interested in discussing "issues" such as pornography, abortion, advertising, rape, personal appearance, and hygiene than in learning about less immediately "relevant" matters. After the first couple of times I taught the course, I realized that the students were, typically, good at articulating their feelings, but far less able to engage in analysis. This meant that assignments to examine the theoretical assumptions of a particular text often resulted in papers revealing "what X [the text] means to me." The discourse of feminism they were picking up elsewhere reinforced their own inclination to concentrate on the confession of personal feelings and to disdain the hard work of intellectual and scholarly critique. Every semester I have had to spend considerable time attempting to undo this tendency, struggling to move students beyond what came naturally to them—voicing opinions on any and every subject, expressing feelings—to what they conspicuously evaded: thoughtful analysis.

Activists will argue that what many women need most is not practice in the subtleties of scholarly analysis, but a nurturing atmosphere capable of leading them to empowerment. But this is a hollow claim. The most distressing aspect of feminist pedagogy may be its tendency to undermine women students' ability to achieve.

If "criticism" is alive and well in Women's Studies in the form of personal assessments by students of one another's degree of feminist enlightenment, it is notably absent as part of a thoughtful intellectual practice. Just as the discourse of feminism today excuses a great many ills, so has it served as an instrument by which students can indulge their own disinclination for hard work. One professor we interviewed—herself a staunch advocate of and participant in the

Women's Studies program at the private "Seven Sisters" college at which she has taught for many years—mentioned her impatience with those students who object to having their writing or other work subjected to criticism because, so they contend, such feedback indicates adherence to the male standards they reject:

> I think it's because we make the students feel safe in doing it. And the other manifestation that I know irritates a lot of my colleagues is that many students assume that feminist teachers don't really mean the rules that they make—"the paper doesn't really have to be in on time," "I don't really have to do all the work," and "oh, but she's a feminist and so her politics will be that she has to be nurturing." That drives us nuts!

A particularly egregious example that this is not merely a "misunderstanding" on the part of students recently appeared on the Women's Studies E-mail list. In a discussion of the "patriarchal assumptions of academia," one contributor offered her own list of just what these assumptions are, and explained the "patriarchal" thinking that lay behind them:

Grading? (hierarchic sorting of students' "worth" on performance measures)

Deadlines? (violence and confrontation implicit in the word)

Focus on performance as opposed to learning? (need for evidence of learning)

Terms? (time chopped up into blocks of arbitrary length)

Specialization vs. generalization? (the very idea of disciplines)

Seeming arbitrary rules of majors and/or graduation?

Focus on preparation for jobs vs. life?

Enculturation to values of rigor, rationality, objectivity, Aristotelian logic?

Enforcement of rules of language and grammar?

Enculturation of rules of citation and promoting "future research"?

The correspondent ended with the question: "Which if any of these are patriarchal in nature, and does it matter?" The fact that it is impossible to tell whether this list is intended as parody or as genuine feminist insight is itself an indication of something deeply amiss within feminism.

The breakdown of a working consensus about the importance of academic achievement is most notable, as we have seen, in the classroom, where those professing feminism act out commitments to constantly challenge "rules and regulations." Not surprisingly, feminist pedagogy encourages faculty to abdicate a "superior" role. Some let undirected classroom discussion go on for an entire semester (which certainly saves the professor much preparation time!). A few take an even more extreme view and do not prepare a syllabus. Encountering such a lack of structure, many of those who enroll in a class, expecting to learn from the professor, may simply decide to drop the course, as one teacher told us happened in her feminist theory class when she informed the students that it was up to them to devise a syllabus for the semester.

Even when professors do not go to such extremes, many seem embarrassed at the thought that they have more knowledge than their students. They work hard to disguise this fact, one technique for doing so being the affirmation that their students' "experience" is as valuable a form of "knowledge" as the intellectual training and specialized learning the professor has (one would hope) painstakingly acquired. Such abdication of expertise, with its concomitant dissolution of identities and roles is, of course, connected to feminism's explicit assault not only on hierarchies generally but also on the boundaries between the public and private, the emotional and the intellectual.

In a 1975 essay, Jo Freeman provides a telling example of a different intellectual climate as she describes a survey conducted at the University of Chicago in 1970 to determine whether women graduate students suffered discrimination or discouragement in pursuing their degrees. The researchers had concluded that, though faculty had offered neither men nor women significant encouragement, such "equality" in fact had a different impact on women than on men because of the "differentiating external environments from which women and men students come." Thus, professors "discriminate against women without really trying" whenever they fail to act positively to help women students overcome this "handicap."

So far, this might sound familiar to today's feminist teachers. But Freeman then moves in quite another direction. In marked contrast to the feminist pedagogical imperatives that developed in the 1980s, she asserts that women, as a group, are "deprived of the rich external environment of high expectations and high encouragement that research indicates is best for personal growth and creative production." "Overt opposition," she continues, "is preferable to motivational malnutrition."[7]

In her particular intellectual setting in the 1970s, Freeman took it for granted that the encouragement women need is provided by the challenge to excel and that teachers' expectations play a prominent role in determining student performance. This is a far cry from today's popular feminist pedagogy, which rejects these "high expectations" or urges women not even to attempt to excel, as such an effort could itself be defined as masculinist or patriarchal.

In Women's Studies' extreme concern for providing students with a sustaining, nonjudgmental, reassuring atmosphere—which can include the tendency to explain away any lack of success as not their own fault—there lurks a highly problematic view of young women. Such educational tactics may seem appropriate for children, who indeed are often short of confidence and need regular and massive doses of encouragement. But to treat university students in this way is to infantilize them, perhaps to drain away their burgeoning confidence by providing too much reassurance, too many acknowledgments that they are not responsible for this or that failure, that someone or something else is to be blamed, and that the academic criteria they are struggling to meet are really obstacles raised against them by an unfeeling patriarchy.

Girls, as they grow up, need to overcome the well-meaning but often ill-advised overprotectiveness of their parents, which sends them the message that they are not quite competent. Do they go to university only to have this message repeated to them in Women's Studies programs?

5

Semantic Sorcery:

Rhetoric Overtakes Reality

WOMEN'S STUDIES originally had two legitimate academic objectives: to find and publicize information about the lives and works of women who had been forgotten or overlooked, and to make women's lives a primary focus of inquiry. But soon the "add women and stir" recipe for doing Women's Studies was rejected as inadequate. As an oft-repeated line in the early 1980s had it, you can't merely *add* the idea that the world is round to the notion that the world is flat. More drastic measures were indicated: the old flat-earthers had to be routed.

Far more important than the recovery of women's lives and past contributions ("excavation work") was the need for a radical reappraisal of all the assumptions and values found in traditional scholarship. As a consequence of this turn in the direction of Women's Studies, what came to be transmitted to students as feminist scholarship was every bit as problematic as the tense and volatile atmosphere of feminist classrooms.

THROWING AWAY THE MASTER'S TOOLS: PLAYING *TOTAL REJ*

TOTAL REJ is our name for the game that results from the feminist move of totally rejecting the masculinist, patriarchal, Eurocentric, capitalistic cultural heritage and trying to invent *de novo* feminist replacements for all that has been discarded.

Earlier generations of feminists believed that if principles of basic decency, justice, and fairness were applied to women, most of women's grievances would be resolved. There was nothing wrong with the principles themselves, according to the older view—it was simply a matter of extending them fairly to women, children, and the disadvantaged.

TOTAL REJ feminists, by contrast, argue that two hundred years of American "enlightenment" have failed to deliver the goods to women—we cannot even pass the Equal Rights Amendment. There are deep reasons, then, why women are justified in doubting that piecemeal modifications of the present society will ever liberate them. Our culture, including all that we are taught in schools and universities, is so infused with patriarchal thinking that it must be torn up root and branch if genuine change is to occur. Everything must go—even the allegedly universal disciplines of logic, mathematics, and science, and the intellectual values of objectivity, clarity, and precision on which the former depend.

A much-beloved aphorism taken from an essay by Audre Lorde is often quoted on this point: "the Master's tools will never dismantle the Master's house."[1] When read in context, it is not at all clear what tools Lorde had in mind. Although her phrase seems to allude to a passage in Frederick Douglass's autobiography, Lorde's intended message is quite different. Douglass fervently believed that the master's tools for enforcing bondage could also become the slave's tools for liberation. He movingly describes overhearing one of his masters explain why slaves should not be allowed to become literate, and then goes on to testify how important it had been to him to learn to read. Lorde proposes a quite different route to liberation. Her remarks appear intended as a call for women not to count on men's help, but to rely on each other for support.

Whatever Lorde's original intention may have been, her words have now been taken up as a slogan by those who find little worth saving in the traditional academic corpus. One contributor to the Women's Studies E-mail list took the suggestion to its drastic conclusion: "I think you could burn the house down. Why would one want to use the master's tools?"

We wish to make it clear that what we are objecting to is the rash nihilism of this game. We have no quarrel with serious debates about feminist challenges to and interventions in traditional disciplines. But in many Women's Studies settings, arguments about traditional knowledge tend to be reduced to avowals of a kind of feminist know-nothingness. This is the posture we characterize as TOTAL REJ.

Students sometimes act as if the invitation to engage in a wholesale condemnation of nonfeminist writings and ideas were to be taken literally. Why should they have to read Darwin, Marx, or Freud when those authors wrote only sexist nonsense? A historical shift has clearly taken place when a Women's Studies student feels justified in submitting a paper (as reported by a political science professor we interviewed) consisting of the single line: "Freud was a cancer-ridden, cigar-smoking misogynist." And how reassuring the thought that one can ignore all science, all economic theory, and all technology because, after all, these brainchildren of "malefactors" just oppress women, as some Women's Studies students now write on their affordable, efficient word processors while listening to a CD as their wrinkle-free jeans are being washed in the laundromat and their Stouffer's spinach soufflé is heating up in the microwave.

What young female students in search of meaningful education most need is broad exposure to countervailing ideas. In a normal program of studies they would indeed receive such exposure, at the very least through distribution requirements in a comprehensive arts and sciences curriculum. But TOTAL REJ encourages them to discredit everything that is not feminist, and the highly charged moralistic atmosphere cultivated by Women's Studies throws up hard-to-surmount barriers around the student who might wish to explore other points of view. One pernicious result of this game is the absence from many Women's Studies programs of anything like encouragement of a love of learning. It is very difficult, after all, to invite students to develop curiosity and the desire to learn while hurling anathemas against the academy.

Not surprisingly, Women's Studies students are often criticized by faculty in other departments (and sometimes, as we have seen, by Women's Studies professors themselves) for their disinclination to think hard and work diligently. A knowing and dismissive sneer is obviously far more economical. An even more predictable effect of TOTAL REJ is the absence of critical thinking about Women's Studies' own pet ideas, claims, and arguments, which must rush in to fill the newly created intellectual void. Nor is this tendency to be found only among students.

Older feminist faculty, the pioneers who started Women's Studies programs, had the benefits of a traditional education. With all its shortcomings, such an education seems to have given them the intellectual tools they needed to make good on their challenges to that very education. These women were not as inclined as younger students or activist staff members to reject "malestream" academic disciplines. It is in large part due to the authority of these older scholars that Women's Studies has come into existence. But, more recently, feminist faculty have not followed their example. One Women's Studies professor we know of—with a doctorate in education, no less—proudly proclaims that all the "old knowledge" must be tossed out. Everyone, she says, is now on an equal intellectual footing, all starting from scratch.

It is, of course, impossible to totally reject one's cultural heritage. Therefore, feminist faculty sometimes simply borrow old ideas from the books of the "fathers," repackage them in feminist jargon, and present them to unwary students and colleagues as the original products of sisterly collaboration. This pretense of intellectual parthenogenesis—a direct outgrowth of TOTAL REJ—has a variety of bad consequences. By spuriously presenting concepts as the offspring of a virgin birth, one cuts off the reader (and the student) from the wealth of prior critical discussions of core ideas. The practice also perpetuates the myth that feminism cannot profit from external input. Not surprisingly, it breeds contempt among academic colleagues in other departments, who may conclude that whatever is worth taking seriously in feminist scholarship is only a cross-dressed version of something created much earlier.

By arguing that feminists have not succeeded in starting *de novo* and have instead drawn selectively on the Western intellectual heritage, we certainly do not mean to suggest that there is nothing new under the feminist sun. Feminist scholars have put forth many original proposals—some of lasting value—and these are readily acknowledged even by feminists who walked away from Women's Studies programs, as we saw earlier. But what is too often missing wherever TOTAL REJ prevails is the appropriate acknowledgment of male precursors, which would help students make connections between Women's Studies and what they learn elsewhere in the university. This omission makes TOTAL REJ a game that subverts, in the name of revolutionary political goals, one of the standard obligations of scholarly integrity: acknowledge your sources.

By claiming that the master's intellectual house must be torn down and that we must start over on a new foundation, feminism has attracted, and has for the most part been receptive to, any number of approaches to knowledge that are alleged to be politically liberating. The popularity of Marxism and of French versions of psychoanalysis seems to be waning now, but cultural relativism, standpoint epistemology, social constructionism, theories of linguistic and cultural hegemony, and other progeny of postmodernism are alive and well in feminist classrooms, and are often uncritically embraced there. Flirtations with exotic intellectual approaches are, of course, endemic in the academy, especially in largely interpretative fields such as literary criticism and film studies. Though these approaches may sometimes irritate nonparticipants (perhaps because they require a lengthy initiation process into their special discourses), they generally do little harm and may even yield genuine insights. In feminist settings, however, they are apt to become more than mischievous. In brief, here's why.

Interpretative frameworks work best when they are used like

proverbs. "Look before you leap" is good advice to contemplate when one is feeling impatient, but on other occasions it is well to remember that "she who hesitates is lost." Likewise, aggressive types who believe that only sticks and stones break bones need to be reminded of the power of language, while folks who think words are more important than deeds should be urged to kick a few stones (as in Samuel Johnson's famous refutation of Bishop Berkeley). Radical approaches to knowledge are most effective when they challenge received orthodoxy. Too much feminist theory, by contrast, employs exotic epistemologies that reinforce, rather than challenge, feminine stereotypes and the gender socialization to which many young female students have been exposed. This is most evident in feminism's uncritical embrace of some peculiar ideas about language.

From at least Victorian days it has been the job of bourgeois women to monitor language and enforce norms of what is socially acceptable. The important things these women needed to know about their world—how to raise children, manage the household, and keep their husbands happy—were learned primarily from small, informal community networks or personal experience, not from books. Deprived of political rights, their most effective means of influencing their environment was through rhetorical manipulation. There is a nice irony in the fact that, like their Victorian foresisters, many feminist academics today are intrigued by approaches that focus entirely on the power of language to shape culture. Just what kinds of games are feminists playing with words?

WORDMAGIC AND OTHER LANGUAGE GAMES

Feminism, like many other political movements today, is in thrall to the notion that linguistic reform will not merely reflect social transformation but will actually bring it about. Feminist activists have used language innovation both to promote new feminist ideas and to shame those who resist their agenda. As a political stratagem, this preoccupation with language has had some success, despite the ridicule now being heaped on politically correct terminology. However, attempts to manipulate language have had a counterproductive impact on feminist research and teaching. WORDMAGIC, our general rubric for the games feminists play with words, hurts women in the long run.

Phony Philology

The study of word origins and the evolution of their meanings is indispensable for the historian of ideas. Philology also offers insights into the cultural significance of contemporary usage. Explaining that *philosophy* comes from *philos*, meaning "fond of," and *sophia*, "wisdom," or that the *nomos* in *astronomy* means "law" is a nice way to start a semester. And it is certainly legitimate and relevant to point out that woman (from *wifmon*) is the qualified or marked form of *man*.

But feminists have turned philology from a scholarly tool into a propaganda weapon by creating a game we call Phony Philology. At first it may be amusing to note that *seminar* is etymologically related to *semen*, and to use this observation to talk about the exclusion of women from higher education. But when feminist editors circle the phrase "X's seminal paper," even when X is a woman, and ask for nonsexist rewording, and when feminist students seriously demand that their seminars be called "ovulars," the emphasis on etymology seems just plain silly.

Words may be clues to attitudes, but the correspondence is not so simple. We speak of *seminal* works, but we also say that a phrase is *pregnant* with implications. One does not get very far arguing that it is the male roots or connotations of academic speech that are responsible for the exclusion of females. For every time someone refers to the *thrust* of an argument, someone else will speak of the *fruitfulness* of a discussion or the importance of being *receptive* to new ideas. Feminine metaphors abound as we thread our way through a difficult passage and peel off layers of meaning.

Once one develops a fixation on male imagery, genuine etymology becomes irrelevant, as in the feminist attempt to call feminist historical research "herstory," an action that is intended to radically modify what is presented in departments where "his-story" has traditionally been taught. Does this also mean that "hermeneutics" is characteristically female? Or could it be that the "her" and the "men" in the word imply a transcendent state of androgyny?

Mary Daly's *Wickedary*, which promises to take the "dick" out of *dictionary*, is a confusing mixture of bad puns and provocative but genuine philology, the latter paradoxically showing traces of Daly's impressive Catholic theological training.[2] But in a day when few students have even a smattering of Greek or Latin, and when most are depressingly unsophisticated speakers of their own language, they cannot easily distinguish tongue-in-cheek etymology from the genuine article. By manipulating philology to fit and advance a political agenda, feminist wordmagicians help cultivate in their students an attitude, at best, of indifference and, at worst, of contempt for intellectual traditions.

Metaphor Madness

Closely related to the game of Phony Philology is Metaphor Madness, which privileges metaphors over precise meanings. Teachers love to share examples of misread metaphors culled from student papers. But sometimes mistakes in the figurative use of language become entrenched. Albert Einstein came to regret having attached the name *Relativity Theory* to his equations, which actually describe certain invariant properties of mechanical systems, because poets and homespun philosophers immediately began to say that Einstein had demonstrated that everything is relative.

As for feminists, they have made the magnification of metaphors into a cottage industry. Looking for hidden positive messages, such as the search for clitoral imagery in Emily Dickinson's poetry (the subject of a paper recently delivered at the Modern Language Association's annual meeting), may lead to a rather skewed view of her verses, but it could also be illuminating. More harm is done when feminists search a text for signs of negative masculinist imagery and then use them to discredit the entire work in which they appear.

This is a favorite device of feminist critics of science. An extended example—given here because it is such a notorious one—will show how this game works. Bacon's *New Organon*, a book on scientific method favorably cited by the founders of England's Royal Society, contains some famous passages in which Bacon speaks of putting Nature on the rack in order to extort her secrets, and of prying into her innermost nooks and crannies. Feminists such as Carolyn Merchant, in her book *The Death of Nature*, claim that this and similar passages in the writings of early scientists strongly suggest that modern science has always treated the natural world contemptuously and has viewed nature as a woman who exists only to be raped.[3] And if it is true that the scientific method was originally conceptualized as a form of rape, is it any wonder that women even today often feel uncomfortable in science classes and believe that science is responsible for our present ecological crises—the rape of Mother Earth?

However, the argument from Bacon's metaphors is very weak. In his day, natural philosophy, science, the nation, justice, and the church were also spoken of as though they were female. Does this mean that a reference to the penetration of Nature by Science alludes to a lesbian affair? Moreover, there are other passages in which Bacon speaks very tenderly of Nature: To be understood, Nature must be obeyed. Feminists might argue that this merely means that Bacon is talking about something more like a date rape; let scientists first try seduction, but if teasing out Nature's secrets doesn't work, put her on the rack! What Bacon really meant to convey by these locutions, however, becomes clear if one actually reads his book and does not merely scan for incriminating metaphors.

The *New Organon* is, first, a sustained attack on the Aristotelian account of knowledge as it had been developed and institutionalized in the Middle Ages, and, second, an attempt to formulate a radically new approach. Aristotle's theory of knowledge was a naturalistic one: only sense organs in their natural state could be trusted. Someone who is drunk or dizzy from spinning around is not a reliable observer. In Bacon's time this sensible-sounding precept was used to discredit Galileo's telescopic observations. And the Aristotelian corollary—that only observations made of systems in their natural state could give knowledge of their normal workings—was used to discourage "artificial" arrangements such as William Harvey's experiments showing that valves in the veins allowed blood to flow in only one direction.

Bacon is saying that we must put Nature on the rack of experimentation and use scientific instruments to penetrate her innermost secrets. The violence of his images is directed at Aristotelians, not women. Since Bacon was also a prominent jurist, his metaphors were undoubtedly rooted in then-current legal debates in England concerning permissible methods of gathering evidence for trials; this is how Bacon's contemporaries probably interpreted his metaphors. If feminists were seriously trying to understand Bacon's writings about science, they would have to read him in this light.

When, however, one's main purpose is political, not scholarly, it is easy enough to construct a "metaphorical case" against almost anyone. And, indeed, feminists have turned metaphor against themselves as they have scrutinized one another's writings for lapses into any of the dreaded -isms.

Linguistic Litmus Tests

Closely related to the game of Metaphor Madness is the feminist habit of applying Linguistic Litmus Tests. Ignoring the proverbial reminder that actions speak louder than words, feminists have transformed the sensible biblical counsel "By their fruits you shall know them" into the more dubious "By their nouns and pronouns you will judge them." Thus, a feminist facilitator at a diversity training workshop attended by one of us told students that any (male) instructor who called women "girls" was not only using "unacceptable" language in the classroom, but was likely to be sexist in other ways as well. Someone asked her, "But what if it were simply a case of a kindly older professor calling his eighteen-year-old students 'girls and guys'?" The reply was firm: there is no excuse for ever referring to women students as "girls." And on the Women's Studies E-mail list, a professor "shared" with everyone her clever solution to a male student's insistence on using the generic *he*: she told him she would not grade his paper until he rewrote it without the offending pronoun.

Many publishing houses now insist on "nonsexist" language in the list of books they publish. We know editors who pride themselves on their rigorous application of this policy. Yet it strikes us as a bizarre laundering of texts whose ideological origins ought to remain open to readers' scrutiny. If a writer genuinely conceives of his [*sic*] argument as applying only to men, or has not extended his research to include women, or otherwise has no interest in women's contributions, would we not want to know it, instead of having the evidence for it excised by diligent editors?

Undoubtedly, lexical choices often suggest a great deal about an individual. And in such cases it is a disservice to readers and listeners if revealing language has been "corrected." On the other hand, while lexical preferences are often very telling, the inferences we draw from them are fallible and, as speakers of so-called Black English will testify, can all too easily be used prejudicially. Moreover, there is an important asymmetry at work here: use of a progressive neologism, one that deviates significantly from the accustomed terms or expressions, is a good indication that the speaker has some knowledge of, and is in sympathy with, the innovative trend. Talk of "womanist" theory, for example, tells us that the speaker is at least vaguely attuned to black feminist perspectives. Negative implications, on the other hand, are more hazardous to draw. Saying "feminist" instead of "womanist" hardly signals racism.

Many of the feminist proposals for altering the English language are good ones and are rapidly catching on. Even the *New York Times* some years ago added the useful honorific *Ms.* to its style sheet. Any individual or group can propose and argue for linguistic changes. Often these shifts affect the cultural and social climate for the better. But feminists go wrong when they conclude that anyone who fails to adopt their proposals should be assumed to discriminate against the group on whose behalf the proposal is made.

The use of a Linguistic Litmus Test is especially ill-advised when one is reading works from other cultures or historical periods; grave misunderstandings, not just howlers, are bound to result. Training students in such habits of mental inflexibility hardly contributes to their capacity to understand the "diversity" of human groups and of past societies.

Accordion Concepts

Phony Philology, Metaphor Madness, Linguistic Litmus Tests— these games are irritating, and they trivialize academic feminism. But there are more serious methodological errors than these at work today, which, as one woman we interviewed sadly put it, turn feminists into "victims of their own rhetoric."

A particulary pernicious game is one we call Accordion Concepts, a label we have borrowed from an essay by Wilfrid Sellars in which he observes that "the term 'theory' is one of those accordion words which, by their expansion and contraction, generate so much philosophical music."[4] Somewhat more formally, we might refer to this game as "The Failure to Draw Distinctions."

When this game is played, concepts are stretched so widely that crucial distinctions are obliterated. Consider two examples: the feminist catchphrase "any woman can be a lesbian" and the "art project" recently exhibited on the University of Maryland campus that listed as "potential rapists" male names pulled randomly from a student directory. The latter action raises all sorts of problems about the legal and ethical limits of "performance art" and the political effectiveness of guerilla theater, but our focus is on how feminist claims such as "all men are potential rapists" or "every woman can be a lesbian" are intended to be understood.

The slogan declaring every woman to be a potential lesbian is taken from a 1975 record album called "Lavender Jane Loves Women." The lyrics to the song, sung by Alix Dobkin, turn the tables on the once-common belief that lesbians, if only they tried hard enough, wouldn't be that way. The song is smart and funny, and it contains no manipulation of meaning.

The game of Accordion Concepts gets under way when academic feminists "theorize" the slogan. An example is Adrienne Rich's redefinition, noted in an earlier chapter, of *lesbian* to include all women who put energy into, or who identify with, the life projects of other women, regardless of whom they happen to sleep with or be in love with.[5] On this redefinition, Catharine MacKinnon, the radical feminist legal theorist who has appeared in newspaper photos arm in arm with her fiancé, Jeffrey Masson, becomes a prototypical lesbian because of her intense political commitments to the cause of women. To be sure, Rich's essay is more subtle than this, because she at least introduces a continuum, permitting the drawing of some distinctions. If taken literally, however—which it often is in Women's Studies courses—her extension-by-definition of *lesbian* rules out the possibility of conceiving either of a nonfeminist lesbian or of a nonlesbian feminist. Such semantic sorcery benefits neither the lesbian rights movement nor the cause of feminism.

Even more mischief is done by feminist identifications of "potential rapists." Again, one could gloss such verbal excesses as mere activist hyperbole: the Maryland students, when interviewed on National Public Radio,[6] said they were only trying to make everyone realize that rape is caused by men's aggression, not by women's imprudence. They were trying to reverse our mothers' warnings that every woman is a potential rape *victim*, focusing attention instead on the *perpetrators*. One could even agree that a woman whose car breaks down on a lonely road at night may be well advised to act as if (almost) every man were a potential rapist. Such commonsensical interpretations of the slogan branding all men as potential rapists do not violate our conceptual categories, at least in the current political context.

Mystification begins as feminist alchemists go to work on it. Here's the trick. First they capitalize on the ambiguity of *potential rapist*. What might this possibly be construed to mean? On one reasonable interpretation, *potential rapist* could be used to describe a man who says he would enjoy forced penetration if he thought he could get away with it, and there is indeed a substantial minority of male undergraduates who have checked this response on surveys of campus attitudes. But most men, contrary to the apparent meaning of the claim that they are all potential rapists, do not in fact express a desire to rape. When confronted with this objection, feminist theorists quickly deny that they think all men have such a yearning. Instead, they say, they are thinking of the masculinist *zeitgeist*, which supposedly determines our cultural milieu so extensively that it makes every man a prospective rapist.

One of the correspondents on the Women's Studies E-mail list, where this subject was discussed at length, offered the following explanation to a feminist man who protested that he did not like being called a potential rapist:

> [Men] are potential rapists because our culture defines traditional male sexuality in such a manner as to glorify violence and the oppression of women. The knowledge that you have overcome this conditioning is very heartening. I know a few other men who have also overcome their conditioning, and are kind and gentle people who would not rape. But they are still potential rapists simply because they are men raised in a patriarchal culture that glorifies violence and conditions both men and women to accept a rape model of sexuality as normal. I agree with you that it does not feel good. It shouldn't feel good. Given your level of sensitivity and knowledge about violence against women, though, I hope you will begin to feel less defensive. It SHOULD make you feel more responsible.

Using this analysis, to say that "X is a *potential* rapist" is to say nothing at all specific about X's individual potentialities. The statement simply conveys the fact that he grew up in a patriarchal society in which, supposedly, rape is normal.

But the "theorizing" of the concept of rape does not stop there. In a radio interview, Robin Morgan proposed that the legal definition of rape be extended to cases where women, though not subjected to forced sex, are cajoled into unwanted sexual activities—cases where, as she put it (alluding to Margaret Atwood's dystopian novel *The Handmaid's Tale*), the woman would rather be playing Scrabble.[7] And Andrea Dworkin and Catharine MacKinnon have long argued that in a patriarchal society all heterosexual intercourse is rape because women, as a group, are not in a strong enough social position to give meaningful consent—an assault on individual female autonomy uncannily reminiscent of old arguments for why women should not have political rights.[8] Obviously, rape is an extremely grave crime, and its definition deserves careful analysis and debate. But serious discussion is not advanced by redefining terms in such a way that every time a feminist woman marries a man she is, strictly speaking, a person on the lesbian continuum marrying a potential rapist. By such definitions we would have to say that every offspring of such a union was conceived in an act of rape. Perhaps some radical feminists do hold such a belief, which may explain their hostility to childbearing.

Most feminists would, of course, neither draw such implications nor endorse them. They want to have it both ways. They would like to retain the charge that rape is a terrible violation of human rights and, at the same time, stretch the legal definition of the crime beyond all reason. But even the rhetorical gains won by this sort of concept stretching can backfire. When birth-control campaigns among disadvantaged groups are labeled "genocide," does this extreme accusation heighten concerns about birth control? Or does it merely diminish the horror of the Holocaust and the slaughter of Armenians? How will victims of a brutal rape feel when they are lumped together with people who suddenly discover that some embarrassing episode on a long-ago date should now be reclassified as "rape"? Whose experience is being trivialized in such careless inflation of language? Will social disapproval of sexual harassment not be lowered when the concept is stretched to include even casual unwanted glances or an unsolicited friendly touch?

One certain result of these exaggerations is the kind of cognitive confusion that inevitably will adversely affect the design of research projects. Imagine trying to discover what it is that makes some men commit rape, in the conventional sense of the term, if *rape* is defined according to Dworkin and MacKinnon. Until the relevant concepts are defined more specifically, skepticism about feminist statistics concerning injustices perpetrated against women is warranted. No matter how firmly people are committed to the improvement of women's condition, they are bound to raise their eyebrows when they discover that in a supposedly scientific study of rape, the act was defined so broadly that nearly half of the victims in the sample were able to say that they continued to date their rapists.[9] The recent adoption of the dramatic term *survivor* for those who have experienced even mild sexual harassment is merely another instance of irresponsible concept stretching.

Because *rapist* and *lesbian* are such highly charged words today, people do notice when they are used indiscriminately. But other instances of concept stretching are less likely to be detected and are, therefore, more difficult to counteract. Consider the compromise position arrived at by contributors to the Women's Studies E-mail list in their vigorous discussions of *potential rapists*:

> I have a comment about how I teach the issue of potential rapist and potential rape victims which might be useful. I do not think all men are potential rapists, but I do tend to believe all people are racists and sexists. To be sexist is not the same as to say a person could or would rape under any circumstances. To be a racist is not to say a person could or would participate in lynching or raping people of races other than one's own. What it means is that all people tend (and I stress that word, "tend") to prefer their own groups (those they are taught to identify with from birth). . . . So . . . I teach my students to be aware of their unavoidable racism, classism, sexism (both women and men) because it is ignorance of those preferences that leads people to participate in racist and sexist and classist activities from a belief that what their group wants, knows, believes, or whatever is a generally acceptable action. We all need to be

aware of our group preferences. . . . If I insist that I am not sexist or racist, that is when I find myself most dangerous.

This correspondent correctly diagnosed the absurdities that result when every male is called a "potential rapist." But she assumes that *sexist* and *racist* can be defined so that they apply to everyone. The justification offered for this assumption is simply that our culture, including our language, is permeated with sexism, racism, and other such attitudes. We grow up in this culture; therefore, all of us are unavoidably sexist, racist, and so on.

In this simplistic feminist worldview, conditions such as racism and sexism are original sins of the soul that all individuals must constantly and publicly confess to in themselves and confront in others. This theological postulate is then invoked to prove that every charge of racism or sexism must be true. One may try to dispute details of who did what to whom, but the answer to the question is always given in the premise that underlies it. Such a move, of course, trivializes the very evils feminism claims to oppose. Whatever is meant by calling Women's Studies programs "racist" (which is a currently fashionable charge), it is surely something other than what a reference to the Ku Klux Klan as a racist organization would signify. Furthermore, so many important differences exist between, say, the men who formed the Tailhook gauntlet and the gay men who provide child care at the Middleway House, a battered women's shelter in Bloomington, Indiana, that one wonders what gain can possibly come from calling both "sexist."

Feminists should ponder this question. Once so vehemently critical of the attempts of anthropologists and philosophers to generalize about the human condition, they are now themselves engaged in a most dubious form of universalizing.

The Power of Naming

According to Genesis 2:19: "[God] brought them unto Adam to see what he would call them: and whatsoever Adam called every living creature, that *was* the name thereof." People of most, perhaps all, cultures believe that having the authority to name something, or even knowing the name of something, gives one power over it. In a recent controversial legal case, when the custody of an adopted baby called "Jessica" was transferred to her biological parents, one of the first steps the latter wanted to take was to rename her. Nor is it a mere accident of history that married women in our culture have traditionally taken on their husband's name, and rarely vice versa.

Feminists, however, carry this faith in the sheer power of names to extreme lengths. Ever since Adam, they argue, it is men who have had the authority to define the world by bestowing names. They go on to claim that liberation will never come until we begin anew and let Eve rename every living creature. This idea is a popular theme in feminist literature. One thinks immediately of Adrienne Rich's *The Dream of a Common Language* and Judy Grahn's *Another Mother Tongue*. Suzette Haden Elgin, the author of novels about a society in which women create their own language, has even written a grammar book for Láadan, a language she invented, one especially well suited, she claims, for expressing the thoughts of feminist women.[10]

So far, so good. A feminist Esperanto (non-Eurocentric, of course) might prove a very interesting experiment, but these imaginative musings are transformed into some very strange political practices. It almost seems as if feminists, at least those within the academy, believe that renaming things *is* liberation. Thus, feminists at one university produced a handbook of "preferred" usage that enjoined professors and students from using *rich* as an honorific—as in "the rich tones of the baritone sax"—and *poor* to denote something undesirable, as in "a poor performance of *Tosca*." To use these words is to be "classist." The example would be merely silly but for the strong suspicion that the language patrols actually believe that the avoidance of such terms will improve the lot of the impoverished.

Critics of the politically correct lexicon have mocked feminist-flavored neologisms such as "differently abled," "physically challenged," and "handicapable," and have deplored heavy-handed attempts to enforce their use. But our objection to the practice is more fundamental: By putting so much energy into the efforts to change languages, feminists are diverting attention from real issues.

Administrators find it much easier and cheaper to rename the office that serves students with special needs (for example, substituting *disabled* for *handicapped* in the title) than to ensure wheelchair accessibility or provide telecommunications devices for the deaf on campus. They find it expedient to require faculty, graduate teaching assistants, and students to attend "sensitivity training" sessions, in which people debate the propriety of hyphenating *African American* (as actually happened at one university). But to imagine that a hyphen will alter anything in the world of social and economic relations is scholasticism masquerading as serious politics.

Early in this century intellectuals were captivated by the so-called Sapir-Whorf hypothesis, according to which the structure and lexicon of a language both molds and reveals a culture's basic categories of thought and perception.[11] People quickly realized that the connection was not perfect: German has no single word for what we call "efficiency," but one can hardly claim that Germans have no such concept. The Hungarian language has no gender, yet patriarchy exists in Hungary nonetheless.

Still, there has always been some plausibility to the view that attitudes and ideas are in some ways influenced by language, and no one could dispute the observation that if a new idea emerges or a new artifact is invented, most likely a new word or phrase will be added to the lexicon. The Sapir-Whorf hypothesis was never intended to suggest a simplistic and unilateral link between language and the world, yet this is how some feminists have been using it. They imagine that if they create new terms and make everyone else use them, social change must follow. In real life, things do not happen in such a predictable way. The result likely to be achieved by the language police is either resentment among those whose language is being regimented or—at best—hypocritical acquiescence by those who can be shamed into compliance. Corporation executives are old hands at awarding employees a fancier title instead of giving them greater responsibility or a raise. Feminists need to recover their senses and *smell* the roses, rather than worry so much about what to call them.

6

BIODENIAL and
Other Subversive Stratagems

TOTAL REJ AND WORDMAGIC are favorites of feminist players, but by no means are they the only games in town. Other, equally obnoxious, games have won fans and participants from among feminist teachers and scholars. In this chapter our primary focus is on feminists' repudiation of the sciences, especially their refusal to grant any explanatory power to biology. This is a posture we call BIODENIAL. Its obverse, social constructionism, is currently the leading contender in the search for an all-encompassing concept capable of sustaining the feminist worldview.

SOCIALLY CONSTRUCTING THE
BIRDS AND THE BEES

It is a basic precept of contemporary feminist thought that both the world and our knowledge of it are socially constructed. But what exactly does this mean? Attempts to answer the question quickly run aground on loose terminology and semantic shifts. *Social construction* is one of those trendy terms in academia today that, while they signal a certain sympathy toward nouveau ideas, have no fixed referent. The core impulse behind its frequent use, however, is easy to detect, and the principle from which it proceeds seems plausible enough. *Social construction* directs attention to those properties of a phenomenon that depend on culture, and are therefore, presumably, amenable to change. Some approaches describing themselves as "social constructionist" are sensible and productive; others lead to extreme or silly conclusions. All too many feminists gravitate to the murky end of this spectrum.

A wide variety of positions fall under the label of "social constructionism," and we begin our discussion with some plausible ones. In his book *Threatened Children*, the sociologist Joel Best argues that what is taken to be a serious social problem at a given period is socially constructed.[1] In other words, the priority ascribed to a problem—for example, the kidnapping of children by strangers—is influenced more by media attention and the rhetorical strategies of activists than by empirical data demonstrating the actual dimensions of the phenomenon. What is being socially constructed is our society's perception of the seriousness of a problem—a problem that is assumed to exist independently of media hype or the preoccupations of our culture. Best's argument is clear and persuasive.

A contrasting, but equally unobjectionable, example of social constructionism is found in a recent newsletter from Iowa featuring a long article on dairy cows. Certain bovine breeds, it appears, have undergone such an intense process of artificial selection, guided by the financial interests of dairy farmers, that they can now hardly survive without being hooked up to milking machines. The cows, in other words, have been genetically constructed to serve a precisely defined social purpose, a process that raises various ethical issues.

In both instances, use of the term *social construction* is uncontroversial. Doubts arise, however, as we move along the spectrum. Michel Foucault's *History of Sexuality* contains the oft-cited claim that no homosexuals existed before the late nineteenth century because "homosexuality" is a social construction contrived by the medical-psychoanalytic disciplines.[2] Much ink has been spilled trying to discover exactly what Foucault meant. Even more puzzling is the question why gay activists should have taken up this claim as a slogan (thereby destroying the continuity between Sappho and Gertrude

Stein or Edward II and Oscar Wilde), but one could supply the following charitable interpretation: Sexual identity, like personal identity in general, is structured by the concepts and beliefs current in the ambient society. The new medical category of "homosexuality as sickness" (as opposed to "homosexuality as sin" or "indulgence" or "sport of nature") was so salient a force that it was incorporated into the very personalities of all people, both homosexuals (who felt afflicted) and heterosexuals (who felt superior by contrast). Foucault might not endorse such a tepid exegesis of his views, and many will find even this modest interpretation historically inaccurate. But at least it puts forward a view worth debating. If a condition is constituted in large part by the beliefs and postulations of the culture within which it exists, then a change in the culture could lead to a reconstruction of the condition, perhaps along more desirable lines.

What are we to make, though, of the claims put forth by certain followers of Foucault? Bruno Latour, for example, contends that no anthrax existed before Pasteur, and Ian Hacking says there were no battered babies before 1962.[3] It is, of course, possible that Latour only wanted to point out that Pasteur's achievement—isolating the anthrax bacillus, growing it in a petri dish, and sharing the specimen with co-workers—was an important contribution to the material culture of science. And perhaps Hacking merely intended to make an assertion similar to Joel Best's, namely, that the battering of babies was not regarded as a serious social problem until physicians defined it as a syndrome in 1962. But each author, in the argument he makes, seems to do his best to block such a charitable interpretation of his work.

If, then, one reads Hacking as making a stronger claim, similar to Foucault's, that the battered-baby problem is constituted in large part by physicians' categorization, does it follow that children would be better off if we changed our conceptual system and ceased speaking of a "syndrome"? In this case it seems that an activist would want to argue that what is at stake here are bruises and broken bones, which exist independently of conceptual schemes, and that willfully causing such injuries is or should be universally condemned. Of course, the die-hard social constructionist could reply that the activist's argument is not meant as a description of reality, but merely as a proposal to the society of readers about an alternative way of constructing the phenomena. We cannot block this rejoinder, but at this point the social constructionist's thesis becomes an idle disclaimer to be appended to every essay.

No other academic program seems to have leaned so heavily and inventively on social constructionism as has Women's Studies. The theoretical bedrock of the current wave of feminism is the claim that gender itself is socially constructed, and that the different roles played by men and women in society, and the personality characteristics, attitudes, and behaviors ascribed to them, derive largely from conventional social arrangements, which vary dramatically from culture to culture. Such differences can be neither explained nor justified by making reference to innate biological sex differences. This is as nontendentious a statement of the social constructionist interpretation of gender as one can make, and we ourselves have used the phrase "social construction of gender" in precisely this sense.

As in the old nature-versus-nurture debates, however, controversies arise about how far the social constructionist approach may be pushed. No one denies, for example, that the division of labor between women and men varies from society to society, and so is, at least in part, socially constructed. But is it legitimate to relate all aspects and expressions of gender to social forces? Does biology have *anything* to do with gender? And if so, what?

Women's Studies is very strongly committed to taking an extreme social constructionist line. Here is a docudrama specimen of the kind of discussion this commitment provokes in introductory classes:

Q: Isn't it a fact that men are stronger and run faster than women, and might not this fact have something to do with traditional work assignments, at least in preindustrial societies?

A: No one knows how strong and fast girls would become if they were encouraged as much as boys are. Besides, women have more endurance and a better ability to survive cold and famine. It is merely a social convention to place such a high value on speed and strength.

Q: But only women get pregnant, and, until recently in human history, infants had to be nursed or they would die. Surely these biological facts explain *some* of the differentiation in gender roles.

A: The effects of pregnancy are certainly socially constructed. Until recently, middle-class women in this country had to quit their jobs as soon as they began to "show." Working-class women or, at earlier times, slaves, by contrast, did heavy work up until it was interrupted by the "labor" of childbirth. It all depends on what society thinks pregnancy consists of.

Q: But even so, those women had to either stay close to home to nurse the baby or else carry the infant with them. Surely it was only rational to take that physical fact into account when setting up a society!

A: You're taking an essentialist, biological determinist line, and we've already seen how this leads to sexism, racism, and homophobia. Besides, what makes you think men can't lactate? Some can, you know. Even scientists admit that. And, anyway, none of this is relevant to the construction of women's roles today in our society.

This exchange represents a relatively moderate defense of claims for the social construction of gender. But Women's Studies abounds with much more startling assertions, such as the insistence of Women's Studies students in a class taught by one of us that the pain of childbirth is socially constructed by patriarchy and would not happen in a feminist society. These same students also argued that there was little infant mortality in the past until childbirth was "medicalized" by men—another notion the students had picked up in an earlier Women's Studies course.

One way feminists have tried to break any possible connection between gender and biological sex is to point to the existence of

societies with three or more genders, such as the *berdache* in some
Native American cultures (on which there is by now a significant literature) or the *Hijras* in India.[4] Another way is to deny the legitimacy of the dichotomous categories of "male" and "female," as
done by Anne Fausto-Sterling. In a recent *New York Times* article,
she noted that as many as 4 percent of neonates are born as hermaphrodites but are surgically altered to force them to conform
physically to male/female body stereotypes. She goes on to argue for
the social acceptance of biologically intermediate sexes.[5]

Bold and speculative claims that challenge current scientific views
are or should be welcome in the academy; they often provide an impe-
tus for investigations that advance knowledge. Valuable insights may
be gained when feminists point out the conventionality of sexual
dimorphism, or propound adventurous theories about the possibility
of parthenogenesis and male lactation, as long as this is done in a
forum where ideas can be critically scrutinized and debated. As the
nineteenth-century philosopher of science William Whewell
observed, truth can survive the struggle, while error will fall apart in
confusion. What we object to is the pedagogical practice of presenting
unsubstantiated ideas to students ill-prepared to examine them, and
dressing these notions up as well-founded and properly documented
feminist correctives to "malestream" prejudice. Equally deplorable is
the habit of branding any disagreements with these ideas as demonstrations of a lack of genuine commitment to feminist aims.

Again, there is nothing wrong with pursuing even crazy-sound-
ing, half-baked ideas. They *may* turn out to be fruitful in some way.
The eccentric German archeologist Heinrich Schliemann believed
the Greek myths and ended up discovering Troy. Perhaps feminist
archeologists will eventually unearth compelling evidence of lost
matriarchies, and feminist biologists will overthrow our current theories of human sexual reproduction. However, it is dishonest not
only to pretend to students that speculative fancies are well established in scientific or scholarly consensus, but also to dismiss criticism of them as inspired by sexism or "backlash," and hence unworthy of reply. In maintaining this pretense, feminist intellectual

separatists are reinforced by a second tenet of constructionism, which is that not only social categories but knowledge itself is socially constructed. If this were taken to be axiomatically true, there would be no reason for attempting to reconcile male-constructed knowledge claims with those put forward by feminists. By embracing such a position, the social constructionist can argue that, in addition to gender itself, our best scientific theories of gender or sex chromosomes or infinite sets are the products of specific cultural beliefs and interests.

As with all the other articles of social constructionism, this claim comes in mild and wild variants. Again we start with the tame versions. We recognize that scientific knowledge or other expert opinion always depends in part on what problems particular patrons of research regard as important at a particular time. The problems favored for investigation may well reflect the patrons' own economic and political interests. Moreover, scientific output is influenced by the technology available to experimenters. In more subtle ways, too, the social context influences how knowledge is constructed. A tradition of open critical debate, and of institutions in which such debates flourish, will lead to a kind of research very different from what can be done in a stifling, suppressive setting where researchers must fear punishment for producing unpopular results. This rather commonsensical view of how knowledge is produced we might call the mild or moderate form of the theory affirming the social construction of knowledge.

But a stronger, more radical social constructionist position holds that all knowledge is so deeply imbued with the cultural norms and personal identities of its producers that it can never be true or—without far-reaching modification—even useful for individuals not belonging to the producers' own group. This more extreme position is invoked in some feminists' wholesale dismissal of science, which would have it that it is neither necessary nor productive to attempt detailed and precise critiques of specific scientific doctrines because all of them are equally tainted by their patriarchal origins. Taking this view, one can reject science and all other forms of specialized knowledge simply by pointing out that they have been constructed by males (and a few women who made their accommodation to the patriarchy) and therefore are *a priori* of dubious worth to feminists.

Students who are invited to accept this radical version of social constructionism, and who act on the invitation, are thereby excused from learning anything beyond that which is offered to them in the setting of Women's Studies. Moreover, they are likely, when emerging from such an education, to distrust and reject whatever deviates from the party line they absorbed in Women's Studies. And there *is* a party line. As will be noted in chapter 7, feminists have, through an NWSA report, made both epistemological relativism and the denial of biology integral parts of the official corpus of feminist theory. Any challenge to these strong forms of social constructionism is taken as a sign of backsliding from feminist commitment.

IS THE MIND THE ONLY SEX ORGAN?

Arguments for the social construction of reality are very old, but it is only since Marx that they have gained the kind of intellectual substance to win them broad support. To a socially conscious and responsible person, it is certainly appealing to be able to demonstrate that a human problem is amenable to remedial action because it has its roots in the conventions of society and culture, and not in some immutable biological order. For progressives, in particular, the promising outlook opened by this demonstration creates the temptation to look for cultural explanations of phenomena and to be intensely suspicious of invocations of biology or other sciences.

As a general argument, however, the case against biology fails. Near-sightedness, for example, leads to all sorts of undesirable social consequences, such as being unable to read or to remove splinters from babies' toes. Near-sightedness is biologically determined, and that very fact helps make it correctable. Xenophobia, on the other hand, is certainly in large measure a social construction, yet we seem to be very slow in correcting this condition.

Feminists would reply that in the case of social differences between men and women, any assignment of these to biology has always oppressed women. Examples of this abound, from the time of Aristotle to the present. But, again, as a generalization, this argument fails. The phenomenon of morning sickness in early pregnancy was for years given a social constructionist interpretation. It was sometimes taken to be a sign of women's innate fragility, an indication of how reproduction put such a strain on women (of a certain class) that they could not possibly bear children and hold down a job at the same time. It has also been construed as a sign of psychological weakness, an indication of women's tendency toward hypochondria and mental instability. But all such constructions can now be relegated to the dustbin, in the light of recent biological research showing how nausea in early pregnancy is triggered by certain substances that are dangerous to the developing fetus. Morning sickness is a natural response that has survival value for the species as a whole, and women can avoid it by following a carefully controlled diet.

In fact, if we want to understand a phenomenon fully, perhaps in order to change it, political touchstones will not lead us to a solution. To reject a promising avenue of research because it smacks of the bugaboo of biological determinism is to privilege dogma over the welfare of the very people one is trying to help.

Feminists who are seriously into BIODENIAL will, of course, look for the ulterior patriarchal motives behind the research on morning sickness just mentioned. They would see this as one more attempt to blame women who bear an unhealthy fetus. This was the knee-jerk response to the research on fetal alcohol syndrome and the adverse effects of nicotine and other drugs. Luckily, the extremists who criticized this research did not draw the most drastic conclusions from their distaste for science; they opted for the slightly more plausible and less harmful argument that patriarchy should be blamed, instead, for driving women to substance abuse in the first place.

BIODENIAL may be part of the reason why feminists have yet to produce a positive model for heterosexual sexuality. If heterosexual intercourse, under patriarchy, is a form of rape, what should it be like in a society based on feminist values? Feminist literary utopias usually simply reverse the present hierarchy, making men into gentle sources of semen, or they dispense with men entirely in favor of parthenogenesis, the merging of ova, or some similar mechanism. Where are the novels or theoretical models that describe healthy relationships between people who are political equals but biologically dimorphous?

Feminists sometimes seem to interpret the sexologists' slogan "The most important sex organ is between the ears" as implying that the mind is the only sex organ. But their position on nature versus nurture is shifty. When it suits them, many feminists—though ostensibly committed to strong social constructionism—surreptitiously slip back into biological essentialism, as, for example, when they totally deny that male-to-female transsexuals, no matter how thouroughly socialized, could ever be "real women."

In a similar vein, one Women's Studies professor reports:

It constantly happens in class that students argue for social constructionism on the one hand but revert to essentialist ideas quite opportunistically. It's as if everything they dislike about "women" gets dismissed as social construction, while all the rest is the Real Thing. As for men, most everything about them is not socially constructed, since that would, in some sense, let them off the hook, so men get heavy doses of essentialist attributions while the students imagine they're espousing a straight constructionist line of analysis.

What amazes me is that these students would rather believe men are evil than that they can change. The intellectual opportunism, as well as the illogicality, of these proceedings are stunning, but any effort to discuss these contradictions in class is, in my experience, futile. People already resistant to unilateral explanations hear the contradictions. The hard-line feminists, on the other hand, simply dismiss the teacher as not feminist enough or not the right kind of feminist for them. Their unwillingness to examine their own ideas is one of the things that clearly sets the Women's Studies students apart from the others.

As an illustration of this tendency, the professor recounted this episode:

> In one recent class on women's fiction, I was discussing a British feminist writer's description of women's complicity in men's wars. From the back of the room, one of the few Women's Studies majors shouted: "That's bull!" When I invited her to elaborate her criticism, she explained that women only supported men's wars as a result of coercion, propaganda, social pressure, and economic insecurity. I agreed that these were real factors, but added that young men might be exposed to comparable pressures—as well as additional ones. This she hotly denied, asserting, in that tone of utter certitude which had by then become familiar to me, that men simply *were* to blame and women simply *were* the victims of patriarchy.

This is not just a matter of impressionable and literal-minded undergraduates speaking from ignorance. Important women scholars who have actively supported feminism have found themselves unwelcome in Women's Studies programs because they did not adhere to social constructionist dogma.

For an extended example of this academic form of shunning, consider the case of the sociologist Alice Rossi, the president (1983–84) of the American Sociological Association (ASA), a pioneer of second-wave feminism, and a founding member, in the mid-1960s, of the National Organization for Women. Professor Rossi explained to us the trajectory that led her away from both

Women's Studies and the usual sociology meetings (she is involved, instead, in international multidisciplinary projects that promote a biopsychosocial approach to human behavior):

> My interests have shifted very much in the direction of trying to build bridges between the biological sciences and the social and behavioral sciences. In fact, my presidential address at ASA was on a biosocial perspective on parenting, which is extremely controversial. And yet the impulse for that really came out of the more radical wing of the feminist movement.
>
> I could not accept the idea that gender differences reflected merely the ghettoization and low status of women huddling together as a discriminated-against group, because I believe that some of the things I admired most in myself and in other women were rooted in more fundamental aspects of gender differences. Once I began thinking seriously about that, I had to inform myself in the areas of neuroendocrinology, reproductive biology, evolutionary theory, and that just led to a different direction of interest, a direction so controversial at that time that I would get notes from former feminist colleagues in the profession and outside it, saying that I had turned conservative and had given up on the "good politics."

Debate became impossible as the pressure increased to deny any biological role in social and individual phenomena. Students who had taken several Women's Studies courses would sometimes come to Professor Rossi's classes with the fixed sense that they had "discussed all that already":

> It was all settled in their minds. You didn't have to know any biology, you didn't have to know anything about genes, you didn't have to know anything about how your hormones worked, what the influence on behavior is, or the lack of influence. I've had endless discussions, not with faculty in Women's Studies but

with students who were in the program, [and when pressed,] they just came back at me all the time with the same argument— "Well, there's no reason to deal with anything biological because that only takes away from the *real* factors. The real things that determine things are social and political." I said, "Look, that's based on an erroneous conception of the relationship between the body and the mind and the spirit. It's a two-way street."

As Professor Rossi sees it, the critique of a strict social constructionist view has significant political (and policy) consequences:

In terms of being interested in activism, if you believe there are some innate tendencies that come out of a very long evolutionary process, then things like unisex education just are not the solution. You need *compensatory education.* I believe that very strongly and deeply. And it isn't just a matter of giving girls a doctor's kit and boys a nurse's role. It's more important than that.

A careful evaluation of Professor Rossi's position can only come in the course of a debate in an appropriate scholarly forum. But we do not for a moment doubt that her views, backed as they are by her substantial research and that of others, deserve to be considered seriously. Once again we observe that feminism, which began its career as an enormous opening out into the world, an expansion— and in many cases, a correction—of existing knowledge and perspectives, has ended up leading to a narrow, blinkered approach. Much of the original feminist work on gender was excellent, but when social constructionism turns doctrinaire, it ceases to be a useful thinking tool and becomes one more intellectual straitjacket to be cast off.

As the flip side of social constructionism, BIODENIAL has done its share to bring on the stultification so pervasive in Women's Studies today. BIODENIAL, however, is not the only self-defeating game feminists play with the vexing problem of gender.

GENDERAGENDA: CLEANSING THE
CURRICULUM OF PHALLIC PHANTASMS

All revolutionaries, political or intellectual, would like to raze the existing system and then build afresh, doing things over according to the revolutionary blueprint. Feminism is no exception, which was our point in describing the game of TOTAL REJ. But it is one thing to call for a brave new feminist world and quite another to actually construct one.

In the heady early days of Women's Studies, gender analysis seemed to cast a totally new light on every subject, and some enthusiasts even talked about establishing feminist universities in which every discipline would be newly founded, using gender as the fundamental and overarching concept. But certain subjects remained more or less impervious to change by either the search-for-missing-women or gender analyses. Because few forgotten women could be reclaimed in the natural sciences and mathematics, some feminists argued that the traditional definition of the scientist was too narrow, and they urged the admission of midwives, lab technicians, and home economists into the pantheon of science. Gender historians uncovered some sexist howlers, such as Aristotle's theory of reproduction, in which a passive, nutritive role was assigned to the female—she was the fertile soil quickened and formed by the male seed. But once one moved from biology to chemistry or physics, what possible relevance could gender have? Goethe may have compared double decomposition reactions to the switching of marital partners, and electricians refer to male and female circuit connectors, but there seemed to be very little gender imagery within the actual *content* of science, except when one was studying sex differences and reproduction. Metaphors were a different matter, of course, and, as we saw in WORDMAGIC, feminists made much of these.

The gender analysts then made a crucial move. Perhaps the place to look for gender in disciplines such as physics and mathematics was not in the subject matter itself, but in the very methods used by scientists and mathematicians as they posed their questions and sought answers. If it could be shown that the entire enterprise of science and mathematics, as well as the traditional canons of rationality embodied in logic and statistics, incorporated patriarchal assumptions, the gender agenda would be vastly expanded. Far from being gender neutral as compared to the humanities, the sciences would at one fell swoop be revealed to be the most sexist disciplines of all. Then it would be obvious why women had traditionally avoided the physical sciences in favor of the liberal arts and "soft" sciences.

There were problems, however. Is there a real difference between the claim that syllogistic reasoning or the methods of controlled experiments are inherently sexist and the arguments of nineteenth-century chauvinists who were sure that the diversion of blood to the womb made women ill-suited for abstract reasoning? Contemporary feminists have never managed to escape from this dilemma, but they have raised enough smoke and mirrors to hide the cracks in their position. It is with such evasive and equivocating moves that the game of GENDERAGENDA is played.

How "Feminine" Tunes Are "Brutally Quashed"

For a relatively simple example of how GENDERAGENDA works, and—presumably—how it is enjoyed, let us examine a recent book on classical music called *Feminine Endings: Music, Gender, and Sexuality*, by Susan McClary.[6] Musicology and music theory are as exacting in their methods as the hard sciences and, one would suppose, just as resistant to the GENDERAGENDA. But such an assumption underestimates the ingenuity of feminist critics, as McClary's book demonstrates.

McClary begins by admitting that she felt envious of friends in literary studies and art history for their ability to use the new tools of feminist criticism in their work. It was difficult for her, at first, to imagine how classical music, with its vaunted attributes of objectivity, universality, and transcendence, could be susceptible to a feminist critique. But once she had pried open the forbidden door, she began to realize that the "structures graphed by theorists . . . are often stained with such things as violence, misogyny, and racism."[7] In the first part of her book, McClary briskly catalogues a number of straightforward complaints: Women musicians have been systematically discouraged from entering the profession or developing their talents, on the sexist grounds that they could not be truly creative. The works of female composers have not received just recognition. The librettos of many operas are egregiously misogynist (Bartók's *Bluebeard's Castle* is described in grisly detail). Furthermore, the technical terminology is sexist: opening themes and strong endings are "masculine," "feminine" endings finish on a weak beat, "feminine" themes are subsidiary, and so on.

So far so good. But not content merely to show (as others have done) that women have not always been made to feel welcome in the classical music scene, McClary goes on to make a move characteristic of GENDERAGENDA. She grants that males prefer the so-called masculine endings, but insists—without offering evidence— that females are in fact more receptive to endings that finish on a weak beat. Therefore, she concludes, the formal structure of classical music is intrinsically gendered and cannot, for this reason, have any universal, objective, transcendental merit rooted in its aesthetic worth. Whatever appeal music has depends on the match between the gender of the composer and that of the listener.

Some extravagant gender interpretations follow. McClary says that "many of Beethoven's symphonies exhibit considerable anxiety with respect to feminine moments and respond to them with extraordinary violence."[8] Furthermore, "Beethoven's Ninth Symphony unleashes one of the most horrifyingly violent episodes in the history of music. . . . The Ninth Symphony is probably our most compelling articulation in music of the contradictory impulses that have organized patriarchal culture since the Enlightenment."[9] In the Unfinished Symphony of the sexually ambiguous Schubert, on the other hand, "it is the lovely, 'feminine' tune which we are encouraged to identify with and which is brutally, tragically quashed."[10] In addition to such observations, McClary describes the radically different formal devices used by contemporary women composers such as Janika Vanderwelde and Laurie Anderson.

It is important that we be very clear as to what makes a book like *Feminine Endings* troubling within the context of Women's Studies. Taken as a speculative musicological exercise, McClary's book might provoke some interesting discussions among experts. Music students familiar with Beethoven and Schubert, and with analyses of their music other than McClary's, will be able to refer to the scores to test her notions of the phallic significance of climaxes in romantic music. They may also ask why Bach and Haydn could express their masculinity in a very different musical idiom. In such a knowledgeable setting, there is no chance that the book will be taken as the new orthodoxy.

But in the happy-go-lucky world of Women's Studies, where interdisciplinarity reigns and no professional caution keeps anyone from using material from fields in which they have little or no learning, the book is likely to be read quite differently. There, it will be taken as showing not only that women have often been excluded from the profession of music, but that the best of classical music contains in its very essence, and expresses in its musical aesthetic, the violence of patriarchal misogyny. Since McClary is obviously inspired by feminist ideas and clearly intends her analysis as a weapon in the liberation of women, her book will be assumed to be useful reading for the aspiring female musician. It may cause some harm there. But its worst injuries will be done to the nonmusicians among Women's Studies students, who will simply add classical music to their already long list of areas with which they need not bother. GENDERAGENDA dictates that no contrary interpretation need be offered, and once again young women will have learned that unless the thing is of woman born, it is worthy only of their contempt.

McClary's book is probably the first comprehensive attempt to apply a gender analysis to music. It is, therefore, not surprising to find that, in its organization and thematic arrangement, it recapitulates the whole history of Women's Studies. It begins with the search for forgotten foremothers, describes how women have been excluded, then looks for and, of course, finds ugly male attributes at the very heart of the activity, and finally declares that women cannot participate successfully without making great compromises (thereby— rather problematically—implying that the forgotten foremothers were dupes, not heroines). The conclusion reached is that if women are to be an authentic part of the music scene, the profession will have to change drastically. Until that happens, women with feminist sensitivities will take up music at their peril.

"Logic . . . Is Insane"

The pattern just described is also present in recent feminist critiques of logic. The old gender stereotype employed to discourage or excuse women from studying logic is a familiar one: women are not adept at abstract thought or formal analysis. Earlier feminists would have bristled at these assumptions. They would have pointed at the sexist content of the homework exercises that, until very recently, were standard fare in logic books. Quite understandably, female students might resent having to analyze the structure of sentences like the following: "If any husband is unsuccessful, then if some wives are ambitious he will be unhappy." "Women without husbands are unhappy unless they have paramours." "If either red-heads are lovely or blondes do not have freckles, then logic is confusing."[11]

However, in a recent book by Andrea Nye, *Words of Power: A Feminist Reading of the History of Logic*,[12] we are given a feminist critique, not of the exclusion of women from logic, but of logic itself. In her first chapter, Nye tells the story of her experiences as a student in her logic class: Only one other woman was in this class. Nye was too unsure of herself to raise her hand. She found it immensely difficult to think in the way required. When confronted with the example "Jones ate fish with ice cream and died," Nye, who had come to philosophy from literature, found her mind wandering off to speculations about why Jones should eat such a bizarre dish and why death was the consequence. The difficulty she experienced in representing the structure of the sentence with p's and q's raised a troubling question in her mind: "Is it because I, as a woman, had a different kind of mind, incapable of abstraction and therefore of theorizing; is it because I was too 'emotional'?"[13]

Many women have had such doubts. The liberal feminist reply to them is to analyze how pedagogical styles in logic classes, as well as societal gender stereotypes, make women feel alienated from logic. Nye's response, however, is to put the shoe of blame on the other foot. She argues that, given its historical development from ancient Greek times, logic, as we know it today, is not only alien to women but also has been, and continues to be, a weapon of oppression used against them.

Nye begins her interpretation of the history of logic with an attack on Aristotle's Law of the Excluded Middle, and concludes by suggesting a link between Frege, a giant of twentieth-century logic, and Hitler:

> Hitler, . . . guided by sentiments not unlike the ones expressed in Frege's diary, worked out the master-logic of National Socialism. . . . National Socialist thought, like Frege's, did not concern itself with empirical content. . . . No personal experience could negate [its] body of truth. The applications of logic to action that Frege had promised came readily to hand. If Jews are a mongrel race, they must be exterminated. "A thought like a hammer" [Frege's phrase] demanded instant obedience to the dictates of logic.[14]

Following this extraordinary association, Nye concludes that "logic in its final perfection is insane."[15]

Nye's unusual reading of the history of logic will be submitted to the normal tribunal of her peers, and the process of critical evaluation has already begun. At the 1992 Pacific regional meeting of the American Philosophical Association, for example, the philosophers Don Levi and Daniel Merrill commented on the book at an Author Meets Critics Symposium. Pointing out that Nye is shifty in her use of the term *logic*—it is absurd to pretend that *Principia Mathematica* and *Mein Kampf* are both logic books in the same sense of the term—they proposed that logic as taught in critical-thinking courses can be a tool of liberation. But, again, it is one thing to submit Nye's book to a panel of philosophers, and another to present it to untrained and suggestible students. We can easily imagine how such a book will be taught in Women's Studies classes. Nonspecialist teachers will mine it for ammunition to use against their usual target. Is it likely that logic will survive such treatment as a subject worth studying, or will it be discarded by the GENDERAGENDA as yet another example of patriarchal thinking?

Opposition to Exact Science

It is interesting to note that in their assault on science, feminists have managed to hold on to many of the stereotypical notions concerning cognitive skills that used to disfigure masculinist thinking on this subject. Take the dichotomies devised long ago to help demonstrate the superiority of the male mind: abstract versus concrete, logical versus intuitive, objective versus subjective, analytical versus synthetic, quantitative versus qualitative. Once these pairs are set up as opposites, ancient gender stereotypes allow the labeling of one pole as "masculine" and the other as "feminine." Not surprisingly, the attributes designated "masculine" are the ones thought of as more characteristic of, and desirable in, science. Females, according to this view of the world, are uncomfortable with quantities (they prefer "so hot I can barely handle it" to "$T = 66°$ C"). They respond naturally to anecdotal evidence but are unmoved by statistical data. And so on.

One would think that those who remain unconvinced by this argument for women's defective reasoning ability would respond by offering counterexamples, such as the market women in Tangiers who compute prices in several currencies without the aid of a calculator, or Katharine Bement Davis's 1926 study of the sex lives of 2,200 women—a survey that predated the Kinsey reports by more than two decades.[16] But the GENDERAGENDA promotes a different strategy: Gladly granting that there is indeed a link between gender and reasoning style, this game preserves the old dualistic categories but reverses the value signs associated with each of them. All the "male" attributes now bear a minus sign, while the "female" attributes are given a plus sign. Thus, intuitive impressions come closer to the truth than logically constructed arguments, and qualitative and anecdotal studies are more humane than—and therefore superior to—statistically rigorous quantitative ones, because the latter ignore the rich peculiarities of individual cases. So the argument rushes to its inevitable conclusion: the very tools of male science are in this way proved deficient and must be replaced by female instruments.

Now, interesting things are to be said about the comparative value of contrasting cognitive styles, and philosophers and scientists have long debated the proper roles they should play. Early in this century the British philosopher of science Norman Campbell argued with Pierre Duhem about the relative merits of physics represented as abstract formulae (the French style) as opposed to physics instantiated in mechanical models (the English style). Long before Barbara McClintock and her "feeling for the organism," scientists spoke eloquently about the need for *Fingerspitzengefühl* and *Empfindung*. Einstein remarked on the importance of having a "nose" for good problems. And biologists have long debated the respective advantages of experimentation and naturalistic inquiry.

Feminists are welcome to enter these discussions, and they may wish to press the argument that the prevailing methodological orthodoxy has sometimes adversely affected women. But nothing is gained by insisting that methodologies are intrinsically gendered and that their value can be determined by their place on the scale of gender stereotypes.

Feminist academics were understandably excited about the significance of gender as a lens through which to view important segments of traditional scholarship. But somewhere along the line they fell victim to a sort of "gendelirium," no longer fueled by solid scholarly achievements but fed by anger and the wish to repudiate wholesale the entire academic tradition. The results have been a few spectacular polemics and some livening up of scholarly journals, but for the Women's Studies student, the outcome has been less fortunate. She learns that traditional disciplines, by the very methodologies they employ, oppress women and that, if she studies them at all, she may lose her feminist soul unless she does so as a subversive agent, a mole burrowing from within to destroy the patriarchal paradigms.

Nor is this burden lifted as the student leaves the university gates. Silvia, the research biologist quoted in chapter 3, spoke to us of the attitudes displayed toward her profession by feminists whom she meets socially:

> There's an antagonism toward people who do science. If I were a sociologist or labeled myself a psychologist—which I sometimes do these days, by the way—or an anthropologist or some of the other disciplines traditionally considered to be more feminine or feminist-oriented, I'd be accepted right away. The problem is that I do biology. Basically, people don't talk to me. There's a general mistrust of anything I do or say. I'm perceived as being poisoned by the patriarchy, because biologists and hard-core scientists are trained in such a way that we're absolutely poisoned, and so we have little or nothing to offer. I find it interesting that women who are medical doctors aren't viewed the same way. I don't know why. Or they may get a similar treatment, but for a different reason—because they are perceived as making a lot of money, and we feminists have the downwardly mobile aspect, too—but not because they've been necessarily poisoned in the way that they think in general. It's almost as if hard-core science and feminism are like oil and water—they simply can't mix, and if you're one, you can't be the other.

In today's professional and graduate schools, logic and science are prerequisites for many fulfilling and important pursuits such as medicine, economics, biochemistry, engineering, law, and computer science. Logic and mathematics often serve as gatekeepers because many students, not only women, find them difficult to master. To tell a young woman to resist logic because it is a tool of domination that will poison her mind is to put yet another barrier in her path. Although the Hippocratic physicians did not always live up to their oath, their injunction to "At least do no harm" has much to commend it. Feminist teachers might think about adopting as their motto "At least do no harm to women," for it is young women who will most suffer from the feminist repudiation of science and critical thinking. In this respect, the presence of feminism in the academy emphatically does not liberate it from past narrowness. Quite the contrary, it introduces a new constriction.

Despite the feminist rhetoric about encouraging a less doctrinaire, more dialogic approach to education, we find, instead, a contemptuous dismissal of great chunks of invaluable knowledge. This affects not only attitudes toward science but, much more generally, the ability to select appropriate research methodologies in all disciplines. Again we cite the words of Professor Rossi:

> I've no argument with good qualitative ethnographic in-depth study—absolutely none. But it's not the be-all and end-all, and what was developing, at least in terms of feminist sociology, was a belief that quantitative work is sexist. I think I'm a good feminist and I am also a good survey designer and a good data analyst and I see things because I *do* have female eyes and a feminist lens, and it has nothing to do with the method. But dismissal of a method just is anathema to me. And that's what I was encountering—*ideological* opposition to quantitative analysis. And the graduate students reflect it. My God, if anything, that's the domain within sociology that women should be encouraged to master. They need to know the possibilities well enough so that they can make a decision—"the problem I'm interested in requires only a personal in-depth approach," fine. But to never learn this method over here, and then not only go your own way but condemn people who made another option—that's intellectual Stalinism to me.

7

"Mirror, Mirror on the Wall":
Feminist Self-Scrutiny

IN THE PRECEDING CHAPTERS we portrayed feminist ideology and its academic pitfalls through a description of games popular in Women's Studies programs. These games are waged more single-mindedly and with greater ferocity in the more self-consciously "political" programs. But they are played, with varying degrees of aggressiveness, everywhere.

At this point in our argument, the sincere feminist reader, one sympathetic to both the legitimate achievements of feminist scholarship and the urgency of the real political and economic obstacles still faced by women, might well be thinking: Yes, you've captured the ethos of all too many Women's Studies programs. But isn't the public perception of an enterprise usually set by the distortions of extremists in its ranks? (This is always an issue in gay-pride marches, for example: How do you keep the media from reporting only on rowdy drag queens, dykes on bikes, and S-M aficionado/as, while overlooking the rank and file?) Surely, such a reader might object, most Women's Studies faculty deplore the games you have described. And now that these idiocies and abuses are being brought to light, will they not move quickly to root them out or at least curtail them?

We sincerely hope our friendly feminist reader is correct in her assumptions. But unfortunately, the actual situation appears to be otherwise. If there is opposition to the processes we have described, it has not been evident in the pronouncements coming out of Women's Studies programs.

To indicate the extent to which the official line is still unreconstructed, let us consider now a report on recent policy trends in Women's Studies programs. This report, along with other internal documents representing attempts by programs to evaluate and improve themselves, suggests that the games feminists play are indeed the current sport of choice in Women's Studies.

ASSESSING WOMEN'S STUDIES

In 1992, the National Women's Studies Association (NWSA), in collaboration with the Association of American Colleges, published the results of a three-year evaluation project financed by the Fund for the Improvement of Postsecondary Education of the U.S. Department of Education. The report was promisingly titled *The Courage to Question* and was issued with a companion volume, *Students at the Center.*[1] The project's goal was to determine how Women's Studies programs across the country were doing, primarily with an eye to improving them. The publication was designed to provide a model for programs seeking to do a self-evaluation. Participating schools included small liberal arts colleges, land-grant universities in the prairies, and inner-city branch campuses.

The Courage to Question and *Students at the Center,* written in an informal and personal style that makes for pleasant reading, are cast as sincere attempts at self-scrutiny on the part of Women's Studies programs. We therefore approached them hoping to find some signs of feminists' attempts to remedy or address some of the difficulties we have been documenting in this book. However, as we read the books it became increasingly clear that the real goal of the self-evaluation was to provide ammunition with which to answer outside critics. Close inspection revealed that the model program goals proposed in these volumes not only fail to alleviate the ideological excesses we have described, but in fact reinforce them.

The authors of the study were evidently pleased with the results they had obtained. The students they polled were, by and large, very positive about their experiences in Women's Studies; some were even ecstatic. They praised the Women's Studies classroom as a place of affirmation and validation where they could find their personal voices and strengthen their identities. They gave high marks to the analyses they were taught to make of sexism, racism, ableism, ageism, classism, and heterosexism. These, they said, revolutionized their views of the world.

All assessments begin by referring to the question of method: How can one best ensure that the data collected and the conclusions drawn are accurate? In *Students at the Center*, Caryn Musil, who edited the two volumes, and the other project directors described their decision to use *feminist* assessment methods: "Feminist assessment begins with and enacts values. It does not presume to be objective in the narrow sense of the word, nor does feminist theory believe there is any such thing as a value-free 'scientific' investigation."[2]

In feminist assessment, narratives count more heavily than statistics, a point the authors drive home with the obligatory reference to the impossibility of dismantling the master's house by using the master's tools.[3] They indicate that evaluation methods "*should be compatible with feminist activist beliefs*" and with the aims of "emancipatory pedagogy."[4] In addition, the assessment should also be based on research that is "central to this interdisciplinary area":

> To be successful, feminist assessment must be compatible with feminist scholarship. It should take into consideration such concepts as maternal thinking, caring, concern and relatedness, and women's ways of knowing or connected learning. These concepts can serve as the theoretical framework for feminist evaluation, a process more concerned with improvement than testing, with nurtured progression than with final judgments.[5]

Since the idea of *connected learning* referred to in this passage plays a central role in *The Courage to Question* and in feminist pedagogy generally, we need to analyze it in some detail. The foundational document on this concept is *Women's Ways of Knowing*, by Mary Field Belenky, Blythe McVicker Clinchy, Nancy Rule Goldberger, and Jill Mattuck Tarule.[6] We argue that the *connected learning* model promoted in *The Courage to Question* is an unfortunate oversimplification of *Women's Ways of Knowing*, but that the latter readily lends itself to such a distortion. It must also be said that *Women's Ways of Knowing* itself is based on inconclusive research and draws too uncritically on the work of Nel Noddings (*Caring*), Sara Ruddick (*Maternal Thinking*), and Carol Gilligan (*In a Different Voice*).[7] Serious flaws in these books, especially Gilligan's, have been repeatedly pointed out in mainstream psychology journals, and even in *Signs*, the premier feminist periodical. But because of the opportunistic eclecticism of Women's Studies (which somehow manages to coexist with academic feminism's doctrinaire assumptions and assertions), these writers' claims are rarely qualified or bracketed. As long as they have intuitive appeal and serve an apparently useful and immediate political purpose, they find wide and uncritical acceptance.

What follows, then, is a case study of how an ideologically inspired conjecture, having evaded the usual mechanisms of scholarly appraisal—largely because Women's Studies rejects these mechanisms—emerged, nearly a decade after its first appearance, as an allegedly well-confirmed discovery, one sound enough to serve as the foundation of far-reaching academic policy.

"WOMEN'S WAYS OF KNOWING"

Women's Ways of Knowing is considered an exemplar of feminist scholarship. Composed collaboratively and dedicated to the four authors' mothers and daughters, it is written in an engaging style without the use of statistics (not even in an appendix), and with surprisingly few qualitative comparisons. The book is based on open-ended interviews with 135 women of diverse ages, classes, ethnic backgrounds, and social circumstances. It offers a blend of quotations from the women themselves with the authors' interpretive comments. These, in turn, are followed by policy recommendations.

The book has been very successful. It received the 1987 Distinguished Publications Award from the Association of Women in Psychology and has become a popular text. For example, in 1993 the biology department at Indiana University used it in a course for prospective teachers, as did the School of Education. The book's authors propound two major theses. One is the descriptive claim that women "have cultivated and learned to value ways [of knowing] which are powerful but have been neglected and denigrated by the dominant intellectual ethos of our time."[8] The second is the pedagogic contention "that educators can help women develop their own authentic voices if they emphasize connection over separation, understanding and acceptance over assessment, and collaboration over debate."[9]

The first mode of knowing described in *Women's Ways of Knowing* is simply called *silence*, which applies to women who think of themselves as "deaf and dumb." They can neither learn by listening to words ("Someone has to show me—not tell me—or I can't get it") nor use language to accomplish their goals. The second mode, called *received knowledge*, grows out of women's passivity: "Hav[ing] no opinions and no voice of their own to guide them, women in this position listen to others for directions as well as for information." Women who take this approach to knowledge are easily confused when experts disagree. When asked what she would do if advisors from a children's center gave conflicting advice, one woman exclaimed, "'Oh, that's never happened! I don't know what I would do.... Maybe I'd go eeny, meeny, miny, mo. I don't know really.'"[10]

The most prevalent mode delineated in *Women's Ways of Knowing* is labeled *subjective knowledge*. One of the few semiquantitative assertions in the book tells us that "of the 135 women ... inter-

viewed, almost half were predominantly subjectivist in their thinking." In this mode, the absolute authority of the expert has been
replaced by an inner voice, variously described by the interviewees
as instinct, intuition, or "know[ing] with my gut": "It's like a certain
feeling that you have inside you." Some of the women classified as
subjective knowers had gained confidence in their "inner voices"
through the process of escaping from physically and sexually abusive
situations. Others had struggled with their fear of being wrong or of
being laughed at. All the women reported a great feeling of elation
and empowerment as they discovered their inner voices and no
longer felt trapped in silence or enthralled by outside authority. But
the authors stress that, at least in our society, these subjectivists are
at a serious disadvantage: "[I]n a world that emphasizes rationalism
and scientific thought, there are bound to be personal and social
costs of a subjectivist epistemology."[11]

A more complex kind of knowing is the mode the authors called
procedural knowing. Women in their survey whose mental habits
exemplified this way of knowing were primarily college students
who were "privileged, bright, white, and young." Often, as a result
of encountering the divergent procedures and methods for investigating the world employed by academic disciplines, such women
have come to realize that neither external authorities nor inner
voices are infallible. They "engage in conscious, deliberate, systematic analysis. They have learned that truth is not immediately accessible, that you cannot 'just know.' Things are not always what they
seem to be. Truth lies hidden beneath the surface, and you must fer-
ret it out."[12]

What makes *procedural knowing* distinctively female? The answer
is that most of the procedural knowers in the sample felt uncomfortable with the methods and approaches they had had to acquire to
succeed in the traditional classroom, and it is assumed that these are
somehow masculine modes. The authors explain:

In general, few of the women we interviewed . . . found argument—reasoned critical discourse—a congenial form of conversa-

tion among friends. The classic dormitory bull session, with students assailing their opponents' logic and attacking their evidence, seems to occur rarely among women, and teachers complain that women students are reluctant to engage in critical debate with peers in class, even when explicitly encouraged to do so.[13]

These students realized that there were often conflicting points of view, and that not all of these could be equally valid. They also thought it worthwhile to try to sort through the positions in hopes of bettering their understanding. But what they were reluctant or unable to do was to separate the ideas from the individuals who held them. "Teachers and fathers and boyfriends assure them that arguments are not between *persons* but between *positions,* but the women continue to fear that someone may get hurt."[14]

Because not all women resist distinguishing thought from thinker, word from speaker, the authors posit two subcategories of *procedural knowing,* as indicated in the following table (based on stages described in *Women's Ways of Knowing*):

MODES OF KNOWING

1. Silence
2. Passive Reception
3. Subjective Knowing
4. Procedural Knowing
   a. Separate
   b. Connected
5. Constructed Knowing

One of these subcategories, which involves separating a critique of ideas from a personal attack on the people who propose them, is called *separate knowing* (4a). This is the traditional approach, but it was not the one that most women in the sample preferred. Instead, they opted for the other subcategory, called *connected knowing* (4b), characterized by the qualities of empathy, trust, and forbearance. Criticism is possible, but only in a supportive setting created once the members of the group have come to know each other well. An art student said, "'[I]f you've gone along since the beginning with the same people it never comes across as this awful criticism.'" And the authors comment: "People could criticize each other's work in this class and accept each other's criticisms because members of the group shared a similar experience. *This is the only sort of expertise connected knowers recognize, the only sort of criticism they easily accept.*" The authors point out that *connected knowing* works well only in small groups whose members are familiar with one another. One student described her seminar in this way: "'It was like a family group trying to work out a family problem, except it was an idea.'" The authors note, however, that "in most educational institutions there is no chance to form such family groups."[15]

Several intellectual and practical factors would seem to limit the applicability of the *connected knowing* model, perhaps even placing those who subscribe to it at a serious disadvantage. By cutting herself off from data gathered by people she does not know personally, or from the ideas of people with whom she cannot empathize, the *connected knower* is severely limiting her sources of information. In other words, she, too, is separating herself! And if women hope to participate in knowledge networks that extend beyond their families or immediate circles—that is, if women want to function effectively in law or politics or in a business larger than a mom-and-pop store—they will have to learn to operate in a broader and more complex arena of information and ideas.

But even in a family situation (as anyone who has lived with an alcoholic relative knows), it is not wise to rely uncritically on empathy, trust, and forbearance. It is somewhat surprising, therefore, to see the authors of *Women's Ways of Knowing* treating *connected knowing* as on a par with, and perhaps even superior to, the *separate knowing* mode. At the very least, it seems to us, they should have urged women (and men, too) to learn to be comfortable with both approaches, and to use each model, as appropriate.

However, the authors stop short of doing this, perhaps because they believe women are extremely comfortable with *connected knowing.* "Women have been practicing this kind of conversation since childhood," they say, and "women seem to take naturally to a nonjudgmental stance."[16] The authors may also prefer the connected mode because of the neat parallels that can be drawn between it and the propositions of Gilligan, Noddings, Ruddick, and others concerning the moral reasoning of women. Gilligan's research, for example, portrays women as so preoccupied with the intricate web of personal relationships that they are unwilling or unable to invoke abstract norms of justice and fairness when reasoning about a moral dilemma such as abortion.

When we return to *The Courage to Question* later in this chapter, we will see that it is *connected knowing* that is taken to be the epistemological goal of Women's Studies. But *Women's Ways of Knowing* still has one more mode to describe: *constructed knowing.* According to the few women who achieve this modality, the transition to it is spurred on by their perception of the inadequacies in *connected knowing. Constructed knowing* seeks—and when it is accomplished, achieves—an accommodation of *all* the components that were selectively invoked in the other modalities. It is a "voice of integration" that "find[s] a place for reason *and* intuition *and* the expertise of others." In addition, "there is ... an emphasis on a never-ending search for truth, which is coordinate with a never-ending quest for learning.... When truth is seen as a process of construction in which the knower participates, a passion for learning is unleashed."[17]

With *constructed knowing* (not to be confused with the social construction of knowledge discussed in chapter 6), we seem to have returned to a conception of knowledge that fits in well with the academic tradition. However, the authors emphasize the differences. "Among women thinking as constructivists ... knowing is not simply an 'objective' procedure but a way of weaving their passions and intellectual life into some recognizable whole." The "empathic potential—the capacity for ... what Ruddick identifies with 'maternal thinking'... —is particularly characteristic of constructivist women," and these women "usually resent the implicit pressure in male-dominated circles to toughen up and fight to get their ideas across." "Constructivist women aspire to work that contributes to the empowerment and improvement in the quality of life of others." These sentences alert us to the realization that this final modality is still tinged with stereotypical feminine virtues—and vices. The authors of *Women's Ways of Knowing* make no attempt to explore exactly how the discordant voices of reason, feeling, authority, and experience are to be brought into harmony; they all must be listened to. We are given a list of ingredients, but the rest of the recipe is missing.[18]

Women's Ways of Knowing effectively documents the severe learning disabilities some women bring with them to Women's Studies classrooms: Such students may be silent; they may only speak by parroting authorities; some may lapse into a solipsistic state of subjectivity; others may be so fragile that they cannot learn without receiving constant support and approbation. The authors make a strong case for the contention that some women have been epistemologically crippled, but they offer no foundation for any claim that the previously ignored "ways of knowing" bestow power on women. Nor do they explore the best techniques for helping learners progress from less to more adequate ways of knowing. And like nearly all feminist research in this area, the authors fail to undertake comparative studies to see whether male students fall into similar patterns.

Women's Ways of Knowing invites the conclusion that some women are attracted to Women's Studies because of a history of personal trauma, and that these students may well have some learning disabilities that will need to be corrected before they can cope with the atmosphere of vigorous debates and critical discourse characteristic of the best university education. In short, the book should be read as a warning that some women need compensatory education, though the authors fail to say which women, how many, or exactly how they can be helped. But, as we will see by returning to *The Courage to Question*, these are not the lessons that Women's Studies faculty have drawn from their reading of *Women's Ways of Knowing*. Instead, they offer it as proof of the superiority of women's wonderfully different and rewarding ways of knowing, and as a celebration of this difference.

THE MISSION OF WOMEN'S STUDIES

As noted earlier, the team that produced *The Courage to Question* followed evaluation procedures growing out of feminist theory and compatible with feminist activism. According to the companion volume, *Students at the Center*, the team decided "not to create a unified, standardized assessment plan."[19] Instead, each participating campus was encouraged to design its own instruments for judging its performance. The consultants, for their part, writing in a chapter titled "Seasoning Your Own Spaghetti Sauce," provide some spices to flavor the various projects, recommending techniques such as open-ended oral interviews and portfolios of student work, as well as the usual questionnaires.

At each of the participating schools, however, the project directors met together on a number of occasions and, after consulting with their local constituencies, drew up a list of key questions intended to guide all seven programs that eventually participated in the assessment project. These questions, indicated in the following list from *The Courage to Question*, provide a summary of the aims and objectives considered essential by this sample of Women's Studies programs. (Numbers have been added for convenience.)

1. Does women's studies cultivate personal empowerment and social responsibility?
2. How successfully does women's studies support students as they express their feminism on campus?
3. Is the authority of experience legitimized and are students urged to comprehend the experience of others?
4. Does women's studies foster connected learning?
5. Are students introduced to the constructed and situated character of disciplinary knowledge?
6. Are students encouraged to reconstruct knowledge from multidisciplinary and cross-cultural perspectives?
7. How do programs navigate tensions between creating safe but challenging classroom space?

8. Finally, how do we shift and make explicit the power relations both in the classroom and the institution?
9. All of these questions [are] understood to be posed within the larger framework in which gender, race, class, sexuality, and other categories of analytic differences intersect.[20]

Nothing in these programmatic questions suggests that it might be the business of Women's Studies to foster research in, or at least make students aware of, women's history, women's literature, or recent social science work on women and gender. Instead, all stated goals seek to promote processes and attitudes, and to stake out psychological and pedagogical "space." Strikingly, these questions assume that an academic department should, as a key part of its mission, support student activism and the shifting of power relations within the institution. Sometimes such efforts take a very concrete form. Hunter College, for example, reported on the establishment of a mentoring program for its students, drawing on "alumnae who are doing feminist advocacy in New York City." The program at the University of Missouri–Columbia listed as its first two goals to "support our students as ambassadors of feminism [and to] continue to address the campus-wide problems of sexism, racism, and other injustices."[21]

The assessors' questions to students were designed to determine how effectively this political agenda was being implemented at the respective institutions. One sample instrument asked: "Can you identify one or two significant experiences at Oberlin (a course, an event, a professor, friendship, membership in political organizations, etc.) that most influenced your feminist consciousness?"[22] The authors of *The Courage to Question* shrug off the concern expressed by a mathematics professor at Oberlin who thought it inappropriate for academic programs to function as political parties.[23] Clearly, political commitment is considered a valuable and central part of the public mission of many Women's Studies programs.

A second major theme of *Students at the Center* is the special quality of feminist pedagogy. Oberlin asked flatly: "Do you believe that women's studies courses differ in pedagogy—in how students learn—from non-women's studies courses? If yes, how?" Old Dominion wanted to know whether "the learning environments were different," and Wellesley asked how the Women's Studies courses had affected the students' personal lives and changed their political beliefs.[24] One of Oberlin's questions encapsulated the central aims of feminist pedagogy, and then asked the student directly how successful she herself thought she had been in achieving them:

> Goals of the Oberlin Women's Studies Program include self empowerment; recognition of differences; collaborative learning; understanding interdisciplinary connections in the analysis of gender, race, class, sexuality; and linking personal with social responsibility. Which of these goals are most important to *you* and which do you feel you have accomplished as a student in Women's Studies?[25]

Many of the buzz words of feminist pedagogy—*empowerment, collaborative learning, personalized learning, connected learning, coming to voice, personal transformation*—evoke memories of progressive education movements dating back at least to John Dewey. When we look carefully at their use in this document, however, we find that the recommended feminist practices are quite different from the rather permissive, individualized, student-centered teaching methods associated with "progressive" education.

First, in feminist pedagogy, students are expected to structure any and all inquiry in terms of overarching concepts such as gender, race, and class (as stated in item 9 of the preceding list). Second, and more important, students are encouraged not only to begin their investigations with personal reflections, but also to continue throughout the stages of their education to make tight connections between what they hear or read and their own day-to-day lives. Third, they are expected, and sometimes required, to voice their personal reactions to their classmates, as well as to listen receptively to the personal comments of others (as in item 3).

Most of the students cited in these assessments were Women's

Studies majors or minors; hence, it is not surprising to learn that they liked this intimate touch. As shown in *The Courage to Question*, they criticized classes that merely talked *about* racism and classism, instead of "really dealing with an issue." What they clearly meant by this expression was "connecting it to one's own experience as oppressed and oppressor." In principle, this sharing of personal viewpoints is intended to lead to "mutual discovery," in the course of which the group generates knowledge about racism, classism, or whatever other -ism is under discussion, by piecing together the testimonials of people in the class who occupy different sites on the web of oppression.[26]

Naturally, when students are actively encouraged by the instructor to relate course materials to their personal lives and speak out about the connection, the classroom atmosphere can get rather intense. All of the participants in the assessment project commented on this (in response to item 7). At Oberlin the atmosphere was described as "searing." Intriguingly, when asked if they felt "pressure to give 'politically correct' answers" in class, 30 percent of the Women's Studies students who participated in the Wellesley study said they "felt silenced or at risk expressing unpopular opinions." An indication of how tense the classroom atmosphere can become appeared in a footnote reporting that, in one Wellesley class, nineteen out of twenty-five students replied yes to a question about pressure to be "politically correct." There is no reason to think that the atmosphere at Wellesley was unusually fervent, but one cannot say for certain, since none of the other assessment teams raised such questions.[27]

Given the intensely experiential character of Women's Studies classes and the pressure faculty exert on students to face up to their status as oppressor or oppressed, it is understandable that, as reported in the study, one of the most satisfying rewards of empowerment that students noted was their increased ability to confront people who told racist or sexist jokes. This response confirms the claim upheld by feminist pedagogues that their classroom techniques are directly conducive to successful activism.

CONNECTED KNOWING AND THE "BELIEVING GAME"

Connected learning, even if seriously oversimplified as a concept by the assessment project, is considered so important by the authors that they include a complete tabular version of it in each volume.[28] Lewis and Clark College used this model explicitly in evaluating student portfolios to determine whether students exhibited signs of *connected knowing*, as was expected of them. In addition, assessment teams were urged to engage themselves in *connected learning* in the process of finding out about their own programs.

The model that forms the basis for the study posits two epistemological styles: *Connected knowers* are said to play a "Believing Game" in which they engage in collaborative inquiry in order to "construct meaning—to understand and to be understood." *Separate knowers*, on the other hand, are playing a "Doubting Game." They are trying to construct truth, rather than meanings, and so they adopt a critical stance as they attempt to prove or disprove claims and refute or convince their adversaries.[29]

Connected knowers are further characterized by a dozen additional oppositions. "Believers" are said to prefer "narrative and contextual" discourse about material to which they feel close attachments. "Doubters" prefer "logical and abstract" reasoning and try to distance themselves from the subject in order to bring "impersonal and universal standards" to bear.[30]

There have been many previous attempts to characterize diverse thinking styles—mathematicians contrast algebraic and geometric approaches, biologists talk about "lumpers" versus "splitters," and there is the old tradition, dating back at least to the Greek mathematician Pappus, of drawing a distinction between analysis and synthesis (or resolution and composition, to use Peripatetic terminology).[31]

But what is unique about the model presented in this two-volume assessment study is the complete repudiation of the path of *separate knowing* that takes as the basis of its authority "mastery of relevant knowledge and methodology." The authors opt instead for basing one's beliefs on "commonality of experience," which may sound innocent enough until one realizes that these shared experiences are to be elicited in an accepting, noncritical atmosphere, in which emotions and feelings are assumed always to "illuminate thought," not cloud it.[32]

Throughout the discussion the goal is to privilege *connected knowing* and to make it the predominant learning mode, not merely give it equal time or due recognition among the variety of epistemologies.

Nowhere in *The Courage to Question* or *Students at the Center* is any recognition given to the most mature model of knowing presented in *Women's Ways of Knowing*—that of *constructed knowing*, the one that attempts to integrate the best features of *connected* and *separate knowing*. As we pointed out, this modality may not match our highest philosophical and scientific norms, but it is certainly much more adequate to them than the *connected knowing* model fostered by the NWSA assessors. The fact that it is not mentioned by the authors tells us much about their assumptions concerning women's mental processes.

If Women's Studies is indeed successful in transforming its students into *connected knowers*, then feminism becomes a Believing Game, one that disdains proof, disproof, and criticism. It incites students to become personally and emotionally invested in the intellectual positions they explore, and it discourages them from trying to detach or distance themselves from the issues under discussion. At most it urges them to modify their own subjective opinions by expanding them so as to include other women's viewpoints, but never are they encouraged to appeal to, or even to recognize, expert learning or to practice methodological rigor. Discourse must never be logical or abstract. It must always be narrative and contextual.

Such a form of inquiry might possibly be useful for a team of feminist evaluators sitting around the kitchen table, or for a family trying to decide where to go on vacation—although even here a bit of detachment and logic often comes in handy. In a situation where the only issue is the reconciliation of preferences, it is perfectly reasonable to try to come up with a solution that includes everybody. But when the conflict is over rival empirical claims or the constitutionality of a proposed ordinance, expert knowledge *is* relevant, and one party's deeply held subjective opinion on the question may simply turn out to be objectively wrong. It is not a crime to have false beliefs—we all have them. Students need to learn to be gracious when refuting other people's pet convictions as well as modest in defending their own. They need to realize that no proofs or disproofs are infallible. But the *last* thing they should be taught is the dangerous proposition that all subjective opinions are equal.

The *connected learning* model goes a long way toward explaining the unstable atmosphere that pervades many Women's Studies classrooms and faculty meetings. As long as positions are not too far apart, the model of sympathetic inclusion works well, and everybody feels validated and cozy. But as soon as sharp conflicts arise, absent the normal modes of conflict resolution—striving for personal detachment, trying to look at the evidence objectively, calling for further study, attempting to be as methodical and logical as possible— the result is likely to be not just a breakdown in sisterly connectedness, but outbursts of extreme rudeness and insoluble conflict.

Defenders of the *connected learning* model might object that recourse to empirical investigations or expertise is never really helpful because, as pointed out in item 5 in the list of key questions ("Are students introduced to the constructed and situated character of disciplinary knowledge?"), all disciplinary knowledge is socially constructed. This elastic notion is repeatedly pressed into service. As reported in *The Courage to Question*, the Lewis and Clark faculty, for example, in describing how student essays were scored, merely said that by the time students were seniors they should have "move[d] ... to a meta-analysis of how knowledge is socially constructed and not simply 'there' to be discovered." Old Dominion was pleased to find that many Women's Studies students had learned that gender is constructed (women do not mother because of maternal instinct), had "realize[d] that sexuality too, is socially constructed," and had in general "switched to socio-cultural as opposed to biological explanations. The troubling exception to this was students' persistence in the belief that violence against women is best explained by the pathological impulsivity and aggressiveness of some males."[33]

We are glad that this team picked up on this common contradiction, but our main worry is that an exaggerated emphasis on social constructionism has contributed significantly to the alienation of Women's Studies students from traditional disciplines. Such an emphasis suggests a rather simple and tempting syllogistic argument:

If all knowledge is socially constructed, and women and blacks were excluded from participation in the construction of the disciplines, then, since any enterprise that excludes women and blacks is sexist and racist, it follows that the knowledge in all books except feminist ones is sexist and racist. Therefore, to use sexist or racist textbooks (except to critique them) is to expose oneself to immoral and misleading tracts. In light of such an argument, is it any surprise that many Women's Studies students consider the only legitimate stance toward most of the courses at the university to be an oppositional one?

CRITICAL THINKING, FEMINIST STYLE

The Courage to Question begins with the acknowledgment that critics accuse Women's Studies of being "a grievance industry" specializing in "oppression studies."[34] A female humanities professor who responded to the survey at Oberlin said: "[It has had a] terrible impact—the program has politicized and ideologized students instead of promoting objectivity in education. . . . I must withdraw my support for this program until it becomes less ideological and more in line with the spirit of true academic excellence at Oberlin."[35]

The advocates' major defense against the charge that they were giving their students "propaganda" and "unintellectual, touchy-freely stuff" and were "silenc[ing] everyone who disagrees" was to claim that Women's Studies teaches its students *critical thinking*.[36]

This phrase appears repeatedly both in students' responses and in the comments of the faculty assessors. Since critical thinking is specifically ruled out by the model of *connected knowing*, one might well wonder exactly what the Women's Studies advocates have in mind when they use this phrase. Perhaps they think that Women's Studies students learn not merely the courage to question, but also the audacity to question everything—because patriarchy is everywhere.

We believe the advocates are right when they contend that this is by and large what their students learn. But we also think that the critics are correct when they object that Women's Studies turns many of the same students into uncritical ideologues. Religious fanatics are adept at thinking and speaking critically about secular society. They are not so inclined to turn their scrutiny on themselves. The skill of Women's Studies students at repudiating all traditional knowledge as socially constructed and their ingenuity in ferreting out the hand of the devil patriarchy in every sin and crime of society are not an exhibition of critical thinking at a very significant level. The fact that students have abandoned received views (and have some good reasons for doing so) is no indication that they have not, at the same time, uncritically locked themselves into another framework, which is at least as deeply flawed. What needs to be investigated is whether students are at all receptive to reasoned arguments against the basic tenets of their own framework or, to the contrary, have learned to deploy various criticism-deflecting strategies in an effort to keep their acquired ideas inviolate. Such an investigation, unfortunately, is nowhere to be found in *The Courage to Question* or *Students at the Center*.

The NWSA report is probably accurate in stating that students who major in Women's Studies are largely getting what they want and what the faculty think is important for them. As long as this is the case, reforms are not likely to come from within. Quite the contrary, one can expect the dominant internal ethos to be further solidified and institutionalized. This is exactly what we find as we turn to the issue of how Women's Studies goes about deciding who and what is to be included in its programs.

"QUALITY CONTROL": BIG SISTER IS WATCHING YOU

Since most courses offered in Women's Studies programs originate in other departments and are only cross-listed with Women's Studies, questions often arise as to which classes should, and which should not, be admitted. In a recent comprehensive essay titled "When Is a Women's Studies Course a 'Women's Studies' Course?: Issues of 'Quality Control' of Cross-listed Courses," Lynne Goodstein of Pennsylvania State University tries to come to grips with the problem of "controlling" the Women's Studies curriculum.[37] Her essay, laudable for its clear and forthright presentation of the issues, warrants close attention here.

Goodstein gives three examples of courses that do *not* count at her university. A course on the biology of sex that devoted equal time to males and females was "declassified" on the grounds that "the bulk of course content" did not focus on women. Her Women's Studies program also rejected a proposed course on the sociology of the family, which, though concentrating on women's experiences, merely gave sociological analyses of women's traditional roles and was not "informed by feminist critiques." Goodstein notes, in this connection, that, to be approved in her program, courses should not merely increase information students possess about women, but should also aim to change students' views of themselves. Merely adding women writers to a literature course is not "feminist," she says. A course must show how gender, race, and class, and not any imputed inferior writing ability, have constrained women's literary production in the past.[38]

In each of these examples one wonders whether the "quality control," for which so much concern is expressed, is not really a euphemism for ideological policing. In fact, the shakiness of the entire effort at quality control is indicated by the shifting vocabulary Goodstein employs to make her argument. Her terms range from "curricular integrity" through "exacting criteria" and "integrity of courses" to a "commitment to feminist theory and pedagogy." The first three of these terms are never defined, merely declared, while the last appears to serve, as Goodstein's careful research has revealed, as the chief touchstone of the effort to set the proper goals for a Women's Studies program. But is there, in reality, general agreement on what these "commitments" are?

The most intriguing part of Goodstein's essay is a description of the seven key points that her program at Penn State designated as essential to Women's Studies courses. A duly appointed Curricular Affairs Committee conducted a survey of all faculty in the program, evaluated the nineteen responses it received, and came up with the following seven themes or goals, which range from the innocuous and tautological to the tenditious and dogmatic. These goals, with some comments of our own, are as follows:

1. *Emphasis on women's status,* arising from the "need to recognize the existence of patriarchal structures in defining values and social roles. It focuses on gender disparities in social power and influence and recognizes that women's status in virtually all contemporary cultures is unsatisfactory and in need of special attention."

2. *Valuing women's perspectives and experience,* affirming "the importance of women's experiences, perspectives, and accomplishments as subjects of study. Emphasis would be placed on the historical role of women in the world, the contributions made by women intellectually, artistically, and politically. To accomplish this goal, the bulk of course content would focus on women."

3. *Praxis:* "This theme reflects an attempt to move beyond analysis into some form of development or change, either personal, social, or political." More than conveying "a passive belief in gender equity," a course incorporating this theme "assumes that women's studies education would encourage students to work toward the realization of these goals." The hint, in this passage, of required political good works is soon undermined by the qualification that "praxis" (contrary to

what the term means) does not necessarily "require that specific projects geared to social action be included in courses. Rather, praxis implies that course participants will be challenged to consider the implications of the material covered for their lives and the lives of others."

4. *Counteracting male bias in scholarship*; that is, rejecting traditional white male Eurocentric values, assumptions, and perspectives in research. This goal "affirms the importance of incorporating the new scholarship on women and feminist critiques of traditional research concerning women and gender into women's studies courses." Here, as elsewhere in the paper, despite the feminist taboo on "linear" and "dichotomous" thinking, a simple opposition is set up between "traditional" male scholarship and the "new scholarship on women." The former is always and necessarily defective, while no indication is given that the latter should ever itself be the object of critique.

5. *Valuing women's self-determination.* Women's studies courses must "empower women students to seek their own paths and define themselves as entities separate and apart from roles that patriarchal societies dictate. [This goal] reflects the corresponding need for courses to encourage reassessment among men students of their perspectives on entitlement to power and privilege." Here again, a gulf exists between, on the one hand, the freedom supposedly offered to female students to select their own paths and, on the other, the pressure to define themselves according to the current feminist line and in opposition to "patriarchal societies" and their decrees. If, for example, a woman were to decide to become a traditional housewife, has she failed to become "empowered"? Has she ceased to "seek her own path"? Will she need additional "feminist pedagogy" to help her recuperate from this expression of disempowerment?

6. *Inclusion of other "isms"* within the concerns of feminism, stressing "the interconnectedness of the operation of sexism

and other 'isms.' [This goal] recognizes that feminism also functions to critique other forms of oppression, including racism, national chauvinism, class and ethnic bias, ageism, heterosexual bias, and other ideologies/institutions that have consciously or unconsciously oppressed and exploited some for the advantage of others. It recognizes the importance of structuring course material which is inclusive across all lines of 'difference.'" A good illustration of what may be called the "totalizing" impulse in feminism, this description also clearly reveals the intellectual arrogance that sometimes seeps into feminism when it represents itself as self-invented, heir to nothing, and stakes its claims so broadly as to encompass all other social and moral concerns.

7. Finally, *feminist pedagogy* "emphasizes the importance of using techniques which recognize and validate students' life experiences as legitimate data. . . . It underscores the need for classes to operate on principles of mutual respect, equalitarianism, a critique of the traditional teacher/student authority relationship, and student empowerment."[39]

None of these seven themes or goals appears to aim at providing students with the intellectual tools that would allow them to make their own analyses. Rather, they all seem designed and intended to enforce what this decade's feminist orthodoxy considers to be appropriate existential models. Goodstein fails to address the dangerous terrain entered by those who take it upon themselves to dictate approaches and course content according to such manifestly ideological criteria.

More alarming still, Goodstein—apparently without meaning to—divulges the inevitable transition to surveillance that must occur if quality control is to be made effective. In order to obtain information for use in the review process, looking at course proposals and syllabi is insufficient. Instead, "treating the instructor rather than the course as the 'unit of analysis' for evaluation is desirable and increases the potential that cross-listed courses will consistently fulfill Women's Studies program goals." But in the end, even this procedure will not suffice, in her view. "[P]robably the most valid means of determining whether a program's goals are met by cross-listed courses" is obtaining information directly from students, since "even personal interviews with instructors are not always adequate, as they yield information about what the instructor says she or he does, not what the instructor actually does." At Penn State, Goodstein reports, the evaluations in use measure "the extent to which students experience a class as embodying feminist pedagogy as well as other aspects of the seven curricular goals."[40]

We have never encountered, in our readings or in our combined four decades of working in the academy, another document like Goodstein's essay. In it, the drive toward "quality control" seems totally unrelated to legitimate concerns about academic standards. Rather, it represents an attempt to define Women's Studies in ideological terms, which is why doctrinaire criteria are considered indispensable. Instead of delimiting the field of study in terms of subject matter, the emphasis unfailingly falls on a *core cluster of perspectives*, which, in the description of them, often reduce to attitudes. This emphasis cannot be defended as promoting "critical awareness" or "analytical abilities" in students, since that awareness and those abilities are being encouraged in one direction only. Nothing is said about promoting a critical examination of feminist discourse itself. In fact, the preferred methods of feminist pedagogy seem expressly designed to make such a critique impossible.

In her conclusions, Goodstein acknowledges that the "healthy and empowering" process of articulating goals can also be frustrating and possibly demoralizing, as it may "bring to light underlying differences among women's studies faculty and between program faculty and others within academic institutions." This admission seems to presuppose that, ideally, Women's Studies faculty should all hold identical views. Her subsequent remark that "unfortunately, there will be no quick solutions to the problem of 'quality control' of cross-listed courses" reveals the blinders that insulate the entire discussion of control over Women's Studies courses.[41] What other field of study would conceivably create this problem for itself? No doubt many people in Women's Studies see nothing awry in Goodstein's description of "quality control," as is confirmed by extensive communications on the Women's Studies E-mail list expressing the same anxiety about how cross-listed courses can be "controlled." But this general agreement, in our view, is a large part of the problem.

. Finally, an important piece is missing from Goodstein's discussion. If surveillance is so indispensable for cross-listed courses, why is it not also necessary for core courses taught by the regular Women's Studies faculty? Surely one cannot assume that all of these individuals, merely because they have appointments or adjunct status in Women's Studies, are in conformity with the feminist perspectives and pedagogical demands set forth in Goodstein's work—unless, of course, such conformity was a condition of employment in Women's Studies in the first place. And what if faculty members in Women's Studies backslide? Shall they, too, then be subject to "quality control"? And shall student spies be commissioned to report back to some central committee on their professors' ideological heresies and pedagogical deviations?

Will Women's Studies, coming full circle, settle comfortably into the practice of bias and ostracism that it originally attacked in androcentric education? If we have moved no farther than "Our picture of the world may be a bit distorted, but it's better than their distortion!" how far have we progressed?

8

Cults, Communes, and Clicks

A CADEMIA, long a sheltered site for radical research and adventurous speculation, has been extremely receptive to the products and producers of feminist theorizing. And this habit of accommodating novelty is appropriate for academics, for it is surely one function of the ivory tower to be an experimental workshop where new ideas are forged, tested, and judged against the old.

There are, however, circumstances in which the spirit of open inquiry essential to the academy is threatened by a worldview. Such a threat materializes when a set of ideas loses its heuristic or experimental character and turns into a dogma that suppresses criticism of itself and blocks alternative paths to discovery. The variants of feminism brought together in Women's Studies programs fit this description of a closed worldview. They are not merely about equal rights for women or the empirical and theoretical study of gender roles and their pervasive effects in society. Feminism aspires to be much more than this. It bids to be a totalizing scheme resting on a grand theory, one that is as all-inclusive as Marxism, as assured of its ability to unmask hidden meanings as Freudian psychology, and as fervent in its condemnation of apostates as evangelical fundamentalism. Feminist theory provides a doctrine of original sin: The world's evils originate in male supremacy. It regards the male's (usually: the white male's) insistence on maintaining his own power as the passkey that unlocks the mysteries of individual actions and institutional behavior. And it offers a prescription for radical change that is as simple as it is drastic: Reject whatever is tainted with patriarchy and replace it with something embodying gynecentric values.

The information we have brought together in this book suggests to us that the feminist persuasions prevailing in U.S. colleges and universities today often lead to consequences deeply subversive of the best academic traditions. Intolerance, anti-intellectualism, and ideological policing produce work that is shaped—we would say, distorted—by an ideological agenda. This may be acceptable in an institution whose denominational affiliations and instructional mission are a matter of record. But it hardly seems appropriate to require teachers in a state university or a private liberal arts college to profess adherence to feminism or to monitor the sex, race, or ethnicity of the authors on their syllabi. Nonetheless, as our investigations have shown, these practices are proudly "owned" by many feminist faculty.

As it pursues such actions, Women's Studies apparently disregards all historical evidence warning of what happens when ideas and those who express them are placed under ideological restrictions. We are concerned that the attempts to set up feminist alternatives to traditional disciplines, each with its own support networks, conferences, and journals, are all too reminiscent of the efforts of "creation scientists" to represent themselves as the intellectual and professional equals of mainstream researchers. In both instances the methods of established science and rigorous intellectual inquiry are dismissed as biased, and radical departures from these methods are proposed to replace them. Creationists say that radioisotope dating must be thrown out because it is sheer atheism to assume that the laws of nature, including those governing radioactive decay, are time invariant. Could God not change the half-life of carbon-14 if he so desired? Many feminists, for their part, find the values of objectivity, parsimony, and consistency shot through with patriarchal bias, and they argue—with breathtaking simplicity of mind—that these intellectual virtues were designed, and are being used, to enforce the entrenched power of the white male European elite.

The harmful pedagogical effects of such positions are obvious. Far too many Women's Studies classes now provide their students with what might be called "negative education." Instead of "learning to learn" (to use a slogan once popular in schools of education), these students are being taught to scorn both the content and methods of the liberal arts and sciences. But the classroom is not the right place for obeisances and anathemas. And it is intolerable that Women's Studies students can come away from their courses with the unshakable conviction that all women are victims, and that victims are, by virtue of their persecuted status, a morally superior breed. It is a fact, however, that Women's Studies classes instruct women in the use of coping strategies to deal with the "oppression" they are being taught to recognize; many feminist teachers pride themselves on this. It should come as no surprise, then, that some students insist on special dispensations to compensate them for past injustices, and claim that if a demand, such as the requirement to become competent in mathematics, is too exacting or a job too taxing, it is because women's different ways of "knowing" and performing are slighted by the entrenched patriarchy (as discussed in chapter 7).

But a feminist education along these lines is sure to impede women's ability to function in the world at large. As a preparation for life, it is counterproductive in the strictest sense of that term. A faculty colleague concerned about the likelihood of this outcome told us about a conversation she had with a graduating senior:

> The student told me she had a good job with a big company in a nearby city—actually it was just what she wanted—better than she had expected. But when I congratulated her, she looked worried.
>
> "Well, there's just one problem," she said. "You know, sexism, job discrimination, all that patriarchal stuff."
>
> I asked her if anything weird had happened at the interview.
>
> She said no, but maybe that was because they saw on her resumé that she had a certificate in Women's Studies and were on good behavior.

I tried to reassure her: "You say they interviewed lots of people for the job? It sounds to me like you were the person they wanted and that they'll make some effort to keep you. I don't think you should expect trouble."

"But it's still a patriarchal world out there," the student said earnestly. "And I'm just afraid that there will be sexist stuff on the job—maybe even stuff that I won't even recognize as being sexist."

I mumbled more words of reassurance, but the image which came to mind was that of certain holy men in India—I think they're called Jains—who walk around with gauze over their mouths to prevent them from accidentally inhaling a gnat and killing it.

We fear that all too often the "empowerment" promised by Women's Studies in fact has undermined students' ability to function effectively and has diminished their life options. Hypersensitizing young women to the obstacles they face may have gained feminism some docile converts, but the initiates have had to pay a steep price.

As a way of trying to map out the main features of the terrain cultivated by Women's Studies, three models seem to us especially useful. One derives from the history of religion; the second, from the experience of communes and utopian social experiments. What these two have in common—with one another and with feminism—can, in turn, be illustrated by a third model, one that has been developed by social psychologists.

TRUE BELIEVERS ALL

Religious movements provide an instructive comparative case to help us make sense of the more disturbing traits of academic feminism. Our frame of reference for drawing analogies and suggesting caveats is the history of Western churches with their tendency to spawn dissenting splinter groups. New movements, whether religious or social, always undergo an initial period of struggle when the intellectual and psychological resources of their members are absorbed by the effort to gain recognition, and when energies are directed mostly against enemies outside the ranks. Ideological positions are kept simple at this stage; there is little discussion of the fine points of belief. Internal cohesion is not difficult to maintain because all who belong accept the movement's survival as a paramount goal. The movement's spokespersons tend to make far-reaching claims for the rights and liberties needed to gain legitimacy, chief among them the freedoms to be self-determining in matters of conscience, to propagate ideas, to voice criticism, and to speak and act on the basis of conviction.

During the period of consolidation that follows, mundane tasks begin to predominate: the need to organize, define the faith, and clarify ambiguities as beliefs are being formalized into a creed. Theological elaboration results from the movement's drive, as it becomes established, to enumerate the articles its followers must accept if they are to remain members in good standing. Hence an orthodoxy arises, as well as a hierarchy of persons entitled to declare and guard it. This development, in turn, leads to attempts to obtain conformity and enforce discipline and—inevitably—to inhibition of deviant beliefs. Tolerance is now seen as worse than weakness; it is a betrayal of the faith. To the true believer, there cannot be more than one valid truth or more than a single way to reach it.

In the later phases of a movement, therefore, declarations of faith tend to be much less inclusive than they had been during the movement's earlier years. Those who cannot agree to them quit, or they are expelled or at least silenced. Means of identifying and separating deviants are implemented so that discipline may be enforced. Deviance itself is demarcated by defining heterodoxy as well as orthodoxy. Proselytizing usually wanes at this stage, as energies are absorbed in the effort to unify and purify the movement internally and as intellectual homogeneity comes to matter more than diversity of ideas and the free discussion of them.

Unless a movement finds some way of accommodating the diversity of views that will always surface in a group not under siege, it survives—if it survives at all—as a sect. A sect sees itself as voluntarily and necessarily separated from the larger society, which it regards as beyond redemption by conversion or other means. Its members are encouraged to view themselves as a righteous remnant. Its saving message, which is utterly exclusive, suppresses debate and criticism. As a result, there is little intellectual development. Ideas tend to atrophy into fundamentalism, showing the mistrust and paranoia that usually accompany a narrow religiosity. Mandated beliefs and coercive institutions are used to erect protective ramparts around the group in order to keep enemies out and followers in. Intolerance is flaunted: one must believe all or one believes nothing. Sects are interesting historical phenomena, and often very moving ones, but because of their intransigence and isolation they have rarely had any major impact on world events.

Such a development is not inevitable. The history of Western religion offers a few notable exceptions to it, such as the Quakers and the Unitarians, whose trajectory from oppositional faction to established denomination evaded the extremes of political orthodoxy and sectarian isolation. But the process described here has been a common one in both the Catholic and Protestant traditions, and its cautionary importance for movements borne by ideological zeal is, we believe, considerable.[1]

It will seem a familiar pattern to many who have been involved with Women's Studies. Similarities are readily apparent. As talk of women's oppression, exclusion, and silencing at the hands of the patriarchy gained prominence in the late 1960s, sufficient cohesion developed for Women's Studies to get under way in the early 1970s— if not yet as a widespread movement, then as a tenacious force and an insistent voice for reform in the academy. Shared beliefs were abundantly supplied by the developing discourse on feminism, in which the imperative to action, when not asserted outright, was always implicit. As the movement gained strength, the emerging agenda, kept simple at first (for example, "integrating women into the curriculum"), expanded in response to the hardening of ideological lines. The sense of mission that legitimized a growing obduracy of thought and speech was noted by most of the women we interviewed, although for some this sense was a nostalgic memory, while for others it acted as an incentive for them to dissent.

Feminism was not slow to develop its corps of theoreticians. But in the accommodating world of Women's Studies, "theory"— recently transmogrified into the more active-sounding "theorizing"—did not always demand a high level of analysis or substantive learning. In many programs, it meant little more than a tethering of precepts to simplistic ideological presuppositions. Instead of expanding intellectual horizons, this, in turn, led to intolerance, the presence and corrosive effect of which were mentioned by nearly everyone we spoke to. Attempts were made to expose and label heterodoxy. Deviant opinion was dismissed as "liberal" or "radical," depending on who was dismissing whom; "false" feminists were distinguished from "true" ones; slanderous comments about one another by faculty members were replicated in students' mean-spirited bad-mouthing and their censorious behavior in the classroom. One professor described her own growing awareness of this process:

> I don't recall now how long it was before I realized that the intolerance and smugness of many of my students was a mirror image of feelings I had experienced privately and had heard my colleagues express publicly. I recalled the sense of self-satisfaction and complacency I felt when another woman— especially one who described herself as a feminist—revealed, through some word or gesture, the "limits" of her feminist understanding compared to my own. In retrospect, it seemed to me that this smugness had, in fact, been an important component of my own identity as a "feminist."

Thus my students taught me, painfully but unmistakably, about another aspect of feminist identity. The lesson should have been obvious from the beginning, given feminism's often illuminating deconstruction of oppositional terms. What I learned was that our own identities as "feminists," too, depend in a deep sense upon the creation and maintenance of a polarization with something that was not-us. And because so many women (in the university and outside of it) were not feminists, or not the right kind of feminist, the opportunities for indulging this private sense of superiority occurred virtually on a daily basis.

Like religious groups as they splinter, feminism also developed competing creeds, each rigidly embraced by its adherents, each dismissive of the others, each undebatable. Not surprisingly, excommunication, in the form of shunning and scapegoating, became common. The effort to propagate ideas broadly—once a major part of the agenda—tended to contract as the curriculum was pitched more and more narrowly to a self-selected audience of students who seek out the program on their own and form a preidentified group of potential converts.

The insularity of such procedures, along with a certain proclivity in the women's movement to separatism, gives Women's Studies programs a strong resemblance to religious sects. But the historical experience of sectarian groups ought to serve as a warning example, as should their tendency to slip into the kind of intellectual fundamentalism in which a handful of unexamined and unquestioned truths is believed to answer every question, solve every problem, and fend off unwelcome criticism from the malevolent forces outside. This may sound excessively alarmist. Women's Studies programs do not, at the moment, have the means to transform their ideas into forced behavior patterns. But we should not therefore be lulled into complacency about the kind of world that would result if the power to impose and control were ever to be given to them.

PROBLEMS IN THE PROMISED LAND

To supplement the religious analogy, we offer another model, again with strikingly suggestive parallels for feminists. This is the model of communes and intentional communities that seclude themselves from the larger world and attempt in their daily lives to act out alternative values.

Women's Studies has always argued that it has fashioned—or at least embraces—a communal ethos. If we take this claim seriously enough to ask how Women's Studies is actually doing as a community, we notice some interesting similarities between the academic programs we have examined and communal groups as studied by historians and sociologists, or as imagined by writers of utopian or dystopian novels. Like most of the communes examined by Rosabeth Moss Kanter, for example, Women's Studies seems to have purchased what little group harmony it has been able to achieve at the cost of setting limits on personal choice and creative debate.[2]

We have also been struck by the prevailing adoption of negative instruments employed by historical communes in their effort to achieve cohesion, among them renunciation of links to the outside world and to one's former life in it,[3] and "mortification" practices such as mutual criticism, surveillance, denunciation of deviants, confession, and so on. These are practices that serve to strip away much of a person's previous identity. They transmit the message, as Kanter says, "that the self is adequate, whole, and fulfilled only when it lives up to the model offered by the community."[4] Here the communal model and the religious cult model clearly meet.

Women's Studies programs not only show some of the isolationist tendencies of experimental communes; they also too often exhibit an anti-intellectualism and, more specifically, an antiscience animus. This is a theme that can also be traced in the history of communes in America and was already evident to scholars long before the present proliferation of emotionally based self-improvement groups brought it to general attention. Such moves are clear reactions against the world "outside," which is viewed, as in the case of religious sectarianism, as antipodal and inimical.

Communes frequently manifest a preference for an activist over a contemplative, or intellectualizing, ethos. As Kanter writes: "The intellectual who sees several sides to every issue may also be out of place in a utopian community."[5] By contrast, the embrace of labor and an "active" life is a common theme in both real and fictive alternative communities. Knowledge is often represented as dangerous to the life of the experiment, and even of the species, as reflected also in the many imaginative post–nuclear holocaust dystopias in which science has proved itself to be the work of the devil and must therefore be stifled. Such scenarios' dislike of the past leads to a suppression of information about it. In Women's Studies, this has sometimes meant that—as we have seen—both specialized expertise and general knowledge are made suspect and are tagged as the products of men, who are blamed for the corruption or suppression of the female wisdom that would have made the world a better place. Antagonism to theory, unless it can simplistically be reduced to practice in accord with the feminist tenets of the moment, is a further aspect of this tendency.

Along with activism, the communal persuasion also favors a drastic leveling of social and personal distinctions—vigorously promoted in actual communes and utopian novels, and often parodied in antiutopian fiction. What is interesting about this for our purposes is that the concept of leveling exists in incipient form in the rhetoric of feminism, and that this sets Women's Studies constantly at odds with the meritocratic principle inescapable in a university—even in the United States, where (unlike the rest of the world) a very large percentage of high school graduates at least enter college. In the academic setting, therefore, the equalizing impulse is fulfilled more by lip service than by structural alterations. As one woman we interviewed noted, the "teaching collective"—comprising faculty, staff, and undergraduate students—in the Women's Studies program of which she was a staff member could not seriously expect faculty to participate in it if salary sharing were implemented. It hardly needs to be said that material and other inequalities persist; that is the reality. In opposition to it, students within Women's Studies programs, caught up in academic feminism's spurious political rhetoric with its promise of leveling, write papers such as one we have read that takes feminism in the academy to task for failing to repudiate academic emphases on effective writing and reading. Such values, the student argued, not only leave dyslexic and other individuals who have communication difficulties at a distinct disadvantage, but also lower their self-esteem.

ARRESTED DEVELOPMENT

A third model, found in the research of black social psychologists working on social identity theory, seems to be especially useful in drawing the lesson of the two analogies presented so far, because it offers a paradigm that has direct relevance to feminism, and also suggests ways in which feminism needs to grow up.

According to this model, as outlined by Audrey Murrell of the University of Pittsburgh, the move from a negative to a positive group identity involves five distinct stages:[6]

1. *preconsciousness*, characterized by denial and feelings of marginalization and alienation because of the stigmatized identity;
2. *emergence/awakening*, in which a critical consciousness dawns;
3. *confrontation/internalization*, the strident militant stage, belligerent and separatist; and
4. *integration*, in which a more holistic view begins to emerge, leading to:
5. *double consciousness*, with separatism now devalued as dual identities become internalized, finally culminating in an identity of a broader sort.

If feminism is viewed in terms of these stages, it becomes obvious that the familiar "click" phenomenon, in which women, having come out of stage one, find their dawning critical consciousness constantly reaffirmed by the sexist world they see around them, is a characteristic manifestation of stage two. Recurring "clicks," in turn, are preconditions of the belligerent stage-three attitude, where rigid distinctions between "us" and "them"—the characteristic dualism of religious and communal movements—are carefully nurtured.

We believe that Women's Studies programs, if they are not strongly focused on educational goals, transform themselves—and not very subtly—into sites of indoctrination to stage-three attitudes. A recent study of the effectiveness of Women's Studies courses in promoting "feminist identity development," using a similar model of stages of development, confirms that these courses are indeed successful in leading students into—but not beyond—stage three.[7] What is chilling to realize, however, is that the authors of this study never question whether such transformation is an appropriate goal of education, or address how it might be said to differ from other forms of indoctrination aimed not merely at the intellect but at the whole person: the creation of a New Man or New Woman. It simply takes for granted that the development of a "feminist identity" is an unproblematic and desirable objective for an academic program to pursue.

Nothing we have seen in our investigations of Women's Studies suggests that the higher stages of identity development, involving synthesis and integration, are anywhere on the horizon. Perhaps young people will simply have to work out a broader, more integrated identity on their own, once they leave the university. This appears to be the only hope. Meanwhile, their training may well have helped them arrive at stage three—but only to remain stuck there.

Nor is this a mere accident. There seems to be a general awareness in feminist circles of the utility of stage three for Women's Studies classrooms. Moreover, when the stages-of-development model is applied to faculty members themselves, we can see that something else, strongly suggestive of manipulation, is going on as stage-three commitments are pursued. Whether Women's Studies professors are genuinely situated at this stage or simply act as if they were—perhaps more effectively to awaken students to women's oppression, or for the satisfaction of enacting their own *echt* feminist personae—is a question we cannot answer.

But stage-three commitments (among both faculty and students) seem predictably to turn the us-versus-them division inward, as if the "them" at the gates are not enough of a threat (perhaps because they are too remote, or perhaps because they are simply too strong) to promote group loyalty and cohesion at the fever pitch at which the greatest emotional intensity can be sustained. As the us-versus-them opposition is replicated within the original grouping, policing actions get under way. This is a form of behavior that, in addition to allowing some people to be censorious and aggressive toward others, reflects a presumption of rights and wrongs: We are right. You are wrong.

Many feminists have trouble swallowing this. As a political science professor from Texas (who has a bumper sticker on her pickup truck saying FEMINIST REDNECK) wrote to us: "At 50 years of age, I have not thrown off the yoke of one master to have it replaced by another, even if its name is feminism." But in such a judgmental climate, appearances of proper group identity must be maintained, hence the endless discussions and criticisms of how particular women dress, look, and behave. Petty surveillance becomes a mechanism for maintaining group solidarity, because it separates authentic members from questionable ones. But it has a costly consequence: Over time, it drives away those who are negatively categorized, and this reduces the group's numbers and alienates potential supporters.

On a more abstract level, censorious vigilantism forecloses discussion of diverging group goals, leads to ever-greater rigidity and uniformity, and saps the group's vitality—a high price to pay for "harmony." At the same time, an excessive concern with the trappings of group identity prompts members to examine not only others but themselves as well. Here, too, the analogy to religious group behavior holds, for punctilious inspection of every aspect of one's inner and outer life has been an obligation placed by the more rigorous movements on their adherents. Calvinists' self-examination and the Jesuits' insistence on the constant exploration of the state of one's soul come to mind as examples. The aim, in each case, was an attentiveness to the self that allowed not the least detail to escape scrutiny.

One feminist scholar, who is now in a Women's Studies program that she strongly supports, recalled precisely such an atmosphere in her consciousness-raising group in the 1970s, as members acted out their stage-three personalities:

Looking back now, I think, psychologically, the vehemence came out of a sense of fragility—in other words: If we don't all agree on this, then something will crumble and I'll slip back into the alienated person that I just escaped from being. So somehow, unless I get validation from everybody else and a mirroring of my choices, I'm in danger of slipping back into patriarchal violence. I'm just guessing that the anger, that you have to do X, you have to see it this way, comes out of feeling, Well, I've only just gotten here, look at the wicked past I've just escaped from, when I was totally socialized into thinking that makeup was fine.

And I remember the kinds of debates we had in my C-R group. There was one woman who wore makeup, and we were down on her like a ton of bricks! We said it was a betrayal of feminism and so forth. At one point she literally said to us, "If you're going to say that I can't put eye makeup on when I come to this group, you're not going to see me." And in fact shortly thereafter she was gone. We didn't ease up.

I look back at that now and I'm horrified at myself. I always associate that with a form of competitiveness, a kind of pressure to be the most pure and the most ideologically untainted, and, now, I just don't see how you can build a movement like that.

Women's Studies programs, in their bunker mentality and tendency to cut themselves off from the rest of the university in the name of feminist commitment, do function in some respects like cults and communes. In saying this, we are by no means deploring the existence of deeply held shared beliefs, or of groups based on them. Communes, in particular, are fascinating social experiments with considerable relevance to feminism. Our point is simply this: It is not, and it should not be, the mission of a university to lock students into one stage of emotional and intellectual development, or to inculcate attitudes of hostility and condescension to all prefeminist knowledge and nonfeminist individuals. To the extent that Women's Studies programs intentionally cultivate such a mentality (and many certainly do), they have no place in the university. Their ostensible reason for promoting such a posture has everything to do with political aims and with the efforts to indoctrinate in accordance with these aims, and very little to do with the goals of a liberal education.

"FOR FEAR OF FINDING SOMETHING WORSE"

Hillaire Belloc once wrote a cautionary tale about a child who ran away from a strict British nanny, only to be eaten by a lion. The poem ends with these words: "And always keep a-hold of Nurse / For fear of finding something worse." We have not investigated the ethos of other kinds of "oppression studies" or "activist" programs in detail, but there are many indications that these are burdened by problems very similar to those of Women's Studies. Conflating Women's Studies with such programs would, we suspect, only make things worse. Ideals turning into frustration, enthusiasm and dedication lapsing into despair, doctrinaire attitudes driving out the spirit of inquiry—it is, alas, a common story.

We were particularly moved by an interview with a woman who began her career as an enthusiastic supporter of a Marxist approach to education but is now surprised to find herself espousing some traditional liberal values. We offer her story as a kind of parable.

Angela is a literature professor who has for years been involved in the Feminist Studies program of a small, private liberal arts college. She was hired nearly fifteen years ago for a position that specified "a Marxist and a feminist." Because of the college's self-conscious stance as a progressive and experimental school, she has encountered many of the problems that also characterize Women's Studies programs, but in a more complex and supposedly more hospitable institutional framework. Her comments have direct bearing on both the possibilities and limitations of a political model of education.

Angela turned down two other offers at more prestigious universities to accept this position, mainly because she wanted to join an "extremely politicized faculty," and the college seemed to offer the possibility of a fully integrated life: "I took the job to sort of 'be' what I was teaching. But now I very much would challenge the idea that you have to be what you teach, or even that I could really fully understand what that might mean." She also imagined that the college would provide a more relaxed atmosphere than that of a research university. This turned out to be wrong. Her teaching load was very demanding because, in addition to conducting classes, professors were expected to work intensively with individual students. She did not find much support for her interest in scholarship:

> There's a kind of surveillance that women do in relation to each other. When some of my work was published and I began giving papers, I very often wouldn't say anything about it at all. It was a kind of underground activity for me. . . . The challenge was to work as hard as the others did, trying to make myself indispensable in that same way, and then to get something going on the outside too. But I did put the teaching first.

The antischolarly bias of the school took the usual form: suspicions and insinuations of "careerism."

> It would have been extremely hard to have just come in with scholarly concerns, because there was a kind of rhetoric about people who are just looking out for themselves or their careers. There's still a lot of that rhetoric of "using" the school to launch a career. I've heard that expression, not applied to me but applied to others. I hope that's changing.

Her women colleagues, even early in their careers, seemed to compete over who was the most tired and stressed out. Less often did they discuss ideas, and her hopes for a lively intellectual exchange at the school were not fulfilled. As for the Feminist Studies program, it showed the usual conflation of functions:

The program was loosely organized, a few years after I came, to do various things. One thing was to be a kind of caucus and to organize around issues like salaries and working conditions, partly because we thought we all actually knew something about overwork. Then there was a loose curricular component, and we also have a women's center which is run separately by a staff person. Anyway, the program has been in crisis for about five years now. It doesn't function so much as an academic program, any more, but as a kind of gathering place.

The naming of the program was itself a deliberate act of proclaiming its politics:

It was called "Feminist Studies" because we perceived that "Women's Studies" sounded like a kind of content rather than an ideology. In other words, there is such a thing as women, and Women's Studies is the study of that thing. And we wanted to distinguish ourselves as a very politically motivated, ideologically motivated group. Ha! I'm laughing because of all the problems that I, at least, didn't foresee in terms of what a political academic culture would be like or could be like.

She offers the following example of how a thoroughly politicized academic culture operates:

At the point at which I started asking myself questions, the issue was no longer senior male colleagues who were teaching courses on autobiography and not putting a single woman on their reading list. Instead, I was seeing myself as a senior colleague looking at a young man who had put two or three women in his syllabus, and the question was: Should he have put in only white women? Did he have a woman of color in his syllabus? Did he have a this, a that? Were all possible, or many possible, sexualities represented?—and so on.

When I found myself in the position of scrutinizing somebody who, in fact, was not my superior, I felt very, very uneasy.
And then, when it became possible to vote against reappoint-
ing somebody on those grounds, I became very unhappy.

Initially, Angela had been enthusiastic about coming to the college as an "ideologically marked person, whose cards were on the
table politically," and excited "about the possibilities of hiring like-
minded people." Her experiences modified her fervor: "But I now
think there are incredible problems with that, that it's gone crazy,
this hiring of people who are only going to be judged on grounds
that are political, ideological." Some people left the college voluntarily because of the pressure they experienced to "be" a particular
kind of person:

There was another case, a woman who left. With her, it wasn't
identity politics in the normal sense, since, as a black woman,
she was formally the right identity. So it was something else.
She said there should be no greater pressure on minorities to
get along with each other than there would be for, say, the
white faculty, white male faculty, or women, or whatever the
category would be, to get along with each other. She used to
wear a T-shirt that said "I am not your Third World expectation," so she was not the most popular person in certain circles
either. There were two negative letters about her in her file. I
remember one of them said, "I have had no experience with
this person, which is odd because I'm a whatever [group mem-
ber]." So this was taken as evidence of her not getting along
with her "community."

Sure, some of this stuff goes on elsewhere, too, and maybe if
I were in a different sort of institution, I would recover my earlier fierceness in terms of an ideological push. But I can only
say now that I've seen something I don't want to be a part of.
It's very troubling.

Would she still consider identity or political commitments to be appropriate criteria for selecting candidates?

> I am not uncomfortable with affirmative action goals in choosing among candidates, as long as these goals are the ones outlined in the affirmative action guidelines of the institution. But I now think that a person's work has got to be judged on its own merits. If someone is a liberal historian, for example, they should be judged in terms of how well they do that kind of history. If you're hiring somebody to teach the history of the novel and they do that very well, and students are generally satisfied, but maybe it's not the kind of literary history I'd prefer, with social history included, or—say—this person is not interested at all in sociology, just very well trained in a kind of formalism, I think that's fine.

Angela has thought carefully about the troubling ways in which identity politics were being played out at her school: "This 'speaking as a . . . ' routine is very familiar. I certainly see knowledge as belonging in a place and specificity. But I also need to see the difference between that and a kind of central casting notion of what intellectual life is." Far from waning or vanishing, however, the "central casting notion" of intellectual life has spread, though Angela cannot be sure whether faculty or students were its original promoters:

> I teach critical theory, and I think there's an ongoing and sometimes very interesting pedagogical problem of responding to demands for a multicultural, multisexual, multiwhatever classroom. In other words, I think the point is well taken that the inclusion of only white women writers in a course is simply not enough, and I never did think it was enough. I especially think that some of the pressure around race and gender and sexuality has been terrific. It brings a very interesting tension to bear. On the other hand, I think that teaching as I do—I team teach

with the philosophers sometimes, and sometimes I teach alone and I do critical theory texts—there is a real problem now in getting students to read texts for the ideas and not simply for the imaginary identity of the author.

I taught a course on postmodernism, and we read a book that emphasized class, written by an economist. And one of the students, a white woman, said, "Why should we care about some white guy in the Midwest who's out of work?" I always feel somewhat disappointed when there isn't more cross-identification in the classroom. I find I spend quite a bit of time trying to displace notions of identity rather than shore them up.

But this narrow-minded categorizing is also found among the faculty:

Let me give you an example. It was a faculty seminar we had, and we read something by a man who happens to be Indian, and there was a scathing critique of this piece done by a colleague who mistook the name and thought it was written by a white Irish guy! It was ridiculous—the author wasn't Irish. But somebody had imagined that he was Irish and white, and had written an essay on multiculturalism and a critique of pluralism. It was very funny, actually, a nice moment for some of us in the seminar.

Identity politics, in Angela's view, has come to replace critical exploration of ideas:

What I just can't stand is a kind of crude bottom line, when people make peremptory challenges and say, "What about such-and-such a group?" Now I think there is a mimicry between our students who do that and a certain style that has developed in the academy. It's got to do with this kind of peremptory challenge, "Well, what about X?"—as if saying it is enough. It isn't seriously about what could be called dialogue.

I'll give you an example. We were reading a work of fiction, and one of the students—a white woman—said, "Well, look, a white woman and a black woman are never going to be equal." And so my colleague with whom I was teaching the course, who's a philosopher, said, "What white woman, or what black woman?" And the student said, with real anger, "Well, a white woman is privileged in this society." Then she repeated that white women always felt superior to black women. I said, "Are you kidding? You mean you can't imagine being in a room with a black woman who was more talented, more beautiful, more elegant, articulate, and whatever, and would make you feel less that way?" And there was complete silence. Then two Indian students who were there started laughing hysterically, and they said, "Yes, we're just so tired of hearing this in the United States. We feel very superior to all of you."

But I think there was a kind of self-satisfaction in the white student's statement, and I asked myself: What is the satisfaction she is feeling? And I'm not sure, except that it is simple, it gives a kind of righteousness to the person who says it.

However, at the same time that rigid lines were being drawn in relation to identity, other boundaries were erased that Angela believed should have been left intact:

I never thought I would hear myself say these things. One sort of boundary has to do with authority—the authority of the various fields. Women's Studies has been a place where a lot of disciplinary boundaries have broken down, and I think in general that's been to the good because of what's happened to people's work and also in terms of the way that's going to impact throughout all the fields. On the other hand, if there is no—or, as at this school, only very little—possibility of making an argument based on knowing something, on having some authority, or even credentials, in a profession—if in fact all of those kinds of authority are broken down—I think there is a real danger. How can you make a case for a program if you recognize no other value than feeling comfortable around somebody?

I'll give you an example. Two years ago I went to a showing of a video that was made about MTV. It points up the sexism that exists on MTV. And the women's center coordinator was there. To my amazement, she stood up and said, "If any of you would like to see this video just with women, you can go to room 101." I was amazed by that. Then, after the video was shown, she said, "If anyone feels uncomfortable, we have co-counselors standing by." I had thought we were going to have an interesting political discussion of that video. "We have co-counselors waiting!" So the whole thing was treated as personal, the discomfort was seen as symptomatic of maybe an individual problem, abuse perhaps, or something in their past, and not a political and intellectual issue about the politics of representation and the industry of popular music, which is what I thought we were going to be talking about. And in fact, many, many people joined this group of women alone, or went to talk to the counselors. And I thought, If this is feminism, it's not what I'm interested in.

Angela tries to walk a fine line between viewing politics as entirely separate from education and yet wanting to preserve some sort of independent space for intellectual work:

I think that what's happened is that there has been such a proliferation of political criticism, political work, that I sometimes feel there just isn't any space to sit back and really reflect, to just be out of the fray, in the sense of *not* having to think about what this might sound like or who I am if I say this, but just to have a little room, in fact, to make some mistakes, some political gaffes if they are that, or to go in a different direction. I think that intellectual work can seem like so many identified points on the map,

so that everything is mapped out too much. There's a kind
of surveillance and a kind of mapping that has gone on.

Angela is clear about who is doing the surveillance:

We are, of ourselves. It's a kind of internalization, finally. I'm not
sure why this hasn't been widely discussed: What's the difference
between lively debate and the kind of devastating character as-
sassination and posturing that I can't stand anymore? I'm so tired
of it. It seems so predictable, it's more like a setup than a real debate. This goes on in scholarly circles, but also in the classroom,
I think. I can imagine if I were teaching a course that had all the
women and men who were interested in women's studies or gender studies, it would be really horrible and impossible and difficult, because of the attitude they would bring.

Still, she has hopes that a different climate will develop:

Maybe now there'll be time out or space or something that I
think a lot of us yearn for right now. Whether that means an
exile or estrangement or whatever, I don't know. But for a lot
of us, I think, there's a certain kind of fatigue.

I can't imagine going back in any institutional way to a kind
of pre-political state—if that ever existed anyway. I cannot
imagine saying, "well, there is some kind of neutral, unpoliti-
cal, or apolitical default you can go back to." But I *can* imagine
in my classes, and I think I do it more and more, trying to
make room for ambiguity, for confusion, for more patient
working-out of issues and not jumping to the bottom line. I see
that as a part of my work, now, as part of my intellectual work,
which I wouldn't have thought of before.

The moral we draw from Angela's story is this: It is not a narrow
emphasis on women that bedevils Women's Studies. The problem is
the whole tangled web of a politicized academy, paradoxically

imbued with solipsistic feel-good practices, which we have tried to unravel in this book. One would find it hard to imagine an environment less likely to lead to an energetic and open-minded pursuit of knowledge.

Conflation of educational and political aims has characterized Women's Studies from the beginning. For many feminists in the academy, this conflation has served as an important source of pride Rarely has it been identified as a problem—certainly not by feminist scholars. Even responsible feminist writers have felt obliged to celebrate the "specialness" of the close link between "scholarly feminism and the activist movement."[8]

The rhetoric of feminism obviously has worked as intended: It has muddied the waters of already difficult concepts such as "excellence in scholarship." Feminist scholars who do not agree with the antischolarly and generally doctrinaire proclivities of their programs, and who do not wish to be constantly embroiled in internal conflicts, tend to walk away—as painful a step as this often is for them to take. And it *is* painful, since it means abandoning students to more militant colleagues, as well as letting go of much that was formerly believed, hoped, and worked for. This book has given instances of their departures. To the remaining true believers, of course, such departures merely serve to confirm that the exiles had never been "real" feminists in the first place.

9

From Dogma to Dialogue:
The Importance of Liberal Values

THE CENTRAL AIMS of feminism (or the women's liberation movement, as it used to be called) were and are exemplary: to end discrimination against women, to protect women from sexual assault and economic exploitation, to transform traditional attitudes about gender roles, to help women gain the confidence and skills they need to pursue their life projects, to make our society truly one of equal opportunity, and to discover what sort of society men and women, working together as equals, might construct. These are noble and urgent goals.

It was also appropriate for feminists in the academy to explore how they might bring their research and teaching to bear on the pressing issues raised by second-wave feminism. And much of the ensuing research on all aspects of women's lives and the effects of gender has been of major significance. But, as we have described in this book, Women's Studies was, from the outset, drawn into an aggressive stance of professing and proselytizing for the feminist movement. The result, as our cautionary tales vividly reveal, has been not only a subversion of scholarship but also a rancorous classroom environment which, far from preparing women students to lead effective lives, disempowers them by depriving them of a liberal education.

We have argued that these highly problematic developments are not the accidental or unintended result of growing pains likely to be remedied once Women's Studies faculty become aware of them. Quite the contrary. They are the direct consequences of a dogmatically entrenched and ultimately debilitating ideology. Many women and liberal male faculty members know all this. But while dismayed by Women's Studies practices, they are hesitant to speak out for fear of being labeled reactionary or antifeminist. Deans and other college and university officials, who are certainly aware that all is not well, prefer to maintain a position of "plausible deniability" similar to the one they favor with respect to flawed collegiate athletic programs. Administrators are under pressure to meet affirmative action goals, and where better to situate a minority representative or woman than in a marginal, nondisciplinary program where "they" teach students primarily like "them"!

So what is to be done? Ultimately, local conditions must dictate particular tactics. In some Women's Studies programs, in universities that have managed to keep their balance, the adherence to rigorous scholarship and open inquiry may be strong enough to sort through the deluge of propaganda being published and taught under the general rubric of Women's Studies and gender studies. In such situations, feminist faculty who have the stomach will stay and fight the good fight—by opposing ideological policing, by refusing to let classrooms be turned into indoctrination sites or therapy sessions, and by resisting politically based hiring.

In conditions where things are too far gone, feminist faculty who are revolted by what is happening in their programs will probably withdraw their support. We hope they will make it clear why they are doing so.

There are now a few possibilities for those feminists who believe in the values of liberal education to organize nationally. The Feminist Anti-Censorship Taskforce (FACT) has for some years provided a feminist voice in opposition to Catharine MacKinnon's and Andrea Dworkin's more visible and audible views on pornography. Just as this book went to press, we learned of the newly formed Women's

Freedom Network, which espouses a philosophy that defines women and men as individuals rather than in terms of gender and believes that there are no "male" or "female" standards of excellence, morality or justice.[1]

Alternative feminist forums are also available at some professional meetings. For example, as the Society for Women in Philosophy (SWIP) turned its attention more and more exclusively to radical feminist issues and modes of philosophizing, many women (and some men), feeling the need for a new type of venue, started the Society for Analytic Feminism (SAF). At this point, the relations between SWIP and SAF are still cordial (and SAF has even been invited to edit an issue of SWIP's journal, *Hypatia*), but there are dramatic differences in both style and content between the two organizations. SAF, for example, routinely has male speakers on its programs, while SWIP has a caucus called NCLI, for the "Not Currently Lesbian Identified."

But, as sensible feminists have known all along, making a society where women have equal opportunities for life, liberty, and the pursuit of happiness is not a project for women only. Too often second-wave feminists have told men of all political persuasions to butt out. This is unwise. On the other hand, we do not want to reproduce the current generation of "wanna-be-sensitive" university men who uncritically acquiesce in the most ludicrous of feminist demands. It is high time that progressive women and men stopped waxing sentimental about both the plight and the latent virtues of the oppressed and started exercising a little tough-minded common sense in proposing realistic, workable reforms.

Given our bleak analysis, friends have asked us, "Aren't you really saying that Women's Studies programs should be disbanded altogether, and that students should no longer be permitted to pursue a bachelor's or a graduate degree in Women's Studies?" We find this question difficult to answer. We do not entirely agree on this between ourselves, and each of us has repeatedly modified her own position. But we can say the following: In the 1970s there was a vigorous debate within the National Women's Studies Association between those who favored a "mainstreaming" strategy for Women's Studies, with the goal of integrating research on women and gender with the general curriculum, and those who favored "autonomy" for Women's Studies, which would separate it from the mainstream. The "mainstreamers" lost the argument, and perhaps, given the climate of the time, they deserved to lose. But things are different now. Whatever the situation was in the 1970s, in today's tense and constrained academic climate it is difficult to justify setting up new degree-granting programs in Women's Studies with tenured lines and professional staff—even at institutions with a record of animosity toward women, for it is exactly in such "chilly climates" that Women's Studies programs are most likely to act as sites for polarization and nonproductive political agitation. It would be far better to introduce courses on women and gender as part of the regular curriculum, insisting on sound scholarship and high professional standards on the part of those who teach and those who learn. Students and faculty should be encouraged to fight sexism and other injustices on their campuses and beyond, but they should not expect to receive academic credit or tenure for doing so. Life, after all, exists outside the academy too. Advocacy is often appropriate, sometimes necessary, in the street. But in the classroom, the more flexible values of liberal education should prevail.

If there is ever to be an enduring field of scholarly research and teaching called Women's Studies, it must find its way out of the ideological maze thrown up by true believers and self-serving activists. The path it must take has to lead, by way of a reconsideration of fashionable feminist phobias, blind spots, and prejudices, to a new (or old!) kind of feminism—a humanistic feminism that can at least recognize within the complex legacy of "patriarchy" the many liberal principles and enlightened attitudes worth preserving.

It is a fact—though feminist ideologues are reluctant to admit it—that feminists have inescapably drawn on liberal ideas as they have attempted to alter curricula and departments. They have had to argue, even when their practices have fallen far short of the ideal, that the education they were offering would prepare young women for the greatest possible number of experiences and activities, and for exercising independent and critical judgment on them. This is precisely what liberal education is about. Feminists have had to demonstrate that traditional education, with its masculinist bias and misogynist prejudices, failed to live up to this standard—failed to live up to its own standard, one might say.

All arguments that support such a position are rooted in liberal values. That is why these values have been so useful, so strong a tool, for feminists. And even the most radical politicos among feminists, those most likely to sneer at every mention of the L-word, grow outraged when they feel their point of view is not being given a fair hearing. For all these reasons, feminism in the academy should abandon its simplistic and debased notion of the "political," its grandiose claims, its know-it-all strictures, and its radical rhetorical flourishes and return to professional practices consistent with the principles of liberal education.

Women's Studies grew out of a political movement. Without that movement, Women's Studies programs probably would not have come into existence at all. But origins and aims are not the same. We live in a culture that holds intellectual and educational work in low esteem. The rhetoric of Women's Studies—the embarrassment some colleagues seem to feel at *not* being political in the approved way—clearly reveals just how *undifferent*, how reflective of the culture at large Women's Studies is. So does the predilection for therapeutic, rather than intellectual, interventions. In too many Women's Studies programs, one does not find a love of learning or a respect for intellectual achievement. But the costs of this uncritical capitulation to the anti-intellectualism of American culture are high indeed.

When insisting that Women's Studies must serve a political or therapeutic purpose, Women's Studies programs are sadly failing to perform what should be one of their vital functions: to act as independent critics of an important political movement that is going on all around us. From this point of view, the statement that Women's Studies is the academic arm of the women's movement, far from being a cause of celebration, actually undermines the great potential utility of Women's Studies as a forum in which criticism and exploration can take place.

But to say this is to resurrect, as we intentionally do, a number of fundamental liberal ideas: tolerance, the cultivation of a distanced and disengaged analysis, and a degree of skepticism toward one's own positions, and not only those of others—traits, in short, that feminists have too often insisted on repudiating because they judged them to be nothing more than fraudulent fronts for academic masculinism. It is ironic, and tragic as well, that feminism, which originally denounced traditional education for its failures to act in accordance with its self-proclaimed precepts of justice, fairness, equality, and dispassionate evaluation, has so enthusiastically trashed the very principles on which its early (and, on the whole, warranted) denunciations rested. As one of the women we interviewed, Anna, the social science professor introduced in chapter 2, put it:

> Liberal is nearly the worst thing you can be. It may be due for a resurrection, but it will probably be some deformed version of liberalism. Certainly I don't know where else people are going to go with their politics but to liberalism. It's not clear to me what else to do with our views than to say: "Well, this needs to all be out in the open, and we need to convince other people of it." And when you start talking like that, that sounds a lot like liberalism.

It is hypocritical, though not altogether surprising, for feminists (especially those most in favor of a politicized program) to join in the derisive dismissal of liberal education now that its utility to them has been exhausted and they are securely entrenched in Women's Studies programs throughout the country. Where they are not in such positions, it is obvious that they must still plead liberal values to make their case. Given the rhetoric prevalent in Women's Studies, however, what is more predictable than that, a little farther down the road, these same petitioners will brand such values, their former allies, as a cowardly failure to challenge the masculine reality?

But this is a self-defeating strategy. Sooner or later, the antiliberal rhetoric will estrange the audience at which it is aimed. As Jeanne, the historian who left Women's Studies, observed:

> I think the university is, now, perhaps the *only* remaining place in society where people can explore ideas and have differences of opinions without consequences for themselves. That is its strength, exactly. And there are few places in society where that is possible. The fact is that at universities we have unusual freedom to say what we believe and to act on that belief. Even junior faculty! To claim otherwise is just crazy.
>
> There are increasing numbers of people—and I'm hearing them, a lot of them are my friends—who are not only critical of these kinds of dogmatic programs, but who are beginning to speak out against them. Whatever courage they needed, whatever critical mass of people needed to develop, I think increasingly there is going to be a critique. And I hear this criticism all over the place.
>
> What that ultimately means, I don't know. I don't think it will mean a return to some prior state, because we have so many people working on women and gender, people who have been influenced by feminist discourse, however they identify themselves. That will not change. That is now institutionalized. But it may be that there will be a rediscovery of disciplines, a reengagement with departments.
>
> You know, all this has been fundamentally destabilizing to my notion of my own politics. I once was a very strong critic of liberalism. I had certain socialist commitments. But now I am much more willing to embrace the label of "liberal" than I ever was in the past. Those liberal values are, to me, in such need of defense, and that's where I find myself at this moment. And I think a lot of us are engaged in a major political shifting, and something will come out of that. People won't be silenced forever on these issues.

Not only women such as Jeanne, however, now find themselves ready to defend liberal values. Angela, the Marxist and feminist humanities professor introduced in chapter 8, slowly discovered the unavoidable conflicts of her political commitments with other values that she only then recognized she held:

> Academic freedom, for instance, is a liberal value that, I thought, was taken for granted, to be defended by other people. I thought it wasn't for me to do. It didn't seem to be anything I'd have to worry about. But I now think that actually preserving the space for academic culture and academic— whatever you want to call it—free speech, is a very important issue. It seems so banal, but I never thought that so much of my institutional thinking and energy would get down to that— that sort of very liberal issue.

Because Women's Studies programs have in so many instances repudiated liberal values and fallen prey to the dangerous amalgamation of political, pop-therapeutic, and educational objectives, they cannot, at this moment, be considered successful. Too many are in crisis, and the causes of the crisis, as we have argued, lie within feminism itself, which should never have been embraced in its ideologically inflamed form by institutions of learning. Those students who seek the single correct path—true believers already or young people demanding the security of ultimate enlightenment—will have to go elsewhere. They can join political groups. Nothing prevents them from becoming activists, even extremists. If feminist seminaries or cadre training camps are to be set up, however, they should be clearly identified as such. It is not the function of a university to sponsor them.

When it becomes impossible to decide whose truth, whose politics, whose identity shall prevail in the academy, what will we then do? Resort to censorship? To arms? Drive people from their jobs? What will we then have? Models abound: the Aryan university of Nazi Germany; Stalinism and Maoism; lily-white institutions in the pre-1960s U.S. South; the purges provoked by McCarthyism; East German universities whose faculties first had to embody Marxist-Leninist truths and were then removed wholesale when that ideology folded; ethnically pure enclaves in the former Yugoslavia. Think about these, and a chamber of horrors opens. We must back away from particular ideologies to see what they all have in common, and that is the tyranny of politicized education by means of indoctrination, and the even more pernicious faith that someone holds the key, knows the truth, has the answers, and is empowered (whether by our will or against it) to impose them on the rest of us.

How can such an arrogation coexist with a genuine call for multiculturalism and diversity? It cannot. Only that weary adjective *liberal*—much maligned and battered but still bravely insisting on tolerance, mutual respect, and an open mind—can lend to education the power to overcome ignorance, prejudice, and hypocrisy.

As long as Women's Studies offers an academic home to the latter traits while distrusting or openly repudiating the former, it will continue to produce students who, like fundamentalists of every stripe, use their small store of fixed ideas to build walls around their tiny enclaves, not realizing that within these walls they themselves must live as prisoners. Women—and men—deserve better.

POSTSCRIPT

IN WRITING THIS BOOK, we found that a tone of irony was often more conducive to our work than one of dejection. But as we approach the end, we cannot avoid expressing the sadness and dismay with which this task has filled us.

Like the other women who walked away, we once shared the great aspirations and hopes that have inspired and sustained Women's Studies programs for over twenty years. We too believed that the lot of women in our society and around the world could be improved through a new kind of teaching and research. No one likes to see dreams turn sour. It is tempting to pretend that something so simple as a renewed faith in sisterhood or a little more patience with one another would set aright the house that feminism has built within the academy. But we are convinced that the task is not so simple and cannot even be broached until the fundamental errors, double standards, false paths, zero-sum games, and pious dead-ends that we have revealed are acknowledged, understood, and repudiated. Until then, stories of pain and disillusionment will continue to emerge.

Just as we were putting the finishing touches to this manuscript, we met a woman in her seventies who told us how, with much anticipation, she had enrolled in a feminist theory class a few years earlier. Straight out of high school she had gone to work in an office and had become involved with union organizing of white-collar women workers like herself. She had been active in women's causes for decades thereafter. The feminist theory course, she thought, would finally place a lifetime of concerns and commitments in a broader perspective. But, though she liked the readings for the course, she found the atmosphere intolerable. After being reduced to tears in one class, she quit attending. In telling us her story, this woman groped for words: "The atmosphere was so . . . so hostile." She did not, however, place the blame for the class's endless divisiveness entirely on the professor. Rather, she said, the professor herself had seemed intimidated by some disruptive women in the class, and had allowed them to take it over and set both the tone and the terms of discussion. "I'm still a feminist," this woman said—as did every one of the other women we spoke with—"but that class can't be what feminism is all about. I went there looking for some answers, and all I found was the same old struggle for power and dominance."

This woman provided us with one more expression of the deep longing many women have to think of themselves as feminists, dedicated to the dramatic overhaul of so many of our society's retrograde attitudes and routine discriminations toward women. She also reveals how natural it is for such women to think that Women's Studies will help them in understanding what has happened historically to women and in thinking clearly about the issues involved. And, finally, she illustrates how amazement and sorrow can replace hope and anticipation once it becomes apparent to them what is really going on in Women's Studies. Such women wonder: Am I crazy? Old-fashioned? Do I still harbor ancient sexist instincts? Am I alone? It is for these women, too, that we have written our book.

To the enemies of all feminist initiatives, the folks who will say, "See, we knew it all along—feminists are a bunch of wild-eyed weirdos," we have this to say: No. You did not read our book carefully. What we are calling attention to are not the deficiencies of the fundamental feminist goals for political and social reform. Nor are we repudiating the study of women's lives or denying the central role of gender in human societies. What we are decrying is the unfortunate path Women's Studies has taken; the attempt to be revolutionary in all respects all at once; the insistence on mixing politics and scholarship in a manner that is detrimental to each; the sacrifice of intellect to emotion; the tendency to turn the very simple basic moral claims of feminism into an esoteric dogma that can be understood only by the indoctrinated and accepted only by the initiated. This is what we are against.

It's all about ends and means. The foes of feminism do not accept the basic goal of the liberation of women from all that impedes their ability to lead full and productive lives. It is the friends of feminism who are best situated to argue about the means for realizing that goal. We are feminists and we are friends of feminism, but we submit that the methods of teaching and research and of self-governance that have become normative in many Women's Studies programs are ill-advised and destructive to women in the long run. That is why we wrote this book.

II

WOMEN'S STUDIES
IN THE NEW MILLENNIUM

10

Rhetoric and Reality in Women's Studies

Daphne Patai

FEMINIST ACTIVISTS in North America frequently complain about the current failure of most women to identify themselves as feminists. Advocates of Women's Studies usually explain away this uncomfortable fact by calling it "backlash" or blaming it on (white) women's false consciousness or adherence to "privilege" of one sort or another. In this chapter, I offer an alternative explanation for public indifference or outright hostility to feminism. I utilize recent books and articles reflecting on Women's Studies, feminist pedagogy, and struggles over who are the "real" feminists today; publications of feminist organizations such as the National Women's Studies Association (NWSA) and the American Association of University Women (AAUW); and the Women's Studies E-Mail List (WMST-L @LISTSERV.UMD.EDU), still run by the indefatigable Joan Korenman, which in 2001 had approximately 4,500 subscribers throughout the world (but concentrated especially in the United States), most of them teaching or studying Women's Studies. In addition, I draw on Women's Studies programs' own mission statements and course descriptions, on advertisements for Women's Studies faculty, and on comments addressed to me personally by Women's Studies' supporters as well as critics. In exploring these materials, I attempt to gauge the status and climate of Women's Studies as an academic endeavor at the beginning of the new millennium.

UNMENTIONABLES

On February 10, 2001, masses of women gathered at Madison Square Garden in a celebration of their vaginas. The occasion was a benefit performance of Eve Ensler's *Vagina Monologues,* a play that, in the words of the writer Dorothy Gallagher, "has grown planetary tentacles and has attracted legions of fans."[1] It is evidently possible to incite 18,000 women, led by the actress Glenn Close, to repeatedly shout "cunt" with great enthusiasm and to join in orgasmic moaning with the "Vulva Choir," made up of seventy famous women. But getting a few notables who participated in the staging of Ensler's ubiquitous play to embrace another controversial though ordinary word—feminism—seems quite a different matter. Sharon Lerner described this V-Day event in the *Village Voice:*

> But even as "hoochie," "pooter," "twat," and "coochi snorcher" rolled off celebrity tongues and Ensler waved a vibrator at her delighted fans, another word seemed to stick in the throats of even the most vagina-loving Hollywood icons: feminist. Ask about it at the Hammerstein Ballroom gala— which, along with the performance, raised more than $2 million to fund antiviolence programs and more V-Day performances—and it's as if you've defamed the clitoris or something.[2]

Many of the comments made by celebrities who took part in V-Day at Madison Square Garden shed interesting light on the image problem confronting feminism at this time. Glenn Close, for example, despite her rhetorical audacity, took the trouble to state that she wanted no part of the "clichéd image of what a feminist would be." What perception of feminists did she have in mind? "They don't like men—you know, kind of, um, butch." As Lerner acidly commented: "So *feminism* stays in the verbal gutter, while Close carries *cunt* to redemption." Talk-show host Ricki Lake was "dodgy" about the term "feminist," but clarified that, though she dislikes labels, she does support women's rights; and the actress Marisa Tomei, somewhat more daringly, admitted to being a feminist—"but without definition."[3]

A more astute appraisal was offered by Isabella Rossellini, who, when asked if she considered herself a feminist, replied: "Well, I don't know what you mean. I would not label tonight a feminist night; it's a women's night. I mean, there are Republican women, there are Democratic women, there are feminist women, and women who don't define themselves, they're just women against violence."[4] Rossellini's answer touches on an important but often overlooked detail: Pro-women activities may indeed encompass a wide range of political postures. The term "feminist," on the other hand, tends to narrow these stances to just a few.

The problem, in short, is that—rightly or wrongly—"feminist" has come to designate particular attitudes and their attendant, if ill-defined, political positions, while in reality women, like men, may be seriously divided about both the directions in which women's status and society in general should be altered, and the means by which such changes should be pursued.

It may be, of course, that these women lauding their vaginas but rejecting the label of feminist are themselves sorely in need of the ministrations of feminism, their very reticence serving as evidence that they are still deeply mired in patriarchal thinking. From such a perspective, their unwillingness to identify themselves as feminists is itself but a symptom of their oppression. Or this recalcitrance may be due to a lamentable desire merely to protect their "privilege." Certainly Women's Studies programs continue to make precisely these claims, as they try to address the recurring problems of student "resistance" in the classroom and, more generally, women's disinclination to wear the badge of "feminism."[5]

But there may be another reason. Perhaps the hesitation on the part of both famous and obscure women to adopt the label tells us something that those engaged in promoting feminism prefer to ignore.

As a point of departure, I note that at this moment the cause of feminist activism in North America seems to depend extensively upon a gross misrepresentation of the status of women. An egregious example is the claim made by some feminist scholars in the United States, presumably with a straight face, that "the academy remains an essentially single sex institution. It is male-dominated, and that domination exerts itself in both numbers and power."[6] Then there is the notorious report published in 1993 by the government-financed Canada Panel on Violence against Women. Two years in the making at a cost of more than $10 million, this report concluded that "Canadian women are all too familiar with inequality and violence which tether them to lives few in the world would choose to lead," a statement so outrageous that the journalist Donna Laframboise was moved to call the report "a national embarrassment."[7] Undeterred, another Canadian academic issued a report, in November 2000, defending Women's Studies and referring to the "plight of women in Canada and around the world."[8]

Such distortions about the status of women should not be seen as a neurotic inability to recognize improvement, and even radical change, in North American society over the past three decades. Rather, the utility of these sorts of claims for feminist activists is transparent. As Cathy Young points out in her book *Ceasefire! Why Women and Men Must Join Forces to Achieve True Equality*, insistence on the pervasiveness of "sexism" helps "keep the movement alive," as feminist activists themselves on occasion admit. Young cites Stanford law professor Deborah Rhode, who in her book *Speaking of Sex*

> frankly acknowledges the stake feminists have in persuading people that women in our culture still suffer inequities that "no just society could tolerate": the more people believe that the "woman problem" has been largely solved, the less they will support feminist political causes. Rhode even concludes that, "ironically enough, [women's] progress has created its own obstacles to further change."[9]

Less surprisingly, but no less reprehensibly, scare tactics are also being employed even by national organizations such as the American Association of University Women. In an October 2000 membership drive, the AAUW sent out an enrollment form headed "I Want to be Part of the Solution!" Next to its check-off box was printed this statement: "**YES!** Enter me as an AAUW member today! It's high time we break the code of silence that perpetuates gender inequality in America!"

Perhaps the exclamation points are meant to strike an emotional chord that will inhibit the recipient of this mailing from asking: What "code of silence" is this? Is it the code of silence that has allowed approximately seven hundred Women's Studies programs and departments to come into existence at American colleges and universities over the past three decades, along with thousands of additional individual courses relating to women? Is it perhaps the code that has produced so extraordinary a burgeoning of women enrolled in graduate programs of all kinds that they are expected by 2006 to reach parity with men in graduate degrees received and are already on the verge of constituting the majority of law students?[10] Or the one that has allowed women, since 1984 (the year in which, for the first time, women slightly surpassed men in college attendance), to enter college at increasingly higher rates than men, rates that in the year 2000 saw over two million more women than men enroll in degree-granting institutions? [11] Or perhaps it's the silence about the fact that women—of all races—graduate from college at steadily higher rates than men, rates that reached 57 percent of all college students in 1998 (as compared with 52 percent in 1985)?[12] These facts go unmentioned. Instead, in the accompanying letter to "Dear Friend," AAUW president Sandy Bernard does not fail to call attention to the "thousand different ways" in which girls' "self-esteem is under attack," a discredited notion that nonetheless continues to play a major tactical role in feminist writing. And how is women's progress viewed by the AAUW? The letter makes it clear that the better things get, the worse they become:

A century ago, AAUW fought for women's right to vote and to pursue a higher education. *Today, we have an even tougher*

challenge—breaking the code of silence on so-called girls' issues like low self-esteem, sexual harassment, violence, eating
disorders, and teen pregnancy.[13] [emphasis in original]

There is a nice irony here: The celebrants of V-Day at Madison
Square Garden deny being thoroughgoing feminists even as they
act out a "transgressive" scenario that Women's Studies feminists
would endorse; meanwhile the AAUW, which used to be a stodgy
organization for academic ladies, now buys into both the substance
and rhetoric of the "victim" feminism promoted by Women's Studies programs.

Far less well publicized is the fact that in August 2000, the National Association for Women in Education, after nearly eighty-five
years of existence, voted for its own dissolution. Initially formed in
1916 as an association of Deans of Women, the group underwent
a series of name changes as its concerns broadened over the years.
Its recent demise is by its own account a result of its very success,
as the *Women in Higher Education* newsletter reported: "With
women now a majority of students and a growing presence among
faculty and top campus administrators, they belong to many other
professional organizations and haven't time to volunteer at
NAWE."[14]

Yet none of this keeps feminist scholars from tirelessly misrepresenting the fragility of their status in academe. Well-known feminist scholars Alice Kessler-Harris and Amy Swerdlow, for example,
in a 1996 essay entitled "Pride and Paradox: Despite Success,
Women's Studies Faces an Uncertain Future," portray Women's
Studies programs as an endangered species. Although they reveal
that three-fourths of their respondents agreed that Women's Studies is "firmly integrated in their institutions," and four-fifths did
not consider it to be any longer at a "critical stage," they somehow
manage to transform these responses into a threat to the survival of
Women's Studies.[15]

Thus, the result of what feminists say and fail to say is a feminism ever more at odds with observable reality, steeped in ever less

authentic-sounding pronouncements of its rationale and objectives. This disjuncture, this "reality gap," in my view helps explain the disinclination of so many women to identify themselves as feminists—even as they enjoy the gains in independence and professional access that have been promoted by feminism. To self-proclaimed feminists, these recusants, both old and young, are, as noted earlier, merely demonstrating the tenacious hold of "resistance," the oft-cited capitulation to "backlash," or a lamentable and self-interested adherence to "privilege." But in issuing such labels, feminists forget that the massive improvements in women's status over the past few decades are due not to feminism alone. The feminist activism of the past few decades was only a part of a much larger story of progress, by no means the whole of it.

The same sort of conflict between rhetoric and reality is apparent in publications issuing from feminist pens, which, even while paying tireless attention to the differences alleged to exist between older and younger feminists, reproduce decades-old orthodoxies. As an example, consider the proposition that white women, "even feminists," are "sometimes loath to admit" their white privilege. This statement was made not in 1970 or 1980, but in early 2001 in a *Ms.* magazine feature titled "Is Feminism a 4-Letter Word?"[16] In her introductory essay to eight women's responses to this question, Jill Nelson tells us: "Like it or not, the word feminist has baggage that we need to unpack, especially when it comes to race," and she goes on to castigate the lack of understanding found among women "privileged by whiteness." Today, Nelson asserts, women of color "hesitate to call themselves feminists to avoid discovery and marginalization by men and women in our own communities. It's not cool to be a feminist."[17]

Is this news? Not quite. Even Nelson admits that the same conversation between white and black women has been going on, with little variation, for thirty years. Why, then, does she repeat these charges? Probably because guilt-tripping has proved to be an effective strategy and hence is immune to revision. Nelson confesses that when she does call herself a feminist, this admission is "greeted with contempt and cries of 'dyke!'" in her communities of color. The truth is, she concludes, "I've met more than a few white women who say they're feminists and aren't, and more than a few sisters who would never call themselves feminists but damn sure are. Ultimately, it's about the work of political, social, and economic equality, whatever we call ourselves."[18]

She is right. And this is precisely what makes Women's Studies programs, which from their inception have defined themselves as the "academic arm of feminism," marginal to most university students, who don't attend college in order to practice politics.[19]

In the same issue of *Ms.*, Paula Rojas, speaking for the feminist collective Sista II Sista, a Brooklyn-based group founded in 1996 to empower young women of color, gives us the tiresome old cant that mainstream feminism "lacks a class and race analysis." She also worries that the "privilege" she enjoyed in going to college, even though it was on a scholarship, "can silence other people."[20] This genuflection is a good example of the impulse toward leveling that seems to underlie so much feminist rhetoric. With "privilege" of one kind or another seen as ubiquitous, and always understood as necessarily reprehensible, one wonders what sort of world these feminists would like to bring about, if they could. Meanwhile, although not a single new thought appears in this entire feature in *Ms.*, the young women who publish there evidently believe they really are making waves. Thus, even as the white actor/singer Betty Buckley denies that there's racism within feminism, which she defines as "equality for all women in all things," Vivien Labaton, director of the Third Wave Foundation, charges that "There's truth to the criticism that 1960s and 1970s feminism did not reflect the concerns of low-income women or women of color." She concludes: "It's up to young women to make this movement what we want it to be."

On the other side, old-timer Mary Kay Blakely insists: "We never said we're only interested in raising white women's paychecks," and "The notion that we were and are a white movement is wrong." And Aileen Hernandez, First Commissioner of the Equal Employment Opportunity Commission (EEOC), points out that there were women of color involved in NOW from the early days. She blames the media for misrepresenting this. But Ingrid River-Dessuit, who calls herself an "activist for women's rights," states that when she thinks of feminists, "the first image that comes to mind is white women. Another is the image of a man-hating dyke. I'm not man-hating, but I am a dyke." She does not relate to "feminism," she asserts, because "the movement doesn't encompass and hasn't really shown interest in all women." Still, the *Ms.* feature ends with Aimee Carrillo Rowe's reiteration of the decades-old accusation that "white women are not investing their lives and emotions in women of color."[21]

What does this habitual accusation reveal about the internal dynamics of feminist politics? Merely that it is not averse to employing the familiar tactic of promoting group unity by focusing on a clearly defined opponent—an opponent against which the forces of good must be rallied. Like the many feminists who cannot survive without the bugbear of patriarchy, women of color also need an official enemy to react against—in this case the image of the supposedly lily-white women's movement. The purely conventional and by-now entirely predictable rhetoric taken by this discussion can be tracked on the Women's Studies E-mail List, where, over the years, the familiar charges (and occasional countercharges) have been vented again and again.

Are women in fact still oppressed by the patriarchy in modern-day America? Listening to what is taught in many Women's Studies courses and what is claimed by women's organizations, the answer would seem to be an incontrovertible YES. Never mind the massive evidence— statistical, judicial, and legislative, as well as anecdotal—of enormous and continuing improvement in women's status in the United States. Society has changed, but feminist activists seem determined either not to notice or not to admit it. Instead, hackneyed stereotypes are repeated as though they were startling insights.

HIERARCHY IS A "GUY THING":
FEMINIST PEDAGOGY

One of the key features of feminism in the academy has been its hostility to individualism and attraction toward collectivism. From the beginning of second wave feminism, as we noted earlier in this book, the demands of "sisterhood" created tensions—and even defections. A notorious case was that involving Ti-Grace Atkinson, founder in 1969 of the radical group The Feminists. As Atkinson's visibility in the media increased, her "sisters" passed a resolution criticizing her "for allowing the media to define her as the group's leader," and demanding that the group remain "leaderless" since anything else would constitute a threat to its commitment to "egalitarianism." The group's members issued a ruling that they would draw lots to determine who would have contact with the media and threatened to expel anyone who disobeyed this injunction. As a result, Atkinson withdrew from the group.[22]

This antagonism toward individual achievement was (and still is) a commonplace in feminist circles, as is apparent also from Susan Brownmiller's recent memoir *In Our Time*. Author of the 1976 bestseller *Against Our Will* (considered a landmark in feminist understanding of rape), Brownmiller found herself accused of racism, homophobia, and that cardinal feminist sin of attempting "to rise to fame on the back of the women's movement." As one "sister" angrily complained to Brownmiller: "Do you have to put your name on your book? . . . Rape doesn't belong to you, it belongs to the movement." Citing this episode in a review entitled "Rape Belongs to Everyone," Wendy Steiner says: "Brownmiller's account [of the women's movement] sounds eerily like a history of Soviet communism, full of rightist deviations, false consciousness and purges."[23] In late 2000, the same antipathy toward individuality surfaced in response to a posting on the Women's Studies E-Mail List by Adam Jones, saying that he considered Camille Paglia's *Sexual Personae* a "towering masterpiece" and the single most important contribution to feminism since Simone de Beauvoir's *The Second Sex*.[24] A heated but not very original discussion then ensued on the subject of male competitiveness and men's (but not women's) natural bent toward hierarchy. Consider historian Rosa Maria Pegueros's riposte:

> I also find the inclination to designate The Best, The Most Important, The Whatever, to be a "guy" thing. It is of no particular use except to establish a particular point of view as The Best Point of View. I, for one, look for the best in all things and all people. Or maybe I should say, MOST people.

Other subscribers joined in, blissfully endorsing gender stereotypes. Lisa Burke responded:

> It can also be argued that "the best, the most important" etc. to which Dr. Pegueros refers is also used to narrow the voices that are heard and listened to, establishing some hierarchy of value on what is said; it is as she clearly points out a mechanism of power and privileging. . . . the notion of having to select from group "X"—and consequently narrow down to—that which is the single best, or the "best of the best," is a mechanism of patriarchy, power, and privilege.[25]

It seemed worrisome to me that such things should be said in an academic forum. I therefore posted the following:

> When the AAUW [American Association of University Women] gives fellowships—in which I sincerely hope they indeed consider the merits of the applications and decide which are the "best" and the "most deserving"—is that an example of a Mechanism of Patriarchy? When Nadine Gordimer and Toni Morrison get the Nobel Prize, are those [decisions] Mechanisms of Patriarchy? When Oprah Winfrey names her book club selection and tens of thousands of people believe her, is that a Mechanism of Patriarchy? When one looks for the "best" surgeon one can find to do one's surgery, is that an M

of P? When one chooses to fly the "safest" airline, is that an M of P? I'm curious as to what sort of world you consider to offer an alternative to this way of doing things.[26]

This led some of the original contributors to attempt to modify their statements. But, while now acknowledging that we all make comparisons, they continued to insist that there is something distinctly patriarchal about the practice of choosing the "best"—or, for that matter, even conceptualizing such a preference.

Not that this was the first (or last) time such statements had appeared on the WMST-List. In 1995, in one memorable posting, philosophy professor Joyce Trebilcot contributed the following observation to a discussion of "intellectuals and elitism": "I have eliminated the term 'intellectual' from my vocabulary because it seems to me to suggest that some women are (not just different from others in a particular way but) superior to others." Making it hard to imagine how she could in good conscience remain in her position as a university professor, Trebilcot went on to say: "To speak of intellectuals, I believe, tends to exclude and depreciate some women, to foster envy and competition, and to encourage conventional achievement within the mainstream."[27]

If claims of this sort occurred only on the admittedly informal medium of a listserve on the Internet, one could ignore them. But they appear also in feminist publications. Such attitudes rest on stereotypes about women, stereotypes that are frequently repeated in discussions of feminist pedagogy. Hence the assertion we find in a recent essay by Carolyn Shrewsbury called "What is Feminist Pedagogy?" that "women seek to build connections. They seek to maintain connections that have been built"[28]—a claim that (as we discussed in chapter 7) has become an orthodoxy in many circles since the publication in 1982 of Carol Gilligan's *In a Different Voice: Psychological Theory and Women's Development*. Some reformers seek to extend these concerns beyond the feminist classroom itself. Thus Jane Roland Martin, a philosopher of education who criticizes "the dogma of god-given subjects," urges all educators to adopt the "three C's": care, concern, and connection.[29]

A recent collection of essays, *Common Ground: Feminist Collaboration in the Academy*, co- edited by Elizabeth G. Peck and JoAnna Stephens Mink, contains the familiar anti-hierarchy rhetoric—as well as the same inevitably inconsistent application of it. The two editors display their own lack of competitiveness by mentioning that, with no prior discussion of name placement, each had listed the other's name first on their proposal for the book.[30] Contributions to the volume rest on the proposition that, as Paula D. Nesbitt and Linda E. Thomas state in their essay, collaborative work, which is "naturally egalitarian," represents a "transformative breakthrough." As Nesbitt and Thomas put it:

> The purpose of collaborative research is to reconstruct the basis of what is considered authoritative knowledge so as to more accurately correspond to the human diversity that constitutes our social reality. . . . Authentic collaborative research is the conception, investigation, and nurturance of ideas through a naturalness of interaction that underlies any concurrent attention to power disparities resulting from the researchers' particular social locations.[31]

For Nesbitt, the white member of the team, collaboration means above all:

> doing my "white" work. Naming this represents an embarrassment, a recognition that what I've perceived as scholarship in general is in fact a very particular perspective through the lens of racial dominance. . . . To go against such a lock-step can be considered treasonous to those who seek to offer European American feminists a certain amount of scholarly security in return for their loyalty.

Apparently unaware of their own recourse to superlatives, Nesbitt and Thomas write:

> Elitism is a characteristic of higher education institutions. What would it mean for an institution to focus less on being

"the biggest and the best" and instead develop leadership that would reconfigure the paradigms that until now have universalized the experiences of a few? . . . Having institutional goals that signal a commitment to transformation will attract some of the finest, most creative minds in the world. Such a community of scholars would be diverse racially and culturally.[32]

In the same volume, Helen Cafferty and Jeanette Clausen, in an essay entitled "What's Feminist about It? Reflections on Collaboration in Editing and Writing," explain that collaborative research is intended to "contribute to a feminist transformation of the academy." They discuss their commitment to "feminist process"—and to "feminist mentoring"—in producing their WIG [Women in German] Yearbook, but complain that authors do not always appreciate their efforts or see them as "nonhierarchical."[33] Being feminist collaborators to them means greater commitment to a "'dialogic' than to a 'hierarchical' mode."[34]

A light-hearted essay on "lesbian collaboration" by Angela M. Estes and Kathleen Margaret Lant comes close to solipsistic self-parody. The authors' aim, they declare, was to "use ourselves as our only field of inquiry." Lovers for five years, friends for a subsequent fifteen, these two English professors reject the "essentialist" view of lesbianism, which they believe to be, like all sexual identity, a social construct. "To conceptualize lesbian collaboration, then, we must answer the questions: What is it like? What does it do? How does it work?" Their response is to use the metaphor of dance: "by dancing in the dark—our desire—our lesbian need and compulsion and energy—moves us together in this choreography of our own." Viewing lesbian collaboration as "choreography," they say, means "locating ourselves in language and moving powerfully through that language." But language tends to "erase the lesbian," even as patriarchal culture itself "denies or demeans the lesbian."[35] How to overcome this dilemma?

The first tactic of lesbian collaboration, then, must be to challenge and subvert the law by forming an improper bond. We dance together. . . . And second, our dance forces an improper bond because it disrupts our culture's most favored view of imaginative creativity—that of the isolated, lonely, creative genius. . . . While our writing must ultimately be brought to conform to certain strictures of patriarchal discourse, our play, our dance in the dark is never constrained by this frigid "enlightenment." Our collaborative sessions are riotous, disorganized, sloppy, and unpredictable. . . . We are frequently unbathed, always disheveled, and completely accepting of each other.[36]

Many of the essays in Peck and Mink's book seem to assume that the male-dominated academy is opposed to collaboration and rarely practices it. It is part of the arrogance of feminist thinking to believe that any practice it adopts or endorses is necessarily a new, original, and, of course, superior one. Oddly enough, when feminists embrace terms such as "superior" or "better," they apparently imagine them to be "non-hierarchical." This is the spirit manifest in Jamie Barlowe and Ruth Hottell's essay "Feminist Theory and Practice and the Pedantic I/Eye." For the authors, the first principle of collaborative feminist teaching is the "relinquishing of pedantic authoritarianism."[37] Within academic feminism, the persistence of this theme—which, absent the hyperbole, merely means the presumption that the teacher has some knowledge and expertise that the students do not—can be gauged by these two authors' citing of a 1969 essay by Constance Penley, who praised the feminist teacher's deliberate "self-undermining of her own authority by refusing to be an 'authority' at all."[38] Relinquishing patriarchal habits of competition, however, does not keep Barlowe and Hottell from boasting, with no awareness of the irony of it: "As our collaborative course took shape in our minds, the College of Arts and Sciences at our university announced a Competition for Teaching Fellowships. The course we proposed was one of two chosen to be funded for that year."

What kind of syllabus won this award? Barlowe and Hottell tell us that they selected "texts representative of the widespread repression of the System," amending their reading lists to include more subversive texts: "To continue in the false vein of objectivity and to deny personal voices," they argue, "is to deny diversity and to contribute to the promulgation of the white, male, heterosexual, bourgeois paradigm of repressive cultures."[39] To supplement their readings, they chose a number of movies which, they insist,

> represent the gynophobia of mainstream films in its violent manifestation—films like *Peeping Tom*, the prototype of the camera as phallic weapon, and *The Big Sleep*, in which women function as "bad girls" who must either be punished/erased from the text or brought back into the confines of the system. We wanted to show our students that exposing the underpinnings at work in hegemonic texts is a transformative, transgressive activity.[40]

And what self-respecting feminist academic today would aspire to be less than transformative and transgressive in her treatment of hegemonic texts?

How important a goal this is can be gauged in a revealing essay by Jane Tompkins, whose pedagogic aim is to go where no teacher has gone before: to the beach. Tompkins's essay "Let's Get Lost" (included in the aptly named 1996 book *Confessions of the Critics*) is a classic in the burgeoning genre I have labeled "nouveau solipsism."[41] It is a meditation on what Tompkins considers the "best course" she ever taught.[42] This course, for undergraduates and graduate students at Duke University, was called "American Literature Unbound," and it consisted of merely two books, to be studied in an "uncluttered, unrushed" way: Herman Melville's *Moby-Dick* and Toni Morrison's *Beloved*. Tompkins prides herself on the lengths to which she has gone in abdicating professorial authority. She disdains teaching her students a lot, or even a little, about literature, but aspires to providing them with nothing less than profound, life-altering experiences. Searching for one such "bonding experience,"[43] Tompkins took her students on an overnight trip to

Ocracoke Island, on the North Carolina coast, to give them the flavor of Melville. While confiding to the reader that she could actually have taught her students quite a bit about Melville, whose work she claims to love, she states that she spoke only once to the class, for fifteen minutes, about the language of *Moby-Dick*. After all, as Tompkins puts it in a flagrant display of how she misunderstands the aims of teaching, "I didn't need to prove to anybody that I could discourse about epistemology or make dutiful observations about structure and point of view."[44] Instead, she let herself just savor "the unbelievable feats of verbal artistry that novel contains"— an experience that, she believes, somehow rubbed off on the class. For the flavor of Toni Morrison's novel, Tompkins took her class on another "fantastic trip"—this time to a plantation, where the class "spent time doing work that slaves had done."

One has to be far advanced in the belief that higher education is utterly insignificant as an intellectual endeavor to embrace such a mode of teaching. Its relationship to feminist pedagogy, on the other hand, is clear: The emphasis on subjective feeling, the abdication of professorial expertise, the failure to demand anything like normal academic work (Tompkins says that, in true communitarian style, she allowed students to grade themselves, collectively— including in their calculations such items as time spent on travel arrangements for the trips—and that she "loved our rebellion against grades and rules and conventional procedures"). Unable to tell us whether the course was a success—since that would imply an acceptance of some criteria for determining the answer —Tompkins is happy in her recollection of the good feelings and bonding that she thought the course had fostered. The students' far more mixed reactions continue to trouble her:

> Why couldn't they see that this *was* the earthly paradise? It *was* what all the theory and criticism of literature was pointing toward, had hoped some day could be achieved? Why couldn't they understand that we're just like the barrier island, the ribbon of sand, that's always being created and destroyed,

always changing, never the same? That we were perfect [*sic*], and that our imperfections were all that we would ever have?[45]

Poor Tompkins. An "outsider" reading this essay can easily discern what actually happened here. The teacher gave in to her *nostalgie de la jeunesse*, wanting somehow to make her students care about her professional persona as much as she did, and she felt that she could accomplish this goal only by abdicating any professional expectations and demeanor—which, meanwhile, fulfilled another agenda of hers. But is this reasonable? Is it appropriate? Are not her students, thirty-some years her juniors, at a different stage of life, one at which a weekend of bonding arranged by their professor may not be what they came to college for? Tompkins' fantasy shows that several decades of feminist rhetoric about non-hierarchical pedagogy can make even learned professionals lose their bearings and give in to the seductiveness of playing guru to students.

Fortunately, rebuttals do occasionally surface in discussions of "feminist pedagogy." On the WMST-List, where comments about women's special practices in the classroom are the norm, a few dissenting voices were heard clearly in late 2001. One woman, discussing the connection between power and knowledge, wrote: "I can remember a couple of grad school courses taught by avowed feminists who would 'decenter' the classroom and, as a result, withhold information from their students. I felt cheated of their *expertise*, which I was paying for with my tuition."[46]

Another woman, evidently realizing that she was at a university, not an ashram, objected strongly and eloquently to the dismissal of male lecturing style that some of the more active listmembers had expressed:

Since starting to learn about feminist pedagogy, I have been given, time and time again, the example of the "lecture" as the ultimate nadir of bad teaching. I find this, frankly, risible. Some of the best and most exciting learning I have ever done in my life, has happened in classrooms where the students sat

in ROWS, not a circle, and looked at a professor who was lecturing. . . .

I think it's unfair and perhaps even irresponsible to claim
that professors who do "straight lectures" have never been
"taught to teach." Lecturing is an art that does, indeed, require
learning. There are excellent lecturers, and rotten ones. Excellent lecturers can really *fire* their students' imaginations, excite
them, inspire them—just as my marvelous lecturing profs at
UCLA did for me. In no way should this method of teaching
be considered "anti feminist" or a sign of "bad teaching."

To take this statement as evidence for an open-mindedness characteristically present in Women's Studies would, however, be a great
error. The same woman was well aware of how atypical her views
were:

I am deeply distressed whenever I see feminist pedagogues
rolling their eyes and waving their hands whenever "lectures"
are mentioned. Let me make this as plain as I can: I would not
be a scholar today if I hadn't had professors who lectured to
me. Listening to them expound on the subject of their expertise—without interruptions, with full freedom to develop
a nuanced and intricate argument with full concentration—
was an experience that could sometimes put me in such a
trance of happiness that I actually jumped out of my seat
when the bell rang. Full hours melted away like ten minutes.
It was a genuine pleasure to see bright, articulate experts reveal the beauties of their field to me. It was inspiring, in the
true sense of the word: it made me feel that the breath of God
was being blown into me. It was like being given a glimpse of
an enormous, endless sea of riches that the professor was
inviting me to explore with him/her.[47]

The more conventional feminist approach, by contrast, is to at
best qualify any endorsement of lecturing as not necessarily inimical

to feminist goals. Thus Berenice Malka Fisher, in her book *No Angel in the Classroom* (2001), offers a bit of faint praise for lecturing as a teaching tool: "Some lecturing styles," she writes,

> may be fairly consistent with certain aspects of consciousness-raising. Feminist lecturers may bring in the experiences of many women; pay attention to feelings and their meaning; search out the relations among experiences, feelings, and feminist theories; and talk about possibilities for action.[48]

"Experiences," "feelings," "relations," and "action" are, of course, the legitimate goals of feminist teaching, perpetually in contrast to the aims of the intractable patriarchy.

WHERE'S THE PATRIARCHY?

In late 2000, an important book was published by the Feminist Press. *The Politics of Women's Studies: Testimony from Thirty Founding Mothers,* edited by long-term feminist activist Florence Howe, is an invaluable source of information about the early years of Women's Studies in the United States. As Howe (who in 1970 co-founded the Feminist Press and stepped down as its director in 2000, having served in that capacity for thirty years), notes in her preface "Everyone a Heroine," the movement called Women's Studies "has altered the curriculum and the style of teaching and produced research that has shifted the paradigms and changed the content of most disciplines."[49]

In addition to its evocation of the exhilaration, passion, and tremendous effort that went into creating Women's Studies, the book provides a revealing portrait of the mental outlook and political purposes that drove these founders of Women's Studies programs at several dozen U.S. universities. It is filled with inspirational, even heroic, narratives that tell of individual commitment, struggle, and success in the building of forces and the discovery of allies dedicated to altering education. In a larger sense, it is also the story of a society undergoing an extraordinary process of change. Contrary to feminists who insist, absurdly, that modern-day universities have remained essentially patriarchal institutions, the stories in this book convey quite a different scene: an entire society on the move, which meant that feminist academics could often count on the active collaboration of well-placed male allies who stimulated institutional receptivity to feminist ideas.

The rapid growth of Women's Studies courses and programs raises questions not usually asked in feminist circles: Where was the much-maligned patriarchy while this unprecedented expansion and reconfiguration of the academy was occurring? Why was the patriarchy not defending its bastions?[50] How can one explain the ready help and willingness to change on the part of male administrators and colleagues described by one after another of the contributors to this volume? The remarkable fact is that feminists succeeded spectacularly. Within the first decade (1970–1980), approximately 350 Women's Studies programs—that is, about half of the currently existing ones—were set in place. There is no history in this book of concerted male resistance, no evidence of a generalized institutional rejection of the efforts of feminist faculty, students, and staff. On the contrary, what all this suggests is a society prepared for change and indeed embracing it, bolstered by legislation endorsed by the "patriarchal" government in Washington, D.C.

In fact, the "politics" announced by the book's title are rarely depicted by its authors, beyond their incantatory references to "patriarchy." Consider the testimony of Mariam K. Chamberlain, who has a Ph.D. in economics. By her own account, she had been unaware of discrimination against women until in 1970, at the age of fifty, she heard about it. At that point, she converted readily and thereafter played an important role in the financing of Women's Studies programs. A project officer at the Ford Foundation (and the sole non-academic represented in the Howe volume), Chamberlain tells us that, between 1971 and 1981 (when she left Ford), the foundation gave grants totaling over $9 million to support women's advancement, more than half of that amount going to Women's Studies programs. Not only does this reveal rapid and early support for Women's Studies, but, equally revealing, according to Chamberlain this largesse was criticized by non-academic feminists who did not have access to such grants.[51]

Although the thirty personal stories in Howe's book implicitly reveal the presence of this favorable climate, the contributors show little recognition of it and display considerable denial—some of it explicit. Instead, the narratives seek to convey struggle and effort—on a grand scale and against formidable and entrenched forces. Seldom is reference made to internal conflicts among female faculty members, or to the many women in academe, past and present, who wanted no involvement with Women's Studies. The chapters also tend to trivialize and gloss over serious intramural conflicts concerning the meaning of feminism. The one exception is the familiar complaint, which we hear a lot about, that Women's Studies was originally "white Women's Studies."

Of course some resistance and opposition to the rising tide of Women's Studies was present, and this prompts several writers to sarcastic descriptions of particular uncooperative administrators. What remains unacknowledged is the extent of support received from male allies, even as it is made obvious that without such allies in high places, feminists in a university world in which hostile males predominated would not have been able to carry the day. And carry the day they did.[52]

Most interestingly, the narrators' stories reveal the pedagogical assumptions and devices that drove Women's Studies from the beginning. These are described in chapter after chapter. Classes sit in a circle. (One professor, Mary Ann Ferguson, discovering feminism at the age of fifty-plus, describes herself in 1970 becoming "a peer" with her students as they formed their circle, regretting only that she wasn't young enough to sit on the floor.)[53] Teachers abdicate their authority. Collective teaching and collective governance structures are set in place, often involving students at all levels, office staff, and women from the "community." Political agreement is expected: All women are assumed to share the communitarian, anti-hierarchical, and pro-consultative convictions and understandings of good feminist politics. This is a hollow posture, however, since women with dissenting ideas (not socialists, say) are treated with no respect and are outside the supposedly democratically diverse academic body imagined by Women's Studies. Margaret Strobel, for example, describing the early program at the University of Illinois at Chicago, states: "Because membership was by invitation only, the Teaching Collective had a high degree of consensus regarding anti-imperialist and largely socialist feminist politics."[54]

Assumptions prevail about honoring experience, about the need for role models, about the imperative of intense study of one's own "position" and "identity." Attention to women of color is deemed obligatory on all. (More recently, this emphasis has been complemented by the study of "whiteness," which in practice means the confession and description of white racism.) Mea culpa attitudes about the presumptive racism of Women's Studies emerge throughout the Howe volume, even though most contributors' accounts of their own programs do not suggest that they excluded women of color in any way.[55]

The ongoing and to this day unvarying "line" on the issue of race within Women's Studies can be fairly gauged by the call for papers in advance of the National Women's Studies Association conference that took place in June 2001 in Minneapolis. This announcement, posted on the Women's Studies E-mail List on October 30, 2000, revealed the usual presuppositions:

> Seeking Abstracts for NWSA Panel on the experiences of women of color in Women's Studies:
> I'm organizing a panel for the National Women's Studies Association Conference (June 14–17, in Minneapolis), to discuss experiences of women of color in Women's Studies. What are the experiences of women of color in the academy, and particularly in WS? How does racism continue to operate, often in subtle and covert forms, in Women's Studies? How are

women of color excluded from and/or tokenized in Women's Studies depts, anthologies, classrooms, etc., and what strategies have you found most effective for challenging such practices? How are our experiences similar, and how might they differ (according to racial/ethnic identity; region; position; context; etc.)? You should feel free to address any aspect of this area (e.g., women of color faculty members; graduate and/or undergraduate students; job market and hiring practices; relationships to curriculum; classroom interactions; mentoring students; etc.). Please consider making use of nontraditional forms of presentation (for example, rather than—or in addition to—reading papers, my hope is that we can collaborate to provide examples and scenarios, and develop frameworks for "reading" the experiences of women of color in WS, to discuss strategies for change).[56]

What accusations of "racism" demonstrate, of course, is that power struggles go on not only between Women's Studies and the rest of the academy but also within Women's Studies itself, as women vie for position and status. But whichever story one tells, white women are always blamed, and no doubt it is partly in an effort to displace that blame that white women continue to repeatedly heap guilt onto the intractable "patriarchy," as if this were a monolithic structure and the academic world were its preeminent site.

Although contributors to the Howe volume describe the insecurity of being untenured, especially in a new field, no countervailing attention is given by these academics to the unusual circumstances that allowed women without Ph.D.s to enter into faculty positions, often bypassing normal academic search procedures, a move possible in this new "discipline" but not elsewhere. It is obvious that many women lacking completed Ph.D.s found Women's Studies programs a friendly and safe haven, and through these programs carved out academic careers for themselves. Nancy Porter, for example, tells us that, though she never finished her Ph.D., she received tenure anyway, having convinced her dean that publications and program development were equivalent to a terminal degree. She retired from Portland State University a full professor.[57]

Porter writes, understandably, as a passionate enthusiast of Women's Studies. She discusses the great things the Women's Studies classroom does for its students, such as make them reconsider their sexual orientation (she herself became a lesbian after her husband left her, she says). In Porter's description of it, the Women's Studies classroom is a place where anything goes: Personal stories of abuse by a boyfriend are as welcome as discussion of the "problematic" of a text.[58] This undiscriminating hospitality to virtually any and all personal subjects a student might wish to raise is characteristic of these "founding mothers"—and of the enterprise they founded. Such a conception—resting as it does on the widespread view of Women's Studies programs as rightly concerned with students' personal lives, as necessarily activist, as emphatically not "merely" intellectual or academic—is clearly articulated in all the chapters of Howe's volume. There is little discussion of any conflict between politics and education, or of the problem of harmonizing educational goals and political ones, or of the perils deeply inherent in the transformation of classrooms into therapeutic "safe spaces," or of what was and is sacrificed to these practices. It is clear that from the beginning these "mothers of Women's Studies" were setting out not only to change the curriculum, but also to change women's lives in the university and outside it. And while some of these aims are laudable, and in fact had broad general support, what made Women's Studies unusual as an academic program was the conviction that the classroom was to be a major weapon in this struggle.

Another example of Women's Studies' insistence, despite its extraordinary success in academe, on cultivating a fortress mentality may be seen in the 1997 *NWSA Backlash Report*, whose most striking feature is its hyperbolic title. Prepared by Diana Scully and Danielle M. Currier, the report summarizes the results of a 1995 survey of 276 Women's Studies programs, departments, and centers (representing 45 percent of the surveys they sent out). Although the survey reveals that there was little evidence of backlash (however loosely the term is defined), this does not prevent the authors from stigmatizing academia as "tradition-bound"—a charge that even a casual look at universities in America today ought easily to refute. The low figures reported for problems encountered should be taken as underrepresentations, the authors tell us. Still, 64 percent of Women's Studies administrators did not indicate any problems.[59]

Despite many pages on outside "instigators" against Women's Studies (in which the National Association of Scholars and the Center for Individual Rights are ludicrously categorized alongside the Ku Klux Klan and neo-Nazi groups as "conservative right organizations" whose goal is "to restore white, Western, male hegemony to the curriculum and to the academy"), the specifics cited by the authors of the *NWSA Backlash Report* tell a different story: Only 24 percent of the 36 percent of administrators reporting problems said they have been "very or somewhat damaged" by "instigators" (most problems having been caused by students or faculty members acting alone). In other words, of the total number of respondents to the survey, less than 9 percent claimed to have experienced problems caused by "instigators." The report ends with an invocation of "The Personal Is the Political," which, we are told, means that

> backlash is not just a personal problem, it is a collective problem that requires political action. What Women's Studies lacks is a collective offensive strategy that is the equivalent of the right wing movement so clearly arrayed against diversity and equality.[60]

Of course, the NWSA, the organization that published the report and that speaks for Women's Studies programs, is precisely such a collective enterprise, which sponsors a large annual meeting of Women's Studies people as well as many publications.

The *NWSA Backlash Report* also finds that a problem "unique" to Women's Studies is what it calls "harassment," especially in the form of "attempts to discredit feminist scholarship and Women's Studies teaching."[61] I will discuss this subject further in the next chapter. For now, it is sufficient to note that because Women's Studies advocates typically treat critics as reactionary enemies, it goes without saying that they are unlikely to grant that there may be good grounds for "discrediting" what passes for feminist scholarship and pedagogy. Increasingly, however, some critical voices have been raised from within Women's Studies circles, as teachers with good feminist credentials speak up.

DISSENTING VOICES

Howe's volume (which, incidentally, contains no contribution by a scientist), despite its triumphant tone, does present several essays by feminists who express one or another unorthodox idea. Inez Martinez, a professor of English at the City University of New York's Kingsborough Community College, criticizes the feminist teacher's self-effacement and posture of "no hierarchy" in her classroom. She recognizes that professors who pretend to know no more than their students cannot educate. She, too, however, ends her piece by celebrating women's activism and the gains made by convincing students how victimized women have been.[62]

A more unusual voice is that of Mimi Reisel Gladstein, an English professor and associate dean at the University of Texas at El Paso, who, as an Ayn Rand enthusiast, sees Rand as a positive model for women, even though Rand's opposition to collectivism and passionate pro-capitalism have made her anathema to most feminist academics. [63]

A very cautious critic is Marilyn Jacoby Boxer, retired from San Diego State University, whose endorsement of rigorous scholarship somehow survives alongside her continuing enthusiasm for Women's Studies. In her chapter in the Howe volume, Boxer incidentally reveals a telling detail: She was hired by San Diego State University (whose Women's Studies program had been instituted in

1970 as "the first integrated program of Women's Studies in the United States") as part of its "try-again" crew, after conflicts and problems led to—in her own words—"the mass resignation of its faculty in the face of a new dean's demand for regularized personnel proceedings" (apparently deemed undesirable by feminists).[64]

In many respects, however, Boxer's is a refreshing voice. She mentions the excellent advice she got from a colleague—advice that is the opposite of Women's Studies usual view, as she acknowledges—to "avoid cronyism" and to learn to separate personal relationships and professional needs. Boxer clearly affirms her belief in the "integrity of academic feminism"—that is, its scholarly integrity. If some feminist scholarship falls short, this, she says, is due to lapses in realization rather than in intention. Her own appraisal of Women's Studies is that it "constitutes an effort to devote women's intellect, fused variously with anger, compassion, and wisdom, to improving the world."[65] Such an idealized view is, however, not borne out by descriptions of actual programs, which, as we shall see later, regularly forget to mention "women's intellect" while focusing all their energies on their own versions of how the world should be "improved."

Most important for my purpose here is the fact that only one contributor to the Howe volume criticizes the key ideas and practices of Women's Studies. This is Nona Glazer, now retired, who was a professor of sociology at Portland State University. Glazer disagreed with many aspects of feminist pedagogy. An advocate of liberal education, she, by her own account, often went "against the grain of feminism." She disliked the drift of the program she cofounded at her university: the "vacuous psychologizing about men," the "whimpering," the "mixing psychobabble with social analysis," the tendency of many younger scholars simply to repeat earlier feminist work, and the hostility toward individually successful women. She deplores the antagonism to intellectual work she heard expressed at Women's Studies conferences. And she declares herself reluctant to see Women's Studies, with its separatism, "become permanent and institutionalized." Instead, she looks forward to a time when we can have "people's studies."[66] That sentiment puts her at odds with the many feminist faculty members worried that the feminist edge of Women's Studies might become dulled as some institutions rename their programs "gender studies."

Glazer is also the sole writer in this 400-page volume to question the feminist mantra of an "integrated analysis" of race, class, gender, and other group markers. ("I never worked through to my satisfaction how to talk or write cogently about gender, race, ethnicity, sexual orientation, and class simultaneously," she admits.) She suggests that this is why she sees Women's Studies as having limits as well as strengths.[67]

Still, Glazer explains that, having distanced herself from her own Women's Studies program, she invariably returned to support it in times of crisis. And, though she remains unhappy that feminism has not "produced an intellectual revolution" capable of completely transforming the curriculum, Glazer considers Women's Studies to have been responsible for her own survival.

Of course there are more critics than these few examples (taken from one book) suggest. But some dissenters—in particular if they are in early stages of their careers and still hoping to obtain employment in Women's Studies—are not willing to identify themselves as such publicly. In the year 2000, during one of the recurring episodes on the Women's Studies E-Mail List in which some messages I sent led to my being characterized as elitist, venal, and right-wing (a good example of what Graham Good describes as "the degeneration of disagreement"),[68] I received several private E-mail messages from women in academe. One was from a graduate student who wrote:

> I must admit that I have pretty much stayed in the closet with my concerns, as far as Women's Studies folks are concerned. As a grad student, and one who hopes to make a home in WS eventually, I don't feel I can risk showing exactly who I am. I just try to teach as well as I can and confine discussions with my fellow instructors and supervisor mostly to issues of pedagogical method rather than course intellectual content or

ideology. I have heard many comments, often while in meetings with all the people teaching [Introduction to Women's
Studies], that have clued me in that "all gender is culturally
constructed" is THE party line that "we all agree on." This is
the biggest area, I believe, where I diverge from the crowd.

Another message was from a teacher of Women's Studies at a state
university. She wrote:

I am still being confronted and challenged by some peers and
some students for not being radical enough (I never discuss
my personal feminist positions because I expect the students
to develop their own understanding of what feminism is, as
well as the ability to articulate and defend their thinking
about it), . . . and of being compromised somehow, because I
have men in my classes and even allow them to speak, which
seems to be a mortal sin. I am so utterly tired of having to defend myself as a "true" feminist, and I'm weary of the battle
from both students and peers, the latter of whom should
know better!
     . . . So, this is the part where I have had difficulty—imag-
ining how to bring about positive changes in the curriculum
of Women's Studies so that it isn't political grandstanding or
propagandizing, so that it is academically based and not a
mini consciousness-raising group, or something that bums
the students out and overwhelms them with an oppressive
sense of dread about sexism. Right now, I am feeling that I
don't really know what Women's Studies is actually about
anymore—and no one here seems to know either (except, of
course, those who want it to be a tool of the gender revolution!). . . . This is a very ill-defined discipline that resembles
a religion more than an academic endeavor. I try to keep it
academic, critical, interesting, intellectual, but the pull is toward convincing students that feminism is something they
should embrace—it's in the core of all the readings, no mat-

ter the overt topic. I can't find an unbiased reader, that actually just presents issues and challenges the students to think critically about them, forcing them to come to their own conclusions. . . . And, I think there are taboo topics in feminist discourse that need to be addressed and thought about for feminism to become real again.

Later, in a more optimistic mood, she wrote again:

My students give me more hope than anything lately that there is hope for feminism. Rather than sneering at them for their belief that they are equal to men—they all enter the class believing this, by the way—I am meeting them right there, RIGHT there, and saying, "you GO girls, but you can't stop there." More than ever, I see how the victim-feminist wallowing of the past decade and a half crushes the spirit and disempowers young women.

A literature professor, the author of several books on women writers, also wrote to me:

I, too, for many years dismissed criticisms of the current feminist movement as right-wing distortions focusing on extremist views. For the past 2–3 years, however, I have become more and more aware that the "extremists" now represent the dominant feminist ideology in academe, and I have become more and more reluctant to associate myself with such views by calling myself a feminist. I wonder if you know of any liberal feminist organization for academic women? I think we need one!

Among younger feminist academics, including those who consider themselves part of the "Third Wave," criticism of feminist orthodoxies is occasionally openly heard. Thus, for example, Joanne Detore-Nakamura, professor at Embry-Riddle Aeronautical University in Florida, in an essay entitled "Why Feminist Isn't Feminist

Enough" states: "In many quarters, despite our best intentions, the feminist movement has become what members hated to begin with—the establishment that censored and silenced differing viewpoints."[69]

Senior scholars, too, are beginning to openly express their dissatisfaction. An important dissenting voice was heard publicly in the Summer 2000 issue of *Signs*, devoted to dozens of essays on feminism and the academy. In a brief piece entitled "Feminism's Perverse Effects," the well-known lesbian critic Elaine Marks, who until her death in late 2001 was the Germaine Brée Professor of French and Women's Studies at the University of Wisconsin, Madison, and a former president of the Modern Language Association of America, complained that she was beginning to feel "isolated in Women's Studies" where she had come to be perceived as "a closet conservative." Why? Because she deplored the prevalence of identity politics, manifest in the habit of reading literature "uniquely for signs of racism, sexism, anti-Semitism, uniquely as a document that reveals underlying discursive and cultural assumptions and presuppositions."[70]

Most shockingly, perhaps, Marks applauded Harold Bloom and other critics with whom she now agreed that "to read in the service of any ideology is not, in my judgment, to read at all." As an example, she described a Women's Studies course she had taught in which white students expressed anger toward Zora Neale Hurston, and toward Professor Marks herself, because Hurston's narrative did not focus on her oppression as a black woman. Marks, at the end of her life, was sufficiently fed up to affirm that the problem is not merely students' scant experience as readers (which makes them unable to recognize echoes of, or references to, other texts in their readings). It is also their bad reading habits, which

> are often supported by ideological positions that students, in some of their classes, are taught to look for in all the texts they read. If the students do not find evidence of racism, sexism, or anti-Semitism, they tend to assume that either the writer or the teacher is guilty of a cover-up.

Marks confessed that she herself used to have similarly politically correct responses. But she was no longer comfortable with them. Hence her decision to go public with some of what she considered to be "the perverse effects of and caveats for feminism at the millennium."

"It is no simple matter," Marks concluded, "in this millennial fin de siècle, to criticize certain tendencies in cultural studies or Women's Studies or ethnic studies without being accused of participating in a conservative political agenda."[71] And she is right. In the topsy-turvy world of feminism and "multiculturalism," to call for an education not simplistically bound to a political agenda *is* tantamount to being "conservative." Furthermore, the observation that "conservative" has become a label of instant dismissal in academe is in itself an example of the current ideological rigidity in the one arena that was supposed to fearlessly and openly explore ideas and knowledge claims. The fact that Marks's criticisms were published in *Signs* will no doubt be used by Women's Studies advocates as evidence of their field's broad tolerance and lack of orthodoxies. But that, of course, would be to disregard the substance of her essay.[72]

Not to be overlooked among significant internal critics of Women's Studies is the sociologist Joan Mandle, author of *Can We Wear Our Pearls and Still Be Feminists? Memoirs of a Campus Struggle,* published in 2000.[73] For six years (1991–97), Mandle was director of the Women's Studies program at Colgate University. A "founding mother" of Sociologists for Women in Society in 1972, Mandle arrived at Colgate with a background in civil-rights and New Left activism. Unafraid of leadership and responsibility, unapologetic about using "I" instead of the politically preferred collectivist "we," critical of the "consensus'" model that she knew could paralyze an organization, impatient with the constant appeals to "community" and "support," she was bound to arouse hostility. She was also enormously successful in making Women's Studies a major presence at Colgate. When ideological purity is the name of the game, however, academic success doesn't count for much. Thus it comes as no surprise to learn that, after six years as director of

Women's Studies, Mandle was replaced, without notice, while on an extended leave.

What were her sins? Rejecting the proposition that separatist "safe spaces" and therapeutic classrooms are legitimate academic goals. Believing that Women's Studies should reach out to members of sororities, even to men, to all parts of the university without restriction. Refusing to see women as fragile and oppressed at Colgate. Above all, insisting on high academic standards and exhibiting a low tolerance for feminist orthodoxies.

Mandle's book is the first full account by a long-term director of a Women's Studies program who, while supporting a non-doctrinaire political agenda for Women's Studies, has substantial criticisms to make of it as an academic enterprise. The significance of her memoir lies in its presentation of a more accurate, less idealized version than the vast majority of narratives of the sorts of struggles that have—and continue to—beset Women's Studies programs. Such struggles are not so much against grudging outsiders (as Howe's volume suggests) as among women for whom the overriding bone of contention has often been the question: What sort of feminists are we?

In an amusing and revealing anecdote on this subject, Mandle describes what happened when, in the mid-1990s, some Women's Studies students from Colgate University attended a conference on global feminism at the State University of New York at New Paltz. Staying with local Women's Studies students, the Colgate women found themselves talked down to by the more assertive SUNY feminists, who fined them (as they did one another) 25 cents for every politically incorrect word uttered, words like "guy," "history," and "straight" (as in giving directions—"just go straight," which carried a three-word, 75-cent fine). Many of the Colgate students were intimidated, but also impressed; some had never met radical lesbians before. Their own feminism seemed pale by comparison. Colgate, they feared, was "not feminist enough." Mandle aptly labels this episode "the punks versus the preppies."[74]

On a more serious note, Mandle's narrative weaves a troubling story of how the self-created marginalization and isolation of some

Women's Studies scholars have served to affirm their identity as "real" feminists and made them fiercely resentful of any encroachment on their turf. Sharing with most feminists the belief that the disadvantages suffered by women justified a separate Women's Studies program, Mandle worked hard to build the program, while urging students to develop the organizational skills they would need to go out and change the world. But that was not enough to salvage her position, as battles raged over who "owned" Women's Studies. Pursuing her vision of Women's Studies, Mandle took on the Women's Resource Center, run by work-study students who did little work and no outreach and had instead formed themselves into a small clique that was not welcoming to others. She incorporated this outfit into a new Center for Women's Studies, whose mission was to be primarily academic. She was also critical of a feminist "theme" dormitory whose ever-dwindling number of residents saw themselves as the only true feminists.

Not that Mandle was alone in observing dissension among women over Women's Studies and its role. Her account of conversations with other Women's Studies directors (in particular, at the 1998 meeting of the National Women's Studies Association in Tempe, Arizona, where a number of women acknowledged the internal difficulties besetting their programs) confirms the frequency of internal discord. But what set Mandle apart from her colleagues was not so much her concerns as her willingness to go public with them. In her book, she defies the accepted adage that to write about problems in Women's Studies is merely to air dirty linen in public and thereby aid Women's Studies' enemies and the "Right."[75]

Most of the conflicts Mandle discusses in her book concerned one essential question: Is Women's Studies an integral part of academe, or should it embrace permanent outsider status? That was and continues to be far from an abstract matter. It raises such concrete problems as: Must Women's Studies adhere to the same standards and goals as the rest of the university (which involve it in competition for excellence)? Or should it create a noncompetitive alternative for women, a different world in which the key values are promoting a sense of community and providing a nurturing environment? These issues are still being argued over—and how one comes down on such questions often reveals a lot about who are considered to be the "real" feminists and who fail the test. At Colgate, after Mandle's ouster, these matters were resolved by the program's rapid reversion to what it had been before her arrival.

As Mandle observes, it's one thing for young female students to be caught up in heated debates over identity and legitimacy, but quite another for female faculty members, supposedly wiser and more knowledgeable, to be forever embroiled in them.[76] There's more than a touch of immaturity to be found in students and faculty members reinforcing in each other a perpetually combative understanding of feminist identity that, on the one hand, wallows in self-pity and vastly exaggerated perceptions of victimhood and, on the other, makes grandiose claims to be creating a new and better world.

Joan Mandle in fact shares most advocates' view of what justified Women's Studies to begin with: the twin historical facts that women have been understudied in the past and that they have been and still are disadvantaged in significant ways in most societies. As noted earlier, she even thinks these two facts warranted separate Women's Studies programs initially. And she believes in the importance of training students to participate in political activism, an essential part of citizenship in her view.

How could such a person come to be ousted from a leadership position in Women's Studies? Obviously, Mandle's commitment to activism on behalf of women was not the right sort of politics. She did not want to dictate the content of feminist political beliefs or the specific direction of activism. She wanted the Women's Studies center to be welcoming even to women wearing high-heeled shoes. She discouraged the atmosphere of exclusivity and the excessive focus on victimization. And it seems that this heterodoxy, in conjunction with her deviation from the therapeutic focus, from the rhetoric of safety and support so common in Women's Studies, and from the insistence on sexuality as a predominant concern, made her unacceptable to some Women's Studies students and to influential feminist faculty.

There's an important lesson in her experience, but I believe Mandle draws a different one from it than I do. What I see is that precisely because political positions can lead to irreconcilable and passionate conflict, the tendency for politicized programs to move from education to indoctrination (which will suppress dissent and promote a sort of unity, or at the very least conformity) is entirely predictable, and the deplorable outcome inevitable. But an educational endeavor that defined itself from its outset as the "academic arm" of a political program will, of course, not be able to avoid such a degeneration.

RECRUITING ADHERENTS

Is there any evidence that Women's Studies as practiced at most universities may be turning to a more intellectual and scholarly focus? One helpful way to assess the current aims of Women's Studies programs is to look at their own mission statements and job descriptions. Judging by their websites, far from even pretending to be engaged above all in the cause of education and learning, many programs seem these days to feel so well-entrenched that they make no bones about the fact that their commitment to feminist activism is *a*, and often *the*, core purpose of their offerings. Thus, again and again one finds in these descriptions the seamless move from "Women's Studies" to "feminism" and from the untiring stress on oppression to the need for political activism to combat it.

Women's Studies websites typically begin with a few paragraphs on "What Is Women's Studies?" At William Paterson University of New Jersey (home of Paula Rothenberg, who has edited volumes of readings that are widely used throughout the country in Women's Studies and "multicultural" courses and whom we will encounter again later in this chapter), we are told that Women's Studies

is an interdisciplinary approach to university study which prepares students to critique power structures relating to sex, sexuality, race, class, age, abilities, belief systems, and other societal institutions. Women's Studies has been defined by the founders of the National Women's Studies Association as an "educational strategy for change with a double purpose: to expose and redress the oppression of women. Women's Studies is the intellectual and research arm of the women's movement."[77]

As if this weren't clear enough, the description goes on to state: "Women's Studies, however, is more than traditionally academic; it is also committed to activism, connecting theory with practice. Hence, Women's Studies students have options to include community work as part of their degree program."

At the University of North Carolina at Chapel Hill, the Women's Studies website begins with the following mission statement:

> The goal of the Curriculum in Women's Studies is to transform the University of North Carolina at Chapel Hill into an institution that takes full account of the perspectives, needs, and interests of women in every dimension of its activities. As a discipline, Women's Studies critiques the traditional curriculum that reflects the biases of white, middle class men and ignores the experiences of other races, other classes, and of women. It offers a methodology that is interdisciplinary, multicultural, and feminist.

In other words, the university is perceived as an inhospitable place for women and other oppressed groups and must be "transformed." One might assume that women at UNC are as aware as everyone else in the country of the enormous gains women and girls have made in education in the past few decades, which have completely altered the lives and prospects of women in the United States. Yet the mission statement rests on an obviously false premise for the sake of presenting a justification for an explicit political agenda.

Here is the University of Arizona at Tucson's Women's Studies website statement:

The Department of Women's Studies at The University of Arizona promotes and supports teaching, research, and outreach. Women's Studies works to contest the historical, ongoing, and pervasive gender-based oppressions within society by evolving a forum for interdisciplinary work. As such, Women's Studies includes but is not limited to: feminist approaches to all possible areas of scholarly investigation; the study of the constitution of women's lives in diverse social contexts; critiques of feminisms; the exploration of women's movements; and the study of the inextricably interconnected processes by which social formations such as gender, race, class, sexuality, and nation are constructed.

Statements like this one sound both grandiose and foolish. Would anyone take seriously a history program that proclaimed its aim to "contest" oppression(s) around the world? And as for "critiques of feminisms," in Women's Studies circles this usually refers merely to competing feminisms (often "theorized" by modifying the word "feminism" through the addition of an adjective such as liberal, radical, socialist, or marxist).

At the University of Massachusetts Amherst, the website announces that the Women's Studies program

is dedicated to the study of women and gender. Gender is the idea of difference between the sexes, and all the assumptions and stereotypes and expectations that accompany these ideas. We look at women and gender issues around the world, but since gender alone does not give a full understanding to women's lives, we consider other factors such as race, class, culture and sexuality. We combine these tools and areas of interest into what we call an "integrative analysis." Our objective is to introduce students to analytical tools and basic approaches to the study of women in a variety of fields.

This belabored description, with its sloppy definition of gender as "the idea of difference between the sexes," is typical of the current emphasis on an "integrated analysis." Judging by similar program and course descriptions all over the country, this integrated analysis amounts to little more than covering all the major identity groups and the -isms to which they are subjected, which, in an endless reiteration, are invoked in program after program and course after course.

Some programs, to be sure, do sound more properly academic— though of course one cannot tell from the mission statements what is actually taught. Still, it is heartening that they evidently do not feel comfortable simply declaring their political objectives. Here, for example, is Princeton's statement:

> The Program in the Study of Women and Gender provides a forum for intellectual exchange on issues of gender relations and sexual politics. Since its establishment in 1981, the program has offered a variety of courses, lectures, exhibitions, and research opportunities relating to questions of gender, sexuality, and society. We seek to encourage open discussion and lively debate among faculty members, undergraduates, and graduate students from all fields of study.

But actual course descriptions at Princeton, as elsewhere, tend to cover the familiar old ground. Thus, a course entitled "Introduction to the Study of Gender" (WOM 201) is described as follows:

> In this course, co-taught by faculty members from different departments, students encounter a variety of primary materials and scholarly methods to obtain a broad picture of the scope and significance of issues associated with the analysis of sexuality and gender. Such a perspective will challenge conventional understandings of psychology, social organization, cultural production, and political participation.

In other words, the same extravagant but by now hollow-sounding claims to be "challenging" all prior knowledge.

It is possible, of course, that these mission statements and descriptions should be taken with a grain of salt, as perhaps idealized or boilerplate versions of what these programs might aspire to, were they in no way constrained by academic standards. But what do we find when we turn to job ads for positions in Women's Studies? A few recent ads, from east to west, should either correct or confirm the impression advanced by the mission statements above.

A position at the University of Southern Maine is advertised as follows:

> The Women's Studies Program . . . invites applications for a one-year fixed length appointment beginning September 1, 2001. Rank is open. Qualifications are a Ph.D. and evidence of excellence in teaching and scholarship. Publications in the field are desirable. We are particularly interested in candidates with a humanities background with expertise in feminist theory and a focus on the experience of women of color and women in global perspectives. The candidate will teach Introduction to Women's Studies and Contemporary Feminist Theories, and will develop and teach courses in areas of specialization, such as immigration, post-colonial theory, globalization, religious studies, cultural studies, and the historical construction of race, gender, and sexuality.[78]

Here is an ad for a position as assistant or associate professor of Women's Studies at Plattsburgh State University of New York:

> Qualifications: Ph.D. in Women's Studies or related area; three years of teaching experience in Women's Studies or related area; record of excellence in teaching; demonstrated administrative and leadership abilities; established, ongoing research agenda; commitment to undergraduate education.

> Responsibilities: Teach already existing courses and develop new ones, depending on area of expertise. The program offers courses in feminist theory and activism, lesbian and gay studies, women

of color in U.S. society, women and popular culture, global perspectives on women's issues, and women and the law.[79]

Another ad, for a tenured professor in "Women's Studies/Black World Studies" at Miami University, Ohio, states:

Seeking candidates with expertise in black feminist/womanist perspectives and knowledgeable in theories which foreground the interactions among race/ethnicity, gender, class and sexuality. . . . Successful candidate will have an excellent record of scholarly productivity and teaching, and must demonstrate a strong commitment to participation in interdisciplinary and collaborative Women's Studies and Black World Studies Programs.[80]

A well-known Women's Studies program, at Minnesota State University, Mankato, in late 2001 advertised a tenure-track position as follows:

The successful candidate will teach general education classes, courses in the undergraduate major, and graduate courses. These include: collective action, feminist pedagogy, feminist theory, research methods, and topical capstone seminars (open specialization). Interdisciplinary, multicultural and international perspectives must be included in teaching. . . .

Based in the College of Social and Behavioral Sciences, the Women's Studies department combines core courses in theory and methodology with interdisciplinary courses and internships in a comprehensive program which is expressly feminist and oriented toward training activists.[81]

And, finally, an early 2002 example from the West Coast:

The Department of Women's Studies at San Diego State University invites applications for a tenure-track position at the rank of Assistant Professor. We seek to strengthen our offerings in the following areas:

- Social Construction of Identity and Body including issues surrounding identity, self-concept, and the body; also, social policy areas such as reproductive issues, aging, mental health, disability, or body image.
- Policy/Law including issues surrounding social activism and public policy, especially in legal studies, immigration, and international parliamentary processes; also public policy areas such as welfare, violence, the sex trade, and other substantive debates in the public arena.
- Science and Technology including history of women/gender in science in relation to access and representation, environmental issues, and technological change; also, epistemology and the critique of dominant scientific models.

The successful candidate will have a Ph.D., Women's Studies preferred, with a minimum of a graduate minor or concentration in Women's Studies required.[82]

The above examples of Women's Studies mission statements and job ads fairly represent the "field" of Women's Studies as described in its own words. They highlight the enormous reach to which it lays claim: all disciplines, all research methodologies, all oppressed groups, all objectionable -isms. Women's studies, in short, seriously aspires to—and seems to believe it can—explain everything, using any and all available means that serve its ideological purposes.

Competence in "feminist theory," in particular (which one feminist scholar has admitted is actually a strategy, an "intervention with definite political . . . aims . . ., intellectual guerrilla warfare"),[83] has become a sine qua non for anyone seeking a position in Women's Studies, though in its more arcane manifestations it often arouses criticism from more practically oriented feminists. As Barrie Thorne, professor of sociology and of Women's Studies at Berkeley, wrote in an essay published in 2000, entitled "A Telling Time for Women's Studies":

> Feminist theory, the most valued academic currency of Women's Studies, has come to signify our shared intellectual life, our claims to legitimacy as a distinctive academic field, and our hierarchies of knowledge. The troubling split between reified theory and other types of feminist knowledge should be more closely scrutinized.[84]

Thorne surveys the enormous successes of Women's Studies, but notes that some fields, such as economics, linguistics, and philosophy, "have been relatively impermeable to feminist insights." This she blames on "congealed" divisions of knowledge, "continuing power of the disciplines" and the devaluing of "interdisciplinary work and also of women and ethnic minorities." On the same page, revealingly, Thorne acknowledges that "we don't even know what interdisciplinarity is"—but affirms that she is exhilarated by it nonetheless and considers it essential for the "ovulars" she has taught since the late 1980s.

The extent to which heady combinations of political and pedagogical aims can warp a scholar's mind is revealed in a memoir published in 2000 by one of the nation's foremost advocates of curricular reform along the lines of race, class, and gender. As an example of the stranglehold this ideology exercises when it is applied unstintingly to an entire human life in virtually all its aspects, one can hardly do better than to cite Paula Rothenberg's recent book *Invisible Privilege: A Memoir about Race, Class, and Gender*. Adopting an attitude of public self-criticism for the "invisible privilege" she enjoyed in the first two areas, contrasted with the lack of privilege she experienced as a woman, Rothenberg has not written a memoir in the conventional sense. Rather, her account is of a life re-scripted, which produces a narrative locked into the grid of race, class, and gender.

Beginning with the very first line—"As the first and, for a while, only child of upper-middle-class, Orthodox Jewish parents growing up in New York City, race and class privilege came easily to me, but it was gender that was always problematic"[85]—we see that race and class will count as plusses to be apologized for, while gender will allow a claim to victimhood throughout this story. And, already on the very next page, we shift seamlessly from Rothenberg's birth and family structure to general comments about female infanticide around the world. Such an approach gives the book a tendentious and apodictic tone, and no doubt makes it eminently useful for Women's Studies courses, which ram home the message incessantly.

Rothenberg tells us, at the outset, that she has spent most of her life attempting to understand the "intersections of race, class, and gender privilege as they have shaped my life and the lives of others." She must be gratified, now, to see this attempt officially written into a large number of Women's Studies courses, and indeed into the general education requirements at many universities. Unlike Nona Glazer, with her confession of confusion about the meaning of an "integrated analysis," Rothenberg believes this "intersection" to be an unfailing intellectual and political tool.

What emerges from Rothenberg's account is a world in which only group identity counts, and individuals, even her own parents, are of interest merely as exemplars of particular identities. This memoir, in fact, lacks humanity. It sees types and categories, not individuals, and few episodes fail to be accompanied by a moralizing bottom line. This culminates in the book's epilogue, in which Rothenberg depicts the deaths of her ailing parents—treated and mistreated by nurse's aides and hired help. Rothenberg uses these episodes as occasions for final comments about race, class, and gender.

The preeminent interest of Rothenberg's memoir, however, lies in its exposé of her views on education, views that, given her high status in educational circles, we would do well to heed. Coming from someone of such prominence, her blatantly anti-intellectual ideas are nothing less than shocking.

Consider Rothenberg's description of what she learned in her high-school English class decades ago. Students read *Beowulf* and Chaucer, were encouraged to imitate their style, and— and this is what Rothenberg most disapproves of—were required to end their book reports with

> a mandatory discussion of the universal themes in the work. In this way, we came to understand that novels and short stories about the trials and tribulations of well-to-do, white men were universal and timeless. In this way, we came to own [*sic*] Ernest Hemingway, Herman Melville, Samuel Butler, William Shakespeare, and a host of other similarly situated [*sic*] writers and adopt their Eurocentric and privileged male view of life and the world as though it were coextensive with reality.[86]

It is hard to imagine a more powerful indictment of Rothenberg's ideas about education and the curriculum than this revealing statement. Whatever the limitations of Rothenberg's education, surely they cannot begin to match the absurdity of her lumping the above-named writers together as "well-to-do, white men," presenting, across the centuries, a uniform "Eurocentric and privileged male view of life and the world." And how ironic that the director of the "New Jersey Project on Inclusive Scholarship, Curriculum, and Teaching" should display so dismissive an attitude toward such a varied group of writers, who in fact wrote such multifaceted works. Is this an example of the sophisticated thinking that lies behind the analysis of the "intersections of race, class, and gender" that undergirds so much contemporary feminist pedagogy?

Presumably Rothenberg did not hold such a narrow perspective when she was in high school. But her drastic re-scripting of old experiences is perhaps inevitable when a new framework imposes itself so violently on one's awareness. In describing herself as a young philosophy teacher, she writes: "I had not yet begun to understand the ways in which the scholarship produced by disciplines as traditionally defined reflected a narrowly male and privileged point of view that was then treated as universal."[87]

To the small extent that this view—axiomatic these days in Women's Studies programs and beyond—has some validity, it would require of its proponents a detailed and differentiated discussion of each field. But Rothenberg, once she made this discovery, did not hesitate to apply it wholesale to all her own teaching. In a revealing illustration of her current educational practice, she describes an episode in which her black students in an introductory philosophy class confessed to her that they could make no sense out of Descartes's *Cogito*. This, she says, "proved to be another turning point in my intellectual life," leading her "to operate from the premise that their [the students'] discomfort was a sign of Descartes's inadequacy," rather than of the students' own shortcomings or inexperience. How to deal with the problem? By telling the students about Descartes's life and personal circumstances, about the "privilege" and "very poor eyesight" that are inevitably reflected in his worldview, about his habit of "staying in bed to 'meditate'" while servants cleaned the floor. "I did this not to dismiss Descartes but to help my students understand that ideas are the products of material reality as well as intellectual engagement"—all of which she construes as presenting ideas to her students "in ways that empowered them." Happily, Rothenberg reassures us that this doesn't mean she taught Descartes, in her words, "as a capitalist running dog"—a reassurance we in fact need after reading these comments:

> The issue is whose "reality" is validated by making Descartes the father of modern philosophy and allowing his questions and, worse yet, his attempts at answers [to] frame the issues for the modern period. By constructing a curriculum—worse yet, a culture—around such an idiosyncratic worldview and then calling it knowledge, we have privileged the distorted perspective of an infinitesimal fraction of the world's population.[88]

Nowhere in Women's Studies' embrace of this sort of application of identity politics is there any sign of recognition of twentieth-century history, which is replete with similar judgments that have disfigured educational, intellectual, and artistic pursuits—and ultimately political life. It is worrying that the feminist literature chooses to ignore notorious predecessors who sound embarrassingly like contemporary feminist and postmodernist critics.[89]

Moreover, to condescend to students, as Rothenberg evidently did to her philosophy class, is to do them a grave disservice. The goal of the university is not to reinforce students' belief that the things they do not know or do not readily understand are frauds not worth bothering about. Yet Women's Studies has too often adopted this latter attitude. Some years ago, when I was still in Women's Studies, a colleague—one of those who had moved up from a staff to a faculty position without having had to go through the usual search process—expressed to me her exhilaration that "we're all starting from zero," that is, that no one's training and knowledge counted for anything because feminism was overturning it all. In the same way, Rothenberg, with her dismissive comments about Descartes, whatever she was doing, was emphatically not teaching her students about philosophy but reaffirming their hunch that they could get along just fine without it.

In recounting her own experiences while doing graduate work with Sidney Hook, Rothenberg states: "As every graduate student knows, the point of writing a dissertation is to earn a degree, not necessarily to say anything that is personally meaningful."[90] The trivial sense in which this statement is true does not obscure the deep cynicism it expresses. Surely a more—dare I say?—objective perspective would reveal that a dissertation is a young scholar's first piece of sustained research, in many instances serving to set that scholar on a lifelong path of intellectual discovery. Perhaps it is because she lacked such a perspective that Rothenberg never completed her Ph.D. Fortunately, she teaches at a university that has no graduate program in philosophy or Women's Studies. But it is small comfort to realize that she has found her niche in politically motivated curricular reform.

To anticipate the objection that Rothenberg is merely one extreme case, in no way indicative of Women's Studies' typical concerns, I turn once again to recent publications on feminist pedagogy.

In 1999, Maralee Mayberry and Ellen Cronan Rose edited a book entitled *Meeting the Challenge: Innovative Feminist Pedagogies in Action*. Among the sixteen essays in this volume, an unquestioned commitment to feminist indoctrination in the classroom is the norm. Some, to be sure, recommend subtlety in achieving this aim. Thus, Sandra Bell, Marina Morrow, and Evangelia Tastsoglou, in their essay "Teaching in Environments of Resistance: Toward a Critical, Feminist, and Antiracist Pedagogy," urge the feminist teacher to refrain "from claims of false consciousness." They advocate a "critical, feminist, and antiracist pedagogical practice,"[91] and they label as "right-wing backlash" the defense of liberal education expressed by critics such as John Fekete, Christina Hoff Sommers, Noretta Koertge, and myself.

Beginning on a reasonable note—as teachers we should "refrain from imposing meaning on our students' experiences"—they go on nonetheless to urge instructors to lead their students "to understand how their experiences are shaped socially." They reflect on "moments" of difficulty in their classrooms "in order to identify the specific factors that undermined our attempts to implement progressive pedagogies," endeavoring to learn from their students' reactions how they might go on with the "struggle toward implementing progressive pedagogical visions."[92]

Another essay, by Jane Rinehart, is even more forthright. She urges Women's Studies faculty and administrators

> to be nimble, shrewd, and creative. What do I mean by that? I think the project of bringing feminism into institutions of higher education is not an all-or-nothing venture. It is more like infiltration and subversion than overt attack. It is disingenuous for us to pretend that we do not want to be at the tables where decisions are made and budgets drawn up.[93]

While admitting that for people like herself, "Women's Studies definitely seemed to be a radical project with potential to change everything in the university and society," Rinehart concedes that, in the face of challenges and incomprehension from other faculty members, "sometimes it is better to leave out the radical impact version of what we are doing in Women's Studies and focus instead on addressing practical concerns about how Women's Studies can make a positive difference in the 'bottom line.'" She advocates making tactical choices such as representing Women's Studies as "a sound investment"—using the sort of language administrators and trustees "find impressive." Women's Studies, she reminds us, "is the academic side of feminism and strives to be connected with its activist side. Both sides are committed to social justice through the elimination of social inequalities between men and women and among women."

In the course of a long discussion of the use of internships as a strategy, Rinehart argues that it is important for Women's Studies not to be separatist, in order to avoid marginalization and trivialization. "Women's Studies educators want both a place at the table and the opportunity to criticize the guest list, place settings, decorations, etiquette, and menu. We are both eager and impertinent dinner partners." Far from being sheep, she states, we want rather to be "wily wolves alert to opportunities for making our way across unfriendly territory." Because administrators and colleagues outside Women's Studies "may not accept the activist orientation of Women's Studies, its desire to turn theories into actions to change cultures and societies," it is more effective for activism to be pursued within the framework of internships, thus reducing "criticism of Women's Studies as insufficiently academic and overly politicized by associating it instead with practical preparation for life after graduation."[94] Although Rinehart worries about whether wolves might become sheep in the process, she thinks it is a risk worth taking.

Annis Hopkins, in her essay "Women's Studies on Television?" agrees that lectures are "authoritarian," but defends them on practical grounds for distance-learning. Motivation, she writes, matters more than method (evidently feminist motivation can make up for "authoritarian" pedagogies). She emphasizes the effectiveness of having guest speakers tell their own stories: "Guests' personal narratives help students to confront oppression as real, not theoretical, as lived, not imagined."[95]

There is surprisingly little to distinguish current feminist rhetoric on the subject of teaching from the essential elements of feminist pedagogy outlined in the 1970s and 1980s, many of which drew on the early twentieth-century Progressive Education movement spearheaded by John Dewey.[96] One can go back to, say, a 1985 essay by Susan Stanford Friedman, which listed as key elements: "non-hierarchical classroom; validation and integration of the personal; commitment to changing students' attitudes toward women, most particularly women's images of themselves and their potential; recognition that no education is value free and that our field operates out of a feminist paradigm (as opposed to the patriarchal paradigm of most classrooms)."[97]

Vehemence in enunciating the tenets of feminist pedagogy was already evident, for example, in Paula Rothenberg's 1988 article "Integrating the Study of Race, Gender, and Class: Some Preliminary Observations," still relevant enough to be reprinted, ten years later, in the volume *The Feminist Teacher Anthology: Pedagogies and Classroom Strategies*. Rothenberg wrote:

> Many of the students I teach . . . are victims of the American dream/Myth of Success. They believe that ability, hard work, and good intentions will be rewarded, that anything is possible. They tell me that they think of themselves as persons or human beings, not women or men, Blacks or whites. And they are often puzzled and angered by my insistence on noticing race, class, and gender differences. They are embarrassed by my inability to look beyond these identifications and even tell me that noticing that someone is Black is itself racist.[98]

Rothenberg's mission, then as now, was to move students "beyond prejudice" to "power." How could she do this? By biting the bullet: "An important task, then, is to persuade students that racism and sexism are powerful forces in today's society." But, alas, the majority of students, then as now, "continue to resist dealing with issues of race, class, and gender as long as those issues are raised in a few isolated courses. Who can blame them?" Rothenberg knows the solution: "Until this content is integrated into the entire curriculum, students will continue to view it as the peculiar concern of a small group of faculty."[99] And such a large-scale integration is precisely what Rothenberg has been doing, as director of the New Jersey Project, the first statewide and state-funded effort to transform the curriculum at all of the state's two- and four-year public and private colleges and universities. We shall see in the next chapter what sorts of strategies feminists are promoting in pursuit of their objective of integrating feminist ideas throughout the "entire curriculum."

Let me offer one final, up-to-the-minute example of feminist pedagogy, from Berenice Malka Fisher's *No Angel in the Classroom* (2001), mentioned earlier in this chapter. Fisher, who is a professor of educational philosophy at New York University, categorically announces the purpose of feminist teaching, which is "to understand women's oppression and promote women's liberation." Having graduated from her earlier years of teaching "as a heterosexual woman fleeing from the domestic fate of the white middle-class women of my generation," she now defines herself as "a lesbian teacher of Women's Studies"—or, as she also puts it later in her book, "a feminist teacher who advocates action." Fisher makes clear what she is writing against: "Classroom discussion divorced from [social] movements ends up serving the dominant educational goal of individual development"—evidently a deplorable thing. Like Rothenberg, Fisher too underwent a process of re-education. In her case, this led not to an unmasking of Descartes but rather to her ability to see Socrates less as a culture hero and more, she says in all seriousness, as an "intellectual batterer."[100]

Feminist pedagogues such as these routinely ignore the contributions of critics—even self-defined feminists—who dispute their pet contentions. One such critic (indispensable reading for every feminist who claims to be a scholar) is philosopher Susan Haack, whose recent book *Manifesto of a Passionate Moderate: Unfashionable Essays* (1998) is filled with challenges to the notion that a "feminist" perspective strengthens intellectual work. To Haack, "the politicization of inquiry, . . . whether in the interests of good political values or bad, is always epistemologically unsound."[101] Haack also points out that "the rubric 'feminist epistemology' is incongruous on its face, in somewhat the way of, say, 'Republican epistemology.'"[102] She explains:

> The profusion of incompatible themes proposed as "feminist epistemology" itself speaks against the ideas of a distinctively female cognitive style. But even if there were such a thing, the case for feminist epistemology would require further argument to show that women's "ways of knowing" . . . represent better procedures of inquiry or subtler standards of justification than the male. And, sure enough, we are told that insights into the theory of knowledge are available to women which are not available, or not easily available, to men.[103]

In another essay, she states:

> I shan't pause to protest the egregious assumption that one thinks with one's skin or one's sex organs. The point I want to stress here is that this form of argument, when applied to the concepts of evidence, truth, etc., is not only fallacious; it is also pragmatically self-undermining. . . . For if there were no genuine inquiry, no objective evidence, we couldn't know what theories are such that their being accepted would conduce to women's interests, nor what women's interests are. [104]

Haack denounces the "ambition of the new, imperialist feminism to colonize epistemology" and then makes the telling comment: "There would be a genuinely feminist epistemology if the idea could be legitimated *that feminist values should determine what theories are accepted*" (her emphasis).[105] And, indeed, precisely such a noxious idea is regularly embraced in Women's Studies circles.

The staples of feminist pedagogy—as both classroom practices and curricular content— have been repeated now for several decades.

They all rest on the increasingly unreal notion that not only American society at large but also the academy is deeply and lastingly antagonistic to women and that this antagonism permeates both the curriculum and knowledge itself. And yet our world has changed so much that feminist pedagogy today is not shy about openly declaring its political goals, confident that the liberal academy will take no action against it. Interestingly, the opposite of "activist" in Women's Studies terms seems to be "careerist," a charge that is normally launched by those who view achieving professional success and status as tantamount to the pursuit of craven self-interest at the expense of fulfilling one's social responsibilities.

But being a professor is indeed a career, and to commit oneself to fostering the intellectual development of one's students is no small or unworthy task. Contrary to what many feminist pedagogues believe, this task requires something other than rampant activism or the kinds of practices condoned by feminist pedagogy. There are vital distinctions between teaching in a university and political campaigning. The important thing is precisely not to deny but to observe such distinctions.[106]

11

Policing the Academy

Daphne Patai

NOT ALL the interventions that feminists bring to the academy take place within the confines of Women's Studies classrooms. An important development since the early 1990s has been the increasing tendency for feminists to argue for sweeping institution-wide implementation of their agenda. Beyond the university, a series of social changes has empowered women and proportionately disempowered men in significant and sometimes frightening ways (e.g., in custody battles, in legislation and funding aiming to stem violence against women, in "sexual harassment" regulations).[1] Within the university, the same shift can be observed. Having firmly established themselves in their own fiefdoms, academic feminists now think in much larger terms. Of course, this aim was implicit, and sometimes explicit, in the very beginning of Women's Studies, when, as we have seen, "transforming the university" was an openly stated goal. But the intended transformation takes on a whole new meaning once we observe some of the efforts actually underway.

One of the more revealing linguistic turns that have occurred in recent years in Women's Studies circles—and one that has greatly facilitated the move toward "transforming" the academy—is the casual substitution of the word "feminist" for "women." Thus, as noted in the preceding chapter, Women's Studies programs (whatever they call themselves) these days explicitly endorse a "feminist" agenda, since to be "pro-woman" in their sights must mean to be "feminist." This shift is a far cry from the sorts of academic-sounding justifications that the "founding mothers" originally offered to university administrations. The meaning of this shift can be observed in several significant and interrelated endeavors made over the past decade or so to ensure that, as women have come to occupy more and higher professorial and administrative positions in the academy, it is not some vague "pro-woman" orientation, but rather a specifically "feminist" one, that directs their activities.[2] How are feminists contriving to change the academy in pursuit of this agenda?

FEMINIST PEDAGOGY REDUX

In 1979, Adrienne Rich wrote a much-quoted passage about the choices facing educators, either "to lend our weight to the forces that indoctrinate women to passivity, self-depreciation, and a sense of powerlessness . . . or to consider what we have to work against, as well as with, in ourselves, in our students, in the content of the curriculum, in the structure of the institution, in society at large."[3]

The passage is interesting for several reasons: On one side there is indoctrination into a variety of harmful beliefs, which is presumably what traditional education is about. On the other side, there is the obligation to "consider" what we have to work against and with in order to subvert and transform the entire enterprise and, indeed, the world. Based on such premises, it made sense for feminist pedagogues to turn education into an artful construction devoted to a justified process of counter-"indoctrination."

Two questions are raised by this approach: First, was the old education really as bad as that? And second, is the proposed "correction" an improvement?

As to the first question, I can safely say—as a product of that bad old education who, along with thousands of other women, came of age in the late-1950s and 1960s and then worked to transform the academy—that the bad old education failed entirely to make us subservient and passive. But I would go further: It failed because that was indeed not its aim, feminist accusations to the contrary notwithstanding. Yes, women faced a variety of obstacles, but the education they received, precisely because it was not driven by gender politics, in fact gave them skills, information, and intellectual horizons that allowed them to shake the world.

Now, as to the new feminist education, is it an improvement? Inasmuch as it introduced women into the curriculum in many legitimate forms, it certainly is—as we have noted throughout this book. But to the extent that it has led teachers to dedicate themselves to inculcating in their students a specifically feminist ideology—and in virtually all their publications and pronouncements feminist pedagogues make it clear that they should—it has to be considered biased and defective.

I cite Rich's decades-old essay because it has remained a touchstone of feminist pedagogy. A recent (1998) collection of essays reprinted from the journal *Feminist Teacher* proves the point. The book's editors assert that these essays, originally published years ago, are still relevant because—so they argue—little has changed. In their introduction, called—typically enough—"Collectively Speaking," the editors give pride of place to Rich's words and then go on to repeat the fundamental tenets of feminist pedagogy. All the key themes encountered in our earlier chapters are here: the importance of "feminist social practice"; the goals of "social transformation," "consciousness-raising," and "social activism"; the belief in the "subjective and communal reality of knowing"; the proudly embraced "cui bono" approach to knowledge; the commitment to improving women's lives inside and outside the classroom; the emphasis on studying the "intersections" of race, class, and gender; the need to address "the undeniable force of sexism and heterosexism in society"; and the concern with "exploring issues of sexuality honestly with students."[4]

If these aims were not so earnestly declared by the authors themselves (who constitute the collective that founded the journal in the 1980s), one might take them as a parody, and as an illustration of why feminist education is not pedagogy at all but—quite intentionally—politics-plus-therapy. Indeed, a listing such as this helps us to understand how particular individuals may protest that "their classroom" is not doing political work, or, alternatively, that it is not aiming to be a therapeutic "safe" space. One can after all stress either strand within feminist pedagogy: the political activism or the more self-absorbed healing approach. Of course, adherents to an ideology that declares "the personal is political" can always argue that even endless discussions of one's self are, at base, political. Thus, four decades after consciousness-raising groups began as a feminist practice, we find them thoroughly established in what are known as Women's Studies programs and the courses they have spawned.

From *The Feminist Teacher Anthology* and other books like it (about which more below), I conclude that feminist teaching is in the strict sense of the word totalitarian—it refuses boundaries, does not respect a private space or inner life on the part of its students, and instead quite explicitly aims to bring all of its concerns—which now go by the code word "multiculturalism" accompanied by a string of other –isms and identities—into a coherent and unified pattern. This is no accident but, as we have seen, a concerted plan, carried out by individual teachers who hope to spread it throughout education, at all levels. Let us examine a number of prominent efforts made in this direction during the past decade.

"ANTI-FEMINIST INTELLECTUAL HARASSMENT"

In 1996, a collection of essays was published entitled *Antifeminism in the Academy.* Beginning with the assertion that "intellectual harassment is the most recent version of antifeminist behavior erupting methodically in the academy and in U.S. society generally,"[5] the book attempts to extend an already dubious concept—hostile environment harassment—to encompass a whole new range of thought and behavior. Delineating the many types of alleged anti-feminist practices perpetrated in colleges, universities, and publishing houses around the country, contributors to this book propose in all seriousness that measures be taken against a new and pervasive kind of offense: "antifeminist intellectual harassment." A prominent place in the events leading up to this suggestion is occupied by Annette Kolodny, well-known feminist literary critic and former dean of the College of Humanities at the University of Arizona in Tucson.

The history of these events is interesting. In 1988, the Modern Language Association's Commission on the Status of Women in the Profession met to discuss the obstacles faced by women in the academy. Quickly, the women present concluded that what might at first seem to be a few isolated incidents of an individual feminist scholar facing "intellectual battery for her presentation of ideas in public" turned out, on closer inspection, to be a major institutional problem that would soon be labeled "antifeminist harassment—a new form of mistreatment that is related to, though different from, sexual harassment."[6]

Asked to define anti-feminist intellectual harassment as a specific and independent category of offenses (and evidently inspired in part by the impressive gains made by women at the University of Minnesota under its Plan II),[7] Annette Kolodny came up with a brief but broad-ranging description, which she presented at the 1991 MLA Convention in San Francisco. Her delineation of this newly discovered and pervasive problem requiring draconian solutions has since found its way, as we shall see later in this chapter, into policy statements adopted by a number of universities.

As Kolodny later described this significant moment in the history of academic feminism, the emphasis in the useful new concept was to be on the word "intellectual," which would set it apart from (but nonetheless associate it with) other kinds of discrimination such as "sexual harassment, emotional battering, and physical threats."[8]

The line of reasoning implicit in this argument is revealing: "Harassment" had proven itself an invaluable concept in the feminist struggle against a stubbornly androcentric world. "Sexual harassment" rules have no doubt proved helpful to women with legitimate complaints, but they have also provided powerful legal weapons to those who simply feel unhappy about one or another aspect of their work or educational life.[9] But however broadly and ambiguously interpreted (as indeed it has been), the qualification "sexual" exempts many unpleasantries that go on in daily life unrelated to sexual overtures. Why should feminists have to tolerate any of these? Kolodny's definition of a new form of harassment represented an enormous potential extension of women's power, allowing any sort of criticism of either women or feminist ideas to fall under the watchful eye of their ideological guardians.

Kolodny's ideas are expounded most recently in her 1998 book, *Failing the Future: A Dean Looks at Higher Education in the Twenty-first Century.* Like the editors of *Antifeminism in the Academy,* Kolodny claims to wish to preserve "academic freedom undiminished by bias, prejudice, or [in her very words] discomfort with difference." But her special understanding of the concept of "academic freedom" emerges at once, as she sets forth the following argument: Since women and minorities (Kolodny's list includes feminists, African Americans, Asian Americans, Native Americans, Latinos, out lesbians and gays, and the disabled) had no role in forming the concept of academic freedom, their interests were protected by it only "insofar as their products and activities *conform to the accepted products and activities of the past.*"[10]

Thus, the concept of academic freedom itself comes under attack while ostensibly being defended. We shall see blatant instances of this assault below, when I consider recent feminist efforts to spread the rhetoric of antifeminist harassment to various universities. All such moves are justified by feminist academicians' repeated claim that there is a powerful "current backlash against feminists and others in the academy."[11] The University of Minnesota Plan II provided a useful model, with its "comprehensive agenda" that included not only pay raises for all women faculty but also "accountability," a daunting concept whose implications were clarified some years later when a similar plan was proposed at six New England land-grant universities. Kolodny's own aim was explicit: Anti-feminist intellectual harassment urgently needs to be defined so it "can be readily recognized and effectively contained." The enormous latitude of Kolodny's definition, as offered in 1991, is self-evident:

> Anti-feminist intellectual harassment, a serious threat to academic freedom, occurs when (1) any policy, action, statement, and/or behavior has the intent or the effect of discouraging or preventing women's freedom of lawful action, freedom of thought, and freedom of expression; (2) *or* when any policy, action, statement, and/or behavior creates an environment in which the appropriate application of feminist theories or methodologies to research, scholarship, and teaching is devalued, discouraged, or altogether thwarted; (3) *or* when any policy, action, statement, and/or behavior creates an environment in which research, scholarship, and teaching pertaining to women, gender, or gender inequities are devalued, discouraged, or altogether thwarted.[12]

Kolodny stresses that she was following the early legal precedents set under Title VII of the 1964 Civil Rights Act, which concentrates on effects and consequences by stipulating "intent OR effect" rather than "intent AND effect." The reasoning is simple. As Kolodny points out, intent is difficult to prove,[13] and therefore those seeking to utilize the new category to protect their ideas, thoughts, and teaching from criticism can far more easily make a case when they are able to rest their claims on the discouragement or devaluing they experience (the "effect"), regardless of the "intent" of the malefactor.

Readers not immersed in the strange world of academic feminism may find it difficult to grasp that the above definition really means what it seems to be saying: that anything, regardless of its intent, which in its effect discourages a *woman's* or a *feminist's* thought or expression is to be held discriminatory. And the definition does not stop there. It would also ban anything that creates an environment that "thwarts," "discourages," or "devalues" either research about women or gender, or the "appropriate" application of feminist theories or methodologies. When, to take a personal example, I participated in a public panel on *Poisoning the Ivy: The Seven Deadly Sins and Other Vices of Higher Education in America*, the book's author, my colleague the sociologist Michael Lewis, might well have felt "discouraged" or "devalued" by my highly critical remarks about what I considered to be his gross misrepresentation of academic life. But as a man and as a writer on academic problems *not* related primarily to gender, he simply had to tolerate my criticisms of his work, however discouraging he may have found them. Some might consider this the normal procedure in academic discussions in which not only praise but also criticism are routinely meted out. But had Michael been Michele, she would, under the Kolodny doctrine, have been entitled to charge me under the broad terms of an anti-feminist intellectual harassment statute. And the other panelists, Robert Jackall and Alan Wolfe, sociologists who faulted Lewis's book for being a poor sociological study, would also have been prohibited from making such criticisms if Michele or her work on gender had been the objects of censure.[14]

Thus, in the name of academic freedom, certain groups and certain ideas are to be protected from criticism. Would a new standard, perhaps that of the "reasonable feminist," need to be created to settle conflicts between critics and victims? What would an "appropriate" application of feminist theories or methodologies be? Who would judge it? And what about those cynics who might object that this whole proposal reveals a pusillanimous and defective understanding of the nature of academic debate? Wouldn't they also instantly fall under the statute's terms?

Kolodny makes clear that the concept of anti-feminist intellectual harassment is meant to raise awareness by identifying a complex problem. Thus, she argues, promotion and tenure procedures could be judged harassing if they fail to recognize such new forms of scholarship and research as interdisciplinary Women's Studies work, or writing computer programs instead of books.[15] She does not explain how her definition will distinguish between those really treated unjustly and those whose work is simply found wanting—and who would surely feel "discouraged and devalued" to hear their colleagues say so. Are certain identity groups, women, and certain subjects, feminism generally, to be beyond reproach?

The chief problems with Kolodny's definition are these: Women may indeed at times be treated unfairly, as men may also be. But how could one possibly prove that "intellectual harassment" is being perpetrated? And even if one could demonstrate discrimination, why should it be prohibited *only* when it is anti-feminist and anti-woman? Why not outlaw any and every form and variety of it—anti-Christian, let's say, or anti-Republican (both popular recent targets on American campuses) or anti-philological or, all-inclusively, anti-old-fashioned or anti-white-male? But Kolodny is not writing a dystopian satire, tempting though it may be to interpret her words as such. Her point is not to imagine amusing scenarios that would unfold as charges and countercharges echo through academic corridors. Her true objective seems quite clear: to inhibit any criticism, trivial or serious, made in good faith or out of pique, that is or can be construed as aimed at women or feminism. It would be unwise to doubt that such a broad new category of harassment, if it were widely adopted, would have this very result—and perhaps already is having such a result, judging from the hesitation of sensible faculty members to criticize feminist initiatives of this sort on their campuses. In the end, offending behavior would not need to actually entail discrimination; it would be sufficient for it to be unpleasant to the recipient, precisely as has happened with the application of the concept of "hostile environment" sexual harassment.

However problematic Kolodny's definition is, it has proved to be more than a one-time shot, as many feminist endorsements of

the concept reveal. At my own university, I had first-hand ac-
quaintance with efforts to implement proposals such as Kolodny's,
when, several years ago, an attempted coup struck New England
universities.[16]

WHY NOT A FEMINIST OVERHAUL
OF HIGHER EDUCATION?

In the earlier chapters of this book, we foresaw potential negative
consequences as a result of the break with Women's Studies that
some scholarly feminists initiated. The most significant of these
consequences was that it left the field clear for the remaining group,
which gets both to define what feminism has become in academe
and to impose that vision on the entire university (see p. 206). How
adamantly feminist professors have gone about doing this can be
seen from the extraordinary effort discussed below.

In 1997, a remarkable document began to circulate among the
six New England land-grant universities. The handiwork of
the New England Council of Land-Grant University Women, a
group formed to develop an "agenda for women," the document,
entitled "Vision 2000," proposed a number of goals designed to
"promote equity for women" in the new millennium. Representatives of campus women's centers, Women's Studies programs,
and commissions and councils on the status of women at the six
universities had developed their proposals over a three-year period. Inspired by a 1993 report produced by a panel of the Faculty Senate at the University of Massachusetts Amherst, and obviously owing much to Kolodny's definition of anti-feminist
intellectual harassment, the group came up with nine long-term
goals followed by detailed guidelines for implementation, to be
achieved by means of a short-term strategy: First, ask each university to endorse the document "in principle," and then work
out specific measures for putting each goal into effect according
to each campus's situation.

This reasonable-sounding approach met with considerable success. Once the presidents of the Universities of Maine, New Hampshire, and Vermont had given the document their personal endorsement, the authors of "Vision 2000" anticipated winning approval by the Council of Presidents of all six land-grant universities at its February 1998 meeting, after which they intended to attempt to persuade university presidents nationwide to endorse the report. When this did not happen quite as anticipated, they continued their piecemeal efforts.[17]

"Vision 2000," it turns out, is a complex and far-reaching attempt at a feminist restructuring of the university. The document makes detailed recommendations covering virtually all aspects of university life, from salaries to course content, from research to teaching styles and campus activities, all of these justified by the by-now familiar phrases invoking the sorry state of women in higher education. Few reasonable observers would accept this claim today, given the well-known increases in female graduation rates and women's entry into professional schools and faculty ranks, but relentless feminist propaganda has succeeded in confusing people about the facts. At the University of Massachusetts Amherst, for example, female students interviewed by a local newspaper at about the time the "Vision 2000" plan was circulating readily asserted that they had not personally encountered any bias in the classroom. Nevertheless, they assumed that such bias exists. Is the assumption correct? It is worth asking that question before endorsing calls for "women-friendly" classrooms and obligatory sensitivity training for professors and others who do not share the goals of "Vision 2000."

Like the endless claims of a "chilly climate" for girls and women in classrooms across America, the charges made in "Vision 2000" presuppose their own validity. The authors of the document rest their case on scare rhetoric that argues that sexual violence is widespread ("Women face sexual violence and sexual harassment in the classroom and in the workplace, and are too often silenced by a system that protects the perpetrators of these crimes"). Concerning academic areas in which women are underrepresented, the report makes the usual leap from disparate outcomes to assumptions of malfeasance: It takes such "disproportions" as a sure sign of discrimination. But might women not be underrepresented in certain fields because of their own preferences? This is a suggestion the mere whiff of which arouses instant dismissal. It is not usual to accuse nursing schools of intentionally discriminating against men; but when numerical imbalances occur in fields in which men predominate, discrimination against women is the immediate charge and its validity treated as a foregone conclusion.

The solutions proposed by "Vision 2000" are as sweeping as its accusations. Training in how to avoid sexual harassment is prescribed for everyone in the university. Disciplinary action (unspecified) taken against offending supervisors must satisfy the injured "supervisee." Unnamed groups shown to be implicated in violence against women at a higher rate than the average for other campus groups "are to be deprived of recognition and support." Campus women's centers are to be established where they do not already exist, and campus leaders are to rely upon them for guidance "in their efforts to encourage, support, and maintain new roles for women."

No less energetic are the changes proposed for the curriculum, which would be transformed "at every level" into one that is "women-friendly and culturally diverse," reflecting "perspectives from scholarship on women and other historically oppressed groups." That process, too, would be "best conducted with guidance from an autonomous Women's Studies site and active Women's Studies scholars." Graduate work in Women's Studies must be made available at each institution, and "equitable recognition" is to be given to the substance and methodologies of work in Women's Studies.

In these and similar ways, "Vision 2000" aimed at nothing less than a feminist overhaul of the entire academic enterprise. After all, the report declared, "women's status within American higher education reflects an intellectual bias that is deeply rooted in the disciplinary methods and social assumptions of university communities." Student evaluations would pose specific questions on the inclusiveness of the curriculum and the "appropriateness of teaching methods to different kinds of students." Presidents and chancellors are to hold "department heads accountable for improvement in achieving gender equity." They are to reward departments that demonstrate measurable progress and "intervene" in those that do not. Faculty members "whose students identify their courses, teaching styles, and mentoring as failing to be inclusive [would] not receive teaching prizes, satisfactory teaching evaluations, or merit raises"—a recommendation effectively encouraging student vigilantism and forcing faculty conformity.

Had these measures been put into effect as proposed, they would have established Women's Studies and its allies in campus women's centers as the arbiters of university policy—with rights of supervision over administrators, faculty members, and programs. And that, obviously, was the intended aim.

It is not possible to understand fully the impulses behind "Vision 2000" without taking a longer-range view of how feminism developed within academe over the past three decades. As we stated earlier in this book (see pp. 209–10), the early 1970s witnessed much debate about which of two strategies feminists should follow: establishing separate Women's Studies programs, or working through existing departments. The Women's Studies route prevailed, and by now about 700 Women's Studies programs and departments exist in American universities, offering undergraduate concentrations and majors and, increasingly, graduate programs as well.[18]

Initially, as we recognized, separate programs were an important asset for helping feminist scholars achieve tenure and promotion that they might well have been denied in other departments. But, as was foreseen in the early debate, that success has had a certain "ghettoizing" effect. Although many institutions now have adopted "diversity" requirements that students can meet by taking Women's Studies courses (and these days one finds such requirements even at community colleges), some areas of the university still remain relatively untouched by feminism. The hard sciences, in particular, have tended to reject (or more often to ignore) the overt politicization imposed by feminist perspectives. When Women's Studies attacks science as "masculinist"—a routine charge in much feminist writing—few faculty members in physics or chemistry seem to notice. To a feminism that rests on a totalizing ideology, such indifference cannot be countenanced. "Vision 2000" was designed to complete the great transformation.

Above all, it was a plan for policing the struggle for gender equity, based on the anachronistic insistence that inequality characterizes women's status in every aspect of university life. Despite masses of evidence to the contrary (some of it available in the book *The Politics of Women's Studies*, discussed in chapter 10), the report depicted faculty members, department chairs, and deans as incapable of doing the right thing without feminist supervision. Although the word "mandatory" did not appear in the document, the spirit that animated it had little of the voluntary in it. As "Vision 2000" made abundantly clear, Women's Studies aimed at nothing less than becoming the central player in the restructuring of university life.[19]

In the earlier chapters of this book, we described the ways in which many Women's Studies programs have allowed the political mission of training feminist cadres to override educational concerns. The strategies of faculty members in these programs—still in force as revealed by my survey of feminist pedagogical literature around the year 2000—have included policing insensitive language, championing research methods deemed congenial to women (such as qualitative over quantitative methods and confessional as opposed to expository writing), and conducting classes as if they were therapy sessions. At my own university, in the mid-1990s, faculty members in Women's Studies supported a radical speech code that would have seriously impeded free expression. They also supported the decision (adopted by the university despite the resistance of the vast majority of faculty members) to have faculty members document, on official, annual-report forms used for promotion, tenure, and salary reviews, their "significant contributions to multiculturalism"[20] in each of the three areas of teaching, research, and service.

But should administrators, department heads, and faculty members really surrender the university to ideologues in their midst? Is claiming the high ground of "equity" sufficient reason to capitulate to a perspective and an agenda not endorsed by most women, let alone men? Women's Studies got its first foothold in academe by invoking the liberal values of tolerance and intellectual openness. Once entrenched, however, and in defiance of both the historical record and common sense, Women's Studies has turned on those very values, rejecting them as helping to sustain the hated status quo. If the university as imagined in "Vision 2000" were to come to pass, the future would look remarkably like Orwell's *Nineteen Eighty-Four*. Would it be any comfort that Big Brother will have turned into Big Sister?

As an illustration of the climate created by such projects to promote women, consider what actually happened when "Vision 2000" was brought to the floor of the Faculty Senate of the University of Massachusetts Amherst. At an initial meeting of the Faculty Senate in December 1997, a particularly illuminating moment occurred when philosophy professor and soon-to-be director of the Women's Studies program Ann Ferguson responded to concerns about how "academic freedom" would fare were the feminist oversight detailed in "Vision 2000" to be adopted. This is what she said: "We can't lose track of the wider goal in order to defend some narrow definition of academic freedom, which might amount to a right not to have to respond to new knowledges that are relevant to someone's own field of expertise."[21]

Having been sent back for review to a number of Faculty Senate committees, the document was once again on the agenda in April 1998. Again, its supporters cast predictable accusations of sexism against its critics.[22] In reply, one faculty senator noted that the document's characterization of the university was severely flawed, in that the university had in fact much reason to celebrate its thorough integration of women. Today, he noted, when he looks at the university administration he sees a female deputy chancellor, vice-chancellor for academic affairs, and provost; a female dean of the graduate school; female deans of the college of humanities and fine arts, natural sciences and mathematics, and school of nursing; a female head of the center for teaching, of the university health services, of the library, of the university's undergraduate advising center; a female dean of students; and so on. The non-discrimination policy in place for many years, he argued, is sufficient to ensure continued progress.

Another speaker stated that the university should disassociate itself from a document as flawed as "Vision 2000" and made a substitute motion. But this was met with an energetic rejoinder by a senator who commented that it would not be wise for UMass to disassociate itself from "Vision 2000." She explained: "I don't want to go on record saying that I—or my institution—can't be held accountable for the way it treats the students, the staff, or the faculty. . . . I'd be happy to invite people into my classes to tell me what I can do better, to serve my women students better, and all my students better. . . . I'd like to think that most faculty feel that way. We want to go on record, especially at this time, as being willing to be held accountable."

But, asked one senator, protesting the sloppiness of the "Vision 2000" document, "what, for example, does it mean that one of the recommendations is to 'foster accountability.' To whom? For what? In what way?" Still another senator objected to the accusatory tone and unsubstantiated statements made in the document, but felt the general principles should be supported.

In response, feminist faculty did not hesitate to recite the usual accusations. One professor commented that the problem lay not so much in the numbers of women on campus, but rather in what was experienced by those, like herself, "actually living the everyday life of a woman in the university, in our programs, in our classroom, in every place where we are."

Perhaps it was through this tactic of gender baiting that the Senate—in blatant disregard of the fact that three of the six committees reporting on the document had not recommended its adoption—was moved to endorse, if not the particulars of the document, at least its nine general principles. Thus, among a faculty of over 1,000 members on the UMass Amherst campus, by a vote of 28 to 7, the motion to adopt the principles articulated in "Vision 2000" was approved. One goal alone was subjected to revision. This was the vague-sounding principle calling for the university to "end gender-bias and discrimination against women in the curriculum," which was opposed by some faculty members because of its hint of obligatory feminist supervision of the curriculum. In its place was put the recommendation to "encourage full integration into the curriculum of relevant scholarship and texts by and about women."[23]

Some months after the event, a colleague wrote to me to explain why he felt the "Vision 2000" episode displayed "contempt for women":

My observation about "contempt for women" stemmed, in part, from the universal (so far as I can tell) rejection of V2K by my six female colleagues in [a social science department] who want nothing to do with the document or its aims, in part from the manifest disregard for the opinion(s) of any woman who did not agree with the document, and in part [from] the failure of the proponents to disseminate the report to the constituencies it was presumably meant to serve (as I observed, the report was not circulated to the faculty, nor was it made available to students—witness [Student Government Association president] Amy Pellegrino's support for postponing action until students could at least read the report [a request that was denied]). From the beginning, I have thought that the V2K exercise betrayed a remarkably patronizing attitude toward female faculty and staff (except, of course, the select few who participated in its drafting and agreed with its characterization of the University).

Why, then, did the Faculty Senate at the University of Massachusetts Amherst vote to adopt the general principles set forth in

"Vision 2000?" No doubt because these goals were thinly disguised as a plea for equal opportunity and fairness—that is, as nothing more than a claim for "equity for women." And who could possibly oppose equity for women? One of the proposal's defenders, who at the time was secretary of the Faculty Senate and hence presided over the April 1998 meeting, likened supporting "Vision 2000" to endorsing "motherhood and apple pie." Refusing to capitulate to this idealized view of a power-seeking document would, of course, have meant both challenging the underlying characterization of the university as a sexist institution and, worse yet, exposing oneself to the imputation that one was a misogynist, a reactionary, and an elitist.

So by presenting a peremptory and very detailed proposal, with recommendations for implementation that were sure to upset most faculty members, the feminist group responsible for the document managed to make endorsement of their nine basic principles—without the accompanying guidelines for implementation—look like the reasonable compromise position. Just what endorsing the principles articulated in "Vision 2000" will mean to the six New England land-grant universities remains to be seen, but academics who value faculty autonomy and academic freedom should not rest easy while "Vision 2000" lurks in the background, waiting to be called into action. Meanwhile, UMass Amherst has inaugurated a series of quasi-mandatory workshops on sexual harassment, and faculty who do not attend these will find that the university will not stand behind them if they are ever accused of sexual harassment.

PROTECTING SOME SPEECH

Many commentators on the contemporary university scene have noted the strange reversals that have characterized academic politics in recent years, as "radicals," "liberals," and "conservatives" have embraced positions and practices that confound all conventional labels. Those who two generations ago participated in or were thrilled by the Berkeley Free Speech Movement are now themselves often the ones insisting on speech codes, harassment policies, and general prescriptions for the "comfort" of women and minorities.

A conference on "Academic Freedom" held in early April 2000, at the State University of New York in Albany, sponsored by the faculty senate of the SUNY system and attended by administrators from many SUNY campuses, brought this development home to me in a very direct way.[24] As I listened to the speakers and to audience responses, it became clear to me that even at a conference addressing the very subject of academic freedom and attended by many stalwarts of the American Association of University Professors (AAUP), a decidedly skewed view of that subject was being played out.

No one present at the conference attacked academic freedom from a conservative point of view. Indeed, it was seen as "conservative" to defend a broad and non-partisan understanding of academic freedom, while the only assaults on academic freedom— never, of course, directly—came from those who had no problems whatsoever with curtailment of speech in the service of harassment policies.

The keynote address was given by Walter P. Metzger, a lifelong AAUP activist and author (with Richard Hofstadter) of the famous work *The Development of Academic Freedom in the United States* (1955).[25] For most in the audience, the part of Metzger's talk that reviewed the history of struggles over academic freedom was probably a familiar tale. Only when he approached the current scene by turning to the culture wars did Professor Metzger begin to tread on contested territory.

Today, he said, threats to academic freedom come not from outside the academy but from those seeking to enforce speech codes and harassment policies relating to race and sex in the name of protecting various identity groups. Although these codes plainly infringe academic freedom, the voice of the professoriate has not been strongly heard in the vigorous disputes over the new academic race and gender speech codes. Even the AAUP's own watchdog Committee A was irresolute until 1994, and to this day it has not disavowed the dangerous concept of "hostile environment" harassment. It had investigated only one case (that of Professor Donald Silva whose use of certain metaphors in the classroom led to charges of sexual harassment at the University of New Hampshire), and ducked the wider question of whether hostile environment statutes are inherently a threat to academic freedom. One academic group alone had a clear-cut response, and that was the much-maligned National Association of Scholars, which openly said the hostile environment concept ought to go. Metzger's comments included the admission that the silence of the profession was his own silence as well. He, too, had been unwilling to make "enemies on the left." Thus, he concluded, psychological intimidation of faculty has worked its way into the academic scene.

Professor Metzger's stature in the profession—and particularly on the issue of academic freedom—is such that his views encountered no audible opposition from the audience. My own presentation, about feminist threats to academic freedom, was received with far less tolerance. But it was above all when Harvey Silverglate spoke, the next morning, that audience reactions revealed just how debased the notion of academic freedom has become in today's academy. The dominant mood at the conference had been anger at the outside forces (corporatization, attacks on tenure, privatization of university services, trustee interference in curricular matters, and the like) that are changing the face of academe. Threats to academic freedom coming from within the academy were ignored. It was to these threats that Silverglate turned in his talk.

Together with Alan Kors (professor of history at the University of Pennsylvania), Silverglate, a Boston attorney and civil libertarian, in 1998 published *The Shadow University: The Betrayal of Liberty on America's Campuses*, [26] an exemplary compilation and analysis of intra-university attacks on academic freedom and freedom of speech, usually undertaken in the name of supposedly progressive aims that rest on identity politics. Silverglate's focus at the Albany conference was on the surreptitious ways in which academic speech codes, having been struck down wherever they underwent legal challenge, have in fact invaded campuses in the guise of harassment policies. These policies typically list "verbal or physical acts" that are to be proscribed. But verbal acts are, of course, speech; hence harassment policies are in fact speech codes, and in this form free expression is being curtailed on college campuses. Silverglate further rejected critical race theorists' notorious defense of a double standard of speech, whereby offensive speech uttered by historically oppressed minorities is protected, while comparable speech by their supposed oppressors can be quashed. This, incidentally, was the very argument explicitly put forth by the administration at my own university in its attempt to introduce a speech code in 1995.

Silverglate's observations did not go over as well as one might have expected in a conference convened precisely to address the subject of academic freedom. Indeed, his clear explanation of how speech codes have transmogrified into harassment policies was something most members of the audience evidently preferred not to hear. One man countered Silverglate's assertion that equality before the law depends on a single standard by observing that equality is a dangerous concept since it leaves inequality untouched. This statement was greeted with applause from the audience. And it was this enthusiastic reaction that formed the predominant image I carried away with me: an academic conference devoted to the defense of academic freedom in which professors, administrators, and AAUP activists applauded an attack on equality in the protection of free speech. Silverglate responded that one does not achieve equality by destroying it. Other members of the audience brought up the demeaning words women students are said to be forced to endure. Silverglate rejected the underlying assumption regarding the precarious position of women students, pointing out as well that most charges of harassment are aimed at what professors say in class. Moreover, if speech codes are indeed a dead issue, as some in the audience had asserted, why, he asked, are they in our college handbooks?

By then it had become obvious that the prevailing view at this conference was that curtailment of free speech is acceptable if the objective is to make minorities and women comfortable in the university. As Silverglate wrote to me after the conference: "All in all, my impression when I left was the same as it was when I arrived—the control of speech and thought is well-advanced in the one place where it should be absent."[27]

In feminist circles, in particular, academic freedom is under attack by feminists not content with sexual harassment policies that are broad, vague, and all-inclusive and whose application routinely violates the due process rights of the accused and the academic freedom of professors and fellow students. In their view, harassment is an ever-expanding threat the depths of which have yet to be plumbed. That such an inflation of the powerful concept of harassment does not immediately evoke dismissal is due to the tacit acceptance of the notion (cited in chapter 10), expressed explicitly in a 1997 essay by Susan J. Scollay and Carolyn S. Bratt, that "the academy remains an essentially single sex institution."[28] The myth of systemic sexism (like the myth of intransigent racism) in the university is thus utilized to justify ever greater encroachments on academic freedom.

As these ideas spread throughout the nation's colleges and universities—and are not resisted by those afraid of antagonizing their feminist colleagues—extraordinary revisions in the notion of academic freedom take place. In the name of a woman-friendly academy, not only can some things *not* be said but other things *must* be said. This is the logic driving feminist demands that feminist methodologies and perspectives—whatever these may be—must be incorporated into all parts of the university.

In an illuminating coincidence, at about the same time as the Albany conference just described, Robert Swope, a senior writing a regular biweekly column for *The Hoya*, Georgetown University's campus newspaper, had his column rejected for lambasting *The Vagina Monologues*, which had been performed on the Georgetown campus, as on hundreds of other colleges throughout the nation.

Earlier in the semester, Swope had published an attack on Women's Studies on *The Hoya* website, declaring that Women's Studies creates "an industry of professional victims," is an "intellectually bankrupt academic fraud" sustained by "cowardly" and "weak-willed" campus administrators, and is generally a "disaster." On February 15, the paper printed a rebuttal by a female associate dean who called Swope's description of Women's Studies "misinformation" and complained that the paper had wasted twenty inches of its space on his views. When Swope later protested the editors' rejection of his column on *The Vagina Monologues,* he was removed as a columnist by the paper's editor.[29]

Events such as these expose as mere frivolous display Stanley Fish's ruminations in 1999 on the vacuity of the liberal commitment to academic freedom. Exclusion is inevitable, Fish affirms, though liberals pretend otherwise. Inclusion is not possible: "All that is possible—all you can work for—is to arrange things so that the exclusions that inevitably occur are favorable to your interests and hostile to the interests of your opponents."[30] (No doubt this explains Fish's efforts, some years ago, to keep National Association of Scholars members, who were on the faculty at Duke University, off tenure committees.)[31] So specious an argument as Fish's would never have been made by anyone who has actually been on the receiving end of forced academic conformity.

The modern university itself stands as a refutation of Fish's claims. Were these claims accurate, feminists would never have established a presence in the academy. Now that they have done so, they can support ill-conceived and dangerous speech codes and sexual harassment policies, try to extend them, and generally attempt to "arrange things"—as Fish describes—in a way "favorable" to their own interests. Many scholars have insisted that academic freedom protects above all people whose thinking challenges orthodoxy. The pertinent questions now are: Which ideas have acquired the status of orthodoxy in today's academy and from which direction are the challenges coming? The answer is clear: The current attacks on academic freedom are launched primarily by what used to be called the Left—and this emphatically includes campus feminists.

One seemingly pathetic but in reality quite chilling example of the current climate involves students' evaluations of their professors. In a language department at one midwestern university, evaluation forms that recently crossed my path contained a section labeled "Sexism Questions," which come in two forms:

1. Do you feel that the materials used in this class (lectures, textbooks, films, etc.) represented the experience of women and minorities in the culture(s) being studied? Please be specific.
2. Do you feel that the instructor has made remarks which have stereotyped or demeaned an individual on the basis of gender, race, or ethnic identification or sexual preference? If so, please explain.

To the first question above, one student responded: "Yes, discussed women, poor, abused, sexuality. Lesbians and gays were underrepresented in textbook and films." Or, as another student put it, "He is very careful!"

The second question elicited comments such as: "[The professor] did not demean anyone, if anything, he supported their cause." Or: "Yes, in particular, the instructor spent a lengthy amount of time demeaning strip bars and the dancers that work there." And "No, he was very careful about not offending anyone."

Yet another example of feminists' contribution to the decline of free speech on campus occurred in relation to quarrels over acceptable speech in the aftermath of the September 11, 2001, terrorist attacks. At my university, the former director of Women's Studies, Ann Ferguson (one of the authors of the "Vision 2000" document), undertook to draft and circulate among the faculty a "statement for peace" that opposed the U.S. military action in Afghanistan and defended the civil rights of those professors who were critical of U.S. policy in response to the attacks.[32] The message contained these words:

We oppose any restriction on our civil liberties of freedom of speech and association, including pressure on individual faculty, staff or students not to openly express their political opinions, no matter how unpopular they are. We believe individuals should suspend "business as usual" and commit themselves to efforts to promote peace and justice.[33]

I was encouraged that Ferguson had perhaps come to see the wisdom of defending the civil liberties of those holding unpopular views. So I wrote her a brief E-mail message, on October 12, 2001:

I address this message to you and all the signatories of the [statement for peace] that is circulating. Leaving aside for the moment the other aspects of this petition, I am struck by a significant inconsistency: You and some of the other people now worrying about threats to the civil rights of those who want to criticize the U.S. response to the terrorist attacks were not equally eager to protect the civil rights of all on campus when it came to a speech code that targeted speech you found offensive. What should I make of this contradictory behavior?

Perhaps I should have anticipated Ferguson's response: "Sometimes speech is harmful action, and when so, should not be automatically protected."[34]

GOING "BOLIVARIAN" WITH A FEMINIST TWIST

In late 2000, reports reached U.S. newspapers regarding the increasing politicization of education in Venezuela, a result of the policies of President Hugo Chávez, who took office in February 1999. Chávez, as explained in the *New York Times*, regarded "integrated education" as a major initiative of his government. In practice, this led to military supervision of the school curriculum. The explicit imposition on all schools of "Bolivarian ideology" (named after Simón Bolívar, father of Venezuelan independence) was criticized by both educators and historians in Venezuela, who objected to projects to rewrite textbooks so that they denigrated the past for the sake of glorifying, by contrast, the current regime. They also objected to proposals requiring military training and indoctrination in all "Bolivarian" schools.[35]

In the United States, it is common for feminists (and other activists) in academe to assert as a self-evident truth that "all education is political." This is the rejoinder I have most frequently encountered when speaking (in public lectures at universities) against the tendency in Women's Studies to make education subservient to a feminist agenda. Although in the first edition of *Professing Feminism* we addressed these issues, we have seen them arise again and again whenever criticisms are made of Women's Studies. As recent examples of this unchanging view within Women's Studies, I will cite a few questions posed to me on an on-line "colloquy" sponsored by the *Chronicle of Higher Education* in October 2000. I quote these exchanges verbatim since both questions and answers were composed under pressure of time and it does not seem fair to reformulate my own responses when questioners cannot reformulate or expand on their questions.

Claire Kaplan, University of Virginia:

My preliminary dissertation research on the experiences of Women's Studies majors, both during their program and after graduation, indicates that this particular area of study leaves students feeling personally empowered and intellectually flexible. The students (present and alumni) I have met so far also feel committed to creating that elusive "better world" for women, and often choose careers that will enable them to do just that.

My question(s): Are not all academic programs ideologically based? Do not all academic programs suffer from internal wrangling and political conflict? Do not leading scholars in most academic disciplines create the expectation that students will learn to "toe the line" in order to be considered serious scholars in the field? Is not the increasing legitimacy of Women's Studies in academe a direct consequence of serious scholarship in the field?

Daphne Patai:

Many fields of study in the humanities and social sciences attempt to expose students to a variety of perspectives without imposing a particular one. Individual teachers may passionately try to convince their students of their own points of view, but few programs as a whole have such an agenda. Women's Studies (like some other identity programs) does, quite explicitly.

The idea that leading scholars are forcing their graduate students to toe a particular line is more parody than reality—and wherever it does happen, it's unfortunate and should be resisted. However, this sounds like a very peculiar defense of Women's Studies. "We force our students to toe the line, but so does everyone else" is hardly a recipe for change or improvement.

There is enormous variety and vigor in the world of scholarship, as well as heated debate. That is all to the good. Women's Studies people always point to the many kinds of "feminismS" that exist and to the many debates within the field. That doesn't change the fact that, as far as the feminist classroom is concerned, there are characteristic feminist approaches and axioms.

The legitimacy that Women's Studies has as a field is due to two things:

1. its role in a great and general transformation of American society, and
2. the excellent work of individual scholars. However, only a small part of this work gets into the classroom, and that part is often distorted and shows up in classrooms

as a feminist bottom-line version mouthed by "multi-disciplinary" teachers who may have little expertise—but strong passions—about the "issues" they teach.

Diana Blaine, University of Southern California:

You argue that Women's Studies courses reflect a unified political agenda. Given the inevitably political nature of deciding what ideas to disseminate, how would you describe the political agenda of non-Women's Studies courses? And why are you more comfortable with the propagation of these unacknowledged agendas than you are with the ideas overtly being articulated in Women's Studies courses?

Daphne Patai:

You presuppose "unacknowledged political agendas" in all programs. I take it, then, that you agree that Women's Studies has a distinct political agenda. You also use the language of "comfort" to describe my position. I tend to disagree with this way of framing the issue. What is the political agenda in deciding to disseminate the Periodic Table?[36] There have been excellent discussions of the meaning of "social construction of knowledge" in relation to the sciences—far different from what students typically get in a Women's Studies course, but I won't get into that here.

I cannot describe "the agenda" of non-Women's Studies courses because, unlike your way of framing the issue, I do not believe there is one such thing, and I don't even believe there are many such things. There may be individual teachers introducing their agendas, but that is not the same thing as a Women's Studies agenda.

The big issue to me is how much politics are we going to deliberately allow into our educational system at this moment in the evolution of our universities, for what purposes, and designed by whom. As long as a thousand flowers bloom, all the political biases can fight it out among themselves. That's far from a Cultural Revolution, à la Mao, which is what I think needs to be avoided at all costs.

I have repeatedly argued that without the existence of a real commitment to liberal education, Women's Studies wouldn't have gotten a foot in the door. It's not the first movement, of course, to use a principle as long as it needed it, and then attack it. Since Women's Studies' other main raison d'être is its avowed claim that it is making the world a better place, I also reject the line of defense you offer. It would be problematic even if I agreed with your premises.

Kristin Rusch, University of Maryland:

Isn't a specifically feminist viewpoint (and variations thereof) a legit perspective to study on the issues you mentioned? Certainly Marxists have something important to say about these issues, as do Freudians, theologians, and others. What's wrong with looking at feminist views on these issues?

Daphne Patai:

There's a big difference between an individual professor bringing her beliefs and convictions to the classroom—whether those are Marxist, Freudian, fundamentalist, or whatever—and the existence of programs devoted to the promotion of a particular ideology. With Women's Studies we have the latter. An example that seems to me appropriate is: do we want to have in secular universities a fundamentalist-studies program that endorses rather than merely studies religious fundamentalism?[37]

Nearly a year after this exchange, the terrorist attacks of September 11, 2001, led to a lengthy discussion on the Women's Studies E-mail List of how to deal with these events in class. Once again, the messages posted demonstrated the tendency in feminist pedagogy to use the classroom for purposes of proselytizing—with the usual anti-U.S. slant. After a day or two of silence (no doubt as most of us sat glued to the television screen), feminist faculty began writing in about this national catastrophe that left our students shaken. Although three listmembers eventually argued that this was not the moment to press professors' political views on students, theirs was a distinctly minority voice,[38] and most messages endorsed the view that the attack had created a pedagogical opportunity not to be missed.

Listmembers' own understandings of the tenor of the debate can be gauged by a posting from Rebecca Wishnant, who summarized the thread up to that point as follows: "I've been very interested in the exchange about whether it is OK to speak with our students right now, in the immediate aftermath of this tragedy, about its roots in US imperialism and terror."[39] The "chickens [are] coming home to roost," another listmember observed. All in all, the predominant tone was one of schadenfreude.

Still, the anti-American/anti-imperialist line, common enough in academe in recent decades, is probably not the most blatant kind of propagandizing that is encouraged in the feminist classroom. Perhaps it is in response to a rise in young women's "resistance" to the feminist message that some teachers resort to ever more extreme examples of the threatening world in which women live. Feminist pedagogy, we are told once again in a recent book reprinting key feminist essays on pedagogy, "emphasizes the sharing of experiences and feelings."[40] In the same volume, Jennifer Scanlon, former director of Women's Studies at SUNY Plattsburgh, makes clear what sorts of "feelings" feminist pedagogy encourages and how it uses political events to arouse them.

Scanlon says she likes to use the Montreal Massacre of 1989 in her introductory Women's Studies classroom to raise the issue of violence against women. Hers is, she says,

> a feminist pedagogical approach that emphasizes discussion and relational thinking, and by remembering the women who died on that day, we can at once pay tribute to a specific group

of victims and name the larger social pathology—misogyny—
that shows no signs of disappearing.

To achieve these ends, Scanlon has devised a formidable classroom ritual: It begins with a reading of the names, ages, and occupations of the women murdered in Montreal. The class then sings
a song called "Montreal, December '89" written by the Australian
Judy Small, which includes the line "What is it about men that
makes them do the things they do?" Refusing to let her students get
away with thinking that the deed was done by one sick man, Scanlon poses questions such as: "What responsibility do all men have
for any male violence?" These questions are meant not to be answered by the students, she says, but rather "to guide their thinking
as we talk about all means of violence against women."[41]
"One of my long-term goals," Scanlon declares, "is that over the
course of the next few weeks the Montreal Massacre will be seen for
what I believe it to be, part of a continuum of violence and hatred
rather than an aberration that will never be repeated." "By using
the Montreal Massacre as a metaphor," she argues, "Women's Studies faculty can open an honest, and revealing, dialogue about violence against women," thereby furthering students' understanding
of women's "struggles to survive, to make their way in the world, to
flourish." Perhaps then, she concludes, students "will understand
better what they really fear when they tell us, 'I'm not a feminist,
but. . . .'"[42]
In an article in the same volume, "Reshaping the Introductory
Women's Studies Course: Dealing Up Front with Anger, Resistance, and Reality," Ardeth Deay and Judith Stitzel complain that
their students "were not making the connections that we wanted
them to make, [and] that the connections did not come automatically." Thus, they concluded that it

was our responsibility to challenge the students' ideology of
individual success and to establish as an underlying theme
of the course the interrelationships of one's own experiences,

the experiences of others of different races and classes, and the patriarchal institutions that shape all experience.

In order to do accomplish this purpose in a non-threatening way, they go on to say, they had to change the "tone" of their class. Their course (at Western Virginia University) is, they note, no longer an elective; it now fulfills a general education requirement.[43]

But it is not only in the realm of politics and institutions that feminists have undertaken to restructure their students' perceptions. As the slogan "the personal is political" is intended perpetually to remind us, it is also at the most intimate and private level that Women's Studies efforts to reorient young minds are under way.

NEW SEXUAL ORTHODOXIES

In chapter six, we discussed the feminist predilection for what we called "biodenial"—the antagonism among feminists to arguments from biology. Why feminists need to adopt a strong social constructionist perspective is no mystery. If one wants to claim that gender "roles" (to use the old-fashioned term) are totally artifacts of culture, one has to contend either that gender has no connection to biology or that the biological account is itself an artifact of culture—or both. My interest here is in noting the effect of social constructionism as a new orthodoxy on feminist teaching and argumentation. The key point is that under the guise of "raising interesting questions" or "challenging conventional ideas," Women's Studies professors impose their defective versions of the "facts" upon their students. The denigration of "facts," "logic" and "rationality"—they often dismissed as forms of "masculinist" linear thinking—is, I believe, in large part driven by feminists' opportunistic desire to leave themselves free to make any claim they wish.

Supported by the spread of social constructionism as a predominant vogue among many academics in our time, any and every aspect of women's lives and being that is thought to need feminist transformation thus can be, and has been, reinterpreted as socially constructed.[44] That this perspective is, inevitably, inconsistently applied—disappearing, for example, when feminists want to stamp men in one or another negative fashion and women in a positive one—does not weaken the powerful hold of the social constructionist line on academic feminism. How this line is applied to the apparently irreducible facticity of biological differences between the sexes can stand as a particularly useful test case, which is why I take it up here in some detail.

In 2001, not for the first time, a discussion took place on the Women's Studies E-Mail List—a crucial resource for Women's Studies faculty, let it be recalled—about the existence of sexual dimorphism. Various listmembers (including faculty members at universities) drew on the work of Anne Fausto-Sterling who, after reviewing the research on infants born with sexual anomalies, has famously argued that there are more than two sexes. Her views (which will be explored at greater length in the next chapter, in the context of feminist critiques of science) have become a touchstone for feminists wishing to insist that sexual dimorphism is itself a social construct. In 2000 Fausto-Sterling had published a large book on this subject, entitled *Sexing the Body: Gender Politics and the Construction of Sexuality*. This book, which met with such approval among sociologists (not, let it be noted, biologists) that it received the Robert K. Merton Award of the American Sociological Association, is a fascinating display of rhetorical sleight of hand, the adroitness of which explains why Women's Studies scholars are not mistaken in taking this work as a biologist's denial of the fact of sexual dimorphism.

By a constant rhetorical slippage from discussions of cultural anthropology and other "social constructionist" disciplines to biology, Fausto-Sterling makes it clear that she is indeed saying that we construct our bodies. In just one of innumerable instances throughout her book, she first asserts that "historians and anthropologists disagree about how to interpret human sexuality across cultures and history"—an unobjectionable statement, focusing on the "meaning" humans attribute to sexual practices. Then, in the same paragraph, she shifts the argument, asserting, on her authority "as a biologist," that: "As we grow and develop, we literally, not just 'discursively' (that is, through language and cultural practices), construct our bodies, incorporating experience into our very flesh. To understand this claim, we must erode the distinctions between the physical and the social body."[45] Which is what her book then sets out to do. Her method is illustrated also by her discussion of hormones, where she baldly asserts that scientists created the category of sex hormones.[46] Here, as elsewhere, Fausto-Sterling has submitted to the lure of postmodernism, which confuses naming with creating. This confusion is vital to her argument.[47]

On the WMST-List, I questioned the utility of spending much precious class time on Fausto-Sterling's views and stated that the mere existence of a very small number of infants born with sexual anomalies in no way challenges the reality of male/female dimorphism.[48] These comments were met with angry denunciations and even with accusations that I was attacking the civil rights of certain minorities. Jessica Fields, of the University of North Carolina at Chapel Hill, wrote in that "some students bring difficult experiences with this two-sex system to our classes, making such conversations difficult. Students for whom the two-sex system has been comfortable and even advantageous may find challenges to it difficult." Thus, she concluded:

I'm surprised that you want not to challenge views of the habitual. This sort of questioning seems fundamental to feminism and to my disciplinary home—sociology. Too often, the habitual is confused with the normal, the acceptable, and the whole of what's possible. My intellectual commitments, coupled with a respect for both students' experiences and their intellectual abilities, make such work basic to the Women's Studies classes I teach.[49]

When I responded that challenging the habitual is one thing, taking the exceptional as typical is quite another, since after all the vast majority of infants are born unproblematically as male or female, I was told by Judith Lorber, founding editor of the journal *Gender & Society*, current president of the Eastern Sociological Society, professor at Brooklyn College and the Graduate Center of CUNY, and author of the book *Paradoxes of Gender*, that

> No one is "unproblematically male or female." Fausto-Sterling, in her new book, *Sexing the Body*, uses intersexuality as an illustration of how sex (bodies, biology) is socially constructed as a binary. Her main point, and that of the feminist social construction perspective, is that all bodies are made, not born, and that they are gendered in crucial ways by the requirements of a gendered social order that categorizes people into two and only two social statuses ("man"/"woman") and also ensures that they can be told apart. Fausto-Sterling shows at length how scientists have themselves socially constructed their version of gendered biology through their experiments with hormones and in the search for brain differences. The feminist social construction view is that bodies and brains develop interactively within a social environment and throughout a lifetime. Gendering is a process rather than a fixed entity, or, as [Judith] Butler says, gender is what we do, not what we are.[50]

As the discussion continued, a new contributor wrote in, providing a brief historical survey of why this argument was so crucial for Women's Studies:

> I have always considered the continuing arguments against biological determinism an (il)logical outgrowth of second wave feminism's claims to complete equality (ideological and physical). Such arguments began, I believe, because men's claim[s] to superiority were based in their physical strength and "superior" intelligence, with the emphasis being on the former

claim. I think that early feminists came up with the "we are physically exactly like men" and the simultaneous "sex, and not only gender is socially constructed" to combat the claim from men's physical/intellectual superiority.

These arguments got us a lot in the 60's and 70's, and I appreciate the ground gained by the second wave feminists who used those arguments, but I believe that feminism should, by now, have been able to outgrow these arguments, rather than cling to them. For one, in terms of sex, and the construction of the male and female body, men and women ARE different. I don't know about you, but I appreciate the difference, and certainly wouldn't want to be a man. Second, I believe that contemporary feminists who cling to the "we are exactly equal and we want equality" argument should consider the implications of this argument. To say that we want to be equal to men centralizes the male as the ideal, and leaves the onus for change on woman. In this instance it is woman then who must strive to demonstrate her equality by moving physically and ideologically towards the male ideal they have set up. Again, I quite simply enjoy being a woman, and wouldn't want to be male, so I feel it's high time that we abandoned the illogicalities of the old argument and moved on to new arguments, which ideally would focus more on women, and not try and make us all into androgyns or men.[51]

The debate went on for days, making little headway and with the "social constructionist" line clearly predominating. Susan Kane, for example, a Women's Studies librarian at the University of Washington Seattle, wrote in as follows:

To refuse to raise the question of whether two sexes do exist biologically seems to impoverish everyone. I also strongly disagree that (undefined) students become hostile to Women Studies because we talk about things, like whether sex exists in fact, that seem counter-intuitive. If a student does not want to encounter information that is new, interesting and possibly contradictory to what they already know, what are they doing in college? Raising questions that challenge social norms does open the discipline to ridicule. But why blame the discipline because some find its questions ridiculous? Research that stays within the bounds of "common sense" and that refuses to ask questions some might find ridiculous is somewhat limited, no?

Kane quoted the key question of my own contribution to the debate: "I raised one issue: why the existence of sexual anomalies in new-borns should be used, in Women's Studies classes, as grounds for attacking the notion that male/female dimorphism is a fact of biology," and then proceeded to respond to it:

> This is the third time that Professor Patai has asserted that sexual dimorphism is a fact of biology. Unlike those opposing her "fact," she has offered no evidence for this assertion.
>
> The disagreement hinges on precisely the question of whether sexual dimorphism is indeed, "a fact of biology." Patai has appealed to common sense. She has told us that we are obsessed with the "abnormal." She has accused us of ignoring "facts" in favor of politics. But she has offered no facts. I have heard no specific arguments on the question at hand. She has offered no counter arguments to her opponents.
>
> Let us work with the question of fact. Are there two biological sexes? Discuss. Should we not make some progress on facts before raising the question of whether someone is being "ridiculous"? Does not the question of "ridiculousness" hinge almost entirely on the question of fact? The fact that Patai offers no evidence for her position makes me fear that she has none. Unable to argue her point on the merits, she resorts to accusations, ridicule, and repeated assertions that she is right. This makes me fearful that it is she who is pursuing a narrow politicized agenda. Logically, I cannot accept the assertion

that she is right without some arguments in her favor. I would like to settle (or at least make further progress on) the question at hand. Patai asserts that sexual dimorphism is a biological fact. Great, I'm ready to listen to her arguments with an open mind. Let's hear it. Convince me.[52]

This in turn led to an astonished response by listmember Elizabeth Keller, a graduate student and teacher of Women's Studies:

Are people disagreeing that human males are ON AVERAGE somewhat larger than human females?[53] That is sexual dimorphism, defined as "differences in physical characteristics between males and females of the same species." The textbook *Introduction to Physical Anthropology* (Robert Jurmain, et al., 2000) states for example that "Growth curves for boys and girls are significantly different, with the adolescent growth spurt occurring approximately two years earlier in girls than in boys (reflected in the fact that the ends of long bones unite earlier in girls than in boys). At birth, there is a slight sexual dimorphism in many body measures (e.g., height, weight, head circumference, and body fat) but the major divergence in these characteristics does not occur until puberty." Please hear me that I am not making any argument whatsoever about the significance or even the magnitude of sexual dimorphism here. I am simply asking how people can deny that sexual dimorphism is (at least for the time being) biological reality?

If there were no such thing as sexual dimorphism, we would not be able to identify skeletons as having belonged to male or female bodies, would we? Yet we do so all the time.

As to the question of "whether two sexes do exist biologically," I just want to say that I don't understand why the fact that a small percentage of babies are born intersexed should obscure the reality that an overwhelming majority of humans are easily categorizable as male or female, by their genitalia and chromosomes at the least. In addition, I don't see how the mysterious and complex continuum of sexual preference, for example, challenges the notion of two sexes. I'm not denying that our culture makes the two sex system rigid and hierarchical, and that many people suffer because they don't fit into box A or B and/or don't want to fit in. I'm only saying that I firmly believe that two (principal) sexes do indeed exist biologically.[54]

Some days later, perhaps finally growing weary of a discussion that seemed to make little headway, Ruthann Masaracchia, who teaches at the University of North Texas, wrote in:

I am a biologist (my Ph.D. was on the metabolism of synthetic estrogens) and a director of Women's Studies. I would like to support [Keller and Patai] and offer my expertise to clarify some of the questions being raised on sexual dimorphism. I think this would work best if those opposing the biological basis of sex would pose one or two direct questions and then those of us trained in this area can attempt to provide the biologists' answer. The lack of basic understanding that has been exhibited in this discussion is somewhat appalling and I hope that much of this is not offered in the classroom as fact. So where would you like to start—dimorphism in utero, chromosomes and chromosomal diversity, differentiation and development? I will try to be succinct but I will also provide some facts that many of you (based on your comments) aren't going to like.

Interestingly, Professor Masaracchia's intervention elicited only a few direct questions. Instead, the discussion quickly turned even more personal, as listmembers did not take well her challenge to their lack of knowledge of basic biology. She posted three very detailed responses to the questions and insults and personal skepticism about her credentials, then withdrew from the discussion.[55]

I recount this episode (one example of many similar debates that take place more or less regularly on the WMST-List) to demonstrate the mood and characteristic response among faculty most involved in teaching Women's Studies. But I hesitate to leave readers with the impression that the above exchange is indicative of a climate of open and lively debate on the WMST-List. In fact, often there is virtual unanimity until I or one of the few other skeptics raise a question or objection. When men have tried to do the same thing, they have found themselves put on "review" status by the list-owner, Joan Korenman, who then vets their messages and usually declines to post them. (This has happened to me as well, on occasion.) James Steiger, professor of psychology at the University of British Columbia, is only one such man, whose postings or attempted postings to the list were often filled with information that challenged the views blithely aired on the list. After many efforts to be heard, Steiger, like most other dissenters, gave up. And this happens to women, too, from time to time. I have been placed on review status in the past, and Ruthann Masaracchia—who represents that rare combination, a Women's Studies director and a biologist—has also had her messages to the list returned, with no explanation from the listowner. It plainly appears that, although many routine bibliographic and other such questions are aired on the WMST-L, the list is not so much an academic forum as a group of like-minded people disinclined to brook opposition.[56]

Aware, of course, that debates such as those on a listserve can be dismissed as "anecdotal," I once again turn to publications on science in the field of Women's Studies. Indicative of the tendency within Women's Studies to dismiss science and put in its place politically more endearing notions is Rebecca M. Herzig's article "What about Biology?' Building Sciences into Introductory Women's Studies Curricula," published in the volume *Feminist Science Studies: A New Generation* (2001),[57] a book that purports to present the latest thinking in this burgeoning new field. In her essay, Herzig describes her Introduction to Women's Studies course at Bates College. After first stating that "at this point in the history of feminist organizing, it is hardly more than a cliché to note that 'woman' does not name a neutral or universal identity," she goes on to explain that nonetheless students typically engage in a "conceptual retreat to the neutral ground of sex"—despite "evident variation in perceptions of 'the' female body."

As was apparent in Susan Kane's comment, quoted above, Women's Studies prides itself on its ability to question any- and everything (except, of course, its root convictions regarding women's oppression and the patriarchy's continuing power). Hence Herzig aims to disturb her students' disinclination to subject "the female body" to critical scrutiny. To do this, she must find a way to dispel students' notion that biology exists "outside the effects of culture and history." Once students start to recognize that not all female bodies menstruate, they are ready to understand that "the female body" turns out "to be equally subject to historical and cultural context." Students still, however, challenge their professor with the question "But what about biology?" And that is what Herzig addresses in the main part of her essay—as she attempts to demonstrate the utility of "feminist science studies" for Women's Studies courses. Using terms that can only confuse students already too ignorant of biology, Herzig provides "modules" complete with guided readings designed to help students "query received knowledge about 'the female body.'" Not surprisingly, the module on "Sexual Dimorphism" relies heavily on readings by Anne Fausto-Sterling and a few others who emphasize the existence of intersexed humans. Thus does Herzig attempt to guide her students through the "problem of materiality." The module's own biases are perhaps not so obvious to young students. Here is how it presents the problem:

> Lurking in most contemporary discussions about gender and sexuality in the United States [but not elsewhere?] is a presumption of the universal, timeless dimorphism between human males and females. How empirically sound are these dualistic categories? What evidence has been presented for and

against universal human sexual dimorphism? How might cross-cultural ethnographic evidence challenge biomedical assumptions of a strict two-sex model? How does the presumption of sexual dimorphism inform our understandings of human sexuality?"[58]

The last question of course gives the agenda away: It is important to attack the notion of biological dimorphism because the fact of dimorphism is essential to our history of sexual reproduction. And sexual reproduction, from a biological point of view, confirms the normalcy, indeed the ordinariness, of heterosexuality, which various famous feminists have interpreted as the "institution" at the root of women's "oppression." Biology presents a particularly intractable problem for this sort of feminist analysis, and it is not surprising, then, that feminists spend considerable energy arguing that biology is merely one more element in the formidable ideology that sustains patriarchy. Readers who note the contradictions evident in Herzig's words should be reassured: These seem not to be a problem for feminists who denounce the existence of biological "facts," on the one hand, while having constant recourse to general and negative characterizations of "males," on the other.[59]

Feminist Science Studies as a whole, as the book's introduction explains, is committed to "progressive, positive readings of science, and of reconstructions of science consistent with feminist theories, ideals, and visions:"[60]

> While we cannot fully predict the future metamorphosis of feminist science studies, each section in this book portrays one of the ways in which feminist science practices are now being forged—through disciplinary border-crossing, interdisciplinary research, pedagogical interventions in the classroom and across disciplines, and community activism.[61]

The three editors describe feminist science studies as a field committed to exploring "situated knowledges," a field under construction, which examines the relationship between feminism and science and "the intersections between race, class, gender, and science and technology," and aims at a "disruption of the dichotomy between scientific inquiry and policy."[62]

In another essay, "Oases in a Desert: Why a Hydrologist Meanders between Science and Women's Studies," Martha Whitaker affirms that Fausto-Sterling's work has been of special importance "in helping me to understand that scientists' analyses and quantification of earth and natural processes *are* social and political processes"[63]—a perfect example of the confusion between the context of science and the content of science.

Another contributor (and one of the book's editors), Banu Subramaniam, in "And the Mirror Cracked! Reflections of Natures and Cultures," aims to go beyond feminist science studies' penchant for "taking apart the visible workings of science to highlight the invisible factors that shaped the interconnections between nature and culture, science and society." Her project "was one of reconstruction—to use these insights of deconstruction to rebuild a practice that was scientifically rigorous but also informed by the rigors of feminist politics and scholarship"—as if the problem were not precisely that the "rigors" of these different endeavors are hardly to be compared.[64]

There is, as noted earlier, a deep and—for many feminists—significant link between attacking the biology of sex differences and undermining the "institution" of heterosexuality, which they see as the linchpin of male dominance. I have documented elsewhere this tendency within feminism; here I will cite only a few expressions of it—leaving aside such notorious figures as Mary Daly, Andrea Dworkin, and Catharine MacKinnon. Marilyn Frye, for example, a well-known professor of Women's Studies at Michigan Sate University, has written:

> Without (hetero)sexual abuse, (hetero)sexual harassment and the (hetero)sexualization of every aspect of female bodies and behaviors, there would not be patriarchy, and whatever

other forms or materializations of oppression might exist, they would not have the shapes, boundaries and dynamics of the racism, nationalism, and so on that we are now familiar with.

As she explains further: "A vital part of making generalized male dominance as close to inevitable as a human construction can be is the naturalization of female heterosexuality. Men have been creating ideologies and political practices which naturalize female heterosexuality continuously in every culture since the dawns of the patriarchies."

And, anticipating the rejoinder that this "naturalization" may indeed be "natural," Frye asserts: "Female heterosexuality is not a biological drive or an individual woman's erotic attraction or attachment to another human animal which happens to be male. Female heterosexuality is a set of social institutions and practices defined and regulated by [patriarchal mores, values, and law]."[65]

Frye presented these views in a speech delivered in 1990 at the National Women's Studies Association conference, but such attitudes have been present in Women's Studies for many years. In a 1984 essay, for example, Joyce Trebilcot, who teaches philosophy and Women's Studies at Washington University in Saint Louis, asked her sisters with a heterosexual past to assume responsibility for their sexual orientation in the present and future. For women who claim not to be sexually aroused by women, Trebilcot provided sage advice: Get your desires in line with your reason. After all, "sexuality is socially constructed." All women, she assured us, can achieve this.[66]

More recently, Robin West, a feminist law professor, has undertaken to analyze what she calls "the harms of consensual sex." While offering a slight qualification—"I want to argue briefly that many (not all) consensual sexual transactions are" harmful to women—she then goes on to make the typical authoritarian-feminist move of claiming that women misunderstand their own experience. As she sees it, the woman who experiences no such harm is actually the one who is most seriously harmed, for such a woman has incorporated a sense of self-negation that makes her incapable of recognizing the injuries she has suffered. West includes among such women those whose decisions to engage in sex are influenced by their "felt or actual dependency upon a partner's affection or economic status."[67]

Lest readers think that arguments such as these come only from a few doctrinaire radical feminists now perhaps out of fashion, I turn to a recent book purporting to be a general reference work, which reveals that statements that once might have been controversial within feminism are these days staples of Women's Studies. The new Houghton Mifflin *Reader's Companion to U.S. Women's History* (1998) contains a telling entry on "Heterosexuality." Composed by E. Kay Trimberger, this entry summarizes current feminist dogma:

> Sexuality is not private, but is political and related to power. "Compulsory heterosexuality" is part of a power structure benefiting heterosexual males at the expense of women and homosexuals. This inequity is justified by an ideology that sees heterosexuality as natural, universal, and biologically necessary, and homosexuality as the opposite. The system also is reinforced by legal sanctions and violence against women (rape, battering, incest, and murder) and against lesbians, gays, and transgendered persons (verbal harassment, physical assault, and murder).

Trimberger makes clear why it is important for feminists to press such an argument: "If our sexuality is socially constructed it can also be de- and reconstructed." [68]

With assertions like these, feminists today are not in a good position to evaluate how much of a role their clearly articulated biases play in alienating masses of women from feminism. As discussed in the preceding chapter, they usually explain such alienation as a sign of timidity or false-consciousness induced by either the patriarchy or the so-called backlash, if not as an outright defense of ignoble privileges. And heterosexual feminists, in turn, too often submit to this stigmatizing of their sexual desires and personal relations and adopt an apologetic stance. After all, as we noted in chapter three, they have been found guilty of "sleeping with the enemy."

But the focus on biology did not arise in a vacuum. It is obvious that Women's Studies has an urgent need to reconstitute everything about men and women's lives that it sees as hindering its own project of social transformation. We will see in the next chapter how tendentious research, undertaken in service to a feminist agenda and spreading its tentacles far outside the university, has been leading to ever stranger results.

12

Feminists Take On Science: Tilting with the Evil Empire

Noretta Koertge

FROM THE VERY BEGINNING, science was the nemesis of Women's Studies. Scientific inquiry embodied all of the so-called masculine virtues that feminism most wanted to challenge—objectivity (vs. subjectivity), the power of reason (instead of intuition), problem solving through logical analysis and the weighing of evidence (vs. conflict resolution through empathy and plumbing the depths of oppression). Given its value system, feminists argued, it was not surprising that scientific practitioners, especially in the physical sciences and engineering, remained overwhelmingly male, even after women had successfully entered other professions, such as law and medicine.

If academic feminists could convincingly demonstrate the gendered nature of science, it would not only complete their research program of revealing the sexist underpinnings of knowledge claims in all the disciplines but also provide the intellectual basis for undermining the hegemony of scientific discourse in society at large. Since science wielded enormous authority in government, law, industry, and the culture at large, challenging its basic values would be an important step in dismantling patriarchy.

And there was an immediate tactical reason for feminists to take on science: The key concept in all Women's Studies research was gender. For too long the experts on gender issues had been sociologists, biologists, and sexologists. Any undermining of science as a whole would make the task of defending feminist conceptions of gender and sexuality easier.

Earlier in this volume, we delineated the various tools that feminists have employed in their assault on the scientific establishment. In describing the lives of women scientists they would not only detail the various obstacles these foremothers encountered (a worthwhile but, sad to say, all too easy task) but also search for ways in which the methods and modes of reasoning that these women worthies used were supposedly different from those of men (cf. the title of Evelyn Fox Keller's biography of Nobel Prize winner Barbara McClintock: *A Feeling for the Organism*). They would attribute a powerful role to the metaphors used to describe both the methods and subject matter of science and remark on their macho associations. From Bacon's comments about "putting Nature on the rack" to the current fascination with the "Big Bang" theory, feminists found science to be saturated with sexist concepts and values.

For a brief introduction to feminist interpretative methods, consider Sharon Traweek's analysis of the terminology used to describe apparatus in high energy physics. In a section titled "Detectors and Desire" she writes:

> The language used by physicists about and around detectors is genital: the imagery of the names SPEAR, SLAC, and PEP is clear as is the reference to the "beam" as "up" or "down.". . . One must see the magnets at LASS to appreciate the labial associations in the detector's name, Large Aperture Solenoid Spectrometer. . . . Ironically, the denial of human agency in the construction of science coexists with the imaging of scientists as male and nature as female. . . . Detectors are the site of their coupling: standing on the massive, throbbing body of the eighty-two-inch bubble chamber at SLAC while watching the accelerated particles from the beam collide twice a second with the superheated hydrogen molecules made this quite clear.[1]

Can this Freudian rhapsody be intended seriously? One wonders what Traweek would say about the genital imagery of vacuum cleaners. Some women prefer uprights, but others like the horizontal type where they can actually manipulate the "wand," moving it "back and forth." Women manifest power over and purify their environment by co-opting the symbols of their oppressors. This is quite clear when one sees them dragging behind them a panting, roaring, dare I say "throbbing" machine, which tries in vain to keep pace with their determined strokes!

Yet Traweek's 1988 book is regarded as a pioneering work in the area of anthropology of science. Traweek is part of the Center for the Cultural Studies of Science, Technology and Medicine at UCLA, and Harvard University Press republished her book in 1995. Some of her comparisons of the career expectations for Japanese and American physicists are indeed interesting. But the sort of feminist analysis illustrated above would certainly distract many readers from the serious parts of her book.

Convinced of the fertility of their approach and the rightness of their cause, feminist scholars have produced an avalanche of articles, monographs, and books about gender and science almost equal in number to feminist publications on literature and art. In Women's Studies circles, feminist scholarship on science is held in very high esteem (we will see why below). Authors such as Sandra Harding, Donna Haraway, Katherine Hayles, Anne Fausto-Sterling, and Evelyn Fox Keller are widely cited. And many have been awarded name chairs in Women's Studies. Feminist accounts of science have also gained a sympathetic audience within schools of education and are often invoked by people working in the area of science and technology studies.

FEMINIST INCURSIONS INTO SCIENCE PEDAGOGY

All too often sentimentally attractive but cognitively bankrupt views find a welcome in the pedagogical establishment. This has certainly been the case with postmodernist and feminist analyses of science. Sometimes the influence is explicit. The 1992 draft of the National Science Education Standards, for example, claimed to be based on a "contemporary approach, called postmodernism, [that] questions the objectivity of observation and the truth of scientific knowledge."[2] And in a recent book review in *Science*, Paul Forman, a historian of science at the Smithsonian, speaks approvingly of "our postmodern world" with its social constructionist epistemology and a "morality-based rather than a truth-based Weltgefuehl."[3] Many science educators now endorse a postmodernist perspective on science which incorporates some of the more extreme feminist views.

For example, students supposedly need to learn that:

- The so-called "laws of nature" are social constructions whose validity depends on consensus. The consensus is driven by interests, not epistemic considerations. "Science is politics by other means."[4]
- There is no legitimate universal science, only local ethnosciences which have been oppressed or colonized.[5]
- The emphasis on so-called scientific objectivity only serves as a cover for exploitation. Instead we need "advocacy research" and "emancipatory science."[6]

These calls for a transformation of the public understanding of science are often accompanied by more or less hostile images of science. For example, Andrew Ross, professor of comparative literature and director of the American Studies Program at NYU, speaks only partly in jest when he dedicates his 1991 book *Strange Weather* to "all the science teachers I never had. [This book] could only have been written without them."[7] There is a general concern that students can too easily be seduced into believing that science gives us an especially reliable way of learning about the world. As we already saw in Part One, feminist writers provide especially vivid examples: "Male science furthers the capitalist, imperialist tradition in which it was begotten: it exploits, rapes, destroys."[8] There is a real fear that scientific ways of knowing can be not only socially destructive but also dangerous to the subjectivity of the individual—especially women.

And although sociologists of science Harry Collins and Trevor Pinch would not describe themselves as being anti-science, their popular book *The Golem: What Everyone Should Know about Science* is constructed around a very ambivalent metaphor:

> Science is a golem. . . . It is powerful. It grows a little more powerful every day. It will follow orders, do your work, and protect you from the ever threatening enemy. But it is clumsy and dangerous. Without control, a golem may destroy its masters with its flailing vigour.[9]

Both postmodernists and feminists call for radical changes in the core methods and norms of science. To cite Ross again: "[We need] different ways of doing science, ways that downgrade methodology, experiment, and manufacturing."[10]

Sue Rosser, a former senior program officer at the National Science Foundation in the United States and now professor of anthropology and Women's Studies at the University of Florida in Gainesville, also would undercut the centrality of the experimental method in her search for a "female-friendly" science: "Well-controlled experiments in a laboratory may provide results that have little application . . . outside the classroom." Instead students should investigate problems of a more "holistic, global scope" using "interactive methods."[11] It is one thing to emphasize the limits of experimentation. It is quite another to recommend not exposing students to its power in ideal circumstances.

And whatever sophisticated caveats one may wish to put on the viability of the fact-value distinction and however difficult it may be ever to live up to the scientific ideal of disinterestedness, it is quite a radical step to call for the deliberate injection of politics into the very formation of scientific hypotheses as does Helen Longino, a professor of philosophy and Women's Studies at Minnesota: "I am suggesting that a feminist scientific practice admits political considerations as relevant constraints on reasoning. . . . If faced with a conflict between [political] commitments and a particular model of brain-behavior, we allow the political commitments to guide the choice."[12]

The influence of these views is very apparent in writings on pedagogical theory, and they are also being taken up by curriculum developers who believe that the concepts of science and mathematics are not congenial with thinking patterns in various local cultures. I will give only two brief illustrations. (For further discussion, see my 1998 essay "Postmodernisms and the Problem of Scientific Literacy.")[13]

First, here is an argument that mathematics conflicts with women's cultural experience. It comes from a Cambridge University Press volume entitled *Equity in Mathematics Education*:

> In the context provided by Irigaray we can see an opposition between the linear time of mathematics problems of related rates, distance formulas, and linear acceleration versus the dominant experiential cyclical time of the menstrual body. Is it obvious to the female mind-body that intervals have endpoints, that parabolas neatly divide the plane, and, indeed, that the linear mathematics of schooling describes the world of experience in intuitively obvious ways?[14]

Similar claims about the incongruity between indigenous modes of thought and mathematics are found in a mathematics newsletter:

> The Western world developed the notion of fractions and decimals out of a need to divide or segment a whole. The Navajo world view consistently appears not to segment the whole of an entity. . . . Non-Euclidean geometry, motion theories, and/or fundamentals of calculus may be naturally compatible with

Navajo spatial knowledge. Math classes should begin with these notions and continue deemphasizing the segmentation of notions into smaller parts.[15]

A startling recommendation for curricular reform follows: "In other words, for some students, it might be appropriate to teach calculus as elementary mathematics, and fractions in college!"[16]

Feminists and postmodernists are even proposing a sort of equal time policy regarding creationism. Barbara Herrnstein Smith, Braxton Craven Professor of Comparative Literature and English and Director of the Center for Interdisciplinary Studies in Science and Cultural Theory at Duke University, takes issue with the usual perspective, articulated in Kitcher's *The Advancement of Science*,[17] that contemporary scientific creationists make "cognitive mistakes" and reason in ways that are not conducive to cognitive progress. Smith finds instead a symmetry between the "epistemic self-privileging" of the disputants. Creationists could offer parallel complaints about their opponents' "ignorance of the Bible, secular humanist prejudice, modern infatuation with evolutionary theory, plus, perhaps, certain sins of sloth and pride."[18] But Smith is overlooking central features of "scientific" creationism. Unlike some of Darwin's theological opponents, these contemporaries are claiming to be relying on empirical considerations, not religious authority, and so it is not question-begging to hold them to the very standard that they proclaim.

Smith argues that the debate about what should be taught in school science classes should *not* focus on the relative scientific merits of evolutionary and creationist biology. It is not clear whether she believes that scientists do not in fact have a strong case for their preference or whether she merely finds them at a rhetorical disadvantage (although given her conception of truth as that which is rhetorically and pragmatically stable, perhaps the distinction is irrelevant). She suggests that instead of appealing to evidence, scientists should rather argue that what is taught in public school science classes should be determined "by members of the relevantly authorized secular epistemic communities." Smith avers that her epistemology does not entail that Might is Right, but by failing to provide a theory that discriminates between diverse modes of rhetorical and pragmatic persuasion she certainly leaves the door open for what she calls "barbarian Might."[19]

Feminists differ in the details of their epistemologies and in their corresponding views of science. (For example, some feminists criticize Smith's cultural relativist stance on clitoridectomy.) But more impressive is the convergence of their views: All feminist commentators on science call for dramatic revisions of traditional scientific norms. They deny the legitimacy of looking for universal, culture-neutral descriptions of nature. And each of these proposals has implications for science education that I would argue harm most the underprivileged and the least powerful members of our society.

THE EMPIRE FIGHTS BACK: GROSS, LEVITT, AND SOKAL

As we have seen, feminist analyses of science became extremely popular in Women's Studies and Cultural Studies circles and influential in schools of education. The reception among historians, philosophers, and sociologists of science—the fields that constitute "Science Studies"—was, however, quite mixed. Many historians of science, always eager to find new raw material and interpretative schemata, found some feminist historiography interesting, although there were grumbles about the fact that many of the authors seemed to think expertise in feminist theory could mask a lack of basic knowledge about the historical period they were addressing. Most philosophers of science, on the other hand, perhaps bored by yet another series of broad-brush attacks on logical positivism and methodological reductionism, simply ignored the attempts to produce a feminist theory of scientific knowledge. Sociologists welcomed essays that illuminated societal influences on science, but many tended to be more intrigued by the internal social structure of science and the relationships between science and government. The reception of feminist analyses of science was much less enthusiastic than had been the case in literature and art, yet they nevertheless seemed to be gaining at least a modicum of respectability within the disciplines that constitute Science Studies.

The situation changed dramatically in 1994 with the appearance of Gross and Levitt's influential polemic against what they called "Higher Superstition." In their hard-hitting book, titled *Higher Superstition: The Academic Left and Its Quarrels with Science*, they clearly traced the conceptual and political links between gender studies, social constructionism, and postmodernism. Drawing on their combined expertise as biologist and mathematician, they catalogued the dozens of basic errors and misunderstandings of the content of science and its history that permeate so much of the most widely regarded feminist accounts. And they implicitly refuted C. P. Snow's suggestion that each of the two cultures was equally ignorant of the other by integrating a good deal of history, philosophy, and political analysis into their attack. *Higher Superstition* was a tour de force.[20]

Once scientists became aware of what people in other parts of the university were saying about their fields, they took action. In 1995, one year later, the New York Academy of Sciences organized a conference called "The Flight from Science and Reason" in which scientists, medical researchers, and also some science studies scholars echoed Gross and Levitt's concerns. Members of the "academic left" were quick to mount a response and in April of 1996 there appeared a special double issue of the journal *Social Text*, dedicated to the so-called Science Wars, which contained rebuttals by many of the people who had been targeted by Gross and Levitt. It began with an introductory essay by Andrew Ross claiming that the rainforest shaman is as relevant to his society as the laboratory scientist is to ours and ended with the now-classic article "Transgressing the Boundaries: Towards a Transformative Hermeneutics of Quantum Gravity" by Alan Sokal, a colleague of Ross at NYU.[21] In the May 1996 issue of *Lingua Franca*, Sokal, a theoretical physicist, revealed that his article was a hoax, part of a little experiment he had conducted to see if *Social Text* would publish sheer nonsense if it were clothed in fashionable jargon and seemed in line with their current ideology. Although the quotations embedded in his essay were all accurate, the conclusions Sokal pretended to draw from them were totally bogus: The axiom of choice in set theory offers no conceivable support for the political project of protecting a pregnant woman's right to choose, and disputes about the possible usefulness of "quantum logic" in no way imply that the assessment of the validity of a deductive argument is the result of social negotiations.

Sokal's parody captured the imagination of the semi-popular media, both here and overseas (see his website at www.physics.nyu .edu/faculty/sokal/ for details) and generated a number of academic books (of which more below). It is tempting to say that this single episode turned the tide against the more radical feminist critiques of science. Where Gross and Levitt had played the "bad cop," Sokal's writing and speaking style was gentle and non-hectoring. Although he pulled no punches in describing what he called "fashionable nonsense," his strategy was to invite people to laugh with him at the foibles that unfettered ideology can lead us into. He had impeccable leftist credentials, having helped develop a mathematics curriculum in Nicaragua during the Sandinista regime, and his primary motive was to advance a leftist agenda. As he wrote in an article shortly after the hoax:

> My main concern isn't to defend science from the barbarian hordes of lit crit (we'll survive just fine, thank you). Rather, my concern is explicitly *political*: to combat a currently fashionable postmodernist/poststructuralist/social-constructivist discourse—and more generally a penchant for subjectivism—which is, I believe, inimical to the values and future of the Left.[22]

Although Sokal certainly didn't single out feminist analyses to bear the brunt of his criticism, in the discussions that took place in the heat of the Science Wars, these feminist commentaries often provided the most egregious and memorable examples of the pitfalls of research guided by activism insufficiently tempered by the traditional norms of scholarship. To cite just one: English professor Katherine Hayles's elaboration of Luce Irigaray's portrayal of the history of hydrodynamics as distorted by males' fascination with "rigid bodies" and "linear models" and their association of fluidity with femininity was marred by a serious misunderstanding of the most basic features of hydrodynamics.[23]

Claims such as those of Carolyn Merchant, a professor of environmental history, philosophy, and ethics at UCLA, who argued in her influential book *The Death of Nature* that the science of matter had been less violent and more in tune with holistic values before the rise of the mechanical philosophy during the time of the Scientific Revolution in the seventeenth century,[24] showed a lack of even the most elementary knowledge of alchemical treatises that described methods for torturing and crucifying base metals.[25] And repeated feminist allegations that the methods of the "New Science" as described by Sir Francis Bacon were inherently misogynist and that Newton's *Principia* might well be called "Newton's 'rape manual'" were easily shown to be based on distorted and highly selective readings of the primary texts.[26]

No longer could allegations of gender bias in both the content and methods of science expect to pass without critical scrutiny as long as they resonated well with the current feminist political agenda. There were now people prepared to take the time to criticize these accounts in detail. And although many feminists continued to shrug off critical responses as the result of "rightwing backlash," at least some became more careful in their presentations. Nevertheless, research habits are difficult to alter and by the end of the twentieth century the canon of Women's Studies contained so much poor scholarship that it was difficult for people who had grown up as scholars in the Women's Studies tradition to make a clean break.

THREE EXAMPLES OF POST–SCIENCE WARS WRITINGS: SCHIEBINGER, POTTER, AND FAUSTO-STERLING

Let us look at some of the best recent work on science that is written from an explicit feminist perspective. I will focus on three recent books that argue for strong influences of gender on the conduct of science, all of which are worth careful reading; none is vulnerable to such immediate criticisms as those discussed above. Yet, I will argue, each is flawed by some of the faulty research strategies that are all too characteristic of feminist work.

Londa Schiebinger's *Has Feminism Changed Science?* was published by Harvard University Press in 1999. It draws many of its examples from the author's earlier books on the history of science, *The Mind Has No Sex? Women and the Origins of Modern Science*[27] and *Nature's Body: Gender in the Making of Modern Science.*[28] In her new book, Schiebinger, who is Edwin E. Sparks Professor for the History of Science at Penn State, comments on sociological studies of the experience of girls and women in science classrooms and laboratories as well as on feminist studies looking for the effect of gender on the substance of scientific claims. It is the latter that are the most controversial.

The second work, *Gender and Boyle's Law of Gases,* is by Elizabeth Potter, a philosopher by training and now the Alice Andrews Quigley Professor of Women's Studies at Mills College. Her book appeared in the Indiana University Press series on *Race, Gender, and Science* in 2001. The last work I will discuss, *Sexing the Body: Gender Politics and the Construction of Sexuality,* has played a central role in discussions about the concept of gender within feminist theory circles. The author, Anne Fausto-Sterling, has appointments in both biology and Women's Studies at Brown University.

I will not attempt here to provide an overall evaluation of the general historical contributions of any of these books. Instead I will use these recent, respectable books in the field to illustrate some general methodological weaknesses that continue to undermine so much of the research in feminist commentaries on science.

Linnaeus, Linguistic Decoding, and Wet Nurses

Schiebinger begins her book with a criticism of various "blind alleys" that feminists have pursued in studying science, including "difference feminism," the search for "women's ways of knowing," and a distrust of quantitative methods, and even voices some areas of agreement with Gross and Levitt's famous contribution to the Science Wars. In her chapter on the effects of gender on physics and math, Schiebinger explicitly refers to Sokal, who she claims is prepared to admit that gender may well have molded parts of the life sciences, but would be dubious of any influence in the physical sciences. Schiebinger, unlike many of her predecessors, grants that there are as yet no convincing examples of the latter. Although she does not explicitly repudiate the purported examples that have been raised by people such as Irigaray and Hayles as well as all of the attempts to show that mathematics is a parochial construction which needs to be supplanted by multicultural perspectives, Schiebinger is very candid that the jury is still out: "Empirical study may reveal that gender does not permeate the most abstract level of human endeavor." And she also emphasizes that the question of gender in science is a complicated one to pursue: "This is a task for the best physicists, philosophers, and historians of science with rigorous training in gender studies of science." This surely counts as a graceful admission that the feminist project of demonstrating the importance of gender in all aspects of science has not been completed and a caution that considerable expertise will be required of those who would endeavor to try.[29]

The rest of Schiebinger's chapter on the physical sciences is devoted to the issue of why they, unlike biology or medicine, are still failing to attract and retain significant numbers of women.

She discusses various possible explanatory factors, such as the on-going history of links to the military and the differential per-formance of males and females on standardized math tests. Whether or not one agrees with every detail of her analysis, one must surely applaud the fact that Schiebinger takes the question of attracting women into science seriously and in no way dis-courages young women from participation in what she describes as "the most abstract level of human endeavor."[30]

Yet there are many places where Schiebinger still follows the more dubious methodologies of feminist analysis. The chapter on biology argues that the method of "linguistic decoding" shows how gender has structured some of the content of that science. She notes that writers such as Gross and Levitt believe that since scientists are trained to disregard metaphorical connotations of the terms they use, they are therefore totally uninfluenced by them. But by pro-posing decodings of the gendered language used by scientists she argues that we cannot just ignore peripheral meanings and conno-tations of terms.

We are not given an account of how to evaluate various linguis-tic decodings and so, before turning to her examples, I would like to raise some general questions about this interpretative method. First, one doesn't need to be a Freudian to readily agree that sexual imagery abounds everywhere—at least in the eye of the observer. As randy teenagers, my classmates and I could hardly contain our ex-citement whenever our English teacher used the word "copula" while diagramming sentences (is that perhaps part of the reason that President Clinton had trouble knowing what the meaning of "is" is?). Our rather nerdy chemistry teacher may never have real-ized our fascination with ionic bonding, what with the chlorine atom that couldn't wait to fill its outer shell and the sodium atom so eager to eject its electron. If he had, he might well have exploited it for pedagogical purposes!

But neither of my examples is a good candidate for gender de-coding because there is no power imbalance. Copulative verbs link equal partners; neither side is "objectified" (in contrast to the sentence on the Catharine MacKinnon T-shirt for sale on the web: "Feminism 101—Subject verb object: Men fuck women"). And although the description of sodium and chlorine's electron configurations is certainly gendered, there is no correlated disparity in reactivity or any other vice or virtue implied—both are poisonous, both are highly active, and neither is particularly hard or unstable or inert.

Schiebinger's examples, by contrast, all involve sexual imagery in situations where there are also implicit differences in power or status. She begins with the by-now legendary example of the intrepid, conquering sperm in pursuit of the big, fat, lazy egg and notes the straightforward gender correlates. She takes Gross and Levitt's point that in the newer politically correct textbooks it is now the egg that is active and selective while the sperm flail around aimlessly. But instead of drawing the conclusion that the scientific account of reproduction can be tarted up for textbook expositions in any number of ways and hence any metaphorical baggage is inessential, she concludes that the second interpretation in fact shows the deep-seated nature of gender stereotypes:

> We might see [the new version of the story] as a narrative of masculinization. Not only is the egg energized, that is, ascribed the valued "active" characteristics of the sperm. Equality—this time for the egg—depends once again on reaffirming masculine virtues. Like women themselves, female biology is here expected to assimilate the values of the dominant culture.[31]

It's not clear what Schiebinger would recommend to the popular science writer—perhaps a variant of the Jack Sprat rhyme where the two sexes are different but cooperating equals? But, of course, in our society there is an asymmetry between being fat and being lean and Schiebinger might well admit that there is in fact no neutral description of reproduction possible and simply take that as evidence that science is inevitably gendered! Her other examples work the same way, although they may seem more forced: "the gendering of the cellular nucleus and the cytoplasm . . . led to the neglect of certain areas of research."[32] This is also the case with her examples of DNA versus RNA and genetics over embryology.

It is easy to make post facto correlations between so-called gendered scientific terms and the amount of research done therein. To extend my own parody of this kind of reasoning, note that most chemistry books follow the historical pattern of beginning with ionic compounds and then turning to organic compounds with covalent bonds. Could this not be construed as a reflection of the assumption in our society that bonding is between opposites (read "heterosexual") and that bonding between like atoms (read "homosexual") is of secondary importance and hence was not a privileged research area until the second half of the nineteenth century—when (can one really say this is a coincidence?) homosexuality began to be openly discussed (also in Germany!) by people such as Ulrichs and Krafft-Ebing?

To continue in this playful mode, one might also try to perform linguistic decodings to discover the influence of race and class. After all, many organic compounds are highly colored (recall aniline dyes), and they are also for the most part less "hierarchical" (recall the egalitarian structure of the benzene ring) than are inorganic compounds, which are either heterosexual dyads (NaCl) or highly centralized (in the stabile sulfate ion the positions of the oxygens are defined in terms of the central sulfur). Small wonder that inorganic chemistry still exerts hegemony over the curriculum in beginning chemistry!

The examples that Schiebinger assembles may well be more plausible than the silly ones that I've just produced, but perhaps my contrived scenario will help remind us that it takes a lot of detailed research to make the case that linguistic devices such as gendered metaphors had a determinative effect on scientific research. And as scientists and others take the trouble to comment on these popular feminist examples, all too many of them turn out to be urban legends. Paul Gross's marvelous (1998) article "Bashful Eggs, Macho

Sperm, and Tonypandy" was probably published too late for Schiebinger to have been aware of it, but there he puts paid to every single feminist claim about the egg/sperm saga, showing, for example, that activity was attributed to the egg at least as far back as 1878 when it was observed to "pull in the sperm," and that it is simply wrong to say that experimental embryology was neglected in the middle part of the twentieth century—Gross himself was involved in such research. If the egg was not neglected, then there is nothing to explain and no need to invoke gendered blindness or any other factor. Gross also traces the spread of the egg/sperm saga from writings of folks in Swarthmore College's Biology and Gender Study Group to a cover story on *Newsweek* magazine. It turns out that the legend of the bashful egg and macho sperm tells us very little about science, but a good deal about gender politics in the last couple of decades.[33]

Schiebinger discusses in considerable detail several places where she sees gender politics playing a role in the work of Linnaeus, famous for the new taxonomic principles he proposed for biology. I will deal briefly with one that illustrates some of the typical moves in feminist historiography, her explanation of why Linneaus chose to designate the class containing quadrupeds and others as *Mammalia*. Schiebinger begins by reminding us that "Linnaeus devised this term, meaning literally 'of the breast', to distinguish the class of animals comprising humans, apes, ungulates, sloths, sea cows, elephants, bats. . . ." She also correctly notes that there were other characteristics that this group shared, such as having hair, three ear bones, and a four-chambered heart, and asks: Why did Linneaus not choose instead *Pilosa* (the hairy ones), *Aurecaviga* (the hollow-eared ones), or *Lactentia* (the suckling ones)? She finds an answer in the gender politics of the time:

If Linnaeus had other valid choices, why did he focus on the maternal breast? His attention to the fully developed female breast had as much to do with unique qualities of the mammal as with eighteenth-century politics of wetnursing, maternal breastfeeding, and the contested role of women in science and broader culture. Linnaeus's choice of the term *Mammalia* presented a problematic outcome for women. By emphasizing how natural it was for females—both human and nonhuman—to suckle and rear their own children, Linneaus's work helped legitimate the restructuring of European society that was then under way.

She then points out that later during the French Revolution there were debates in the legislature about whether "the breasted ones" should become citizens and be given public rights or encouraged to take up their "natural" duties in the home.[34] One immediate observation about this line of argument: It begins by trying to make the case that gender considerations influenced the scientific decision, but ends up by merely claiming that, after the decision was made, it in fact had an impact on the political situation. All too often sociologists of knowledge end there and assume that if a scientific choice benefits X, then anticipation of this later consequence must have been part of the reason for the choice in the first place. Schiebinger, to her immense credit, however, does make it plausible that Linnaeus might have foreseen the political ramifications of his choice by documenting his active involvement in the campaign against wet-nursing.

But let us now revisit the basic assumption that triggers this whole analysis, namely that there was no scientific reason for picking *Mammalia* as the name of the taxonomic category. First, a little debating point: If the scientists had chosen to focus on hirsuteness instead, might not feminists immediately conclude that this was a case of privileging a gendered characteristic? But the main point is this: Scientists generally set up their classifications schemes in a way that will facilitate theory building about the items being classified. Thus Aristotle noted that some animals were warm-blooded and some cold-blooded, in part because heat was an important active principle in his account of the world. He also distinguished between oviparous and viviparous animals because he felt that reproduction was an important characteristic of living things.

Any viable new classification would also have to reflect characteristics that were thought to be biologically important. As far as I know, there was no reason at the time for thinking that having hair or certain kinds of ears were fundamental biological properties. Having a heart with four chambers seems closer to the central processes of life, although it is not as easy to detect (practical considerations would also militate against using the number of chambers in the ear). Providing food for offspring certainly would count as a biologically important function and it certainly makes sense for a taxonomist to focus on the body part (breasts) vs. the process (suckling). So it seems that there are clear theoretical and pragmatic reasons for the choice Linnaeus made. There is no explanatory gap that cries out for explanation from external considerations.

Another debating point: What if Linneaus had not chosen *Mammalia*? Could feminists not then propose that it was fear of attributing too much centrality to female-gendered body parts that drove his decision? This surely was the tactic taken in the sperm/egg story, where focusing on the sperm was taken to be an indication of the superiority of maleness. To be consistent, shouldn't one also argue that focusing on the breast was an indication of the importance of femaleness? Once again we see how easy it is to produce a gendered "decoding" of episodes in the history of science no matter what happens. And as Popper long ago argued, using the cases of Marxism and Freudianism, any world view that can "explain" every conceivable event actually explains nothing.

Boyle, Chastity, and the Gender of the Gas Law

Let us now turn to the second case study claiming that gender played a crucial role in the development of scientific ideas. Elizabeth Potter was trained as a philosopher, but recently she has turned her attention to the historical role of Sir Robert Boyle. In the introduction to her new book she explains part of her motivation. In the 1980s she heard Evelyn Fox Keller speak at a conference on gender and science. In the discussion that followed, a man in the audience, after failing to refute the examples given by the speaker, got in the last word to the effect that "you folks will never show that gender affects something like Boyle's Law!" Potter writes, "This book is a response to that challenge."[35]

Potter's basic thesis is that at the time when Boyle was studying gases, discovering among other things the inverse relationship between volume and pressure that we now call Boyle's Law, there existed an alternative account put forward by a Jesuit named Linus that was on a par from a scientific point of view. The only reason for preferring Boyle's account, according to Potter, had to do with class and gender politics. A secondary thesis concerns Boyle's views on the suitability of women to do science.

Before describing Potter's work in more detail, I should point out that there is a very active Boyle "industry" in history of science today, including recent books directly relevant to Potter's claims by Peter Anstey, Rose-Mary Sargent, and Larry Principe. Furthermore, Boyle himself was a prolific writer—the new edition of his works, edited by Hunter and Davis, now runs to fourteen volumes. These considerations make it difficult to propose a definitive summary of Boyle's attitudes or views on anything! To Potter's credit, she has responded to criticisms of her earlier claims and has introduced some modifications and qualifications. She now recognizes that Boyle was not an unmitigated male chauvinist (for example, he explicitly discussed the equality of women in the preface to his "Martyrdom of Theodora"). She also now realizes that despite being the father of the mechanical philosophy, he did not view matter in purely mechanical terms but attributed "activity" to it. This receptivity to criticism puts her writing into what I am calling the "postwar" category—that is, following the Science Wars—but it still bears the hallmarks of the distorting influence of feminist research traditions. I will not attempt a thoroughgoing evaluation of the book, but I will list a few typical feminist errors.

Let me begin with a criticism that may sound a bit pedantic. In more than one place (cf. p. ix and p. 35) Potter mistakenly identifies Boyle's Law ($pv = k$) with what we now call the Ideal Gas Law, which includes the effect of temperature. However, the exact nature of the dependence of the volume of gases on temperature (called Charles' Law) was only discovered late in the eighteenth century. To make matters worse, Potter gives the wrong equation for the Ideal Gas Law. She writes it as $pvt = k$ instead of $pv = kT$ (where the capital letter denotes absolute temperature), thus suggesting that pressure is *inversely* proportional to temperature. One might be inclined to overlook this blunder except for the following considerations: As was already indicated, Potter's case hinges on the assumption that Boyle's account was scientifically on a par with Linus's alternative. But one of the factors that complicated the interpretation of experimental data in Boyle's time was the fact that the exact influence of temperature was not known. Thus Boyle's opponents could argue that when Pascal's barometer fell as it was carried up the Puy-de-Dôme mountain, the cause might have been the drop in temperature, not the drop in pressure. There are other places in the book where Potter does state Boyle's Law correctly (e.g., p. 183, in the conclusion), but nevertheless this confusion about the basic science that is the topic of her book is worrisome. And it is all too reminiscent of more egregious cases of feminists' ignorance of the most rudimentary scientific aspects of the subject matter they are critiquing. (See, for example, Sullivan's 1998 bill of indictment against Katherine Hayles on hydrodynamics.)

As we will now see, Potter, like feminist commentators on Bacon, is also tripped up by not having sufficient knowledge of the historical context. Let us begin with her claim about Boyle's general views on gender and science. Here is her summary of her position:

Boyle helped to construct a new science which required that facts be produced through experiments properly conducted and attested, and that the new man of science be a chaste, modest heterosexual who desires yet eschews a sexually dangerous yet chaste and modest woman.[36]

She then provides a nice anecdote as part of her argument for the claim that Boyle thought women had no place in the laboratory. Once when he was demonstrating his vacuum pump to an assemblage of gentle people and showed the effect of evacuating a jar on a small animal, a gentlewoman present made him stop the experiment (luckily the bird revived); Boyle writes that they had to wait until the ladies retired before the science demonstration could proceed. Potter concludes that Boyle thought that the presence of women would not only threaten the male scientists' chastity but also interfere in a very direct way with the impersonal manipulations required by his vision of the mechanical philosophy.[37]

However, this episode seems less compelling when we learn that Boyle himself frequently stopped experiments before the animal died and noted that some of the experiments performed by Hooke on dogs were so gruesome that they made him feel uncomfortable.[38] Furthermore, others shared Boyle's scruples. After Hooke performed one such experiment in front of the Royal Society, Thomas Birch reports that he wrote Boyle about his reluctance to conduct such experiments, saying he would "hardly be induced to make any further trials of this kind, because of the torture of the creature."[39]

The attitude of scientists at that time toward experimentation with animals is more ambivalent than Potter's story would lead us to believe, and although she might attribute Boyle's hesitation to a weak heterosexual identity (he never married and was a bit prissy), it's hard to extend that explanation to the tough-minded Hooke— or Priestley, who several decades later expressed concerns about the treatment of mice in studies of respiration!

Anyone doing history is vulnerable to having their interpretation refuted by facts of which they were unaware. Feminists or others doing history for strong ideological reasons may be unusually susceptible to this fate. If one takes as axiomatic certain assumptions about historical development (for example, that science is unfriendly to women), and if one is also convinced that all previous work by historians has been slanted against one's favorite oppressed group, it is easy to become rather cavalier in one's treatment of extant historical knowledge and to draw quick conclusions from historical data that do in fact seem to fit one's preconceived model. The story of the treatment of experimental animals deserves to be told in more detail, and it may well turn out to have interesting parallels with the history of women's participation in science; but that case must be carefully made. It cannot be deduced a priori from current conceptions of gender stereotypes.

Let us now comment briefly on Potter's central claim: There was, she says, no scientific reason at the time to prefer Boyle's account of the behavior of gases to that of Linus. She argues that: "[Boyle's] commitment was based not only on the empirical adequacy of his hypothesis, but also on its religious and political meaning, including its implications for gender politics."[40]

We first note that unlike many contemporary commentators on science who are radical constructionists, Potter believes that experimental data do play an important role in the acceptance of hypotheses in science. In fact, within the spectrum of feminist epistemologists, Potter is usually regarded as a feminist empiricist. But she believes, as well, that in this particular episode, class and gender also played an important role.

Even the most sympathetic reader would have to admit, however, that the connection between gender and Boyle's Law that Potter posits is a rather indirect one. The links in the chain go something like this:

1. During the time of the English Civil War, social radicals proposed egalitarian ideals regarding women and common folk.
2. The radicals were sympathetic to animism and hylozoism, the doctrine that "Nature is a spirit who infuses and guides the world." [41]

3. The aristocratic Boyle was not sympathetic to the social radicals' political agenda nor to the philosophy of animism and hylozoism.

4. As a Jesuit, Linus was not sympathetic to the social radical agenda, but his non-mechanical account of the behavior of gases that retained the idea that Nature abhors a vacuum could be viewed as compatible with hylozoism.

5. Although Boyle may have had metaphysical reasons for opposing hylozoism, he also opposed it because of its association with the social radicals who promoted gender and class equity.

6. One reason Boyle had for opposing Linus's account was the belief that acceptance of a non-mechanical account of gases might give aid to or confer credibility on the social radicals' movement.

For our purposes here we can cede Potter's first four points, but notice that the example of Linus immediately triggers our suspicion that the philosophy of hylozoism was not uniquely and perhaps not even strongly associated with the radicals' cause. The major problems arise in steps 5 and 6 of the argument, and they are worth discussing because they are typical of feminist historiography.

It is an irony that so many commentators today who bash science for being too "positivistic" themselves seem to assume that the only legitimate scientific reason for preferring one hypothesis to another is its present empirical adequacy. But scientists and philosophers of science, even at the height of logical positivism, have articulated other desiderata, such as linguistic or conceptual simplicity, ease of computation and openness to experimental test, or heuristic potential, which play a role in choosing which research programs to pursue. Boyle was very aware of this type of consideration—he spoke in terms of the "intelligibility" of a theory—and this was one of the respects in which he found the mechanical philosophy superior to the animistic one. And as we all know from Molière's joke about opium being a soporific because it possessed the dormative virtue, non-scientists could also appreciate the force of Boyle's requirement of intelligibility.

By adopting an overly restrictive view of what counts as a scientific reason for preferring one research program over another, feminists too quickly conclude that non-scientific factors must be playing a major role and then go looking for how gender politics must therefore be implicated.

So my response to #5 is that Boyle had very strong scientific reasons for opposing hylozoism and, given that it was an old approach that pre-dated the contemporary radical movement (Boyle often appeals to the history of scientific ideas in his treatises) and was not confined to them (Linus is one of many examples), it seems quite a stretch to suppose that Boyle's concern about gender politics played a part in either his dislike of hylozoism or his defense of his theory of gases!

Potter, of course, can correctly point out that neither I nor anyone else can prove that gender played zero role in this incident. She is correct, but what *can* easily be established, I think, is that there are no gaps in a straightforward explanation of his behavior that involves only the usual scientific considerations. I will not attempt to spell out the full details of such an explanation here, but if I were to do so it would involve showing how Potter's confusion between Boyle's Law and the Ideal Gas Law mentioned above and her downplaying of the ad hoc character of Linus's theory led her to the erroneous conclusion that from a scientific viewpoint the Linus and Boyle accounts were on a par. I, unlike Potter, am persuaded by Boyle's own careful and detailed refutation of the Linus proposal and conclude that Boyle in fact had good scientific reasons for preferring his account.

Now feminists can always claim that scientific decisions are overdetermined, so that although there may be scientific considerations sufficient to explain the adoption of a certain approach, the story can be enriched by pointing to gender or political factors that militate in the same direction. But as I pointed out in the Schiebinger account of *Mammalia* above, one can always generate a gender story once one knows the scientific outcome. Hence additional work is required to make the gendered history more than an imaginative adornment.

Once again we find that feminist case studies are raising some interesting new questions, but their overall value as history is seriously marred by ideological blinders and distorting methodologies. The two examples discussed so far both try to show the influence of male gender perspectives in the past. We now turn to a case where there is a call to reform current biological concepts in order to bring them into accord with a female-gendered point of view.

Multiplying Sexes, Multiplying Genders

Anne Fausto-Sterling's new book, *Sexing the Body: Gender Politics and the Construction of Sexuality*, is literally a heavyweight contribution to feminist theory. Six years in the making, it consists of close to five hundred pages, nearly half of which are devoted to scholarly footnotes. And Fausto-Sterling, who continues to hold an appointment in the Biology Department at Brown University, can speak with some authority on the scientific subjects she addresses. As a result, the book has justifiably generated a great deal of discussion both inside and outside of Women's Studies circles. (Like any expert, however, she can easily lose her way when she ventures too far afield. For example, she uncritically accepts as reliable evidence for the extreme malleability of human nature reports about feral children who were raised by wolves and could supposedly run faster on four legs than most humans can on two.)[42]

Many of the book's explicit claims are very strong and relatively easy to summarize: Dualistic conceptions of both sex and gender are not justified by our knowledge of biology. They are in fact kept in place by politics of a retrogressive kind and should be replaced by a new, less rigid, systems account of gender, sex, and sexuality that would recognize both the vast variability and multi-dimensional nature of all such aspects of human beings. The harm done by trying to force people into our present impoverished categories is especially striking in the case of intersexed neonates whose genitals are excised or mutilated until they fit one of the two sexual stereotypes. And all of us suffer more or less from the Procrustean forces that shape our gender identities and sexual preferences.

One can, however, share Fausto-Sterling's social concerns without buying into any of her historical or philosophical analysis. Take, for example, the case of the intersexed babies: As Fausto-Sterling and other recent critics have pointed out, there is now much empirical evidence that the sex-selection operations are unsuccessful. Furthermore, there are ethical reasons for not undertaking cosmetic surgery without a high level of informed consent. So why shouldn't we just educate both the medical profession and the public at large to facts about intersexed humans? Why do we have to revolutionize our conceptions of male and female?

The reason seems to hinge on Fausto-Sterling's conviction that as long as we take the two-sex system to be the norm, then folks who don't fit the types will be stigmatized. So she calls for two simultaneous reforms: Society should stop forcing people to declare themselves male or female on birth certificates and passports, and scientists should give up the fiction that homo sapiens is a two-sexed species. Ditto for gonads, hormones, and sex chromosomes. Until we give up the underlying binary biological concepts, it will be difficult to loosen up our conceptions of gender and sexual orientation. She envisions a utopia in which people can locate themselves along a continuum of possible genders and sexualities and may change their location dramatically over their life span.

Most of the book consists of a historical review of research on reproduction, sexual development, sex hormones, sexual behavior, studies of sex differences in brain structure, and so on. With each topic Fausto-Sterling argues that binary conceptions of sex have led the biologists astray and that there is no basis in nature for the two-sex system. Gender politics was constantly intervening and shaping the outcome.

Before we look at some detailed examples from her narrative, I'd like to list some problematic and puzzling features of her overall line of argument. First of all, it is surely worth noting that it was scientists themselves who gave us precise descriptions of the variants of intersexed humans that so bewilder Olympic committees and obstetricians. Folklore posits hermaphrodites and third sexes, but it took rather sophisticated biological techniques for us to know about XYY chromosomes and congenital adrenal hyperplasia. And long before the Internet made visible the subcultures of people who are sexually attracted to amputees or of females who like to play male drag queens, anthropologists and sex researchers were charting exotic sexual practices and paraphilias. What an irony that the scientists whom Fausto-Sterling sees as most blinkered by their rigid binary categories turn out to be the very ones who consistently inform feminists and the rest of us about the variety and complexity of human bodies and behavior!

Second, it is not at all clear what sort of new conceptual system Fausto-Sterling is advocating. We get some vague analogies—the interplay of genes and environment should be viewed sort of like a Moebius strip or a tesselated Escher figure; an interdisciplinary approach to gender might be represented by nested Russian dolls. None of this is spelled out. It is also not clear how thoroughgoing the repudiation of our traditional conceptions would be. We would no longer speak of two sexes or two genders or male and female hormones—that much is clear. But could we still speak of men and women (as long as we weren't filling out birth certificates)? Perhaps in the utopia she envisages people could choose what they want to be thought of and it would be a social faux pas not to respect their wishes, just as today Miss Manners tells us to address thank you notes as Mrs./Ms./Miss according to the preferences of the recipients.

Third, even if Fausto-Sterling were right to say that scientists should give up all talk of two sexes (I shall argue below that she is mistaken), how naive to assume that if scientists regimented their categories differently, ordinary people would follow suit. Most of us now remember that whales are not fish, although we can sympathize with the small child who upon getting a big lecture about whales being mammals responded wisely, "Well, they still swim and live in the ocean." But few of us feel comfortable calling window glass a liquid or saying that a circle is a special case of an ellipse; and although most of us are firmly committed to heliocentrism, we nevertheless cannot just look at the sun at dawn (I must not say sunrise) and feel that the earth is turning under it towards the east. Whatever the technical definitions may be, in most situations we rely on prototypes, and these reflect what is common and useful in our experience. And so for most people, the first thing they think of when you say "bird" will not be a penguin and their prototypical mammal will not be a whale. And I daresay people will continue to anticipate that a newborn is either a boy or a girl no matter how much sympathy they have for intersexed children.

Fausto-Sterling, herself, repeatedly exemplifies how difficult it is to adopt her own proposals in a consistent manner. For example, after nearly two hundred pages of berating scientists for their talk of male and female sex hormones and putting a great deal of emphasis on the facts that a variety of organs, including the adrenal gland, can synthesize these growth steroids and that all human bodies contain both estrogen and testosterone, Fausto-Sterling finally proposes that they should be renamed: "Let's agree to call them steroid hormones and nothing else." Yet in the very next paragraph she writes: "Under the right circumstances these hormones can dramatically affect sexual development at both the anatomical and the behavioral level. They are present in different quantities and often affect the same tissues differently in *conventional males and females.*"

And a couple of chapters later, when summarizing social science research about the interactions between boys and girls, she writes about teenagers: "During the years of hormonal hell, they return to each other for sex and socializing."[43] Evidently in the brave new feminist world it may still be a useful convention to label parts of the continuum as male/female or boy/girl and talk about their sharply different reactions to certain hormones; but we must not, of course, talk about two sexes or two kinds of sex hormones. This is starting to sound a bit like semantic covers on Victorian piano legs!

So even before looking at the details of Fausto-Sterling's argument all sorts of skeptical questions arise. More difficulties quickly emerge as we analyze her historical narrative. Fausto-Sterling, like many other feminist historians, adopts a historiographic methodology reminiscent of Jung's theory of synchronicity. They look for meaningful coincidences and assume that these reveal causal connections. Fausto-Sterling uses the following narrative technique repeatedly: She picks an interesting episode in the history of science, juxtaposes an account of the gender politics operating somewhere in society at the period in question, and then opines that it can't just be a coincidence that these two things happened at about the same time.

Here's an example of this interpretative method at work. In an introduction to a section called "Purifying" she gives us a hint of how the narrative will go:

In 1920, the male hormone turned boys into men, and the female hormone made women out of the girls. Feminists had won a major political victory in getting the right to vote, and America had rid her shores of many foreign radicals. But out of this apparent calm, a new unrest soon broke loose. While feminism struggled to maintain its newfound identity, women's roles continued to change and sex hormones started to multiply.[44]

We then get a reasonable history of how scientists kept discovering unexpected facts about the hormones—they were made in various parts of the body, they had diverse effects, they were found in both men and women. Scientists disagreed about how best to describe them. Here is what Fausto-Sterling says about the two major positions:

Because of their loyalty to a two-gender system, some scientists resisted the implications of new experiments that produced increasingly contradictory evidence about the uniqueness of male and female hormones. . . . But scientists are a diverse lot, and not everyone responded to the new results by trying to fit them into the dominant gender system.

One might then expect Fausto-Sterling to back off her claims about the strong role of gender. But, no, on the next page she says "Diversity in scientific voices paralleled diversity within feminism itself" and refers to Eleanor Roosevelt's 1940 call for solidarity: Women must become more conscious of themselves as women and of their ability to function as a group. And then we read on the following page Fausto-Sterling's startling conclusion about the scientific situation in 1936: "Amid such gender turmoil, it was never possible to resolve the identity of the sex hormones."[45]

Despite Fausto-Sterling's continual reminders that the two historical accounts she has pieced together really work like a Moebius strip, the two strands function as completely separate accounts. She might be able to make a weak case that when scientists first discovered hormones their conjectures about them were influenced by the two-gender system. However, even at the earliest stages there were good scientific reasons for thinking in terms of a male hormone and a female hormone simply because the first samples were isolated from men's urine and women's urine respectively!

Neither this historical episode nor any of the others Fausto-Sterling presents gives us reason to believe that gender politics played a role of any significance in the construction of the science involved. I would have frankly expected to find more of a role, but Fausto-Sterling presents us, almost despite herself, with enough historical detail to refute her own broad claims.

But let us leave the historical, descriptive part of her book aside and look at her philosophical, normative proposals. Certainly there would be no scientific harm done if we were to stop talking about sex hormones and talk of steroid hormones instead. And we know from science itself that any adequate account of the origins and functions of these chemicals will certainly be very complex indeed. Ditto for the varieties of intersexed babies, and what, following

Freud, we might call the polymorphous perversity of genders and sexualities. Why shouldn't biologists just gracefully admit that, strictly speaking, homo sapiens is *not* a two-sexed species?

In many parts of science this proposal would not lead to a catastrophe. After all, one of the hallmarks of modern biology is thinking in terms of populations instead of type specimens, and social scientists almost always find that they need to work with cluster concepts instead of simple conjunctions of necessary and sufficient conditions. Sexologists and psychologists have for some time been using multi-dimensional schemes to talk about both sex and gender. (See, for example, the Kinsey Institute volumes edited by Reinisch et al.)[46]

But there is one central part of modern biology that could not give up its talk of two sexes and still retain its explanatory power, and that is evolutionary theory. There are major differences in the evolutionary path of species that reproduce asexually and species where two sexes are required for reproduction. In fact, producing mathematical models of just how much difference it makes in the rates of variation and adaptation when offspring share genetic materials from both parents has been one of the major achievements of biological theory. Species that reproduce sexually tend to be rather good at sorting out which of their conspecifics belong to which sex, and this often is associated with quite a marked sexual dimorphism.

New technologies may make it possible in the future to have reproduction without the involvement of people of two different sexes, but it is undeniable that the evolution of our present bodies and minds happened within a species that had two clearly distinct and easily recognizable sexes. Just as there are a variety of scenarios that show how having a few non-reproducing homosexuals around could be of adaptive value (see, for example, Ruse),[47] there may well be evolutionary explanations of why a species that produced the occasional sterile or intersexed child could be viable; but none of this would gainsay the central importance of thinking of homo sapiens as a two-sexed species.

Once again we find that the feminist case studies are raising some interesting new questions, but their overall value as history is seriously marred by ideological blinders and distorting methodologies. But perhaps this is all starting to sound too much like one of those local spats for which the ivory tower is notorious. Does it really have much impact on the students who imbibe the feminist take on science and its history?

THE CHILLY CLIMATE WITHIN WOMEN'S STUDIES FOR SCIENCE STUDENTS

In 1994 I wrote an opinion piece for the *Chronicle of Higher Education* called "Are Feminists Alienating Women from the Sciences?" remarking that the feminist denigration of traditional scientific values such as logic, quantitative reasoning, universality, and objectivity, coupled with feminists' flamboyant assertions about the ubiquity of sexism in science, might well discourage young women from even contemplating a major in scientific disciplines and interfere with their scientific training if they did. I wrote that they might well believe that "Any feminist who wants to pursue a scientific career [would] have to think of herself as a missionary and exercise vigilance to keep from going native! By implication, the feminist credentials of any woman who does manage to succeed in science today are open to question."[48]

As the title indicates, this little piece was intended to be speculative and provocative, and it did indeed provoke remonstrances from women scientists who considered themselves to be staunch feminists. There is no denying, as I actually said in the body of the essay, that feminism in general has helped eliminate barriers for women scientists as well as providing useful coping tactics. So groups such as AWIS (American Women in Science) and WPHYS (Women in Physics) run useful discussion lists, organize babysitting and room-sharing for women attending conferences, and promote the inclusion of women in various professional activities.

They are feminist in the traditional sense of the word and certainly do *not* alienate young women. But they rarely raise any of the issues so dear to the hearts of Women's Studies commentators on science. (Here is one case where they did: Someone on the WPHYS listserve asked for an introductory physics textbook that introduced optics before mechanics, reasoning that young women might find it more congenial to study waves before having to deal with collisions of rigid bodies. But this query elicited little discussion and soon the discussion list turned to nitty gritty issues, such as how to help women students prepare for and feel less anxious about Graduate Record Exams.)

A more descriptive title for what I was really concerned about would have been "Are Women's Studies Courses Now Driving Women Away from Science?" Earlier chapters in this volume present personal narratives that suggest that Women's Studies is contributing to the alienation of women from science. There is now additional relevant evidence.

A useful preliminary study of the impact of various strands of feminism on young women scientists today is presented in Angela Pattatucci's fascinating collection of autobiographical narratives.[49] This is a collection of tales of troubles and triumph from women in the natural sciences. On the face of it, their experiences are quite varied: some are engineers and others biologists; some have successful research careers and others have switched to science journalism or science teaching; some are upbeat (one titles her story "I Dared to Be Different"), while another calls her contribution "A Woman's Story of Disillusionment." Nevertheless, common patterns emerge. Nearly all of the contributors mention being interested in science and encouraged by family or teachers at an early age. However, as they grew older most encountered either professors or peers who discouraged them in ways that are either directly or indirectly related to gender. Many of those who emerged victorious talk about finding support—sometimes from a husband or friends, sometimes from a group of other women in science or a research mentor.

I think it would be fair to say that virtually all of the women in this sample have something good to say about the general feminist ethos that has pervaded the American scene in the last thirty years. It has made them better able to recognize and deal with gender discrimination. An example of what I mean by the general influence of feminism occurs in the entry titled "Who's Afraid of Virginia Woolf Now?" There Angela Rella, an undergraduate who chose to do a double major in electrical engineering and English literature, relates that she "look[s] toward two things to clear [her] mind: numbers and Virginia Woolf."[50]

However, when we look at the impact of Women's Studies and feminist theory on the lives of these scientists, a very mixed picture emerges. First of all, of the twenty women who contribute autobiographical sketches to Pattatucci's volume on women in science, only three make any mention whatsoever of academic feminism. (I am not including the editor here.) The reactions of these three range from extremely positive to extremely negative. Nina Wokhlu, a student in medical school, makes a brief positive comment:

> In trying to survive my male-dominated classes, I desensitized myself to any unpleasant circumstances. However, I eventually enrolled in a campus women's studies course. This was one of the most positive experiences that I can remember. My original feelings and sensitivities were rekindled. I remembered who I was and what my purpose was.[51]

Suzanne Franks, now a medical writer, gives a ringing endorsement of the helpful feminist insights and friendly classmates she found:

> I attended the History of Feminist Thought graduate seminar and grew as a person, finding some of the answers, or explanations, for which I was looking. . . . The friends that I made . . . helped me make sense of, and endure, what transpired during this ordeal [she describes the gender hostility of one of

the professors on her qualifying exam committee] . . . If I had not received [this] support and encouragement . . . I believe that I would have quit graduate school.

However, even Franks's positive protocol gives a hint of possible sources of discomfort for young women aspiring to be scientists when they encounter women's studies:

I just showed up on the first day of class and announced that I wanted to participate, much to the consternation of the instructor. [She] let me sit in that first day, but mentioned that she wanted to speak with me later regarding my participation. During our meeting, she outlined the difficulties I might experience in the class. She advised that I would be asked to consider things that I had not encountered in my science education, noting that the questions addressed would not have the hard answers characteristic of an equation or engineering problem. In desperation—for I feared she was saying I could not participate—I babbled about the Heisenberg uncertainty principle in quantum mechanics, and how this prepared me to think in the ways she was saying were needed.

Suzanne Franks eventually did talk her way into the course (which was taught by Jean O'Barr, director of Women's Studies at Duke) and says, "the opportunity forever changed my life." She eventually left bench science and is now very active in promoting feminist reforms of science education. Franks emphasizes that

women's studies was not asking me to reject science or to replace the traditional definition of success with a different and equally rigid one. Women's studies was not asking me to be a failure. Instead it asked something much more difficult of me . . . to develop my own personal and particular answers to . . . questions [about what my life's goals were to be].[52]

The most extended and negative discussion of Women's Studies comes from Donna Riley, a doctoral student in engineering at Carnegie Mellon University. Titled "Feminist/Scientist: Ambiguities and Contradictions," Riley's story begins with a description of her experience of leaving an all-girl high school in Pasadena and entering the chemical engineering department at Princeton: "It felt like running into an ivy-covered brick wall." The entire engineering school had only one female faculty out of a hundred, and she was untenured. However, when Riley signed up for a Women's Studies class on the history of gender and science, she discovered a different kind of isolation:

> In a class of anthropologists, sociologists, and historians, I was the sole engineer. . . . Once again, I found myself having to prove my abilities—this time not as a woman in a hostile field but as an engineer in foreign territory. . . . I had awkward interactions with some students who assumed I had no background in basic feminist theory. They seemed to think that if my perspective differed from the readings, it was because I did not understand it, or because I had sold out to the male engineering patriarchy. If, on the other hand, my women's studies classmates disagreed with the readings, their comments were taken as informed criticisms. In that respect, I felt excluded from the lively classroom debates. This type of isolation crystallized in my interactions with some feminists on campus who viewed science as inherently and irreparably oppressive to women.

She also found this attitude instantiated within academic books such as *Gyn/Ecology* and describes the position presented there by Mary Daly this way:

> According to Mary Daly, all female gynecologists who have been educated in mainstream American medical schools are "token torturers" of women, liaisons to the patriarchy. There

is no room in Daly's view for female gynecologists to use powerful knowledge men have monopolized, subverting it to help other women.

Riley survived this double onslaught, partly by finding a female scientist to mentor her independent research during her junior year and partly by working with a Committee on the Status of Women to improve the retention rates of women science students at Princeton. She concludes:

> Forces from all sides set up obstacles: sexist men say that women cannot do science; technophobic feminists demand women abandon science in order to withdraw energy from the patriarchy; antifeminist women in science attack feminist scientists as weak, whiny victims. . . . All I can do is rise up defiantly, and say, "I'm going to do it anyway."[53]

What a tragedy when the latest incarnations of "women's liberation" turn out to be yet another obstacle in the path of aspiring young female scientists! But even sadder are the effects on the large numbers of students who come into Women's Studies with little previous knowledge of or interest in science. For them, radical feminist accounts of the content and methods of science may well come across not as provocative challenges to scientific orthodoxy but as a canon of well-established truths.

A good example of how this works is provided by the discussion on the WMST-List of Fausto-Sterling's controversial ideas, described in chapter 11. In principle, seriously flawed perspectives such as those of Fausto-Sterling could provide a useful means for provoking students to re-examine standard concepts of sex and gender, just as expositions of "creation science" can be used as a way to get students to think critically about the evidential basis for Darwinian theory. Philosophers are quite accustomed to proposing all sorts of strange theories or thought experiments as a foil to promote the critical examination of commonsense beliefs. But that is *not* what is happening in Women's Studies. Instead Fausto-Sterling's rejection of sexual dimorphism is presented as *the* scientific theory of choice, and it is then taken not only as a basis for activism on behalf of intersexed people but also as a foundation for feminist theorizing about sex and gender. When it is perceived as convenient for feminist purposes, it is all too common for Women's Studies to adopt fringe views within science or about science without taking cognizance of their controversial status.

WOMEN'S STUDIES VIS-À-VIS SCIENCE STUDIES?

Our story of recent feminist approaches to science is a tangle of quite diverse strands. Much nonsense is still being written. But there are now feminist writers producing work of a caliber that can make an impact on the traditional disciplines constituting science studies. Certainly historical studies of the role of women scientists and the history of ideas about sex and gender have enriched the history of science. Sociologists who study career paths in the sciences and the roles of mentors and invisible colleagues now realize that gender is an important variable. Feminist theorizing about the epistemology and methodology of science has been less successful, but feminist reflections on issues of ethics, social responsibility, and technology assessment have contributed to the increasing discussion of such topics by philosophers of science.

But in order to continue making contributions feminist writers are going to have to interact with a wider scholarly audience. Criticism within feminist circles is still overwhelmingly concerned with issues of political correctness or nuances of feminist theory. If feminists want criticism of the strength of their arguments or the historical bases for their claims, they will have to heed the comments of scholars outside of academic feminism. Will they be receptive to dialogue with those who do not share their ideological goals and methods?

The past record is not good. Although academic feminism has been extraordinarily successful in exporting its ideas to other parts of the university, it has been loath to engage in critical dialogue with traditional disciplines or to import ideas from them. So Women's Studies programs remain rather small, for the most part, while dozens of courses having to do with sex, gender, race, and class are taught throughout the university. Yet those courses are often not even cross-listed for Women's Studies credit. (At my university the English Department offers a concentration in feminist approaches to literature entirely separate from course offerings in Women's Studies.) And whereas it is common these days for textbooks and research articles to make some mention of feminist perspectives, even if only to criticize them, feminist writers typically do not cite any criticisms of their views that come from outside feminist circles. As I pointed out above, Schiebinger and Potter are unusual in the fact that they do take cognizance of other commentators.

Just because science and science education are deemed to be so important in our society (feminists are right about the high value that is placed on science as a source of knowledge in our society), feminist distortions of the content, methods, and even history of science will not benefit from benign neglect. The frank debate inspired by Sokal's hoax paper and the Science Wars has alerted more people to what is at stake. Until recently it may have seemed that the value placed on rational discourse in our society was on the wane, but it now appears that the winds of relativism and the privileging of political agendas over empirical adequacy have only succeeded in fanning the embers of the Enlightenment back into flame. Feminist scholarship has now had three decades in which to get over some of its growing pains. It is surely time to move from a defensive separatist stance toward a new era of cooperation.

Here again, however, one cannot be overly optimistic. Consider, for example, both the tone and the substance of the opening words by Janet Kourany, the convener of a panel on Feminist Philosophy of Science at a meeting in 2001: "What does feminism contribute to philosophy of science? Why be modest? Feminism contributes nothing less than a new program for philosophy of science—a program for a socially responsible philosophy of science." Kourany believes that "for the most part. . . . science has done more to perpetuate and add to the problems women confront than to solve them. . . ." The only remedy, she argues, is the sort of thoroughgoing reconceptualization provided by feminists.[54]

This grandiose claim about feminist contributions is not only egregiously incorrect as an account of the historical development of philosophy of science in the past one hundred years but also a rhetorical disaster. It would be both more truthful and more productive for feminists to trace continuities between their projects and those of other philosophers of science, past and present. Feminists could learn much from the writings of Karl Popper on the fallibility of science, from Bertrand Russell's critique of the romanticist fear of science, from the analysis of the role of values in science provided by Hempel, Rudner, Kuhn, and Laudan, from John Searle's account of the construction of social facts, and from Feyerabend's quixotic search for an anarchist epistemology. If feminists really want to "lead the way" into the new millennium, they would do well to avail themselves of the intellectual resources of the tradition they wish to lead.

Newton, who was not known for his modesty, once said that if he had seen a little further than some of his predecessors, it was because he "stood on the shoulders of giants." Feminists have taken the initiative in searching for giantesses and pointing out that women hold up half the sky. They have been extraordinarily successful in introducing both women worthies and a recognition of the role of gender into both the university and the K-12 curriculum. Isn't it now time for academic feminists to stop trying to play with half a deck? Separatism and appeals for solidarity may be useful when a movement is just beginning. But in the realm of ideas they are a recipe for dogmatism and stagnation.

But most distressing about Kourany's salvo is the claim that science has generally done more to create problems for women than to solve them. Kourany, a professor affiliated with the History and Philosophy of Science Program at Notre Dame University, is well aware of the positive impact of medical science on women's life span and reproductive freedom, and she knows that technological advances have made brute upper body strength a less important factor in survival, thus turning dozens of physically grueling jobs into occupations open to a much wider pool of people. Yet she cannot resist a rhetorical flourish reinforcing the Women's Studies commonplace that science and technology are inimical to women.

This chapter has argued that feminist views of scientific inquiry are seriously skewed.[55] Feminists themselves grant the importance of science in contemporary society—that is one reason they are so eager to challenge its authority. But even if their evaluation of science were correct, it always helps to recognize the strengths as well as the weaknesses of one's adversaries. That they have failed to do. And in the process they are alienating a generation of Women's Studies students from an understanding of both the content and methodology of the sciences.

Conclusion

W ENDED the first edition of this book (1994) on an ambivalent note. After all, things change rapidly in new fields, and it is not unreasonable to suspect that the excesses one observes might be due to mere growing pains. We saw our work not as an attack on the field of Women's Studies, but as a description and analysis that, we hoped, would cause colleagues to reflect on the programs they were building and the education they were proudly offering.

Now, early in the new millennium, our exploration of the current state of Women's Studies provides no grounds for revising the criticisms we presented in earlier chapters of this book. On the contrary, in many ways things have gotten worse. From the vantage point of the year 2002, it appears that feminist pedagogy has acquired a much stronger hold on the academy than we realized previously. In the form of required "diversity" courses, it is reaching large numbers of students who would not voluntarily seek out Women's Studies in the curriculum. "Women's Centers" abound and spread their alarmist message of a "chilly" and dangerous climate for women on campus and beyond. Their work is often replicated in supposedly academic Women's Studies programs. "Sexual harassment" is presented as endemic on college campuses, "training" in how to avoid it is sometimes obligatory on faculty and staff, and harassment policies are in place that target "verbal acts" (including professors' lectures) as much as the very rare instances of actual sexual assault.

In 1994, *Professing Feminism* was roundly denounced by most feminist academics and their supporters as false, biased, distorted, poorly researched, and generally reprehensible. Many critics called our use of (anonymous) personal narratives—a technique otherwise warmly embraced in Women's Studies circles—"anecdotal," our sources "atypical," and ourselves "reactionary."[1] Thus, one overriding question about the first edition of *Professing Feminism* emerged in the months and years following the book's original publication: Was our portrait of what went on in Women's Studies by and large accurate? Was Women's Studies really like that? Writing about Women's Studies with the benefits of another eight years of evidence, we have no hesitation in answering yes, noting that the institutional problems we described in the foregoing chapters are by now even easier to discern than they were in the early 1990s.

The reactions to the first edition gave us a good deal of insight into the defense mechanisms of Women's Studies faculty. First and predominantly, there was a massive denial of the accuracy of our representation of Women's Studies. This was the typical response of Women's Studies professors and program directors, of many reviewers affiliated with Women's Studies, and of most feminist faculty we met over the subsequent years. What was especially revealing was a crucial inconsistency evident in their reactions. With respect to virtually every important issue we raised, the denial that this is in fact a problem in Women's Studies has rested on two different and mutually exclusive claims. The first is that what we critique simply does not exist. There is no pattern of propagandizing, of male-bashing, of intolerance, of debasement of academic standards. The second claim, resting—fascinatingly—on a diametrically opposite contention, is that all education, all programs, are equally political and politicized, equally biased, and that Women's Studies, while indeed manifesting some of the features we criticized, acts in no way differently from the rest of the academy; it simply does it in an open way and with new targets.

There were, however, a few feminist reviewers and scholars who affirmed the validity of many aspects of our critique, or who acknowledged its accuracy in describing some Women's Studies programs or practitioners, but insisted these were far from the norm. They claimed, in other words, that our portrait, while not altogether false, was entirely unrepresentative. One particularly interesting example—more revealing than most because it noticed the dichotomy described above—is provided by Carol Sternhell's review, in 1994, of *Professing Feminism* along with other books on feminism published in the same year. Sternhell argued that, although we "offer a convincing critique of some currently popular foolishness," our book was on the whole unconvincing because— she asserted—it is atypical of what takes place in Women's Studies: "For every Women's Studies teacher who claims that what 'women need most is not practice in the subtleties of scholarly analysis, but a nurturing atmosphere capable of leading them to empowerment' [a quote from us], there are twenty feminist scholars gagging in the ladies' room."[2]

If this was indeed Sternhell's conviction at that time, we hate to think how she must be feeling today, when writing that celebrates "feminist pedagogy" has turned into a flourishing growth industry and book after book on the subject confirms our original views of it. As we demonstrated in chapters 11 and 12, feminist scholars do not hesitate to make more and more extreme pronouncements, and their views are then incorporated as "ground truth" by Women's Studies teachers who enthusiastically embrace multi-disciplinarity as a compensation for a lack of basic knowledge of the relevant parent disciplines.

In light of the environment described in the preceding chapters, there is scant reason to believe that critiques such as ours will help to bring about substantive change to Women's Studies programs. The one incontrovertible fact that we take from our research over the past two decades is that most feminists in Women's Studies genuinely

believe that their "good" politics justify any and all of their pedagogical practices and research approaches, no matter how questionable these might otherwise be. The theories as well as the practices of
feminist pedagogy are explicitly intended to change students' political attitudes—but this can only come at the expense of conveying
full and balanced information to them. Feminists claim that they are
justified in presenting one-sided perspectives because they need to
counterbalance the patriarchal ideology that purportedly infects the
rest of what these young women are learning. The result is frequently
a mild (or not so mild) form of brainwashing. Feminist research demands loyalty to an ideological agenda rather than empirical adequacy and logical consistency. And if one raises this as a criticism, the
defense is that feminism prides itself on subverting and challenging
the norms of academic inquiry. In addition, "academic service" now
means efforts to install feminist values in all aspects of university life
and beyond.

Thus, the conclusions we offer after our second field trip into
the strange world of Women's Studies are discouraging ones indeed. What morals, then, can we draw from our sorry saga? How
did this situation arise in the first place? What can be done? Is it
too late to intervene? First it is important to note that, from the
beginning, a number of factors predisposed Women's Studies to
end up as an administrative and academic trouble spot. We summarize these as follows:

The field started as a response to a social problem that required
multi-disciplinary expertise. Yet it is notoriously difficult within a
university setting to tackle such issues. True, there are now successful programs in environmental studies and criminal justice; but few
such programs have the ideological rigidity and push to conformity of Women's Studies.

The women who began Women's Studies often did not include
scholars with the sort of expertise required to address the problem
of gender inequities. There were many representatives from the humanities, but few social scientists, law faculty, or political scientists,
and still fewer with any knowledge of biology and other sciences.

As a consequence, Women's Studies relied heavily on interpretive methodologies current in literary criticism and on overly simplified bottom-line summaries of scholarship in other fields.

At the beginning and for most of its existence Women's Studies was receptive to ideas and strategies that had been developed by feminist activists outside of the university. (Imagine what an environmental studies program would be like if half of the people attending their scholarly conferences were from Earth First or the Earth Liberation Front.) Thus, by defining itself as the academic arm of the women's movement Women's Studies gained a great deal of passion and energy but also lost significant intellectual autonomy.

Ironically, at the same time, the new theoretical developments that go under the general rubric of postmodernism resulted in a lot of esoteric theorizing that was disdained by activists in the field but had to be defended to students and colleagues as highly relevant to the analysis of problems facing women. The ensuing tensions resulted in more extreme claims on both sides.

Women's Studies also provided a convenient place to satisfy demands for affirmative action hires. A strange symbiotic relationship developed between Women's Studies units and university administrators. Deans were hard pressed to employ and retain women faculty; Women's Studies programs—when they controlled faculty lines—were often eager to hire activists or people with unusual, even marginal, credentials.

As Women's Studies became institutionalized it provided a channel for women academics both in Women's Studies and in other departments to get tenure and promotion. Women who chose this route, as long as they conformed to the ideological standards of Women's Studies and played the identity game, could often get by with a publication record that would not satisfy the requirements of other departments.

This, in turn, tended to discourage scholarly communication between Women's Studies and other disciplines, and what should have been a truly multi-disciplinary enterprise tended to become an

insular enclave, focused on retaining its power base. The characteristics of this self-isolation persist to this day, as do its effects in and
on the university.

The almost inevitable consequence of the compounding of all
these factors is the presence within the academy of an academic
field that often fails to merit the respect of colleagues and students.
This, then, creates a situation in which the problematic traits noted
above are reinforced while feminists multiply their search for other
ways of extracting from colleagues the regard and appreciation they
have not legitimately earned.

The general conclusion we draw from our work is, therefore,
clear: Serious intrinsic and systemic weaknesses deform scholarship and teaching in Women's Studies, and it is the entire history
of academic feminism that has made such an outcome extremely
likely. These weaknesses are harmful not only to Women's Studies
itself but to the whole university. Still, we do not recommend declaring war on Women's Studies units—for all sorts of reasons.
First of all, we gladly acknowledge that some scholarship coming
from Women's Studies has been valuable. Second, we recognize
that gadflies, mavericks, and contrarians with radical viewpoints
have an important role to play in university life. And, finally, in a
more practical vein, we are well aware that once a university department or program is established it is practically impossible to
dismantle it if the incumbents do not agree. The institutional in-
ertia (more than hostility) that made it laborious to set up
Women's Studies programs in the first place is now protecting the
existing units from extinction.

But this in no way implies that the academic profession should
just turn a blind eye. Rather, it is our duty as professors, university
administrators, student advisors, and journal editors to be engaged
in an ongoing and vigorous critical debate with our colleagues in
Women's Studies.

However much we applaud the idealism and good intentions of
some of our colleagues in Women's Studies, we must also hold
them accountable if the programs they sustain exhibit doubtful

standards of scholarship or embrace questionable teaching practices. This means, for example, that deans and curriculum committees should look closely at descriptions of proposed courses and proposed majors. Do the faculty involved have the expertise to do what they say they want to do? It also means that tenure committees should look just as carefully at the quality of research and teaching of Women's Studies faculty as they do those of other people. The often-heard claim that the field has its own standards should not be allowed to function as an excuse for inadequate work.

At professional meetings and conferences, there should be a concerted effort to integrate feminist research into the substance of the academic discipline instead of setting up parallel programs where feminists can do their own thing protected from the scrutiny of their peers. And in integrated sessions, where feminist panelists join other, perhaps more traditional scholars, participants should stop the condescending practice of letting feeble or dubious assertions go by if they are well intentioned or claim privileges associated with identity status. This is the best way to reinforce the good work that is being produced and to reduce the influence of bad work.

Equally important, in discussions of departmental and university policy all efforts at guilt-tripping male and female colleagues (men, for the history of the world; women, with a demand for solidarity because "we are all women") should be rejected. No concessions based on past injustices should be made. The fact that women are still being treated unfairly in some respects and in some places is no reason to cut Women's Studies programs any slack when it comes to the evaluation of the research, teaching, or service they provide. Nor should we credit Women's Studies faculty and advocates with any special insight and competence when it comes to making recommendations for university-wide policies on curriculum, campus life, and professorial conduct.

In view of the situation described in the preceding chapters, what, finally, is our vision of the future of Women's Studies? We hope that it will become obsolete, and this for two principal reasons. First,

Women's Studies' legitimate mission of directing more academic attention within relevant disciplines to the study of the role of women and gender has been richly accomplished. The early founders' hopes of "mainstreaming" the study of women have been realized beyond their wildest dreams. The second reason is that the political issues that Women's Studies programs have traditionally raised have now entered public discourse, where they are directly and deeply influential on public policy, for good or ill. We think it was never entirely appropriate for an academic program to function as a center for political action. But there is certainly no justification whatsoever now for maintaining these entrenched ideological havens in the midst of our institutions of learning.

In the end, the best of what Women's Studies has achieved will spread throughout the university and the society at large, and the worst of what it does—its substitution of indoctrination for education, its ideological heavy-handedness, its intolerant prescriptions for how women should live and relate to men, its insistence on "support" and "comfort" as what women need and want in academe, and its attack on and dismissals of intellectual standards, "malestream" knowledge, and "Western" epistemology—will come to be recognized as marks of a debased education belonging to a particular historical moment, an education to be deplored and left behind.

NOTES

1. Introduction to the
World of Women's Studies

1. Cited in Adena Bargad and Janet Shibley Hyde, "Women's Studies: A Study of Feminist Identity Development in Women," *Psychology of Women Quarterly* 15 (1991): 181.

3. Ideology and Identity:
Playing the Oppression Sweepstakes

1. Adrienne Rich, *On Lies, Secrets, and Silence: Selected Prose 1966–1978* (New York: Norton, 1979), p. 189.

2. Renée R. Anspach, "From Stigma to Identity Politics: Political Activism among the Physically Disabled and Former Mental Patients," *Social Science and Medicine* 13A (1979): 765.

3. Quoted in Allan Hunter, "Missing in Action: Radical Feminism and/or Poststructuralist Feminism in the Academy," unpublished ms., Department of Sociology, SUNY Stony Brook, Summer 1992, p. 13.

4. Ibid., pp. 1–2.

5. Erving Goffman, *Stigma: Notes on the Management of Spoiled Identity* (Englewood Cliffs, N.J.: Prentice-Hall, 1963).

6. Rich's essay was first published in *Signs: Journal of Women in Culture and Society* 5:4 (1980): 631–60. It is reprinted in *Powers of Desire: The Politics of Sexuality*, ed. Ann Snitow, Christine Stansell, and Sharon Thompson (New York: Monthly Review Press, 1983), pp. 177–205.

7. Lillian Faderman, *Odd Girls and Twilight Lovers: A History of Lesbian Life in Twentieth-Century America* (New York: Columbia University Press, 1991), p. 212.

8. Combahee River Collective, "A Black Feminist Statement," reprinted in *Feminist Frameworks: Alternative Theoretical Accounts of the Relations between Women and Men*, 2d ed., ed. Alison M. Jaggar and Paula S. Rothenberg (New York: McGraw-Hill, 1984), p. 204.

9. Alice Walker, *In Search of Our Mothers' Gardens: Womanist Prose* (New York: Harcourt Brace Jovanovich, 1984).

10. On this subject, see Daphne Patai, "Sick and Tired of Scholars' Nouveau Solipsism," *Chronicle of Higher Education*, February 23, 1994, p. A52.

11. In *Mothering: Essays in Feminist Theory*, ed. Joyce Trebilcot (Totowa, N.J.: Rowman & Allanheld, 1983), p. 332.

12. One of us heard her make this statement in public lectures at Indiana University in 1986 and at the University of Massachusetts in 1993.

13. Mario Vargas Llosa, "El intelectual barato," in *Contra viento y marea*, vol. 2 (Barcelona: Seix Barral, 1986), p. 151 (our translation). In this article, written in May 1979, Vargas Llosa affirms that he heard Baldwin say these words, but does not specify where or when. Our thanks to Will Corral of Stanford University for bringing this passage to our attention.

4. Proselytizing and Policing in the Feminist Classroom

1. Aphorism cited in Mary Field Belenky, Blythe McVicker Clinchy, Nancy Rule Goldberger, and Jill Mattuck Tarule, *Women's Ways of Knowing: The Development of Self, Voice and Mind* (New York: Basic Books, 1986), p. 214. See also Nel Noddings, *Caring: A Feminine Approach to Ethics and Moral Education* (Berkeley: University of California Press, 1984).

2. Naomi Littlebear, *Hermanas: Songs Written by Naomi Martinez Littlebear* (Portland, Oregon: printed by Olive Press, distributed by Riverbear Music, 1979).

3. Plato, *Republic*, IV.439.

4. Aristotle, *Nichomachaean Ethics*, IV.5.3.

5. Susan Swartzlander, Diana Pace, and Virginia Lee Stamler, "The Ethics of Requiring Students to Write about Their Personal Lives,"

Chronicle of Higher Education, February 17, 1993, p. B1.

6. See John Eisenberg and Gailand MacQueen, *Don't Teach That!* (Don Mill, Ontario: General Publishing, 1972).

7. Jo Freeman, "How to Discriminate against Women without Really Trying," in *Women: A Feminist Perspective*, ed. Jo Freeman, 2d ed. (Palo Alto, Calif.: Mayfield, 1979), pp. 217–32.

5. Semantic Sorcery: Rhetoric Overtakes Reality

1. Audre Lorde, "The Master's Tools Will Never Dismantle the Master's House," reprinted in *This Bridge Called My Back: Writings by Radical Women of Color*, ed. Cherríe Moraga and Gloria Anzaldúa (Watertown, Mass.: Persephone Press, 1981), pp. 98–101. We are grateful to the Women's Studies E-mail list for the many interesting comments posted about the essay, and especially for the information concerning Frederick Douglass's quite different view of the "master's tools." We note, however, how quickly the comments appreciative of Lorde's phrase degenerated into a reductio ad absurdum, by which it would be impossible for women to use language at all, let alone typewriters and computers.

2. Mary Daly, *Websters' First New Intergalactic Wickedary of the English Language* (Boston: Beacon Press, 1987).

3. Carolyn Merchant, *The Death of Nature: Women, Ecology and the Scientific Revolution* (San Francisco: Harper & Row, 1980). A further appraisal of this view appears in Noretta Koertge, "Methodology, Ideology and Feminist Critiques of Science," in *PSA 1980: Proceedings of the 1980 Biennial Meeting of the Philosophy of Science Association,* vol. 2, ed. Peter Asquith and Ronald Giere (East Lansing, Mich.: Philosophy of Science Association, 1980), pp. 346–59.

4. Wilfrid Sellars, "Scientific Realism or Irenic Instrumentalism," in *Boston Studies in the Philosophy of Science*, vol. 2: *In Honor of Philipp Frank*, ed. Robert S. Cohen and Marx W. Wartofsky (New York: Humanities Press, 1965), p. 172.

5. Adrienne Rich, "Compulsory Heterosexuality and Lesbian Existence," in *Signs: Journal of Women in Culture and Society* 5:4 (1980): 631–60. It is reprinted in *Powers of Desire: The Politics of Sexuality*, ed. Ann Snitow, Christine Stansell, and Sharon Thompson (New York: Monthly Review Press, 1983), pp. 177–205.

6. National Public Radio, "Morning Edition," September 1, 1993.

7. Ibid.

8. See, for example, Andrea Dworkin, *Intercourse* (New York: Free Press, 1987), and Catharine A. MacKinnon, *Feminism Unmodified: Discourses on Life and Law* (Cambridge: Harvard University Press, 1986).

9. See Mary P. Koss, "Hidden Rape, Sexual Aggression and Victimization in a National Sample of Students in Higher Education," in *Rape and Sexual Assault*, vol. 2, ed. Ann Wolbert Burgess (New York: Garland, 1988), p. 16. For critiques of this and other rape surveys, see Neil Gilbert, "Realities and Mythologies of Rape," *Society* (May/June 1992): 4–10; and Del Thiessen and Robert K. Young, "Investigating Sexual Coercion," *Society* (March/April 1994): 60–64.

10. See Adrienne Rich, *The Dream of a Common Language: Poems, 1974–1977* (New York: Norton, 1978); Judy Grahn, *Another Mother Tongue: Gay Words, Gay Worlds* (Boston: Beacon Press, 1984); and Suzette Haden Elgin, *A First Dictionary and Grammar of Láadan* (Madison, Wis.: Society for Furtherance and Study of Fantasy and Science Fiction, 1985).

11. See *Selected Writings of Edward Sapir in Language, Culture and Personality*, ed. David G. Mandelbaum (Berkeley: University of California Press, 1949); Benjamin Lee Whorf, *Language, Thought and Reality*, ed. John B. Carroll (Cambridge: MIT Press, 1956). For a summary of recent assessments of the hypothesis, see Jean Aitchison, "Sapir-Worf Hypothesis," in *The Oxford Companion to the English Language*, ed. Tom McArthur (New York: Oxford University Press, 1992), p. 886.

6. BIODENIAL and Other Subversive Stratagems

1. Joel Best, *Threatened Children: Rhetoric and Concern about Child-Victims* (Chicago: University of Chicago Press, 1990).

2. Michel Foucault, *The History of Sexuality*, vol. 1 (New York: Pantheon, 1978).

3. See Bruno Latour, *The Pasteurization of France* (Cambridge: Harvard University Press, 1988), pp. 84–93; and Ian Hacking, "The Sociology of Knowledge and Child Abuse," *Noûs* 22 (1988): 53–63.

4. See Serena Nanda, *Neither Man nor Woman: The Hijras of India* (Belmont, Calif.: Wadsworth, 1990).

5. Anne Fausto-Sterling, "How Many Sexes Are There?" *New York Times*, March 12, 1993, p. A29(L).

6. Susan McClary, *Feminine Endings: Music, Gender, and Sexuality* (Minneapolis: University of Minnesota Press, 1991).

7. Ibid., p. 4.

8. Ibid., p. 69.

9. Ibid., pp. 128–29.

10. Ibid., p. 69.

11. These examples are taken from, respectively, Irving M. Copi, *Symbolic Logic* (New York: Macmillan, 1954), p. 89; Donald Kalish and Richard Montague, *Logic: Techniques of Formal Reasoning* (New York: Harcourt, Brace & World, 1964), p. 98; and Patrick Suppes, *Introduction to Logic* (Princeton, N.J.: Nostrand, 1957), p. 18. A spirited defense of the importance of logic and reason for feminism is made by Janet Radcliffe Richards in *The Sceptical Feminist: A Philosophical Enquiry* (London: Routledge & Kegan Paul, 1981).

12. Andrea Nye, *Words of Power: A Feminist Reading of the History of Logic* (New York: Routledge, 1990).

13. Ibid., p. 2.

14. Ibid., p. 169.

15. Ibid., p. 171.

16. Katharine Bement Davis, *Factors in the Sex Life of Twenty-two Hundred Women* (New York: Harper & Row, 1929).

7. "Mirror, Mirror on the Wall": Feminist Self-Scrutiny

1. Caryn McTighe Musil, ed., *The Courage to Question: Women's Studies and Student Learning* (Washington, D.C.: Association of American Colleges, 1992); and Musil, ed., *Students at the Center: Feminist Assessment* (Washington, D.C.: Association of American Colleges, 1992).

2. *Students at the Center*, p. 35.

3. Ibid., p. 43.

4. Ibid., pp. 33 (emphasis in original); 35.

5. Ibid., p. 35.

6. Mary Field Belenky, Blythe McVicker Clinchy, Nancy Rule Goldberger, and Jill Mattuck Tarule, *Women's Ways of Knowing: The Development of Self, Voice, and Mind* (New York: Basic Books, 1986). Although this book was slow to gain recognition, it is now a standard feminist text. It began to be cited frequently in 1990. The Arts and Humanities Citation Index lists 29 citations for 1990, 27 for 1991, and

40 for 1992. The Social Science Citations Index provides even more impressive figures, with 88 citations in 1991 and another 88 in 1992. Dozens of reviews also began to appear in 1991.

7. Nel Noddings, *Caring: A Feminine Approach to Ethics and Moral Education* (Berkeley: University of California Press, 1984); Sara Ruddick, *Maternal Thinking: Towards a Politics of Peace* (Boston: Beacon Press, 1989); Carol Gilligan, *In a Different Voice: Psychological Theory and Women's Development* (Cambridge: Harvard University Press, 1982).

8. *Women's Ways of Knowing*, p. ix.

9. Ibid., p. 229.

10. Ibid., pp. 24; 40; 41.

11. Ibid., pp. 55; 52–53; 69; 55.

12. Ibid., pp. 87; 93–94.

13. Ibid., p. 105.

14. Ibid. (emphasis in original).

15. Ibid., pp. 115–17; 118; 118 (emphasis added); 119; 120.

16. Ibid., pp. 114; 116.

17. Ibid., pp. 133 (emphasis in original); 140.

18. Ibid., pp. 141; 143, 146; 152.

19. *Students at the Center*, p. 51.

20. Ibid., p. 8.

21. Ibid., pp. 152; 182.

22. Ibid., p. 101.

23. *The Courage to Question*, p. 165.

24. *Students at the Center*, pp. 98; 92; 94.

25. Ibid., p. 101.

26. *The Courage to Question*, pp. 191; 119.

27. Ibid., pp. 172; 120; 128.

28. See *The Courage to Question*, p. 77, and *Students at the Center*, pp. 88–89.

29. See table entitled "Characteristics of Connected and Separate Knowing" in *Students at the Center*, p. 88.

30. Ibid., p. 89.

31. For a brief discussion of these dichotomies, see Noretta Koertge, "Analysis as a Method of Discovery During the Scientific Revolution," in *Scientific Discovery, Logic, and Rationality*, ed. Thomas Nickles (Dordrecht: D. Reidel, 1980), pp. 139–57.

32. *Students at the Center*, pp. 88–89.

33. *The Courage to Question,* pp. 53; 89.
34. Ibid., p. 1.
35. Ibid., p. 165.
36. Ibid., p. 1.
37. Lynne Goodstein, "When Is a Women's Studies Course a 'Women's Studies' Course?: Issues of 'Quality Control' of Cross-listed Courses," in *Re-Visioning Knowledge and the Curriculum: Feminist Perspectives,* ed. J. R. Ladenson, K. Geissler, L. Fine, and M. Anderson (East Lansing: Michigan State University Press, forthcoming). We appreciate Professor Goodstein's willingness to share this essay with us before its publication. Page numbers refer to the typescript.
38. Ibid., pp. 13; 10.
39. Ibid., pp. 13–15.
40. Ibid., pp. 16–17; 17.
41. Ibid., p. 21.

8. Cults, Communes, and Clicks

1. Our thanks to Kathleen Lowney, associate professor of sociology at Valdosta State University, for her informative comments on cults and sects.
2. Rosabeth Moss Kanter, *Commitment and Community: Communes and Utopias in Sociological Perspective* (Cambridge, Mass.: Harvard University Press, 1972), p. 57. For a trenchant critique of communitarian arguments recently advanced by philosophers and sociologists such as Alasdair MacIntyre, Charles Taylor, and Robert N. Bellah, see Derek L. Phillips, *Looking Backward: A Critical Appraisal of Communitarian Thought* (Princeton: Princeton University Press, 1993).
3. Kanter, *Commitment and Community,* pp. 82–91.
4. Ibid., p. 103.
5. Ibid., p. 222.
6. The following outline is based on a lecture by Audrey Murrell, "The Many Faces of Group Identification," at the University of Massachusetts at Amherst, March 10, 1993. Murrell draws on such work as: William E. Cross, "Negro-to-Black Conversion Experience: Toward a Psychology of Black Liberation," *Black World* 20 (1971): 13–27; William S. Hall, William E. Cross, Jr., and Roy Freedle, "Stages in the Development of Black Awareness: An Exploratory Investigation," in *Black Psychology,* ed. Reginald L. Jones (New York: Harper & Row,

1972), pp.156–65; and William E. Cross, "The Thomas and Cross Models of Psychological Nigrescence: A Review," *Journal of Black Psychology* 5 (1978): 13–31

7. Adena Bargad and Janet Shibley Hyde, "Women's Studies: A Study of Feminist Identity Development in Women," *Psychology of Women Quarterly* 15 (1991): 181–201.

8. Ellen Carol DuBois et al., *Feminist Scholarship: Kindling in the Groves of Academe* (Urbana: University of Illinois Press, 1985), p. 202.

9. From Dogma to Dialogue:
The Importance of Liberal Values

1. The Women's Freedom Network is a 1500-member, Washington-based organization of which Rita Simon, a sociologist at American University, is president. Their address is Women's Freedom Network, Suite 179, 4410 Massachusetts Ave. NW, Washington, D.C. 20016

10. Rhetoric and Reality
in Women's Studies

1. Dorothy Gallagher, "Lifestyles of Rich and Famous Vaginas," *Areté* (Spring-Summer 2001): 18. My thanks to Richard P. Brickner for bringing this essay to my attention. A new twist on the wildly popular *Vagina Monologues*, which is performed yearly on hundreds of college campuses, has recently appeared, in the form of a comic rejoinder, *My Johnson Speaks*, by Dave Goodman and Bert "Chili" Challis. Will this play, premiering in January 2002, be adopted on the college circuit? Another "V-Day Challenge" was launched in 2002 by feminists who are "intersex" (i.e., born with biological anomalies that lead them to have both male and female sexual characteristics), who say they are hurt by the play and by audience reactions. As one message to the Women's Studies E-mail List (WMST-L, 1/07/02) put it, these activists seek to use V-Day as an opportunity to raise awareness about the experiences of intersex people and to build greater alliances between feminist anti-violence activists and intersex activists. [Emi] Koyama continues: "V-Day is not just a performance, but a movement—the global movement

to stop violence against women and girls." As such, it needs to "hold itself accountable for damages it causes [by its implication that all women need a vagina], however unintentional that may be."

2. See Sharon Lerner, "Clit Club: V-Day's Charismatic Cuntism Rocks the Garden," *Village Voice*, February 20, 2001, p. 60.

3. Ibid., p. 63.

4. Ibid., p. 63.

5. On the Women's Studies E-Mail List (WMST-L@LISTSERV.UMD. EDU) there are frequent and repetitious discussions of what to do about student "resistance," which seems to be a problem year after year. Contributors to these discussions invariably attribute this resistance to "backlash," bad public relations, misapprehension about what feminism is, or students' desire to "protect their privilege"—never to any possible failing of Women's Studies courses or pedagogy, which are always assumed to be "challenging" in appropriate ways. I refer readers to the WMST-L archives, an invaluable source of information about both the ideology and rhetoric driving feminists in academe. Feminist journals, meanwhile, go on pretending that it is the "mainstream media" that considers "feminist" a "dirty word." See, for example, the mailing in January 2002 from the journal *Sojourner: Feminist News, Culture & Commentary*, which sent a letter soliciting subscriptions that began with the sentences: "Come on, I dare you! Say it with me: the F-word, a word that scares the mainstream media and makes politicians cringe."

6. Susan J. Scollay and Carolyn S. Bratt, "Untying the Gordian Knot of Academic Sexual Harassment," in *Sexual Harassment on Campus: A Guide for Administrators, Faculty, and Students,* ed. Bernice R. Sandler and Robert J. Shoops (Boston: Allyn & Bacon, 1997), p. 274. Such attitudes are also reflected in the efforts of campus feminists to set themselves up as watchdogs over the entire university. See chapter 11, "Policing the Academy."

7. Donna Laframboise, *The Princess at the Window: A New Gender Morality* (Toronto: Penguin Books, 1996), pp. 41–42.

8. Pamela den Ouden, "Naming Women's Studies: Maintaining Perspective," November 2000, available on-line at http://www.fsj.nlc.bc.ca/staffpages/pdenoudn/wmst/naming.htm. This report includes a listing of undergraduate and graduate programs in Women's Studies at Canadian universities.

9. Cathy Young, *Ceasefire! Why Women and Men Must Join Forces to Achieve True Equality* (New York: The Free Press, 1999), pp. 80–81. Citation from Deborah L. Rhode, *Speaking of Sex: The Denial of Gender Inequality* (Cambridge, Mass.: Harvard University Press, 1997). Young's book is a thoroughly researched and carefully thought-through analysis of feminist complaints, "scare statistics," and misrepresentations. She is equally impatient with the effort of recent men's movement advocates to reverse the hyperbole and make men out to be society's victims.

10. U.S. Department of Education, *Digest of Education Statistics* (Washington, D.C.: National Center for Education Statistics). Cited in *About Women on Campus* 6, no. 2 (Spring 1997): 7. See also "Women Are Close to Being Majority of Law Students," *New York Times*, March 26, 2001, p. A1.

11. See National Center for Education Statistics, Tables 11 and 13, available at http://nces.ed.gov/pubs2001/2001046.pdf.

12. U.S. Department of Education, *Projection of Education Statistics to 2010* (Washington, D.C.: National Center for Education Statistics), Chapter 2. Available at: http://nces.ed.gov/pubs2000/projections/chapter2.html. Whether one uses low, middle, or high alternative rates of change, projected growth in enrollment of women exceeds that of men. Chapter 4 of the same document tells us that the number of Ph.D.s awarded to women increased by 73 percent between 1984–1985 and 1997–1998, at which time women received 42 percent of all doctorates awarded.

13. American Association of University Women, October 2000 membership drive letter.

14. See "NAWE Members to Vote on Dissolution," p. 3, and Mary Dee, "NAWE: A Victim of Women's Success on Campus," p. 24, both in *Women in Higher Education*, August 2000. My thanks to Cynthia Welch, of the University of Wisconsin—Eau Claire, for making this document available to me. Dee writes: "A tribute to its success is that women on campus are no longer stuck in one office, but integrated into virtually every facet of academic and administrative service:

- Women administrators are on the rise. Almost 20 percent of colleges and universities have a woman president, and those lacking women in top leadership are suspect.
- Women faculty are major forces in many of the professional associations in the disciplines.

- Women head many mainstream national associations. . . . most have a women's caucus to reflect their concerns.
- Women are the majority of students on campus, and receive the majority of bachelor's and master's degrees, and soon doctorates and professional degrees."

The NAWE suffered from "declines in membership, loss of market niche, competition from academic and professional disciplines, and a societal shift away from single-sex organizations." Dee draws on the work of Lynn M. Gangone, executive director of NAWE, whose 1999 doctoral dissertation in education explains how and why NAWE had outlived its purpose.

15. Alice Kessler-Harris and Amy Swerdlow, "Pride and Paradox: Despite Success, Women's Studies Faces an Uncertain Future," *Chronicle of Higher Education*, April 26, 1996.

16. *Ms.*, February/March 2001, pp. 46–55.

17. Jill Nelson, "Call Me Woman," in *Ms.*, February/March 2001, p. 48.

18. Ibid., p. 49.

19. At my own university, the University of Massachusetts Amherst, several hundred students a year enroll in Women's Studies courses. But, as is increasingly common throughout the country, this is in large part because certain low-level Women's Studies courses fulfil the university's general education requirement in the area of "diversity." The number of majors, however, is small, having moved back and forth at the 30 to 35 mark for the past decade. See University of Massachusetts Amherst, Office of Institutional Research, Department Profiles, 1/25/01.

20. *Ms.*, February/March 2001, p. 50. For a telling example of the prevalence of academic rhetoric even in activist groups, see Genan Zilkha, "'Womanism in Brooklyn' Examines Feminism," in the *Brown Daily Herald*, April 21, 2001, describing an event at which Adjoa Jones de Almeida, a Brown alumna, and Melissa Reyes discussed the goals and problems of Sista II Sista. This is how they initiated a discussion with participants at the event: "Think of a time in your life when you were caught at the intersection of multiple levels of oppression. . . . Think for a second about daily interactions you've had in your life when you were dealing with multiple levels of oppression . . . as complex people coming from a variety of contexts."

21. *Ms.*, February/March 2001, pp. 53; 55; 54; 55.

22. See Alice Echols's account of this episode, in *Daring to Be Bad: Radical Feminism in America, 1967–1975* (Minneapolis: University of Minnesota Press, 1989), p. 181.

23. Wendy Steiner, "Rape Belongs to Everyone," *TLS*, April 6, 2001, p. 10.

24. See discussion on WMST-L, October 6–10, 2000.

25. WMST-L, October 9, 2000.

26. WMST-L, October 9, 2000.

27. WMST-L, February 23, 1995. Seven years later, a similar discussion occurred again (see WMST-List, mid-February 2002), with several listmembers expressing their hesitation to name particular books or figures as "founders of feminist theory" since to do so was "hierarchical" and contrary to the supposed feminist principle of communitarianism.

28. Carolyn M. Shrewsbury, "What Is Feminist Pedagogy?" *Women's Studies Quarterly* 25:1 and 2 (1997): 170.

29. Jane Roland Martin, *Changing the Educational Landscape: Philosophy, Women, and Curriculum* (New York: Routledge, 1994), pp. 188–91; cited by Marilyn J. Boxer, *When Women Ask the Questions: Creating Women's Studies in Academia* (Baltimore: The Johns Hopkins University Press, 1998), pp. 58–59; 252.

30. Elizabeth G. Peck and JoAnna Stephens Mink, eds., *Common Ground: Feminist Collaboration in the Academy* (Albany: State University of New York Press, 1998), p. 3.

31. Paula D. Nesbitt and Linda E. Thomas, "Beyond Feminism: An Intercultural Challenge for Transforming the Academy," in Peck and Mink, p. 32. Unfortunately, this passage sounds as if it were indeed written by a committee.

32. Ibid., pp. 39; 48

33. Helen Cafferty and Jeanette Clausen, "What's Feminist about It? Reflections on Collaboration in Editing and Writing," in Peck and Mink, pp. 81–98.

34. Ibid., pp. 88; 89; 96.

35. Angela M. Estes and Kathleen Margaret Lant, "Lesbian Collaboration and the Choreography of Desire," in Peck and Mink, pp. 156; 160.

36. Ibid., pp. 161; 163. But, they add, the choreography of their lesbian collaboration, which liberates them "from the patriarchal codes that keep us from finding ourselves as subjects in language" is not enough. It is "les-

bian laughter" that provides "the most powerful aspect of our collaboration" (pp. 163; 64).

37. Jamie Barlowe and Ruth Hottell, "Feminist Theory and Practice and the Pedantic I/Eye," in Peck and Mink, p. 274.

38. Ibid., p. 274. The citation is from Constance Penley, *The Future of an Illusion: Film, Feminism, and Psychoanalysis* (Minneapolis: University of Minnesota Press, 1969), p. 174.

39. Barlowe and Hotell, in Peck and Mink, pp. 275; 278. Equally fascinating, in this 1998 essay the authors argue for the importance of including "personal narratives"—as if this had not been a common, indeed celebrated, feminist methodology for at least the preceding twenty-five years.

40. Ibid., p. 276. See also *Is Academic Feminism Dead? Theory in Practice,* ed. The Social Justice Group at the Center of Advanced Feminist Studies, University of Minnesota (New York: New York University Press, 2000), which celebrates the "transgressive scholarship" offered by this collection, made possible by the "generous support" of the Rockefeller Foundation (p. vii). The brief introduction is a virtual catalogue of trendy academic terms and proper political views (see pp. 1–3). The question posed by the book's title is, of course, answered in the negative: "feminist critical engagement with the university and the rest of society, far from being either dead or deadly, is both vital and vitalizing" (p. 3).

41. Daphne Patai, "Sick and Tired of Scholars' Nouveau Solipsism," *Chronicle of Higher Education*, February 23, 1994, p. A52.

42. Jane Tompkins, "Let's Get Lost," in *Confessions of the Critics*, ed. H. Aram Veeser (New York: Routledge, 1996), p. 268.

43. Ibid., p. 270.

44. Berenice Malka Fisher, *No Angel in the Classroom: Teaching Through Feminist Discourse* (Lanham, Md.: Rowman & Littlefield, 2001), p. 198, discusses the pressures on feminist academics, especially if they are also women of color, lesbians, and/or from working-class backgrounds, to "demonstrate [their] expertise." Unemployment and ostracism are the risks incurred by daring women whose teaching doesn't confirm their claim to expertise, Fisher informs us , as if the expectation of professional competence in the exercise of one's chosen profession were simply an old prejudice designed to harm women.

45. Tompkins, p. 275; 277; 281, emphasis in original.

46. Julie K. Daniels to WMST-L, December 17, 2001; her emphasis.

47. Ilana Nash to WMST-L, December 17, 2001.

48. Fisher, *No Angel in the Classroom*, p. 50.

49. Florence Howe, ed., *The Politics of Women's Studies: Testimony from Thirty Founding Mothers* (New York: Feminist Press, 2000), p. xi.

50. This question can be posed, as well, in relation to the much publicized mea culpa by the Massachusetts Institute of Technology, which in March 1999 published a study confessing to institutionalized gender discrimination against female science faculty. The "MIT Study on the Status of Women Faculty" appeared as a Special Edition of *The MIT Faculty Newsletter* 11:4 (March 1999), available at: http://web.mit.edu/fnl/women/women.html. The study group was chaired by Nancy Hopkins, professor of biology and the initiator of complaints of discrimination. The Dean of the School of Science, Robert J. Birgeneau, described the study as "data-driven and that's a very MIT thing." See Carey Goldberg, "M.I.T. Admits Discrimination against Female Professors," *New York Times*, March 23, 1999, p. A1. This claim, however, has been decisively refuted. See Judith S. Kleinfeld, "MIT Tarnishes its Reputation with Gender Junk Science," Special Report to the Independent Women's Forum, December 1999; and Patricia Hausman and James H. Steiger, "Confession Without Guilt? M.I.T. Jumped the Gun to Avoid a Sex-Discrimination Controversy, but Shot Itself in the Foot," Special Report to the Independent Women's Forum, February 2001.

Why did MIT confess to gender discrimination when it has not provided any data to substantiate the charge? Evidently there are more rewards for simply complying with women's demands and complaints than contesting them. Thus, shortly after the MIT confession, Birgeneau moved on to become president of the University of Toronto. The MIT report inspired the presidents of nine major universities to adopt a statement pledging to work toward gender equity. In writing about the joint statement issued by the presidents, Cathy Young questioned whether this was a triumph of gender justice or gender politics. Young contacted a dozen women scientists at universities for their views. The majority, she reports, responded that "they had never felt mistreated or marginalized because of their gender." Some who felt that women in science did experience some difficulties conceded that the problems often were "fuzzy" and subjective. As astronomer Pamela Bjorkman, of the California Institute of Technology, told Young, "Most academics seem to feel they're getting a raw deal." See Cathy Young, "Fuzzy Math on Women," *The Boston Globe*, February 7, 2001.

51. Mariam K. Chamberlain, "There Were Godmothers, Too," in Howe, pp. 353–64.

52. See, for example, Elizabeth Lapovsky Kennedy, "Dreams of Social Justice," in Howe, pp. 243–63. Kennedy tells us that at SUNY Buffalo, the number of Women's Studies courses grew from "several in 1970 to almost sixty courses in 1971–72" (p. 253) and points out that these courses were "not that different from those offered today."

53. Mary Anne Ferguson, "Awakening," in Howe, pp. 73–74.

54. Margaret Strobel, "The Academy and the Activist: Collective Practice and Multicultural Focus," in Howe, p. 161.

55. Nellie McKay, of the University of Wisconsin—Madison, and Beverly Guy-Sheftall, of Spelman College, express some of the standard and by now axiomatic beliefs held in Women's Studies. The ubiquity of white women's "conscious or unconscious" racism is one of these; the invisibility of black women is another. See Nellie Y. McKay, "Charting a Personal Journey: A Road to Women's Studies," in Howe, pp. 204–15, and Beverly Guy-Sheftall, "Other Mothers of Women's Studies," in Howe, pp. 216–26. Despite the conventional claims that Women's Studies was originally "white Women's Studies," several chapters in Howe's book show that this was not the case. Intriguingly, Elizabeth Lapovsky Kennedy blames this widespread impression on the tendency of writing about the 1970s women's movement to focus only on gender, when in fact the movement as she experienced it engaged in much antiracist and anticapitalist work as well.

Beverly Guy-Sheftall tells us that she almost didn't participate in Howe's volume, because she was hesitant to be involved in still another book on Women's Studies that would be largely by and about white women. Elsewhere she comments that black women's presence in Women's Studies was atypical. If the latter was the case (and simple demographics would suggest that it must have been), these small numbers are not necessarily a sign of discrimination. A basic conflict constantly appears between claiming, or implying the claim, that discrimination exists and marginalizes black women from Women's Studies and the simple recognition of numerical disparities. The point seems to be that minorities (whether of race or sexual orientation) need to be massively overrepresented in Women's Studies in the United States if accusations of racism, homophobia, and tokenism are not constantly to be cast—and, indeed, this overrepresentation is readily found when one surveys the course offerings and course contents of Women's Studies programs today.

For an important new book on the self-defeating effects of the "racial etiquette" currently in place, See Elisabeth Lasch-Quinn, *Race Experts: How Racial Etiquette, Sensitivity Training, and New Age Therapy Hijacked the Civil Rights Revolution* (New York: W. W. Norton, 2001). Lasch-Quinn does not specifically address feminism and Women's Studies programs, but her analysis clearly applies to them as well.

56. Patricia L. Duncan to WMST-L, October 30, 2000.

57. Nancy Porter, "The Ground Revisited," in Howe, p. 350.

58. Ibid., p. 352.

59. Diana Scully and Danielle M. Currier: *The NWSA Backlash Report: Problems, Instigators, and Strategies* (College Park, Md.: National Women's Studies Association, 1997), pp. 33; 34.

60. Ibid., pp. 40; 64; 66; 88. Of special interest are the long quotations from NAS and CIR documents, in which one finds no objectionable words but rather strong defenses of liberal and inclusive education and of academic freedom, and criticisms of politicized education. Evidently the authors of the *Backlash Report* believe such affirmations represent reactionary threats to Women's Studies. It should be noted that Scully and Currier rely extensively on Ellen Messer-Davidow's 1993 essay "Manufacturing the Attack on Liberalized Higher Education," *Social Text* (Fall, 1993): 40–80.

61. Ibid., p. 41.

62. Inez Martinez, "An Odyssey," in Howe, pp. 110–11; 114.

63. Mimi Reisel Gladstein, "The Deodorant of Success," in Howe, pp. 119–129. Gladstein is also unusual in that her "then" photograph is the only one in the volume that includes a man.

64. Marilyn Jacoby Boxer, "Modern Woman Not Lost," in Howe, p. 234. Boxer is the author of *When Women Ask the Questions: Creating Women's Studies in Academia* (Baltimore: The Johns Hopkins University Press, 1998), a celebratory and yet somewhat critical account of the development of Women's Studies.

65. Boxer, in Howe, pp. 236; 237; 242.

66. Nona Glazer, "Making a Place," in Howe, pp. 339; 344.

67. Ibid., pp. 344; 343.

68. Graham Good, *Humanism Betrayed: Theory, Ideology, and Culture in the Contemporary University* (Montreal: McGill-Queen's University Press, 2001), p. 48. Good describes the numerous strategies by which substantive challenges can be disregarded while critics are subjected to rhetorical ploys which "place" them rather than respond to their arguments.

69. Joanne Detore-Nakamura, "When Our Feminism Isn't Feminist Enough," in *Fractured Feminisms*, ed. Gil Haroia and Laura Gray Rosendale (Albany: State University of New York Press, forthcoming 2003). My thanks to Nakamura for providing me with an early draft of her essay, in which she describes many experiences of feminist intolerance and goes so far as to defend Christina Hoff Sommers against blatant misrepresentations of her work. At the same time, Nakamura points out that at community colleges in the south, Women's Studies, even of the most moderate sort, still has to fight for recognition and resources. I have no doubt that this is an accurate description of some schools. What is regrettable is that feminist militance at other schools does nothing to help this situation, since it merely provides a negative example.

70. Elaine Marks, "Feminism's Perverse Effects," in *Signs: Journal of Women in Culture and Society* 25:4 (Summer 2000): 1162.

71. Marks, pp. 1165–66; 1163.

72. A very interesting version of the same criticism appears in a review by K. Anthony Appiah of Susan Gubar's book *Critical Condition: Feminism at the Turn of the Century*. Appiah notes that Gubar's book is in part an apologia and reveals the pressures she evidently felt to defend not her mind but her very soul from the negative judgments of other feminists, simply because of her critical responses to feminists who had attacked her work. He writes:

> Discriminating between what is and isn't worthwhile is the purpose of intellectual judgment. Why, then, could [Gubar] not criticize her critics without having her character impugned? The answer is, in part, that the intertwining of academic and social agendas has given rise to an outlandish rhetorical inflation. . . . Individuals get taken for kinds: a particular third world literary feminist theorist comes to represent all women of color. Not teaching Jeannette Winterson is taken to mean excluding her from the canon, which is easily inflated into excluding lesbians from it; and soon we have unqualified talk of the "exclusion" of lesbians—or gays or blacks—which sounds as though you're keeping them out of the class, or the university, or running them out of the neighborhood. This is indeed moralism; but it is moralism run amok.

See Appiah's "Battle of the Bien-Pensant," *New York Review of Books*, April 27, 2000, pp. 42–44.

A related criticism, excellently argued, has been available for years on William C. Dowling's website. See his essay "The Genetic Fallacy," available at: http://www.rci.rutgers.edu/~wcd/gender.htm. Men making such criticisms, of course, are more vulnerable to dismissal than is Marks.

73. Joan Mandle, *Can We Wear Our Pearls and Still Be Feminists? Memoirs of a Campus Struggle* (Columbia: University of Missouri Press, 2000).

74. Ibid., pp. 158–61.

75. Ibid., p. 2.

76. Joan Mandle, in private correspondence with the author, October 2000.

77. For an interesting reflection on similar notions, prevalent among Women's Studies faculty, about scholarship, clearly designed to decrease and redefine its role in academe, see the 1999 NWSA document "Defining Women's Studies Scholarship: A Statement of the National Women's Studies Association Task Force on Faculty Roles and Rewards, " drafted by Marjorie Pryse et al. Available at: http://www.nwsa.org/taskforce.htm. See also chapter 11 in this volume on feminist efforts to enforce these perspectives in academe.

78. WMST-L, February 12, 2001.

79. WMST-L, December 7, 2001.

80. *Chronicle of Higher Education*, October 6, 2000, p. C118.

81. WMST-L, November 11, 2001.

82. WMST-L, January 7, 2002.

83. Elizabeth Gross, cited by Susan Haack, "Knowledge and Propaganda: Reflections of an Old Feminist," in *Manifesto of a Passionate Moderate: Unfashionable Essays (*Chicago: The University of Chicago Press, 1998), p. 132.

84. Barrie Thorne, "A Telling Time for Women's Studies," *Signs: Journal of Women in Culture and Society* 25:4 (2000): 1186.

85. Paula Rothenberg, *Invisible Privilege: A Memoir about Race, Class, and Gender* (Lawrence: University Press of Kansas, 2000), p. 9.

86. Ibid., pp. 70–71.

87. Ibid., p. 125.

88. Ibid., pp. 121; 122.

89. For example: "Science is a social phenomenon, and like every other social phenomenon is limited by the benefit or injury it confers on the community." Adolf Hitler went on to say:

> The simple question that precedes every scientific activity is: who is it who wants to know something, who is it who wants to find how

he stands in the world around him? It follows necessarily that there can only be the science of a particular type of humanity and of a particular age. It is reasonable to say that there is a Nordic science, and a National Socialist science, which are bound to be opposed to the Liberal-Jewish science.

Quoted in Hermann Rauschning, *The Voice of Destruction* (New York: G. P. Putnam's Sons, 1940), p. 223.

90. Rothenberg, p. 126.

91. Sandra Bell, Marina Morrow, and Evangelia Tastsoglou, "Teaching in Environments of Resistance: Toward a Critical, Feminist, and Anti-racist Pedagogy," in *Meeting the Challenge: Innovative Feminist Pedagogies in Action*, ed. Maralee Mayberry and Ellen Cronan Rose (New York: Routledge, 1999), p. 25.

92. Ibid., pp. 26; 25.

93. Jane A. Rinehart, "Feminist Wolves in Sheep's Disguise: Learning Communities and Internships," in Mayberry and Rose, p. 65.

94. Ibid., pp. 64; 89–91.

95. Annis Hopkins, "Women's Studies on Television?" in Mayberry and Rose, pp. 129; 130.

96. See Diane Ravitch's indispensable *Left Back: A Century of Failed School Reforms* (New York: Simon & Schuster, 2000).

97. Susan Stanford Friedman, cited in Jeanne Brady, *Schooling Young Children: A Feminist Pedagogy for Liberatory Learning* (Albany: State University of New York Press, 1996), p. 100. Among other recent books on feminist pedagogy I have consulted, all of which confirm the portrait of feminist pedagogy presented here, are: Gail E. Cohee et al., *The Feminist Teacher Anthology: Pedagogies and Classroom Strategies* (New York: Teachers College Press, Athene Series, 1998), which brings together nineteen older articles published in the journal *Feminist Teacher*; Cheryl L. Sattler, *Talking about a Revolution: The Politics and Practice of Feminist Teaching* (Cresskill, N.J.: Hampton Press, 1997); and Amanda Coffey and Sara Delamont, *Feminism and the Classroom Teacher: Research, Praxis, Pedagogy* (London: Routledge Falmer, 2000). This last title—whose introduction states: "This book explores the consequences and risks of confronting patriarchy and critiquing malestream knowledge in the classroom" (p. 1)—demonstrates that the familiar rhetoric is alive and well in England a well as in the United States. In particular, Coffey and Delamont argue,

"heterosexism" must constantly be challenged in the classroom (p. 73). These are books I picked out more or less at random at my university library from an ever-growing number of current works on feminist pedagogy. The mere existence of such a large number of books on this subject is, of course, indicative of the growth of academic feminism.

98. Paula Rothenberg, "Integrating the Study of Race, Gender, and Class: Some Preliminary Observations," reprinted in Cohee et al., *The Feminist Teacher Anthology*, p. 138.

99. Ibid., pp. 140; 148.

100. Fisher, pp. 50; 77; 51; 161. Fisher also attempts to embrace the postmodernist rhetoric that attacks the notion of a coherent self and urges teachers and students to explore "the multiplicity of selves"—by which, however, as her book makes clear, she has in mind merely competing or interlocking identities of race, class, sexual preference, ethnicity, and so on.

101. Susan Haack, "Science as Social?—Yes and No," in *Manifesto of a Passionate Moderate: Unfashionable Essays* (Chicago: University of Chicago Press), p. 119. For similar criticisms, see Ellen R. Klein, *Feminism under Fire* (New York: Prometheus Books, 1996).

102. Haack, "Knowledge and Propaganda: Reflections of an Old Feminist," in *Manifesto*, p. 124.

103. Ibid., p. 126.

104. Haack, "Science as Social," p. 118.

105. Haack, "Knowledge and Propaganda," p. 128.

106. Too late for more than a brief mention in this note, I learned of two books that confirm both the success of Women's Studies programs and the existence of unease and criticism about the "professionalization" of the field, which is seen as having been achieved at the expense of still greater activism. According to Scott McLemee, "Hot Type," *Chronicle of Higher Education*, February 8, 2002, p. A17, Ellen Messer-Davidow, a professor of English at the University of Minnesota–Twin Cities, in her book *Disciplining Feminism: From Social Activism to Academic Discourse* (Durham: Duke University Press, 2002), discusses the contradictions created by feminism's success in the academy. On the one hand, she celebrates the work that, starting with a handful of founding mothers, has grown into hundreds of Women's Studies programs and scores of feminist research centers, as well as "'thousands of academic-feminist presses, book series, journals, and newsletters.'" On the other hand, she is frustrated by the insularity and esoteric topics on which feminist scholarship sometimes now focuses,

and misses the days when scholarship was no end in itself but merely one aspect of a political movement. Similar criticisms are evidently voiced by Elisabeth Armstrong, a professor of Women's Studies at Smith College, in her book *The Retreat From Organization: U.S. Feminism Reconceptualized* (Albany: State University of New York Press, 2002), who studies the activist work of early second-wave feminists and wonders if their academic counterparts today still want and are able to be leaders. In both cases, it appears clear that conflicts still exist between the two parts of the expression "feminist scholar." One obvious solution, in my view, is to recognize that the "feminist" part properly belongs in the public arena in which political positions can be debated and fought over, while the "scholar" should predominate in an academic setting. But many Women's Studies programs and teachers, as we have seen, explicitly deplore drawing such a distinction.

11. Policing the Academy

1. See Cathy Young's *Ceasefire! Why Women and Men Must Join Forces to Achieve True Equality* (New York: Free Press, 1999) for a thorough appraisal of these developments. By her logical and fair-minded approach, Young manages to offend both left and right.

2. See, for example, Joyce Antler, "Whither Women's Studies: A Women's Studies University?" *Academe*, July-August 1995, pp. 36–38, who first celebrates the mainstreaming project designed to transform the general curriculum through the "integration of material about women and gender," but in the next breath discusses as a single unit "women's studies and feminist theory" (p. 37). She clarifies further: "Despite current threats to affirmative action, . . . feminist scholarship has found a solid footing in the academy and will provide an important aspect of the education and future employment of coming generations of academicians. Such an institutional rooting of feminist theory on the graduate as well as undergraduate level is the surest way to secure and enhance the potential of academic women" (p. 38).

3. Adrienne Rich, "Claiming an Education," in *On Lies, Secrets, and Silence: Selected Prose, 1966–1978* (New York: Norton, 1979), p. 240.

4. Gail E. Cohee et al., "Collectively Speaking," in *The Feminist Teacher Anthology: Pedagogies and Classroom Strategies*, ed. Gail E. Cohee et al. (New York: Teachers College Press, Athene Series, 1998), p. 3.

5. *Antifeminism in the Academy*, ed. VèVè Clark, Shirley Nelson Garner, Margaret Higgonet, and Ketu H. Katrak (New York: Routledge, 1996), p. ix.

6. Ibid., p. xi.

7. See Shirley Nelson Garner, "Transforming Antifeminist Culture in the Academy," in *Antifeminism in the Academy*, pp. 201–17. The article draws heavily on Janet Spector's "The Minnesota Plan II: A Project to Improve the University Environment for Women Faculty, Administrators, and Academic Professional Staff," *Women's Studies Quarterly* 18:1–2 (1990): 189–203. Another fascinating aspect of *Antifeminism in the Academy* is the claim put forth in all seriousness by Elaine Ginsberg and Sara Lennox, in their essay "Antifeminism in Scholarship and Publishing," pp. 169–99, that "Despite the boom in feminist book publishing, we want to argue in this essay that feminist scholarship remains under siege on a number of fronts" (p. 169). They then go on to delineate the "new forms of antifeminism," which they see as "part of a coordinated, well-funded, and highly visible conservative campaign to discredit scholarly and curricular changes in the academy since the sixties." The newest wave, they argue, is the "antifeminism that cloaks itself in the vestments of feminism," that is, feminists who criticize feminism (p. 170). Antifeminism, they conclude, "is a hot commodity in the media world of the early 1990s, and feminists will have to muster all their resources to combat it" (p. 189).

Despite such assertions, the enormous success of feminism in publishing is reflected on all fronts. There are many lengthy bibliographies of feminist works now available, and countless publishers have Women's Studies or feminist lists—as well as, of course, lists in gay, lesbian, and transgendered studies. For a study of the periodical literature, see Kristin H. Gerhard, ed., *Women's Studies Serials: A Quarter Century of Development* (New York: Haworth Press, 1998), a volume simultaneously published in *The Serials Librarian* 35: 1–2 (1998). For an analytical treatment of the practices that set Women's Studies journals apart from other academic publications, see Blaise Cronin, Elisabeth Davenport, and Anna Martinson, "Women's Studies: Bibliometric and Content Analysis of the Formative Years," *Journal of Documentation*, 53:2 (March 1997): 123–38. They used bibliometric techniques "to expose the underlying social structure of a field by describing patterns of publication, co-authorship, citation, and acknowledgement" in three leading journals (p. 123). Cronin et al. comment on the "ironic reversal" accomplished in these journals, which have an enormous preponderance of females among their authors (p. 133). This was in striking contrast to journals in the related field of sociology, which showed much less gender exclusivity. The authors see this as in keeping with the "affirmative action agenda" revealed by a content analysis of editorials in their sample, whose avowed intent is to give women a greater voice in academic journals. They point out, however, that this agenda is "premised on incompatible objectives, the advancement of women in an institution, academe, which these same women seek to subvert." The ensuing ambivalence produces publications that adhere to the forms of scholarly publication while, as their study shows, employing an emotional register and other features that deviate from scholarly norms (p. 136).

8. Annette Kolodny, *Failing the Future: A Dean Looks at Higher Education in the Twenty-first Century* (Durham: Duke University Press, 1998), p. 103.

9. On this subject, see Daphne Patai, *Heterophobia: Sexual Harassment and the Future of Feminism* (Lanham, Md.: Rowman & Littlefield, 1998).

10. Kolodny, pp. 103; 104 (emphasis in original).

11. Garner, in Clark et al., p. 213, endorsing other contributors in the volume who, she says, "continually" refer to this backlash.

12. Kolodny, p. 105

13. Ibid., pp. 105–6.

14. See my review-essay "The Professor as Hooker," *Sexuality & Culture* 5:1 (Winter 2001): 99–104.

15. Kolodny, p. 106.

16. The following discussion of "Vision 2000" is adapted from Daphne Patai, "Why Not a Feminist Overhaul of Higher Education?" *Chronicle of Higher Education*, January 23, 1998, p. A56. See also Sen. Doc. No. 98–015, "Special Report of the Status of Women Council Concerning the Vision 2000," presented at the 548th regular meeting of the faculty senate, University of Massachusetts Amherst, December 4, 1997.

17. See the letter by Neil R. Wylie, executive officer of the New England Council of Presidents, *Chronicle of Higher Education*, January 28, 1998. Virtually the identical letter was sent to each publication that had aired a critical column about "Vision 2000," including the *Boston Globe* and *U.S. News and World Report*. Earlier in the month (before my article appeared in the *Chronicle* and the issue was picked up by journalists), however, Wylie had written a far friendlier-sounding letter to Jane Stapleton, coordinator of the University of New Hampshire's President's Commision on the Status of

Women. Dated January 7, 1998, this letter, after citing the Council of Presidents' formal statement of support for the nine principles, stated:

> Because of the unique history and circumstances of each institution, the Council of Presidents did not feel it would be helpful to have a group discussion with representatives from several institutions. *Vision 2000* has articulated many important concerns, and suggested possible approaches toward solutions. Each president or chancellor will consider the recommendations in the context of his or her own university, will work with the women's leadership on the campus, and will continue to move in appropriate ways toward the objectives expressed in *Vision 2000*.

Most interesting is that certain phrases suggestive of capitulation to the demands of "Vision 2000," including the key phrase that each president "will work with the women's leadership on the campus," were eliminated from the letters sent late in January. Meanwhile, though women's centers are perhaps not being consulted by university presidents on a regular basis, the federal government has made a good deal of money available to campus women's centers. Under the Violence against Women Act passed in the year 2000, the Justice Department awarded over $162 million to be used for improving training, reporting, prosecution, and response to domestic violence, sexual assault, and stalking. Of this, $6.8 million in federal funding was awarded to twenty colleges and universities in nineteen states to improve assistance to victims of sexual assault, domestic violence, and stalking. This was the second year that the Violence against Women Office awarded Grants to Combat Violent Crimes against Women on Campuses to institutions of higher education. At the University of Massachusetts Amherst, the Everywoman's Center, an advocacy group not known for common sense, received approximately $400,000 of this largesse, which will enable it to offer help and "training" to faculty, staff, and students. This is the same group that was central to the effort to pass the "Vision 2000" plan. For a discussion of the exaggerated claims of violence against women on which such advocacy groups depend, see Cathy Young, *Cease-fire!* (as in note 1).

18. For current information on Women's Studies programs, see Gerri Gribi's listing of Women's Studies programs in the U.S. Also available at http://creativefolk.com/directories.html or Joan Korenman's site at:

http://research.umbc.edu/~korenman/wmst/programs.html. Korenman also provides links to: Smith College's *Links to Graduate Programs in Women's Studies*, the University of Illinois' *Searchable Database of Women's Studies Programs*, and John Younger's *Programs in Gender and Lesbian, Gay, and Bisexual Studies at Universities in the USA and Canada*.

19. For an interesting example of the devastation suffered by an academic department when ideological policing is allowed free rein, see Graham Good's discussion of the infamous McEwen Report about the political science department at the University of British Columbia in Vancouver, in his *Humanism Betrayed: Theory, Ideology, and Culture in the Contemporary University* (Montreal: McGill-Queen's University Press, 2001), pp. 9–21.

20. On this subject, see my essay "The Vaguest Measure of Faculty Merit," in *Academic Questions* 12:1 (Winter 1998–99): 35–42.

21. See Records of the Faculty Senate meeting of December 4, 1997, University of Massachusetts Amherst. When Ferguson's comment was quoted in a column by John Leo in *U.S. News and World Report*, January 19, 1998, she denied having made it. I was present at the meeting when she originally made the statement, but I nonetheless sought out the taped version of the meeting and listened to it, thus confirming her precise words.

22. See Minutes of the Faculty Senate, April 9, 1998, University of Massachusetts Amherst. A comparison of these minutes with the tape of this meeting reveals that the minutes present a biased and sanitized version that conveys little of the conflict the "Vision 2000" document generated.

23. Faculty members can and do in fact lose their jobs because of feminist attacks on their approach to the "curriculum." See, for example, the case of the well-known drama professor Jared Sakren at Arizona State University, who was terminated over the emphasis on Shakespeare and other classical writers in his teaching and producing. See the American Association of University Professors' 1997 account of the case, at www.aaupaz .org/UWBC_add.htm, and also: David Kalstein, "Academic Freedom Under Fire," Boundless Webzine, available at http://www.boundless .org/1999/departments/isms/a0000053.html. Sakren sued the university and settled out of court in 2001 for $395,000, approximately six years' worth of salary. See Andrea Billups, "Shakespeare Settles Out of Court," in Boundless Webzine, available at http://www.boundless.org/2000/departments/isms/a0000358.html.

24. For a more detailed account of this conference, in which some of the following comments first appeared, see my "Speak Freely, Professor—Within the Speech Code," *Chronicle of Higher Education,* June 9, 2000, p. B7–8.

25. Walter P. Metzger and Richard Hofstadter, *The Development of Academic Freedom in the United States* (New York: Columbia University Press, 1955).

26. Alan Charles Kors and Harvey A. Silverglate, *The Shadow University: The Betrayal of Liberty on America's Campuses* (New York: The Free Press, 1998). Kors and Silverglate went on to found FIRE—The Foundation for Individual Rights in Education—which receives hundreds of appeals a year from students and faculty of all political persuasions whose free speech rights are being infringed. (Disclosure statement: I am on the advisory board of this organization.) See their website: www.thefire.org for information about free speech battles in which FIRE is involved.

27. Harvey Silverglate, E-mail correspondence, April 10, 2000.

28. Susan J. Scollay and Carolyn S. Bratt, "Untying the Gordian Knot of Academic Sexual Harassment," in *Sexual Harassment on Campus: A Guide for Administrators, Faculty, and Students,* ed. Bernice R. Sandler and Robert J. Shoops (Boston: Allyn & Bacon, 1997), p. 274.

29. "Nothing could be clearer: *The Hoya* should grant ample space only to voices conforming to orthodox feminism," noted Camille Paglia in her article on this episode, "Imagination Unleashed in All Its Perverse Glory," in *Salon,* April 5, 2000. Available at http://www.salon.com/people/col/pagl/2000/04/05/mcmedia/index1.html. See also the Foundation for Individual Rights in Education's documents in regard to this case, available at http://www.thefire.org/issues/gtown040700.php3.

30. Stanley Fish, "Academic Freedom: When Sauce for the Goose Isn't Sauce for the Gander," *Chronicle of Higher Education,* November 26, 1999, pp. B4–B6.

31. Michael Bérubé alludes to this episode in "The Culture Wars Are 10 Years Old. Has the Right Won the Struggle Over P.C., Multiculturalism, and the Canon?" *Village Voice,* February 21–27, 2001. Available at http://www.villagevoice.com/issues/0108/berube.shtml

32. The immediate occasion for this "statement for peace" was a local situation. By sheer bad timing, on the evening of September 10, Jennie Traschen, a professor of physics at the University of Massachusetts Amherst, attended a town meeting at which disagreement was aired over

how often American flags ought to be flown on lamp posts along the town's main streets. Traschen had no hesitation in voicing her view that the American flag "is a symbol of terrorism and death and fear and destruction and oppression." After September 11, Traschen received threatening letters and phone calls and appealed to the police for protection. See Jerry Guidera and Robert Tomsho, *The Wall Street Journal*, October 2, 2001.

33. E-mail correspondence, October 12, 2001.

34. Ferguson, E-mail correspondence, October 13, 2001, responding to Patai's message of October 12, 2001.

35. Larry Rohter, "Salutes, Some Skeptical, as Schools Go 'Bolivarian,'" *New York Times*, November 9, 2000; and Larry Rohter, "Venezuela Leader Broadens Focus on Reshaping Schools," *New York Times*, May 7, 2001.

36. Diana Blaine undertook to respond to this question with the following comment: "Doesn't the teaching of the periodic table imply that 'man's' appropriate relationship with 'nature' is one of dominance? And that we should search for the meaning of existence through science? Since when are such humanist assertions free from political implications?"

37. In her book *When Women Ask the Questions*, mentioned above, Marilyn Boxer responds to our critique (the merits of which she in part recognizes) with the statement that the features we discuss—"overpersonalization, service learning of dubious academic merit, politically charged classrooms"—are, as she puts it, "endemic in the academy" (p. 212). Once again, I note the oddness of exculpating feminist teaching for its duplication of problems that supposedly already characterize the academy. Boxer, at the same time, acknowledges and lauds the unusual goals of Women's Studies. She asked several acquaintances who have chaired Women's Studies programs: "Is teaching women's studies a political act?" All, she states, answered in a split second with a resounding "Yes!" (p. 187). In Boxer's view, "Women's studies need not indoctrinate" (p. 189), and, she admits, there is a "kernel of truth" (p. 201) in the accusation that "women's studies suppresses dissent." While acknowledging that the "tendency toward 'narrow politics' and 'political correctness,' which has on occasion [*sic*] led to extremes in women's studies settings that range from program staff meetings to national conferences, clearly exists," Boxer conspicuously omits, in this acknowledgment, "the classroom" as a key area where this "tendency" toward extremes does great damage. Boxer's real concern is revealed when she says: "But it is also possible to distort the prevalence and

impact of the negative and use it to rationalize opposition to all feminist-inspired education" (p. 202).

38. These three were Rose Maria Pegueros of the University of Rhode Island, Viki Soady, director of Women's Studies at Valdosta State University, and I.

39. Rebecca Wishnant to WMST-L, September 15, 2001.

40. Berenice Fisher, "Enhancing Feminist Pedagogy: Multimedia Workshops on Women's Experience with the Newspaper and Home," in Cohee et al., *The Feminist Teacher Anthology*, p. 100.

41. Jennifer Scanlon, "Educating the Living, Remembering the Dead: The Montreal Massacre as Metaphor," in Cohee et al., *The Feminist Teacher Anthology*, pp. 226; 227. This question might make one wonder why feminists never raise the issue of the responsibility all women bear for the fact that some women abuse and even kill their children.

42. Ibid., pp. 232–33.

43. Ardeth Deay and Judith Stitzel, "Reshaping the Introductory Women's Studies Course: Dealing Up Front with Anger, Resistance, and Reality," in Cohee et al., *The Feminist Teacher Anthology*, pp. 87–88.

44. On this subject, see Paul A. Boghossian, "What Is Social Construction: Flaws and Contradictions in the Claim that Scientific Beliefs Are 'Merely Locally Accepted,'" *TLS*, February 23, 2001, pp. 6–8. Boghossian explains: "We commonly distinguish between what philosophers of science call the 'context of discovery' and what they call the 'context of justification.' And while it's plausible that social values play a role in the context of discovery, it's not plausible that they play a role in the context of justification. Social constructionists about knowledge deny this; for them it is naïve to suppose that while social values may enter into the one context, they need not enter into the other" (p. 7). He then goes on to address this argument in detail.

For an intriguing and amusing analysis of what may lie behind excessive adherence to social constructionism, see Ian Craib, "Social Constructionism as a Social Psychosis," *Sociology* 31:1 (February 1997): 1–15. Craib asks what anxieties might give rise to comforting collective beliefs not open to rational debate and suggests that extreme social constructionism (which he calls a "manic psychosis") allows us to fantasize control over change that we do not, in fact, possess (pp. 10, 11).

45. Anne Fausto-Sterling, *Sexing the Body: Gender Politics and the Construction of Sexuality* (New York: Basic Books, 2000), p. 20.

46. Ibid., p. 28. Meanwhile, aging radical feminists are occasionally forced to come to grips with reality. Robin Morgan, for example, said in an interview in February 2001: "I was one of the women who marched around before menopause saying 'menopause is socially constructed, and if women were able to lead meaningful lives, we would never [suffer] from menopause.' Well, excuse me. I certainly got my comeuppance, and it had nothing to do with social construction." "Robin Morgan, Activist as Ever," interviewed by Carol Anne Douglas, *Off Our Backs*, February 2001, pp. 4; 5; and 14.

47. An apt rejoinder to Fausto-Sterling's views is David Barash's letter to the editor of the *New York Times* (January 9, 2002), in response to an interview with Fausto-Sterling, on January 2, 2001. Barash, the author of several dozen books on biology, psychology, and peace studies, acknowledged the interest of examining intermediate cases of all natural phenomena. He then commented, "Nonetheless, scientists and laypeople alike would be seriously misled if they were to respond to the existence of rare in-between cases by questioning the legitimacy, or even the existence, of the baseline situations from which these cases depart. Imagine a meteorologist who was so intrigued with dawn and dusk that she insisted that we abandon the categories day and night, or that we consider them to be 'socially constructed.'" While often claiming to have superseded a simple distinction between the biological and the social, feminists' real agenda clearly emerges in their own discussions of this subject. See, for example, the special issue on "The Science and Politics of the Search for Sex Differences," *NWSA Journal* 12:3 (Fall 2000), whose very title gives away its bias.

48. See, for example, my postings to WMST-L on February 19, 2001.

49. Jessica Fields to WMST-L, February 19, 2001.

50. Judith Lorber to WMST, February 20, 2001, responding to my message of February 19, 2001.

51. Samantha Holt to WMST-L, February 21, 2001.

52. Susan Kane to WMST-L, February 24, 2001.

53. On the subject of male/female size, the usual feminist response is that given in an earlier discussion several years ago, when Ruby Rohrlich wrote: "Sexual dimorphism may derive from social values. If these start to include preference for height, then over generations women choose taller men . . . . This becomes incorporated eventually as sexual dimorphism" (Ruby Rohrlich to WMST-L, May 25, 1999).

I confess to having made precisely this sort of argument in "feminist theory" courses that I used to teach in the 1980s, before it became embarrassingly apparent to me that I, like many other humanities-trained Women's Studies professors, was talking about things of which I had little actual knowledge or understanding. This is one of the predictable features of Women's Studies programs that value a generalized feminist perspective above disciplinary expertise and that even attack the latter notion in order the better to pursue their agenda.

54. Elizabeth Keller to WMST-L, February 25, 2001.

55. Ruthann Masaracchia to WMST-L, March 01, 2001.

56. A new feature of the WMST-List allows listmembers to very easily locate past messages and discussions. See http://research.umbc.edu/~korenman/wmst/interface.html.

57. Rebecca M. Herzig, "What About Biology? Building Sciences into Introductory Women's Studies Curricula," in *Feminist Science Studies: A New Generation*, ed. Maralee Mayberry, Banu Subramaniam, and Lisa H. Weasel (New York: Routledge, 2001), pp. 183–92.

58. Ibid., pp. 183; 184; 185; 187; 189; 186–87.

59. See, for example, Doris Lessing's comments at the Edinburgh Books Festival in August 2001 that men are "continually demeaned and insulted" by women: "I was in a class of 9- and 10-year olds, girls and boys, and this young woman was telling these kids that the reason for wars was the innately violent nature of men." And "You could see the little girls, fat with complacency and conceit, while the little boys sat there crumpled, apologising for their existence, thinking this was going to be the pattern of their lives." "The most stupid, ill-educated and nasty woman can rubbish the nicest, kindest and most intelligent man and no one protests." Lessing contrasted these practices with the lack of action on child care, which she called "the real liberation." See Fiachra Gibbons, "Lay Off Men, Lessing Tells Feminists," *The Guardian*, August 14, 2001. Available at http://books.guardian.co.uk/Print/0,3858,4238674,00.html.

Still on the subject of feminist stereotypes of men, Alice Echols, in *Daring to Be Bad: Radical Feminism in America, 1967–1975* (Minneapolis: University of Minnesota Press, 1989), pp. 362–63, notes that a confusion between essentialism and social constructionism characterizes radical feminists such as Andrea Dworkin and Catharine MacKinnon, who, while indignantly proclaiming that they were not essentialists, see male dominance as "eternal and unchanging." Echols comments that if the so-cial structure is "as impervious to change as [they] suggest, it might as well be biologically fixed." Today, though few professors identify themselves as "radical feminists," positions that used to be identified with radical femi-nists appear institutionalized within Women's Studies programs.

60. Maralee Mayberry, Banu Subramaniam, and Lisa H. Weasel, "Ad-ventures across Natures and Cultures: An Introduction," in Mayberry et al., p. 10.

61. Ibid., p. 3. Interestingly, in the entire book there is no mention even of well-known critics of feminist science studies such as Gross and Levitt (about whom see chapter 12). Instead, the same few feminist science scholars (Barad, Bleier, Fausto-Sterling, Fox Keller, Haraway, Harding) are cited again and again. For analysis of the retrograde effects on less de-veloped countries of anti-Western, anti-science postmodernist fashions, see the important work of Meera Nanda, for example: "The Epistemic Charity of the Social Constructivist Critics of Science and Why the Third World Should Refuse the Offer," in *A House Built on Sand: Exposing Post-modernist Myths about Science*, ed. Noretta Koertge (New York: Oxford University Press, 1998), pp. 286–311.

62. Mayberry et al., pp. 5; 6.

63. Martha P. L. Whitaker, "Oases in a Desert: Why a Hydrologist Me-anders between Science and Women's Studies," in Mayberry et al., p. 49.

64. Banu Subramaniam, "And the Mirror Cracked! Reflections of Na-tures and Cultures," in Mayberry et al., p. 57. See Raymond Tallis, "Evi-dence-based and Evidence-free Generalisations," in *The Raymond Tallis Reader*, ed. Michael Grant (Hampshire: Palgrave, 2000), pp. 309–29, for a brief but telling description of the crucial distinction between these two modes of inquiry. Tallis is both a physician and a prolific critic of post-modernism.

65. Marilyn Frye, "Willful Virgin, or Do You Have to Be a Lesbian to Be a Feminist?" in *Willful Virgin: Essays in Feminism, 1976–1992* (Free-dom, Calif.: Crossing Press, 1992), pp. 130–32. For a more detailed dis-cussion of this subject, including the occasional feminist challenges to such viewpoints, see my *Heterophobia: Sexual Harassment and the Future of Feminism*, especially chapter 6.

66. Joyce Trebilcot, "Taking Responsibility for Sexuality," in *Philosophy and Sex*, rev. ed., ed. Robert Baker and Frederick Elliston (Buffalo, New York: Prometheus Books, 1984), pp. 421–27.

67. Robin West, "The Harms of Consensual Sex," *APA [American Philosophical Association] Newsletter on Feminism and Philosophy, and Philosophy and Law* 94:2 (Spring 1995): 53–54.

68. E. Kay Trimberger, "Heterosexuality," in *Reader's Companion to U.S. Women's History*, ed. Wilma Mankiller et al. (Boston: Houghton Mifflin, 1998), p. 255. Adrienne Rich's concept of "compulsory heterosexuality" is discussed in chapter 3. This view is now also an orthodoxy of Queer pedagogy. See, for example, the description by Professor Deborah Carlin (director of graduate studies in the English Department at UMass Amherst) of her graduate course entitled "Queer Theory," which refers to the "fallacious belief that heterosexuality is *innate* or *natural*" (her emphasis). English 891B, Spring 1996.

12. Feminists Take on Science: Tilting with the Evil Empire

1. Sharon Traweek, *Beamtimes and Lifetimes: The World of High Energy Physicists* (Cambridge, Mass.: Harvard University Press, 1988), pp. 551–60.

2. Gerald Holton, "Science Education and the Sense of Self," in *The Flight from Science and Reason*, ed. Paul R. Gross, Norman Levitt, and Martin W. Lewis (Baltimore, Md.: Johns Hopkins University Press, 1997).

3. Paul Forman, "Assailing the Seasons," *Science* 276 (1997): 750–752.

4. Sandra Harding, *Whose Science? Whose Knowledge? Thinking from Women's Lives* (Ithaca, N.Y.: Cornell University Press, 1991).

5. Ashis Nandy, *Science, Hegemony and Violence: A Requiem for Modernity* (New Delhi: Oxford University Press, 1989).

6. Steven Fuller, *Philosophy, Rhetoric, and the End of Knowledge: The Coming of Science and Technology Studies* (Madison: University of Wisconsin Press, 1993).

7. Andrew Ross, *Strange Weather: Culture, Science and Technology in the Age of Limits* (London: Verso, 1991).

8. Kathy Overfield, "Dirty Fingers, Grime and Slag Heaps: Purity and the Scientific Ethic," in *Men's Studies Modified: The Impact of Feminism on the Academic Disciplines,* ed. Dale Spender (New York: Pergamon Press, 1981), pp. 237–248.

9. Harry Collins and Trevor Pinch, *The Golem: What Everyone Should Know about Science* (Cambridge: Cambridge University Press, 1993), p. 1.

10. Andrew Ross, "Introduction," *Social Text* 46/47 (Spring/Summer 1996), p. 4.

11. Sue V. Rosser, "Female-Friendly Science: Including Women in Curricular Content and Pedagogy in Science," *Journal of General Education* 42 (1990): 213.

12. Helen Longino, *Science as Social Knowledge* (Princeton, N.J.: Princeton University Press, 1990), pp. 191; 193.

13. Noretta Koertge, "Postmodernisms and the Problem of Scientific Literacy," in *A House Built on Sand: Exposing Postmodernist Myths about Science,* ed. Noretta Koertge (Oxford: Oxford University Press, 1998), pp. 257–71.

14. Susan Damarin, "Gender and Mathematics from a Feminist Standpoint," in Walter G. Secada, et al., *New Directions for Equity in Mathematics Education* (Cambridge: Cambridge University Press, 1995)p. 242.

15. Bonnie Jean Shulman, "Implications of Feminist Critiques of Science for the Teaching of Mathematics and Science," *Journal of Women and Minorities in Science and Engineering* 1 (1994): 4.

16. Ibid., p. 5.

17. Philip Kitcher, *The Advancement of Science: Science without Legend, Objectivity without Illusions* (Oxford: Oxford University Press, 1993).

18. Barbara Herrnstein Smith, *Belief and Resistance: Dynamics of Contemporary Intellectual Controversy* (Cambridge, Mass.: Harvard University Press, 1997), pp. 144–45.

19. Ibid., pp. 151; 118. For further discussion, see my review of her book in *British Journal for the Philosophy of Science* 50/4 (1999): 601–06.

20. Paul R. Gross and Norman Levitt, *Higher Superstition: The Academic Left and Its Quarrels with Science* (Baltimore: The Johns Hopkins University Press, 1994).

21. Alan Sokal, "Transgressing the Boundaries: Toward a Transformative Hermeneutics of Quantum Gravity," *Social Text* 46/47 (Spring/Summer 1996): 217–52.

22. Reprinted in Alan Sokal and Jean Bricmont, *Fashionable Nonsense: Postmodern Intellectuals' Abuse of Science* (New York: Picador Books, 1998), pp. 269–70; italics in original.

23. Philip Sullivan, "An Engineer Dissects Two Case Studies: Hayles on Fluid Mechanics, and MacKenzie on Statistics," in Koertge, ed., *A House Built on Sand*, pp. 71–98.

24. Carolyn Merchant, *The Death of Nature: Women, Ecology, and the Scientific Revolution* (San Francisco: Harper, 1990).

25. See William Newman, "Alchemy, Domination, and Gender," in Koertge, ed., *A House Built on Sand*, pp. 216–26.

26. See Alan Soble, "In Defense of Bacon," in Koertge, ed., *A House Built on Sand*, pp. 195–215.

27. Londa Schiebinger, *The Mind Has No Sex? Women in the Origins of Modern Science* (Cambridge, Mass.: Harvard University Press, 1989).

28. Londa Schiebinger, *Nature's Body: Gender in the Making of Modern Science* (Boston: Beacon Press, 1993).

29. Londa Schiebinger, *Has Feminism Changed Science?* (Cambridge, Mass.: Harvard University Press, 1999), pp. 3–6; 2; 159; 178.

30. Ibid., p. 178.

31. Ibid., p. 146.

32. Ibid., p. 147.

33. Paul R. Gross, "Bashful Eggs, Macho Sperm, and Tonypandy," in Koertge, ed., *A House Built on Sand*, pp. 59–70.

34. Schiebinger, *Has Feminism Changed Science?* pp. 152; 154; 155.

35. Elizabeth Potter, *Gender and Boyle's Law of Gases* (Bloomington: Indiana University Press, 2001), p. ix.

36. Ibid., p. 4.

37. Ibid., p. 17.

38. Rose-Mary Sargent, "Boyle on Animals," E-mail correspondence, May 21, 2001.

39. Nicole Howard, "Cruelty to Animals," E-mail correspondence, May 21, 2001.

40. Potter, p. 184.

41. Ibid., p. 22.

42. Anne Fausto-Sterling, *Sexing the Body: Gender Politics and the Construction of Sexuality* (New York: Basic Books, 2000), pp. 238–39.

43. Ibid., p. 193, my italics; 244.

44. Ibid., p. 179.

45. Ibid., pp. 191; 192; 193.

46. June Machover Reinisch, Leonard A. Rosenblum, and Stephanie A. Sanders, *Masculinity/Femininity : Basic Perspectives* (New York : Oxford University Press, 1987); and June Machover Reinisch, David P. McWhirter, and Stephanie A. Sanders, *Homosexuality/Heterosexuality: Concepts of Sexual Orientation* (New York: Oxford University Press, 1990).

47. Michael Ruse, "Are There Gay Genes? Sociobiology and Homosexuality," in *Nature and Causes of Homosexuality: A Philosophic and Scientific Inquiry,* ed. Noretta Koertge (New York: The Haworth Press., 1981).

48. Noretta Koertge, "Are Feminists Alienating Women from the Sciences?" *The Chronicle of Higher Education,* September 15, 1994, p. A80.

49. Angela M. Pattatucci, ed., *Women in Science: Meeting Career Challenges* (Thousand Oaks, Calif.: Sage Publications, 1998).

50. Angela Rella, "Who's Afraid of Virginia Woolf Now?" in Pattatucci, p. 175.

51. Nina Wokhlu, "My First Experience as a Woman Scientist," in Pattatucci, p. 139.

52. Suzanne E. Franks, "One Woman's Life in Science," in Pattatucci, pp. 123; 122; 132.

53. Donna Riley, "Feminist/Scientist: Ambiguities and Contradictions," in Pattatucci, pp. 182; 183–84; 187.

54. Janet A. Kourany, "What Does Feminism Contribute to Philosophy of Science?" Pacific Division, American Philosophical Association Meeting, 2001.

55. See also my articles: "Science, Values and the Value of Science," *Philosophy of Science* 67 (Proceedings, 2000): S45–47, and "'New Age' Philosophies of Science: Constructivism, Feminism and Postmodernism," *British Journal for the Philosophy of Science* 51 (2000): 667–83.

Conclusion

1. See, for recent and typical examples, Sue V. Rosser, "Warming Up the Classroom," in *The Feminist Teacher Anthology: Pedagogies and Classroom Strategies,* ed. Gail E. Cohee et al. (New York: Teachers College Press, Athene Series, 1998). pp. 31–44. Rosser warns against a "strong backlash movement" and names Patai and Koertge as "individuals who call themselves feminists and identify as Women's Studies faculty" but nonetheless "have attacked notions of gender equity in curriculum and pedagogy" (pp. 31, 32). Bernice Malka Fisher, *No Angel in the Classroom: Teaching through Feminist Discourse* (Rowman & Littlefield, 2001), p. 15, also criticizes *Professing Feminism* and says our use of examples from disgruntled students "reeked of political reaction and left little room to discuss the complex political and pedagogical questions that feminist as well

as nonfeminist teachers often address." And even well-known scholars such as Alice Kessler-Harris and Amy Swerdlow are content to misrepresent our criticisms. In a 1996 essay entitled "Pride and Paradox: Despite Success, Women's Studies Faces an Uncertain Future" (*Chronicle of Higher Education*, April 26, 1966), they accuse us of "repudiating the study of women's lives or denying the central role of gender in human affairs." Christina Hoff Sommers, of course, is the critic whose work is most distorted and vilified by feminist reviewers, who typically dismiss her publications on the basis of which groups supported her research and by casting aspersions on her supposed politics. Sternhell, in the review under discussion below, notes that Sommers's book *Who Stole Feminism?* and ours make many overlapping criticisms of Women's Studies, but she feels no need to address Sommers's work in any detail and instead engages in an ad feminam dismissal of Sommers.

2. Carol Sternhell, *The Women's Review of Books* 12:3 (December 1994): 1–4, which discusses *Professing Feminism* as well as Christina Hoff Sommers, *Who Stole Feminism? How Women Have Betrayed Women* (New York: Simon & Schuster, 1994), and Frances A. Maher and Mary Kay Thompson Tetreault, *The Feminist Classroom* (New York: BasicBooks, 1994).

Index

About the Authors

Daphne Patai is Professor in the Department of Spanish and Portuguese at the University of Massachusetts Amherst, where she also spent ten years in the Women's Studies Program. A recipient of Guggenheim, National Endowment for the Humanities, and National Humanities Center fellowships, she is the author and editor of, among other books, *The Orwell Mystique* (1984), *Brazilian Women Speak* (1998), *Women's Words: The Feminist Practice of Oral History* (1991, with Sherna Berger Gluck), *Rediscovering Forgotten Radicals: British Women Writers 1889–1939* (1993, with Angela Ingram), and *Heterophobia: Sexual Harassment and the Future of Feminism* (1998). Her book *What Price Utopia? Essays by a Recovering Feminist* will be published in 2003. She is currently coediting, with Will Corral, a volume of critical essays on literary theory.

Noretta Koertge is a member of the Department of History and Philosophy of Science at Indiana University, Bloomington. Her research interests include both the historical and normative aspects of scientific methodology. Her novels, *Who Was That Masked Woman?* (1981) and *Valley of the Amazons* (1984), explore the ethos of the early feminist movement. She edited *Nature and Causes of Homosexuality: A Philosophic and Scientific Inquiry* (1981) and *A House*

Built on Sand: Exposing Postmodernist Myths about Science (1998) and is coeditor (with Cassandra Pinnick and Robert Almeder) of *Scrutinizing Feminist Epistemology: An Examination of Gender in Science* (2003). She is currently editor-in-chief of *Philosophy of Science,* the official journal of the Philosophy of Science Association.